# Faith and Fath

## Parish Politics in Hitler's Germany

**Kyle Jantzen**

**Fortress Press**
MINNEAPOLIS

FAITH AND FATHERLAND
Parish Politics in Hitler's Germany

Cover image: National bishop Friedrich Coch giving a Nazi salute, Dresden, 10 December 1933 © Gedenkstaette Deutscher Wiederstand.
Cover design: Christa Rubsam
Book design: Michelle L. N. Cook
Frontispiece: Photo © Bettman/CORBIS.
Maps: Lucidity Information Design

*Library of Congress Cataloging-in-Publication Data*
Jantzen, Kyle, 1966-
  Faith and fatherland: parish politics in Hitler's Germany / by Kyle Jantzen.
    p. cm.
  Includes bibliographical references and index.
  ISBN 978-0-8006-2358-6 (pbk.: alk. paper)
  1. Church history—Germany—20th century. 2. Christianity and politics—
Germany—History—20th century. 3. National socialism and religion. I. Title.
  BR856.J36 2008
  274.3'0823—dc22        2007052793

Manufactured in the U.S.A.

12    11    10    09    08    1    2    3    4    5    6    7    8    9    10

# Contents

*Young German Christians give the Nazi salute at a rally
in front of a new Christian Nazi flag, circa 1933-38.*

# Preface

 **What is it that we want from the past but explanations** of who we are and how our world came to be as it is? This holds true for us as individuals and families, for churches and businesses, and for whole societies. In times of personal crisis or political upheaval, answering such elemental questions—*Who are we?* and *How did we get here?*—becomes even more urgent. For historians who explore these issues of identity and development in our collective past, it has become increasingly clear that the first half of the twentieth century was a pivotal moment in Western and world history. The confidence and optimism of a century of European progress and world domination were shattered by the blood-letting catastrophe of the First World War. In the turbulent years that followed, extremist political movements flooded across Europe and spilled over into the rest of the world. On the left, communist dictatorships seized power in the former Russian empire and, ultimately, over all of Eastern Europe, much of Asia, and regions beyond. On the right, fascist, National Socialist, and conservative military dictatorships ruled in Italy, Germany, Spain, and several other European states, as well as parts of Africa, Asia, and (not least) Latin America.

In the history of this political polarization, no nation or event has retained as strong a grip on our imaginations as the Germany of Adolf Hitler. Whether it is the eye-catching spectacle of old National Socialist propaganda films, the obsessive figure of Hitler himself, the crusading ideology of the Second World War, or the unfathomable evil of the Holocaust, we are drawn again and again to the Third Reich. And so the scholarly and popular historical literature on National Socialism and the Holocaust continues to grow at a steady and surprising rate, fueled in recent decades by the memoirs of the aging participants in the events of the 1930s and 1940s.

Even as we survey our vast storehouse of knowledge about the Third Reich, we realize that after sixty years' worth of books, films, museums, and monuments, we have yet to plumb the depths of the Hitler phenomenon. Even after analyzing the ideological, sociological, and historical roots, trunk, and branches of National Socialism, we remain at many points unsatisfied with our answers. And so we keep on asking, How could such a barbaric movement have taken hold of such a technologically advanced and culturally sophisticated society as that of Germany? How could German Jews, numerically so insignificant, have become such an obsession for the government and public alike, driving Germans (and later, of course, many other Europeans with them) to such depths of inhumanity? Deeper still lie harder questions: How can human beings do these things to one another? Where does such evil come from? And, for some, where was God? These questions first drew me into the study of National Socialism and the Holocaust, and they continue to propel my teaching and research in the field.

For Christians (or, for that matter, for observers or critics of the faith), the role of the Roman Catholic and Protestant churches in Nazi Germany and the Holocaust remains a perplexing and embarrassing problem, not least because of the popular and theologically proper expectation that Christians are called to a higher standard of morality than others. Why then, we ask, did so few dedicated, influential Christians speak out against the hatred, violence, and national idolatry of Adolf Hitler and his movement? How did so few pastors and parishioners appear to feel any discomfort with the rejection and even public mockery of traditional Christian virtues like love, hospitality, mercy, humility, and kindness? Even more troubling, how could Christians in the Third Reich hold on to such mutually exclusive sets of values—so we would argue, in hindsight—as those of Jesus Christ and Adolf Hitler, of the cross and the swastika? And what does all this say about the human capacity for inconsistency, self-deception, and moral breakdown? This book is an attempt to address these questions.

In *Faith and Fatherland*, I have chosen to study the church history of the Third Reich at the local level, focusing on Lutheran parishes and church districts from across Germany. This is because I am interested in the personal decisions people make and the practical outworking of large political or religious issues in the ordinary realm of everyday life. I am forever fascinated and frequently dismayed by the diverse responses to National Socialism among pastors and parishioners in 1930s Germany. I believe, however, that those diverse responses are keys with which to open doors of exploration into our collective past and into the larger question of how good and evil are worked out in our individual and collective humanity.

Over the course of this long project, I have acquired many debts of thanks, both personal and professional. I wish to express my appreciation to editors Julie O'Brien and Michael West at Fortress Press for taking on my book and seeing it to completion. I would also like to thank my *Doktorvater*, Dr. Peter Hoffmann of McGill

University, for his patience, timely advice, and deep engagement with this material, and for his example of a consistently superior standard of scholarship. I am also grateful to the archivists, churchmen, and officials who assisted me in Germany, particularly at the Dekanatsamt and Stadtarchiv in Ravensburg, the Domstiftsarchiv in Brandenburg, the Evangelisches Zentralarchiv in Berlin, and the Kirchenkreisamt in Pirna. Special thanks go to Dr. Karlheinz Blaschke of the Technische Universität Dresden for opening the doors to several Saxon church districts, Frau Christiane Mokroß of the Evangelisches Zentralarchiv in Berlin for her patient guidance into the Old Prussian Union Church records, and to Dr. Wolfgang Schössler of the Domstiftsarchiv Brandenburg for permitting me to work on days when the archive was not normally open.

I would also like to thank Drs. John Conway of the University of British Columbia, Doris Bergen of the University of Toronto, John Delaney of Kutztown University, Don Dietrich of Boston College, and the late Dave De Brou of the University of Saskatchewan, for guidance, encouragement, and stimulating scholarly exchanges. More generally, my thanks go out to my past professors, friends, and colleagues at the University of Saskatchewan and at McGill University for teaching me and giving me opportunities to teach, and to my current colleagues and students at Ambrose University College for ongoing support and encouragement. Special thanks to the Franciscan friars at St. Michael's Retreat in Lumsden, Saskatchewan, whose gracious hospitality, peaceful surroundings, and delicious food have made my numerous writing and editing "retreats" more pleasant than I could have hoped or imagined. While all of these individuals have contributed to this study in one way or another, none of them is responsible for its contents, interpretations, or errors, each of which is the responsibility of the author.

More personally, I would like to express my deep gratitude to my parents, parents-in-law, and family, for their understanding, patience, and support (material and moral) for my academic career. I want especially to remember my late mother, whose interest in my studies I miss deeply. I would also like to thank the many church friends in Saskatoon, Montreal, Regina, and High River, for fellowship and encouragement over the years. Special thanks to Dr. Mark Baker for being a mentor in the mid-1990s, and to Pastor Arni Schmeichel for timely advice in the dark days of 1998.

Finally, I dedicate this book to my wife, Colleen, and our children: Elizabeth, Matthew, Sarah, and John. Colleen, thank you for your sharp editorial eyes, for putting up with the unconventional life we lead, and for your commitment to walk beside me all these years. Kids, please don't let your rooms look like my office.

As ever, praise to the God of Psalm 111:10; Proverbs 2:6; and Colossians 2:2-3.

# Introduction

## The Church Struggle

This book has its origins in my desire to understand Christian responses to National Socialism in Germany and to investigate the impact of the German Church Struggle (*Kirchenkampf*) on Protestant parish clergy and their congregations. After more than half a century, a rich interpretive tradition has grown up around the Church Struggle. Coined by the church leaders who lived and worked in the Third Reich, the term *Church Struggle* captured the rising tension and open conflict among clergy and laity within the churches, and also between church leaders and members of both the Hitler government and the ruling National Socialist German Workers' Party (NSDAP, or Nazi Party).

Although the Church Struggle lasted until the end of the Third Reich, the years 1933 to 1935 were most intense, when institutional Protestantism was split over the campaign to establish a comprehensive German Protestant Reich (or National) Church. From early on, however, the Church Struggle consisted of more than just a theological or church-political feud. As Hitler, the NSDAP, and its political police interfered ever more directly in the affairs of the Protestant churches in Germany, the Church Struggle evolved into a semipublic quarrel between the churches and the National Socialist regime, primarily over the extent to which the Nazi Party and state could or should control the religious realm in Germany. Conflict arose over issues such as the application of new civil service regulations within the churches, the role of the churches in the celebration of national holidays, the publication of church news, the religious and ideological education of children and youths, and the implementation of Nazi racial policy.

No discussion of National Socialism and German religious life would be complete without reference to the ideological roots of National Socialism and its

1

leader, Adolf Hitler. National Socialism was in large part a movement of protest: anti-Bolshevik, anti-Western, anti-capitalist, anti-liberal, anti-democratic, anti-internationalist, anti-pacifist, and above all, anti-Semitic. The basis of Adolf Hitler's worldview consisted of what he termed "the basic principle of the blood." The Aryan race, of which the German nation or ethnic community (*Volk*) was the most perfect embodiment, was alleged to be a free, strong, creative master race that stood above any other. According to Hitler, however, the Germans had been neglecting their duty to cultivate the purity of their race and were consequently succumbing to foreign influences. Among these influences, the greatest threat to the continued existence of the German race was the Jews, an allegedly degenerate race that produced no creative ideas of its own but infiltrated and weakened the blood of other races caught up in a Darwinist struggle to survive and thrive in the world.

Hitler and his followers asserted that the disastrous influence of the Jews was exemplified by the humiliating Versailles *Diktat* (with its war-guilt lie and outrageous demand for reparations) imposed on a Germany that had never *really* been defeated in the First World War. National Socialists rejected the Weimar Republic for its Enlightenment rationalism; its weak, Western parliamentary government; and its hedonistic, individualistic culture. For Hitler and his associates, the solution to this un-German political and cultural degeneration was to return to an authoritarian form of government, in which the Nazi Party would coordinate and centralize all aspects of German life. Such a regime would serve the romanticized ideal of a German national community (*Volksgemeinschaft*) and remove the Jews from German society—in what manner was not initially clear.

Based on such a narrow sense of racial superiority, Nazi ideology violated many core Christian doctrines, such as the common sinfulness of all humanity, the universal judgment of God, the salvation of all humanity through the sacrificial death of God's Son, Jesus Christ, and the mission of the church to live as the unified body of Christ on earth. However, several factors inclined parish ministers (and many of their parishioners) to favor the authoritarian solutions that the German National People's Party (*Deutschnationale Volkspartei*, or DNVP) and the Nazi Party offered in the late 1920s and early 1930s. For one, Protestant pastors feared they were losing their place in society, especially after the long-standing union of throne and altar was dissolved by the Social Democratic Party, which led the Weimar coalitions of the 1920s. Moreover, clergy feared the real and imagined threat of atheistic Communism in Germany and fell back on their traditional social, cultural, and political conservatism.

Already before 1933, but especially during the Nazi seizure of power, Protestants who were inclined toward Hitler and his movement argued that fundamental changes were needed in the organization and even the theology of the German churches, in order to align them with the racial and authoritarian values of the Third Reich. Great numbers of these clergy and laity flocked to the deceptively named *German Christian Movement*. (In this book, the words *German Christian* always refer to the members of the Faith Movement of the German Christians, and never merely to Germans who identified themselves as Christians.) German Christians wholeheartedly endorsed National Socialism and the government of Adolf Hitler. Influenced by the political theology of the day, they believed in a unique German spiritual destiny and aimed to conform their faith to the image of the Nazi state. To that end, German Christians worked to place the new Reich Church under the unrestricted authority of a Reich bishop. Radical German Christians who congregated in the "Thuringian" or "National Church" wings of the movement also argued that God was calling the German nation or ethnic community (*Volk*) into a congregation of blood and faith, and that God had created Germans with a particular national mission that was now embodied by Adolf Hitler and the Nazi Party. In keeping with the party's doctrine of "positive Christianity," Thuringian and National Church German Christians sought to rid Christianity of all its Jewish elements and envisioned a time when their movement would bridge the chasm between Protestantism and Catholicism, rendering obsolete that long-standing confessional division in German society.

The illusion that Adolf Hitler and the NSDAP offered a preferred future for the Protestant churches was reinforced by the National Socialists' vague language and promising symbolism. Article 24 of the NSDAP Program of 1920 proclaimed the independence of the party from traditional confessional churches but advocated a form of "positive Christianity" that would correspond to the sensibilities of the German racial community. On March 21, 1933, Hitler held the opening of the new parliament (*Reichstag*) and installation of the new government at the famous Garrison Church in Potsdam and gave his address from the lectern normally reserved for biblical readings. Two days later, he proclaimed that Protestantism and Roman Catholicism would be pillars of the Third Reich. Leaders in the NSDAP encouraged party members to participate in church life as part of the recovery of traditional German values and the struggle against godless Bolshevism. Christian ministers could even request a parish Bible with a handwritten dedication from Hitler. Church leaders responded positively to these signals: German Catholic bishops retracted their prohibition against joining the NSDAP, and Protestants welcomed the "national renewal" and the positive changes they saw in the nation and state.

During and after their seizure of power, leading National Socialists avoided any direct confrontation with the churches. In July 1933, the long-awaited signing of a Reich Concordat between the German government and the Holy See purported to guarantee the religious rights of Catholics in Nazi Germany. Among Protestants, there was almost nothing but praise for the order and tradition the new government stood for. The only sign of trouble concerned the proposed replacement of the twenty-eight Protestant regional churches with a single Reich Church, which was not so much a point of conflict between the Nazi state and Protestants as it was an inner-church battle brought on by the agitation of the German Christian Movement.

When the German Christians began to call for a unitary Reich Church to supersede the regional churches, they pretended that there would be little if any theological consequence to the "external" reform they proposed. They argued that the church needed to keep in step with the new regime by abandoning parliamentary forms of government for a hierarchical structure ruled by an authoritarian Reich bishop. After negotiations between representatives of the German Protestant Church Federation and the regional churches, on July 11, 1933, a new church constitution was agreed upon, creating the German Protestant Reich Church and granting the Reich bishop powerful executive authority. In the national church elections that followed, German Christians swept to victory, thanks in part to the employment of the NSDAP campaign machine on their behalf and to the endorsement of Adolf Hitler in a national radio broadcast on the eve of the vote. German Christian agitation dominated the various regional church synods that followed, most notably the Prussian "Brown" Synod and the Reich Synod, both held in September 1933. As a result of the elections and synods, German Christians took control of almost every regional church government as well as the new Reich Church government. Former military chaplain Ludwig Müller was elected Reich bishop and began the task of gathering the German regional churches into his fold.

These developments did not go unopposed. Karl Barth, a Swiss theologian and professor at Bonn University, unleashed a scathing attack against the false teaching of the German Christians, calling upon the church to defend its historic teachings. Pastor Martin Niemöller of the affluent Berlin parish of Dahlem launched the Gospel and Church Party (*Evangelium und Kirche*) to oppose the German Christians in the July 1933 church elections. He walked out of the Prussian Synod in protest against its overt Nazi orientation and subsequently founded the Pastors' Emergency League on September 11, 1933.

The Emergency League bound together Protestant ministers who vowed that they would base their preaching solely on the Bible and Reformation Confessions. It was formed in protest against the German Christian demand that the Aryan Paragraph, which banned Jews from careers in the civil service, be applied in the churches. Within a week, the membership of the Pastors' Emergency League had grown to two thousand. By the beginning of 1934, at least seven thousand ministers had signed on.

The stunning growth of the Pastors' Emergency League was fueled by the increasing radicalism of the German Christians. One watershed event was the infamous Sport Palace speech of Berlin German Christian leader Dr. Reinhold Krause, on November 13, 1933. Speaking to twenty thousand German Christians in Berlin, Krause demanded the creation of a commanding Reich Church and advocated the de-Jewification of Christianity through the purging of the Old Testament and the teachings of the "Rabbi Paul," a significant portion of the New Testament. Gospel portrayals of the meek, suffering, and crucified Christ were to be exchanged for those of a forceful, heroic Jesus more akin to the needs of the "Nordic spirit." Krause even argued that fanatical support for the Nazi "national renewal" ought to be the criterion for membership in the Protestant clergy.

The results of Krause's speech were disastrous for the German Christians: an immediate, mass exodus of clergy from the movement; the distancing of Hitler and NSDAP leaders; and the forced resignation of Reich Bishop Ludwig Müller (who was also Hitler's plenipotentiary for Protestant church affairs) from his headship over the German Christian Movement.

By 1934, it was clear that neither Reich Bishop Müller nor the German Christians were going to unify German Protestantism peacefully. Consequently, on January 4, Müller adopted a harsher approach, as evidenced in his *Decree for the Restoration of Orderly Conditions in the German Evangelical Church*, popularly known as the *Muzzling Decree*. This edict prohibited two broad categories of activity: any political action in the churches or any criticism of the German church leadership or constitution. In defiant response, thousands of Protestant ministers read an illegal pulpit declaration from the Pastors' Emergency League, resulting in fines, suspensions, and the harassment of rebellious clergy by members of the Gestapo.

In March 1934, Reich Bishop Müller launched a bid to incorporate resistant regional churches into his new Reich Church, culminating in the forcible takeover of three churches and the suspension of their dissident leaders: Bishops Theophil Wurm of Württemberg, Hans Meiser of Bavaria, and August Marahrens of the Hanover Lutheran church. This action was so patently un-Christian in nature and aroused such widespread opposition to Müller's plans that it sabotaged any hope of creating a single Reich Church. Müller's campaign was broken off toward the end of 1934, never to be completed.

Meanwhile, since the beginning of 1934, independent "Confessing synods" had been established by ministers and laypeople who opposed the German Christian (and National Socialist) attempt to coordinate and centralize their churches. On April 22, 1934, representatives from these synods founded the Confessing Church at a special service in the city of Ulm. In May, representatives from its member synods met at a national gathering in Barmen, Westphalia. Under the guidance of Reformed theologian Karl Barth, the Barmen Synod issued a declaration that rejected four main ideas of the German Christians: first, that divine revelation existed outside of Scripture (that is, in the German racial community); second, that Jesus Christ was not lord of all aspects of life; third, that the form of the church's message and structural organization ought to be determined by the political trends of the day; and fourth, that the state could exceed its own realm and claim to be the sole authority in life.

A second national Confessing Church synod took place in November 1934 at Dahlem, in Berlin. It established a Provisional (or Emergency) Church Leadership that claimed to be a replacement for the corrupted Reich Church government dominated by German Christians. In March 1935, Prussian members of the Confessing Church went so far as to issue a pulpit declaration denouncing Nazi racial ideology and the new heathenism emerging in Germany. As a result of reading this statement, roughly seven hundred Confessing pastors were thrown in jail.

The emergence of the Confessing Church signaled the obvious failure of Reich Bishop Müller's work and convinced Hitler to turn instead to Nazi lawyer Hans Kerrl for solutions to the ecclesiastical division. Appointed Reich Minister for Church Affairs in July 1935, Kerrl immediately amnestied all Protestant clergy from the judicial punishments of the Müller era and reinstated the authority of the regional churches (ending the Reich Church experiment). Next, between October 1935 and March 1936, Kerrl established church committees at the Reich and regional church levels. These committees included representatives from across the Protestant church-political spectrum. Though extremists in both the German Christian and Confessing Church camps scorned the church committees, on the whole their creation ushered in a more settled phase in the Church Struggle.

The use of church committees to manage church-political division was only temporarily successful, however, in part because forces in the Nazi Party were growing ever more antagonistic toward dissident or nonconformist church leaders. In 1935, state and party officials, including members of the Gestapo, began to harass clergy. They initiated judicial proceedings in the Special Courts against priests and pastors, disseminated racial and anticlerical propaganda, secularized public education, restricted church meetings, and suppressed the church press. This was nothing less than an organized campaign to marginalize the German churches, with the ultimate goal of excluding them from German society altogether.

Within the Confessing Church, the creation of the church committees induced a theological and tactical crisis that split the Provisional Church Leadership. On one side were Martin Niemöller and his colleagues from the Dahlem Confessing Synod, who tended to be more Reformed in their theology and were sharply critical of the official church government. These were the church leaders who had been the driving force behind the original Barmen Declaration. On the other side were three powerful regional church bishops—Wurm, Meiser, and Marahrens—the heads of the so-called intact regional churches of Württemberg, Bavaria, and Hanover, which were not under German Christian control. The three bishops were reluctant to challenge the authority of the official church and the Reich government that stood behind it by declaring the Confessing Church to be *the* legitimate church government in Germany and therefore rejecting the authority of the existing Protestant hierarchy. Rather, they favored cooperation with Reich Minister Kerrl and his policy of pacification. Niemöller and his followers denounced this idea as an alliance with German Christian heresy and broke away from the three powerful bishops, establishing a Second Provisional Church Leadership. In response, Bishops Wurm, Meiser, and Marahrens formed the Council of the Evangelical Lutheran Church of Germany, a moderate body that continued to support Kerrl's church committees.

The Second Provisional Church Leadership of the Confessing Church was serious about its rejection of the institutional authority of the Protestant regional churches and its criticism of the church policy of the NSDAP. On June 4, 1936, Confessing Church leaders issued a private memorandum to Hitler, expressing alarm at the apparent attempt to de-Christianize Germany. They denounced the vague and unorthodox interpretations of "positive Christianity," the repeated interference of the Nazi Party and state in the internal life of the churches, and the ongoing drive to eliminate confessional public schools. Above all else, they castigated Nazi racial politics as idolatry:

> When blood, race, nationality, and honor are thus raised to the rank of qualities that guarantee eternity, the Evangelical Christian is bound, by the First Commandment, to reject the assumption. When the "Aryan" human being is glorified, God's Word bears witness to the sinfulness of all men. When, within the compass of the National Socialist view of life, an anti-Semitism is forced upon the Christian that binds him to hatred of the Jew, the Christian injunction to love one's neighbor still stands, for him, opposed to it.[1]

Although this memorandum was intended to be a private submission to Adolf Hitler, copies were soon circulated. Within days of its submission to the Reich Chancellery, the American State Department knew of its existence and English Bishop George Bell of Chichester had seen a copy. The *New York Herald Tribune* noted the existence of the memorandum on July 16 and published an English translation of the full text on July 28. Five days earlier, the *Basler Nachrichten* had published the full German text.

Already from 1935, the Confessing Church grew increasingly active in the training of new clergy, establishing its own church training colleges in Berlin and Elberfeld, and founding seminaries, the most famous of which was Dietrich Bonhoeffer's Finkenwalde Seminary in Pomerania. Though an SS (Schutzstaffel, or "defense squadron") decree outlawed these seminaries on August 29, 1937, Confessing Church leaders continued to train young theological candidates in secret well into the Second World War.

Caught between the opposition of the Confessing Church and the radicals within the NSDAP, Reich Minister Kerrl spent the bulk of 1936 trying to convince everyone who would listen that National Socialism and Christianity were inseparable, indeed vital to each other's survival. Meanwhile, government decrees established church finance departments to tighten fiscal control over dissenters in the regional churches and church legal bureaus to enforce the administrative will of the Reich bishop over dissenting clergy. Within the Reich Church Committee, frustration over the impossibility of uniting the political and theological diversity of German Christians, neutrals, and supporters of the Confessing Church led to the widespread resignation of committee members in February 1937. With Kerrl threatening the regional church committees, Hitler suddenly intervened, overruling his minister and announcing that new church elections would take place, leading to a new general synod empowered to draft a new church constitution. Very quickly, it was clear that nothing would come of Hitler's announcement. The ensuing election campaign only reconfirmed the deep divisions in the church between the German Christians and the Confessing Church, forcing the indefinite postponement of the elections.

In part, this was the result of the growing rift between Hitler and the churches. In 1936, church leaders from both confessions had affirmed their support for the Nazi struggle against Bolshevism during the Spanish Civil War, though in both cases statements of support were coupled with demands that the National Socialists tone down their ideological and bureaucratic opposition to Christianity. After the Roman Catholic encyclical of Pope Pius XI *Mit brennender Sorge* of March 21, 1937, Hitler gave up the idea that either the Roman Catholic or the disunited Protestant churches would ever unconditionally support his regime, and he no longer concerned himself with the churches.

Reich Minister Kerrl, who had reassumed executive control over the churches during the abortive church election campaign, tried to regain both his authority within the churches and his prestige within the Nazi Party by ordering the arrest of almost fifty leading members of the Confessing Church, including Brandenburg General Superintendent Dr. Otto Dibelius and Berlin pastor Martin Niemöller. In the summer and fall of 1937, roughly seven hundred more Confessing Church pastors were arrested, most for refusing to submit church collections to their official church governing bodies. As a result, many pastors were forbidden to teach religious instruction in German public schools, and measures were taken to terminate the employment of pastors trained and examined for ordination by the illegal Confessing Church seminaries and councils. This process culminated with Kerrl handing over control of the German Protestant Church to Dr. Friedrich Werner, the German Christian president of the Old Prussian Union Church.

Werner was supposed to control the external administration of the church, which included the discipline of pastors. In April 1938, he responded by promulgating a decree demanding that all Protestant clergy swear an oath of allegiance to the Führer as an expression of gratitude for the recent German annexation of Austria. Once again, while most ministers agreed with this measure, a minority in the Confessing Church refused, adding yet another front upon which the Church Struggle was contested.

The infamy of the Church Struggle reached its height in 1938 with the trial and acquittal of Martin Niemöller, leader of the Confessing Church. Upon his release, Niemöller was promptly seized by Gestapo agents and detained in concentration camps, where he remained until 1945. By mid-1938, however, the Nazi regime was increasingly preparing for war and was decreasingly prepared to antagonize large segments of German society. Thus, while the Gestapo continued to harass clergy, publicly the regime backed away from its earlier anti-Christian extremes.

For their part, Protestant leaders were generally supportive of Hitler's foreign policy, praising the annexation of Austrian and Czech territory and the outbreak of war against Poland. German Christians were the most eager to prove their loyalty to the regime, volunteering for front-line duty and positions in the military chaplaincy. At the outset of the campaign against Soviet Russia in June 1941, the executive council of the German Protestant Church—the federal umbrella organization for all of German Protestantism—was quick to assure Hitler of its ongoing support for the war effort.

The introduction of the war in the east also provided the opportune moment for the Nazi regime to implement its most radical solution to the "Jewish Question": annihilation. Since the beginning of the Nazi era, political anti-Semitism had rekindled an old problem for the German churches. The long history of Christian anti-Judaism in Germany (as elsewhere), coupled with increasing cultural, economic, and racial forms of anti-Semitism that emerged in the later nineteenth century meant that German Protestants generally held ambivalent or antipathetic attitudes toward Jews. For many pastors and parishioners, the "Jewish Question" that obsessed National Socialists held little meaning. Some church leaders spoke directly to the issue but sent mixed messages about the nature of Jewish identity that gave little guidance to confused parishioners inundated with party propaganda depicting Jews as vermin or forms of disease that threatened the existence of the Aryan race. In 1933, for instance, no less a figure than Martin Niemöller preached that the Jews stood as outcasts under God's punishment while he was fighting tooth and nail to prevent the application of anti-Semitic legislation in the churches. Apart from the 1936 memorandum to Hitler (which was not even intended to be public), there was scant public protest among Protestants against any government measures taken against the Jews, from legal and social marginalization of the early Nazi years to the Nuremberg racial laws of 1935 to the "Kristallnacht" Pogrom of November 9–10, 1938, when SA (Sturmabteilung, or "Storm Troopers") and SS gangs destroyed Jewish homes, shops, and synagogues throughout Germany. There were, however, a few notable exceptions. In Berlin, Roman Catholic provost Bernhard Lichtenberg led his congregation in public intercession for the Jewish victims of the pogrom. He was subsequently arrested and died while in detention. Also in Berlin, Protestant pastor Heinrich Grüber established and operated an office to help Jews escape from Germany, until he was arrested in 1940.

Protestant and Roman Catholic church leaders were somewhat more active, however, in their opposition to the Nazi policy of euthanasia that was implemented at the beginning of the Second World War. Roman Catholic Bishop Clemens August von Galen of Münster and Protestant Bishop Wurm of Württemberg were among the boldest opponents of the organized murder of physically and mentally handicapped and mentally ill Germans. Von Galen preached a famous sermon in August 1941 that was quickly circulated throughout the country in printed form, while Wurm wrote pointed private letters of protest to Nazi leaders, including Hitler himself. Sadly, these men and others like them constituted but a small minority within the German churches.

War and conquest served to demonstrate the ultimately anti-Christian nature of the Nazi movement. The constant stream of propaganda, the antagonistic statements of Nazi leaders toward Christianity, and a policy of outright de-Christianization in the Warthegau region of occupied Poland demonstrated that Protestants who believed that the Christian religion was an integral force within National Socialism were profoundly mistaken.

The end of the Second World War brought the German Church Struggle to a close—at least in the western part of the country. As in other sectors of German society, however, the postwar denazification process failed adequately to punish or even expose the active or tacit support of Hitler by German Protestants. Alarmingly, very few Christian clergy sympathetic to National Socialism were suspended from their positions or otherwise punished. Sadly, this was true even for the most outspoken champions of Hitler and Nazi racial ideology who had inhabited the German Christian Movement.

## Questions of Interpretation

In the course of investigating the German Church Struggle, I have sought answers to a series of fundamental questions about Protestant Christianity in Nazi Germany. In the first instance, how was the seizure of power by Hitler and his National Socialists received by pastors and parishioners? What meaning did it hold for them, and how did it affect their religious lives? What did they think National Socialists stood for? How did Protestants feel about Nazi values, such as authoritarian rule and racial purity, and how important were these values in local church affairs? Then, given the polarization of German Protestantism in the Third Reich, what role did moderates play in parish life? Did they accommodate, enable, or undermine church-political extremists, whether on the side of the German Christians or the Confessing Church? And how did church-political tensions affect relations between local ministerial colleagues? Finally, to what extent did patterns of church-political conflict simply trickle down from the higher levels of church government? Were national-level conflicts simply replayed locally, or were there deeply felt local concerns that reshaped the Church Struggle at the parish level? Was it simply that national and regional church leaders determined the course of parish life, or were the personalities of parish clergy and key parishioners more important in shaping the Church Struggle as it unfolded across Nazi Germany?

To answer these questions, this book will follow the lives of German Lutherans in the church districts connected to three large towns: Nauen, on the northwest outskirts of Berlin, in Brandenburg; Pirna, on the southeast outskirts of Dresden, in Saxony; and Ravensburg, in the southernmost part of Württemberg. By comparing and contrasting these districts, I will examine a range of themes and situations: the eagerness of pastors for the revitalization of Germany under the Nazi movement; the transformation of local church conditions during the Nazi seizure of power; the politicization of the appointment process for parish clergy; the ambivalence of Christians to the challenge of Nazi racial policy; and, not least, the trials and temptations of parish life during the Third Reich. Through this study, I hope to add to our present understanding of both the German Church Struggle and the history of everyday life under National Socialism, by showing how the religious upheavals of this era became a lived reality for some of the more than sixty million Protestants in Hitler's Germany.

Taken as a whole, *Faith and Fatherland* offers a reading of the German Church Struggle that emerges "from the bottom up." It is intended to be an alternative (or at least a complement) to the preponderance of "top-down" histories of the German Church Struggle that examine Nazi church policy and Protestant institutional or theological responses only at the highest levels. By uncovering key issues that were unmistakably significant for Protestant parishioners across Germany, my hope is that general readers will find that this book offers an informative glimpse into the world of German Protestants in the 1930s. Specialists will find that it addresses the field of Church Struggle literature from four angles.

First, the local church history of Nauen, Pirna, and Ravensburg confirms the general impression that Protestantism, hampered by its cultural and theological traditions, largely failed to resist or even critique the Nazi state. This includes, for the most part, the Confessing Church.[2] Most of the parish clergy in this book were conservatives who publicly welcomed the accession of Hitler and the National Socialists. They exhibited a Protestant-nationalist worldview that dated back to the nineteenth century, a mentality that historian Klaus Scholder has described as "the distinctive expression of the character of the Protestant church and piety." It was, as he has argued, based on notions like "the 'German God'; the Germans as his chosen people, chosen for their piety, honesty and loyalty; German history as the place of his revolution; political unity and freedom as the fulfilment of his will and order."[3] This was certainly the dominant view of things in 1933. For many, it was a conviction that persisted until the later 1930s, and even to 1945.

Many pastors disagreed publicly with the centralization and reorganization of their churches in the style of Nazi authoritarianism. Often, though, this disagreement was simply grounded in the desire for church independence from state interference. Only rarely did clergy or laity raise specific theological objections to the influence of Nazi ideology within their churches, such as the hatred and violence at the core of National Socialism, or even its idolatrous exaltation of the nation. On the other hand, perhaps the very act of defending the church against the totalitarian claims of the state was the greatest support that Christian leaders could have given to the forces of opposition, as Hans Rothfels argued already in 1948.[4] If Rothfels was right, then it can be said that Confessing Church clergy in districts like Nauen, Pirna, and Ravensburg gave decisive support to their parishioners in the creation of moral and theological boundaries across which Nazism could not trespass. They demonstrated courageous conviction in perilous times and stand as representatives of a "good Germany" that was not corrupted under Hitler. Still, as will become clear in the pages to follow, they remained the small minority, the noble exception. In the main, institutional Protestantism either tacitly accepted or actively collaborated with the Nazi government.

Second, the local church history of Nauen, Pirna, and Ravensburg demonstrates that relationships within both the German Christian and Confessing Church factions were more complex than first assumed by historians of the Church Struggle. Neither of the two movements should be understood as a uniform or unified camp. In this regard, Andreas Kersting has rightly criticized both Klaus Scholder and Kurt Meier for failing to differentiate sufficiently between the *members* of the Confessing Church, who denied the legitimacy of the regional church governments, and *supporters* of the Confessing Church, who refused to make a complete break with regional and national church authorities. Over time, Confessing Church members under the Second Provisional Church Government argued that their *church* (which opponents called a *front*) had become the sole legitimate German Protestant Church. This was based on their fidelity to Scripture and Reformation Confessions, as articulated in the declarations of not only the Barmen but also the Dahlem Synod. It was also based on their contention that the existing regional church governments had embraced heresy and had thus made themselves illegitimate. Confessing Church supporters, on the other hand, while sympathetic to the Barmen and Dahlem critiques of the institutional churches, continued to work with the national and regional church committees in the spring of 1936, pursued other conciliatory measures thereafter, and never repudiated the legal authority of the regional and national churches. In this regard, Hartmut Ludwig carries Kersting's contention further, asserting that the commonly held notion that these two groups (members and supporters) were simply two factions *within* the Confessing Church was a historical myth created by supporters (many of whom had risen to positions of ecclesiastical authority) after 1945 for political purposes.[5]

What is true at the national level is even truer at the local level, where members and supporters of the Confessing Church worked side by side, but often in tension. Indeed, in the uneven reality of church-political life in the parishes, it was the fact that the Confessing Church *supporters* retained their connection with the regional church authorities that often made the work of the Confessing Church *members* possible. For that reason, Ludwig has called upon historians to write "a history of the Confessing Church 'from below' . . . a history of the daily life [*Alltagsgeschichte*] of the Confessing Church."[6] Entering into that daily world of German Protestants illuminates many gradations within the church-political spectrum, as well as the inconsistencies with which pastors and parishioners thought and acted, shifting their positions and living in ways that defy our subsequent attempts to pigeonhole them into neat theological or church-political categories. The more nuances of this ecclesiastical *Alltagsgeschichte* we can master, the clearer will be our overall picture of the Protestant experience in Nazi Germany.

Third, by interweaving the three local church histories of Nauen, Pirna, and Ravensburg, we can broaden our historical understanding of the overall Protestant experience in the Third Reich. This book is the first study I know of that engages in a detailed comparison of the Church Struggle in geographically and church-politically varied districts and parishes, and thus reveals a fascinating diversity inherent in the German Church Struggle that is often unaccounted for in the literature of the field.

Fourth, *Faith and Fatherland* addresses the current renewal of the debate about the relationship between Nazism and Christianity. Over the past decade, scholars have increasingly suggested that Nazism was a political religion—an ideological rival to Christianity. Given the deification of the so-called Aryan race, the ideology of blood and soil, the status of Hitler and his book *Mein Kampf*, and the complex liturgy and symbolism employed by the NSDAP, this view has much to recommend it. More recently, however, this view has been challenged by the provocative interpretation of Richard Steigmann-Gall in his book *The Holy Reich*. Steigmann-Gall takes the bold position that leading National Socialists not only identified themselves as Christians but also strove to unite the German nation into an anti-Semitic, anti-liberal, and anti-Marxist racial community that would be loyal to God and committed to overcoming existing confessional divisions—a task at least some of them saw as the completion of the Protestant Reformation in Germany. To be sure, this view has come under heavy criticism, some of it justified.[7] However, the words and actions of parish clergy from Nauen, Pirna, and Ravensburg suggest that many of them believed that supporting Nazism was consistent with their practice of Christianity and raise the possibility that they too believed that Hitler and the Nazis were engaged in a movement that complemented, if not flowed out of, their faith. Whether or not leading National Socialists formed their early political views from Christian or pseudo-Christian sources, by the later 1930s they had clearly abandoned such a position and were deeply antagonistic toward the faith.

## Sources and Terminology

For the purpose of investigating these questions, I have employed a wide range of ecclesiastical archival sources, including the Evangelisches Zentralarchiv in Berlin, the main repository of the Old Prussian Union Church, and the Landeskirchliches Archiv in Stuttgart, Württemberg. The bulk of the primary source material came, however, from three smaller archives: the Brandenburg Domstiftsarchiv, a repository for many rural church districts and parishes in the region west of Berlin, along with two district church archives in Pirna and Ravensburg. I consulted also the city archives in Pirna and Ravensburg and the state archive of Saxony. Supplementing the diverse and plentiful correspondence among parish pastors, district superintendents, and regional church authorities were district circular letters, parish newsletters, statistical reports, sermons and clerical addresses, and newspaper accounts of parish meetings and other newsworthy items from local church life.

Here it is appropriate to insert a note about German ecclesiastical terminology, the complexity and confusion of which is legendary. Indeed, no less an authority than the 1925 *Church Yearbook* decried "the excessive variety in the terms for church ministries and authorities," and joked that one would need a lexicon just to understand them.[8] For the sake of simplicity, I use *Saxon Lutheran Church* or *Saxon Church* in place of *Saxon Evangelical-Lutheran Land Church* to denote the state-supported church in Saxony. Likewise, I employ *Württemberg Protestant Church* or *Württemberg Church* in place of the formal name *Württemberg Evangelical Land Church*. Alongside these, the long form of *Brandenburg Church Province of the Old Prussian Union Church* is frequently shortened to *Brandenburg Church Province*.

The German word *Land* refers to any one of the states that amalgamated to form the united Germany of 1871 and have constituted it since then. In ecclesiastical usage, *Land* refers to the churches from those territories, as well as to churches from various smaller German territories that existed prior to unification but were eventually subsumed by larger *Länder*. I have followed the common convention that finds the word *regional* to be a more descriptive term for these twenty-eight formerly established (and still state-supported) churches that existed in the Germany of 1933.

Another point of confusion is the German word *evangelisch*, properly translated as *evangelical*, a Reformation-era label for the German churches commonly described in English as Protestant. In British and North American usage, however, the term *evangelical* refers to a modern church movement that is distinct from these Lutheran and Reformed traditions that date from the sixteenth century. Therefore, I generally use *Protestant* rather than *evangelical*, and omit either term from the names of the regional churches when their inclusion would seem redundant. Finally, also for the sake of simplicity, I have chosen to use the title *district superintendent* or simply *superintendent* to describe the clergy placed in leadership over each church district, though their German titles vary from *Dekan* in Württemberg to *Superintendent* in Brandenburg and both *Superintendent* and *Ephorus* in Saxony.

## Nauen, Pirna, and Ravensburg

Before proceeding to the analysis of the district and parish contexts in which the Church Struggle unfolded in Nauen, Pirna, and Ravensburg, it will be helpful to introduce briefly the three church districts and their parishes. All were rural or semirural in nature, with small-town and village churches that were important institutions in local life. Their pastors and lay leaders were prominent people in the community.

The Nauen church district was located in the Berlin-Brandenburg Church Province, one of nine provinces in the massive Old Prussian Union Church, the largest Protestant regional church in Germany by far. Nauen is located just northwest of Berlin, not far from Falkensee and Oranienburg. Because the Nauen church district had incorporated parishes from the Spandau and Fehrbellin districts in 1929, it was one of the largest church districts in all of Brandenburg during the 1930s—about twenty miles wide. Most of its twenty-five parishes were situated in tiny farming villages located in the flat, marshy Havelländ and Rhin Marsh zone that lay just beyond the outskirts of the German capital. The district superintendent in Nauen reported to councilors in the Brandenburg Consistory (the provincial church governing body), who reported in turn to councilors on the Superior Church Council of the Old Prussian Union Church. Both the consistory and the Superior Church Council were based in Berlin. The head of the Old Prussian Union Church during the Nazi era was President Friedrich Werner.

The Pirna church district was located in the Saxon Lutheran Church. Pirna is immediately southeast of Dresden. During the Nazi era, the church district stretched along the River Elbe toward the Czechoslovak border. Containing thirty-nine parishes, the district measured more than twenty miles from west to east and almost as much along its north-south axis. Only a few parishes lay to the west of Pirna, on the outskirts of Dresden itself. Most were centered in the small towns set into the rugged Elbe sandstone hills known as the Saxon Switzerland. The district superintendent in Pirna reported to authorities in the Saxon Church Office in Dresden. The head of the Saxon Lutheran Church during the Nazi era was the Lutheran bishop Friedrich Coch.

The Ravensburg church district was located in the Württemberg Protestant Church. Ravensburg is fully eighty miles from the regional church capital of Stuttgart (further still via road and train routes), situated in the southeast corner of Württemberg. The southern border of the church district was the *Bodensee* (Lake Constance), across which lay Switzerland. East of the district sat the southern tip of Bavaria and, a few kilometers farther on, Austria. The eleven parishes in the

Ravensburg district were centered in substantial towns, which served a host of smaller *filial* or *diaspora* communities in which tiny groups of Protestants typically met in smaller prayer halls scattered about the country. The district was also home to several Protestant special care institutions for physically and mentally handicapped Germans. The district superintendent in Ravensburg reported to councilors on the Superior Church Council in Stuttgart. The head of the Württemberg Protestant Church during the Nazi era was the Lutheran bishop Theophil Wurm.

Taken as a whole, these church districts represent an intriguing range of historical characters, parish institutions, and ecclesiastical problems. Their diversity in terms of geography, culture, confessionalism, government, and church polity will accentuate both the uniqueness of parish life and the presence of common experiences. All this, I hope, will contribute to a more nuanced understanding of the German Church Struggle and the religious component of the history of everyday life in Hitler's Germany.

# chapter one

# Faith and Fatherland
# through the Eyes of Clergy

 **"The face of the new Germany shall be that of a** Christian nation!" Those were the words of the German Protestant Reich bishop, repeated in a sermon by Super- intendent Hermann Ströle of Ravensburg in November 1933.[1] In uttering them, Ströle identified himself with the so-called *national renewal*, the radical transformation of German politics and society undertaken by Adolf Hitler and his National Socialist government in 1933. Like so many other pastors, he embraced the new religious nationalism founded on the ideas that Protestantism was revealed most fully in the German nation and that German nationalism was incomplete without the ethical foundation and symbolic presence of Protestantism. This illustrates one of the nagging questions about the German Church Struggle: How and why did the German Protestant clergy catch such a potent strain of religious nationalism?

As we probe the religious nationalism of Protestant clergy in Nauen, Pirna, and Ravensburg, more questions arise: What motivated Protestant ministers to embrace the national renewal sweeping across Germany in 1933? To what extent did their nationalist sentiments imply direct support for Hitler and National Socialism? What role did they see their churches playing in a National Socialist Germany? Were any clergy opposed to serving the national renewal, and if so, why? Finally, were there substantial differences between the nationalist rhetoric employed by clergy in different parts of the Reich, or did they all tend to think and speak the same way?

## Motivations

If Protestant pastors were excited about the new political climate in German society under Hitler, it was largely due to four factors: First, many believed that the national renewal of 1933 would bring with it a parallel moral renewal of the German people. Second, Protestant clergy perceived that the Führer, Adolf Hitler, was calling them into a partnership in which they could assist him as local leaders in this hoped-for renewal. Third, they were keenly sensitive to the political danger of Communism and grateful for the Nazi success at crushing the radical left. Fourth, Protestant pastors were predisposed toward authoritarian politics on the basis of a series of important, if problematic, concepts in Lutheran theology.

## National and Moral Renewal

In Nauen, Pirna, and Ravensburg, no event was more important to publicizing the religious national enthusiasm of 1933 than the annual district church assemblies. Behind the patriotic rhetoric of these meetings was the conviction that Germany was on the verge of a profound moral renewal that would accompany the national renewal already under way. In fact, all three district superintendents made that point in their keynote speeches. In Nauen, Brandenburg, Superintendent Graßhoff explained that the present task of the church was "the inner restoration of the German soul and of our beloved Protestant church." In language that echoed the biblical language of salvation as new creation, he declared: "God has spoken to our German nation through a great transformation. An epoch in German history has come to an end, a new period has begun." Graßhoff hailed the end of political grumbling, class conflict, moral laxity, and godlessness in Germany, while looking ahead to a new era of sobriety, discipline, strong leadership, and a nation willing to follow. Noting the astonishing speed at which this transition was already occurring around him, Graßhoff exclaimed: "What a miracle has come over us."[2]

For the Nauen superintendent, this new atmosphere in Germany was only the beginning of a revolutionary spiritual resurrection of the national community. Moral renewal would produce a profound new national character in Germany, marked by dependability, loyalty, and a strong sense of German racial identity. Graßhoff hoped this deeper transformation would save Germany from the threat of national decline, and so he challenged the clergy and lay leaders from Nauen to capitalize on the opportunity for moral renewal created by the new political environment:

> The decision about whether or not the new structure of our state will be blessed by God lies in our hands. God has given our nation a great opportunity. If we Christians fail now, then the final end of all the external state structure is in vain. Then the West will indeed finally crumble, just as the Roman Empire crumbled.[3]

On that sober note, Graßhoff closed his speech, a powerful amalgam of patriotic fervor and spiritual energy that fit seamlessly with the popular political mood of 1933.

Similar in tone was the address delivered by Superintendent Maximilian (Max) Zweynert to the clergy and church leaders gathered at his district church assembly in Pirna, Saxony. Speaking on behalf of his audience, he proclaimed, "We place ourselves without reserve behind the Reich government and are determined to support it with all [our] forces in the fulfillment of its responsible work for the national and moral renewal of our nation."[4] Finally, in Ravensburg, Superintendent Hermann Ströle was only slightly less enthusiastic in his praise of the new political developments. Although in the past he had been skeptical of the ability of the churches to influence their surrounding culture, Ströle publicly thanked God, "the guide of history," for allowing German Protestants to experience the new state unfolding before them. He described the renewed unity of the German nation as "a miracle," an incredible recovery from the brink of civil war, and rejoiced to see the fear of God taken seriously in Germany again. Importantly, he connected this development explicitly with the emergence of the Nazi government and hopes for a revitalized role for Protestant Christianity: "With the new state, *a spiritual change* is also being generated. Through this spiritual change, *the church will be called to a new, great service* . . . for our nation."[5]

In their affirmations of national and moral renewal, all three district superintendents were only echoing the laudatory tone set by higher church leaders. In Brandenburg, General Superintendent Otto Dibelius praised the Nazi political victory as the return of "a parliamentary majority with a consciously nationalist attitude," then added, "There will only be a few of us . . . who do not delight in this change with all their hearts." Dibelius's remarks paled in comparison to the April 11, 1933, Easter message of the leaders of the Old Prussian Superior Church Council, who described the German nation as "a people to whom God has spoken by means of a great turning point in history." The church leaders continued, asserting:

> We know that we are at one with all Protestant fellow believers in joy at the awakening of the deepest powers of our nation to a patriotic consciousness, to a true community of the *Volk*, and to a religious revival. . . . In the conviction that the renewal of the *Volk* and Reich can be achieved and secured only by these powers, the church knows itself bound in gratitude to the leadership of the new Germany. It is joyfully prepared to co-operate in the national and moral renewal of our people.[6]

Things were no different in Saxony, where Bishop Ludwig Ihmels asserted that no one could have imagined "that so quickly a completely new beginning of the patriotic ethos would seize the widest circles of the German nation." He then encouraged Saxon Lutheran clergy to participate in the joy that God had given their nation and to use their preaching to anchor the new sociopolitical developments in God.[7] Ihmels's successor, Friedrich Coch, a leading figure in the German Christian

Movement, was more radical still, attacking the opponents of reorganizing the churches and issuing a new set of guiding principles for the Saxon regional church, designed to bring it into line with National Socialist ideology and practice.

In Württemberg, church president Theophil Wurm estimated in February 1933 that at least 80 percent of convinced Protestants in Germany supported Hitler and other conservative political leaders, while he himself gave thanks to the Führer "for salvation out of very serious danger." Wurm praised the Nazi movement because it had "broken the back of terror," united disparate social classes, and taken on "the struggle against the influences destructive of our cultural life," words that his audience would have understood as anti-socialist and anti-Jewish. When in July 1933, Wurm exchanged the title church president for bishop, National Socialists in Württemberg celebrated the move as an ecclesiastical application of the authoritarian Führer principle.[8] Just like other church leaders, Wurm believed that together the Nazi movement and the Protestant churches could effect a deep transformation of German life.

The union of the national and moral renewal of Germany was a hope that filtered down from regional and national church leaders to the Protestant superintendents and ministers at the district and parish levels. This was especially so in the early years of the Third Reich, when clergy enjoyed the growth of popular interest in the churches. Superintendent Graßhoff of Nauen described the 1933 political turnaround as "a very gratifying influence," while his colleague, Pastor Herbert Kahle of Linum, was even more forthright: "The spiritual forces of faith, of confidence and of obedience are beginning to come alive again." Pastor Lux of Groß Behnitz agreed with his colleagues that the new connection between the Protestant church and the life of the nation was heartwarming, noting that the national renewal was generating a new level of public confidence in the church.[9]

The figure of Martin Luther was key to this linking of national and moral renewal at the parish level. The 450th anniversary of the reformer's birth, in November 1933, enabled clergy to connect the life of Luther with the lives of Protestants in the Third Reich. Pastors in Pirna gave public lectures on topics such as "Luther, the German Man," "Luther as Fighter [Kämpfer]," "Luther and the State," and "Luther and the German Home."[10] For parishioners, these lectures established the central position of the great Protestant reformer in the new religious nationalism of the Third Reich and fostered the notion of Hitler's national and religious renewal as a completion of the Protestant Reformation of the sixteenth century.

Such events were not isolated occurrences. In fact, national leaders in the German Christian Movement had planned since early summer 1933 to transform the November Luther celebration into a great mission to the German nation, and to link their movement "increasingly closely with the figure of Luther." German Christians planned to turn Luther into "the spiritual patron of the new Reich Church" and to make the 1933 anniversary celebrations into "a triumph of the *völkisch* Luther."[11]

Judging by the events in Ravensburg, Württemberg, leaders in the Nazi Party there also hoped to celebrate Luther as a German national and religious hero. The November anniversary church service was packed, in part because of the presence of the local SA, *Stahlhelm* army veterans, SA Reserve, SS and National Socialist Motor Corps, along with the local chapters of the Hitler Youth and the League of German Girls. These groups created a powerful impression, entering the church in their formations, complete with their distinctive uniforms and flags, and proceeding ceremoniously to their assigned places behind the altar. Other symbolic elements in the service included a Bach prelude, the performance of a Luther hymn, and the ceremonial display of the parish copy of the 1530 Augsburg Confession. Taken together, they created a powerful atmosphere for Superintendent Hermann Ströle's sermon, which described Luther's "soul-battle" and applied the reformer's life and words to Germany in 1933. In this and other meetings, Luther was presented as the model union of Christianity and Germanness, and an important figure for the new revival of German national life under Hitler.[12]

Ströle reiterated his support for National Socialist rule as a means to national and moral reform in August 1934 in the form of a Württemberg church proclamation endorsing Hitler's plan to assume the political authority of the deceased Reich president Paul von Hindenburg. Ströle not only circulated the proclamation to his clergy but also edited his own copy of the document to emphasize the divine sanction upon Hitler's rule: "We are all living witnesses of this powerful transformation, which we piously regard as the gracious act of God." Such words recalled the religious and political excitement of the past year even as they implied Ströle's present satisfaction with Hitler's ambitious and unconstitutional assumption of presidential powers. As if to emphasize the point, Ströle underlined another section of the proclamation that called for the "undivided loyalty of the entire nation."[13]

In early 1935, church trustee David Kuhn, from the neighboring town of Kilegg, added his voice to the chorus of approval for Hitler and his German national renewal. In a breathless letter to Superintendent Ströle, Kuhn argued for the need to deepen the spiritual bond between the Protestant churches and the Nazi state. The connection between national and moral renewal could hardly have been closer in Kuhn's mind, as he listed a pantheon of German heroes: Luther, Goethe, Schiller, Bismarck, Hindenburg, and Hitler. His point was simply and forcefully to say "that the Führer follows a high calling for the shaping of the German destiny." It followed naturally for Kuhn that there could be no criticism of anyone's faith in the Führer.

Kuhn went on to advance ideas commonly held by radicals from the German Christian Movement: Hitler was accomplishing what had not been done before, reversing the shameful confessional division of Germany and giving race, blood, earth, and the natural forces of the German nation their due. In time, he argued, the Führer's will would be accomplished and Germans would abandon their particular religious confessions and adhere to a single religion centered on Christ: "This *spiritual melding together* of the nation is a *necessity* which will be made a reality in a short time. Of that I am convinced." Hitler would win this spiritual struggle and create a united church, "the yearning of all who really love the German nation." Kuhn's hope was that Protestant ministers would soon catch Luther's spirit and place themselves at the disposal of the Führer. Summing up his adulation of the Nazi leader, Kuhn asserted: "Adolf Hitler is a 'doer of the word'! He is genuine! The nation feels that he is genuine and consequently it holds so firmly and tightly to him."[14]

In one fell swoop, Kuhn had encapsulated the sentiment that was driving clergy in Nauen, Pirna, and Ravensburg to welcome the Nazi national renewal as a catalyst to a new moral or spiritual renewal of Germany. At its extreme, this belief encompassed the notion that Hitler was not only the political savior of Germany but also its spiritual savior. At the very minimum, this belief led clergy to appreciate the benefits of National Socialist rule under the firm leadership of Adolf Hitler and to expect that it would lead to a revival in the fortunes of the churches.

## The Call of the Führer

Protestant pastors were motivated to adopt a strongly nationalist stance in the early years of the Third Reich not only because they believed that the national renewal would lead to a moral renewal but also because they were convinced that Adolf Hitler was calling them and their churches to help him save Germany. They believed that the National Socialist leader was appealing personally to the churches to enter a working partnership with him in order to renew public standards and political life. Hitler and other leading Nazis encouraged this belief—whether it was true or not is another question—in the positive, inviting language they employed during the National Socialist seizure of power in early 1933. For instance, in a radio speech delivered by Hitler on February 1, a day after he had assumed the chancellorship of Germany, he promised that his government would "preserve and protect the fundamentals on which the strength of our nation rests. It will preserve and protect Christianity, which is the basis of our system of morality."[15] The speech was then published in the leading Nazi newspaper, the *Völkischer Beobachter*, so that its content was widely circulated.

Two weeks later, in mid-February, Hitler made what amounted to a profession of faith, when he stated during a speech in Stuttgart:

> Today Christians and no international atheists stand at the head of Germany. I speak not just of Christianity; no, I also pledge that I will never tie myself to parties who want to destroy Christianity. . . . We want to fill our culture again with the Christian spirit, not just theoretically. No, we want to burn out the rotten developments in literature, in the theater, in the press—in short, burn

out this poison which has entered into our whole life and culture during these past fourteen years.[16]

Then, at the opening of the new national parliament on March 21, Hitler and Hindenburg both participated in a highly symbolic ceremony at the Potsdam Garrison Church. It was a theatrical portrayal of the new National Socialist regime that suggested its roots lay in the religious and military tradition of Imperial Germany. On the day after this elaborate ceremony, Hitler continued his promising tone during his opening address to the national parliament. As in earlier speeches, he reiterated his government's intention to undertake a twin revolution of German political and moral life, and then appeared to call on German Christendom for help when he added, "The [Reich] government regards the two Christian Confessions as the weightiest factor for the maintenance of our nationality." Hitler went on to promise that his government would abide by all agreements with the churches in order to ensure their proper influence in education and maintain an honest spirit of cooperation between the state and the churches. In return, he asked only that the churches respect the state's work for national and moral renewal.[17]

Protestant ministers from the Nauen, Pirna, and Ravensburg districts responded eagerly (and naively, as it would turn out) to these words. In the Nauen district, Pastor Kahle of Linum reported appreciatively that his parishioners had "joyfully greeted the fact that the National Socialist state considered the religious and moral forces of the gospel necessary for the recovery of the health of the nation." Another pastor told a Nauen women's group that "the young chancellor of the nation openly professed his faith in God and promoted the work of the Christian churches" and interpreted Hitler's words as a call for Protestant women to minister to the national community—not least in their role as the mothers of the next generation, where their efforts would "create the ground on which the young Germany can truly prosper."[18]

Pastors in the Pirna district had an easy time interpreting Hitler's message to the churches, particularly when the conference of Saxon church superintendents sent a congratulatory proclamation to Hitler, pledging their service to the Fatherland and thanking "the new Führer, whom divine predestination has given to the German nation in the Reich and [in Saxony]," for his Christian statesmanship and respect for the churches. Echoing this, one Pirna area pastor told his colleagues that Hitler's appointment was a divine event that compelled Saxon Lutherans to join in the national renewal: "The development of current conditions, the extreme spiritual and mental crisis of our nation and the call of the Führer are utterly unavoidable demands on the church and all its officeholders to do the utmost possible to unite our nation in a great Protestant national church, to gather our fellow members of the nation into a living community."[19] This was not simply the hope for a general moral renewal, but the conviction that Hitler was appealing directly to the churches to engage in the renewal of German society.

This sentiment was repeated in August 1934, when Saxon Lutheran church leaders rushed to offer their support for Hitler's assumption of the powers of deceased Reich president Hindenburg. In an August 19 pulpit statement meant to prepare Saxons to vote yes in that day's plebiscite to ratify Hitler's expanded powers, pastors described Hitler in glowing terms, as the one "whose love and concern extends to all, even to the least of his fellow members of the national community." As the one "whose thoughts revolve solely around the freedom, honor, and greatness of the German nation," Hitler's only goal was "Germany, nothing but Germany!" The pulpit statement went on to praise Hitler for making the German nation healthier, more content, stronger, and more united as each month passed. Most important, however, the proclamation hailed Hitler as a Christian statesman who based both his work and the new Germany on the ideal of *positive Christianity*, and who wanted to draw on the moral forces of the Christian churches to help him. To drive home the spiritual importance of Hitler's regime, Saxon pastors closed their pulpit address with a word of thanks to God "for the salvation of [Saxony] out of a very dark, very difficult time through Adolf Hitler." They continued, "We know [Hitler] as one given to us by God, we have borne his work as Führer of the National Socialist Movement and as Chancellor of the German Reich in praying hearts, we declare again and again our human respect, our Christian obedience, and our allegiance to him."[20]

This powerful clerical blessing of Hitler's regime was nothing less than the outgrowth of the belief that Hitler had called upon the Christian leaders to help him reform the German nation. Voting for Hitler in the plebiscite to ratify his new authority was the natural response for Saxon Lutherans, once their parish clergy had spoken in this way.

On other occasions, clergy in Pirna took their response to the perceived call of Hitler even further. The fullest expression of this sentiment was given by Pastor Paul Kühnel of Zschachwitz, between Pirna and Dresden, in February 1934 in a lecture entitled "The German Protestant Church and the National Socialist State." Speaking to his fellows pastors from around Pirna, Kühnel argued that, despite its long history of preaching obedience to the state, the German church had not yet fully submitted to the Nazi state. Kühnel called for a complete incorporation of the church into the National Socialist state, by which he meant the dissolution of the church and the sacralization of the state. In order to prepare itself for this eventuality, the church would need to learn what it meant to accept the total claim of the state. As he explained, the church would need to place itself "beside, over, under, in the state," through an intimate relationship of trust (in contrast to the legal rigidity of a Catholic-style concordat). In Kühnel's view, such an intimate relationship between church and state was highly feasible in Saxony, since the government of the Saxon Lutheran Church was both National Socialist in its orientation and faithful to its confession of faith. His ultimate goal was the creation of a single, Lutheran, pro-Nazi Reich Church under the leadership of the German Christian movement.[21]

If anything, as time wore on, these Lutheran pastors argued even more vociferously that Hitler had indeed called the Protestant churches to assist his national renewal by providing the moral fiber needed to hold the new Germany together. In 1934, a pastor from Struppen, near Pirna, insisted that the call of the Führer placed "totally irrefutable demands on the church and all its officials to do the utmost to unite our nation, if at all possible, into a great Protestant national church, to gather our fellow members of the nation into a living community."[22]

One way that Pirna clergy responded to this supposed call from Hitler was to give spiritual legitimacy to the successful political events in Germany. Thus, in 1935, Saxon pastors prayed for the return of the Saar province and rang bells to mark the January plebiscite that paved the way for that to happen.[23] In 1938, Pirna superintendent Heinrich Leichte gathered pastors from across the district together to promote the reelection of National Socialists in the upcoming April 10 national election. Leichte's pastors were overwhelmingly sympathetic, and even pastors from the Confessing Church who rejected Leichte's authority fell into line. In this regard, the response of Pastor Franz Ploedterll of Königstein is telling. Because of their church-political differences, Ploedterll had absolutely no intention of attending Leichte's political meeting. Still, he wanted Leichte to know that he would answer the question of April 10, 1938—in other words, the question of Germany's future under Adolf Hitler—with a yes, both "as a pastor of the German Protestant church and also as a member of the German national community and a Lutheran Christian." For Ploedterll, there was "no other possibility at all, than to joyfully march along in the unity front of the entire nation under the motto to which we are called: 'One nation, one Reich, one Führer.'"[24] Although Ploedterll belonged to the outlawed Confessing Church, Hitler's call to advance the German national community still resonated deeply with him. His support for Hitler's regime remained firm, even in 1938, long after the regime had revealed itself as an enemy of the churches and of the orthodox Christian faith for which the Confessing Church stood.

In Ravensburg, clergy responded to Hitler and his call to German Protestants in much the same way. Ravensburg superintendent Hermann Ströle explained to his district church leaders in December 1933 how the Nazi state was eager to receive the political service of the church, "as our Führer Adolf Hitler has stated again and again." One of his colleagues, Pastor Armbruster of Wälde-Winterbach, took that message to heart and proceeded to fill his parish newsletter with hymns of praise to the Führer, driven by Hitler's word that "the forces of Christianity are indispensable" to National Socialist rule. Other pastors were of a similar mind: one emphasized the church's responsibility to unite itself with the German liberation under Hitler's leadership; another proclaimed that it was Hitler's conviction that the political renewal be rooted in spiritual revival and asserted that the Führer wanted the Germans to be "renewed people." Only Pastor Karl Steger of Friedrichshafen expressed any reservation at all about Hitler's religious attitude. Ironically, this was not because Steger thought that Hitler harbored any animosity toward the churches, but only because he feared Hitler might be overly friendly to his Roman Catholic co-religionists, at the expense of Protestants. Even in 1936, by which time it was clear to everyone that Nazi agencies and officials were growing increasingly hostile to the churches, Superintendent Ströle took refuge in the three-year-old promises of the Führer, asserting, "I cannot believe that the Führer wants [to destroy the churches]. On many important days, he has stated that our nation has in Christendom a source of the deepest spiritual forces."[25]

Nor were these local clergy alone in holding on to Hitler's 1933 promises. Four years into the reign of Hitler, church officials in Berlin distributed a poster of heartening quotations taken from the Führer's speeches, highlighting Hitler's piety and his former declarations about the importance of the churches in the Third Reich. That they sent the poster out in 1937, well after events had revealed Hitler's interest in the churches to be a fantasy, testified to the strength of desire among Protestant clergy to belong to the Third Reich, to participate in the mythical Nazi vision of national and moral renewal in Germany.[26]

## The Threat of Bolshevism

German Protestant clergy also found motivation for their religious nationalism in the Nazi success at crushing Communism in Germany. Like their Catholic counterparts, Protestant pastors feared and loathed Bolshevism for its atheistic and revolutionary doctrine. Already in 1932, Superintendent Hermann Ströle of Ravensburg publicly identified the Communist movement as a grave danger to both Christianity and the German nation. Driven by what he called their "fanatical enmity with God," communists blew up churches in Russia and threatened the life of the parish and the family in Germany. In the early years of the Third Reich, clergy from all three districts urged one another to smash Marxist ideology by drawing the German nation back to its Christian foundation in the churches. Pastors criticized the shoddy effort put out in the struggle against Bolshevism and unbelief, lamented the dreadful living conditions of Germans suffering under Soviet rule, and remembered the earlier struggles of the church against Communism, free thought, and political terror in the Weimar Republic. Pastor Karl Steger of Friedrichshafen, Württemberg, summed up the situation from the perspective of the pastors: "[God], through our Führer, saved us from the Bolshevist terror at the last minute."[27]

Anti-Bolshevism was a regular feature in the local church press. Articles such as "About the Battle of Bolshevism against Religion and Church" described crimes against German farmers in the Soviet Union accompanied by the customary condemnation of the godlessness of the communist state and reminder of Adolf Hitler's determination to avert Bolshevism in Germany. Indeed, German newspapers and periodicals of all kinds played up this religious aspect of anti-Communism, offering their readers illustrated front-page articles about communists burning churches and murdering clergy in both Soviet Russia and republican Spain.

Much more than a passing phase, the anti-communist zeal of the clergy from Nauen, Pirna, and Ravensburg persisted deep into Hitler's reign. Public warnings about communist threats in Germany and words of praise for the National Socialist victory over the Left continued to appear throughout the 1930s, as in the case of a 1938 Advent sermon preached by Pastor Friedrich Siems of Nauen. Siems, an outspoken nationalist and anti-Semite, had been a Nazi Party member since before 1933 and was also a local party official. As he spoke, Siems reminded his parishioners of Hitler's (and Christ's) saving work. In the process, he linked the rise of Hitler, the defeat of Communism, and the salvation of the churches:

> We were once close to a red dictatorship of the kind which, in Spain and Russia, has burnt churches, murdered clergy, and denied God. We thank God that he granted our Führer to lead us from the abyss that sought to swallow us and the life of our churches. He has led us onto solid ground, where our church stands secure.[28]

In response to this kindness toward the churches, Siems declared to his congregation that he was resolved to follow Hitler as the all-time greatest unifying and healing force that God had ever raised up in Germany, a bold display of less religious nationalism founded on anti-Communism.

## Lutheran Theology

Protestant theology also played a role in stirring up religious nationalism among pastors, who took their cues from leading theologians such as Paul Althaus, Werner Elert, Emanuel Hirsch, and Friedrich Gogarten. These scholars were predisposed to support Hitler and National Socialism, owing in part to three emphases in the German theology of the day: the dual revelation of the law and the gospel, the traditional Lutheran doctrine of the two kingdoms, and the theology of the orders of creation.[29]

First, Lutheran theologians argued that God's revelation to humanity consisted of two parts: the law and the gospel. Rather than understanding the gospel as a fulfillment of the Mosaic law, they argued that the gospel message of the atoning death of Jesus Christ—the act of divine grace that fulfilled the requirement of divine justice for human sin—functioned merely to provide forgiveness for violations of the law and to help humans obey it more consistently. Even for members of the church, life on earth still revolved around the dictates of the law, not around any fundamental new order of grace. According to Elert and Gogarten, the gospel of Christ had no redeeming effect *at all* on the temporal realm. In other words, it placed no new ethical demands on the social, economic, or political aspects of life.

Thus, as Althaus argued, the law was the original revelation of God's demanding will, which contained all of God's ethical obligations for humans. Hirsch and Elert agreed and added that the law was made known not only historically in God's covenant with Israel but also in nature. Gogarten defined this more specifically when he asserted that the law was revealed in the blood (that is, in race), in the soil, and in the history of the nation. The consequence of such a position, he insisted, was that the political demands of any particular nation amounted to the law of God.

These propositions about the dualism of the law and the gospel led to the theological grounding of Christian ethics in the new ideological values and legal mores of Nazi Germany. If God was the sole guide of history and the unique force behind any existing political power, then political history and contemporary politics were simply ongoing revelations of God's law.[30]

Second, Althaus and other theologians used the Lutheran doctrine of the two kingdoms to reinforce this division between the eternal, spiritual kingdom of God ruled directly by Christ (according to the grace of the gospel) and the temporal, political kingdom of this world ruled (indirectly by God) through the coercive power of the state and its laws. Indeed, Althaus warned that the kingdom of Christ and the kingdom of the world "must be strictly distinguished and may not be mixed." The consequences of this position were paralyzing for German Lutherans. On the one hand, they remained theologically detached from politics, since the metaphysical realm of the kingdom of Christ, in which the gospel ruled, was deemed not to have any prescriptive authority in the realm of the kingdom of the world, in which the law ruled. On the other hand, Lutherans remained passively obedient to the state, since both the gospel and the law enjoined them as individuals to obey their earthly rulers, as stated for instance in Romans 13.[31] In this manner, the law-gospel dualism and the theology of the two kingdoms combined to keep Lutherans distanced from any truly Christian critique of Nazi political extremism.

Third, by the 1930s, a good many German Lutheran theologians were consumed with the study of the theology of the orders of creation, the idea that God had ordained that his divine nature would be continuously revealed to humanity in various aspects of life in the natural world: blood (race), soil, gender, marriage, and (not least) the state.

Effectively then, academics like Althaus, Elert, Hirsch, and Gogarten provided German Protestants with the theological justification for Nazi ideology and cloaked that justification in language very close to that used by Hitler and other party leaders. In parishes throughout the districts of Nauen, Pirna, and Ravensburg, ministers influenced by these intellectual trends frequently spoke in similar terms.

The effect was a kind of Protestant blessing of Aryan racial ideology, as illustrated by a lecture that Dr. Ernst Ranft gave to his fellow ministers in the Pirna district at the beginning of 1934, "The German Evangelical Church and the National Socialist State." Ranft, pastor in the Helmsdorf parish, began by comparing church-state relations in different eras of German history, then emphasized two new factors in church-state relations in Hitler's Reich: first, the emergence of the total claim of the National Socialist state; and, second, the new primacy of the national community over the individual. In language that echoed the theologian Friedrich Gogarten, Pastor Ranft spelled out the implications of Nazi totalitarianism: "The total claim of the state comes up against the total claim of God," he observed. "For that reason, it is necessary to bring state and church into the right relationship with one another," and all the more so because religion in Adolf Hitler's state was a national matter, not a private matter. Ranft encapsulated this new relationship in a tidy slogan: "Total Church in the Total State." As he explained, the church had to have absolute confidence in the state and learn how "to recognize the total claim of God in the total claim of the state." To drive home his point, Ranft drew an extraordinary comparison between Christianity and National Socialism: "Just as the church remembers its eternal foundation in the sacrificial death of Jesus, so the Third Reich has its eternal foundation in the sacrificial death of the Fallen," the men who died fighting for the Nazi cause in the years before 1933.[32] For Ranft, the duty of the German church was expressed in its highest form as service to the German nation, and spiritual salvation through Christ was superseded by a racially-based salvation through National Socialism.

In the Brandenburg Church Province, similar theological ideas were at work. For instance, in conversation with a visiting Swedish journalist in 1938, Pastor Friedrich Siems of Nauen used both Luther's two-kingdoms doctrine and the theology of the orders of creation in explaining his perspectives on politics and race. Drawing from Matthew 22:21 ("Give therefore to the emperor the things that are the emperor's, and to God the things that are God's"), Siems used Christ's identification of the two kingdoms (God and Rome) to argue that Protestant ministers ought to steer clear of political activity: "We pastors have other things to do than to occupy ourselves with politics, if we want to give to God what is God's. Our struggle belongs to another realm than the political." However, like the prominent theologians who argued against political engagement while simultaneously praising contemporary political developments they saw as beneficial, Siems immediately followed up his disavowal of political activity with expressions of adulation for Hitler's saving work in Germany. For Siems, the Führer was clearly a dynamic expression of God's providential rule over the kingdom of this world. Hitler ruled with God's help and lived a life that was nothing less than a model of dedicated service.[33]

In his dialogue with the journalist, Siems then used the theology of the orders of creation to assert that the welfare of the German nation would be secured only through the creation of a strong, united national church in which both Protestants and Catholics would feel at home. In the process, Siems gave distinct priority to his German racial community over his Christian spiritual community: "We serve God as we serve our brothers—in the first place, those who stand nearby in our own home nation."

But what did that mean? Siems went on to explain that the Christian's first duty was to his or her fatherland. National identity was God-given. In turn, nations had a duty to prepare themselves for various God-given roles on earth, and the churches could help by organizing themselves around the nation, and particularly by encouraging the maintenance of blood purity among their parishioners. Siems argued that blood purity was a divine order, a Christian duty that was threatened by the presence of Jews in the German Reich. Attacking Jews as both the root and strength of Bolshevism and the high priests and servants of capitalistic mammon, Siems asserted that it was a God-pleasing work to transfer them from Germany into their own colony somewhere else.

Siems returned to the theme of the Jews in 1939 in a letter in which he questioned Jesus' racial identity, arguing that "the founder of Christianity had nothing, really nothing at all to do with the Jewish people, rather they were always his sharpest opponents. . . . The personality of Christ is too great and too holy for us to bring it into connection with [Jews, who have] become a curse for the whole world."[34] So, just as Christ opposed "the Jews" on religious grounds, German Protestants were justified in driving off Jews on the grounds of preserving the divine order of race. Indeed, they would be serving God in the process!

One of the clearest cases in which the theology of the orders of creation was used to legitimize important aspects of Nazi ideology took place in 1936, when Pastor Adolf Wertz of Isny presented a treatise entitled "State and Church" before a monthly conference of clergy from across the Ravensburg district. His starting point was the conviction that God had created humanity with the need for blood-bound community, expressed in the blood union of marriage and the blood ties of the nation: "National uniformity of the blood, national character is God-willed."[35]

Once the blood ties of marriage and nation were established, the next "God-given expression of the human will to live" that Wertz examined was the economy, and farming in particular: "The human is bound to the earth [*Erde*], more precisely to the soil [*Boden*]," he declared. The Bible affirmed the high value of land, which made the farmer the foundation of the entire economy. Farmers were vital, he claimed, because it was God's will that the economy "goes out from the soil and returns to the soil." Wertz then drew together his first two ideas: "Just as human existence takes place in the realm of the blood, in marriage, family and nation, so also in work, [human existence takes place] principally in work with the soil."

From there, Wertz proceeded to argue that it was God's will that the human being "should and must be a ruler." Human (and particularly male) mastery was exercised over nature, in marriage and the family, and also within the blood-bound national community, in the form of political authority.[36] Wertz performed the ultimate service that a Protestant cleric could offer National Socialism. He presented a theological justification for the three core values of the Nazi movement: blood, soil, and authority.

The theological preoccupation of Protestant clergy with national themes was not limited to individual talks and sermons but appears time and again in the themes taken up in the monthly pastoral conferences in all three districts. It was the discussion that never ended, and it demonstrates how intellectually predisposed Lutheran pastors were to endorse the ideology and rule of National Socialism. Combined with the pastors' belief in the possibility of the national and moral renewal of the German nation, the belief in the Führer's call to a partnership with the churches, and religiously motivated anti-Communism, political theology provided the basis for a persistent and persuasive clerical nationalism that pervaded the three church districts of Nauen, Pirna, and Ravensburg.

## Clerical Support for National Socialism

Protestant clergy with strongly nationalistic views were unlikely to be critics of the National Socialist regime, but did that necessarily mean that they were National Socialists themselves? Answering that subtle question is not as easy as it might seem, because not all nationalists were direct supporters of the Nazi Party. Many were simply traditional conservatives who cherished the nation, who used some of the same language as National Socialists, but whose beliefs were incompatible with the radical agenda of Hitler and his movement. Certainly, as we have seen, some Lutheran ministers openly celebrated the leadership of Hitler and argued that the church needed to coordinate itself with the structure and values of the Nazi state. But beyond those self-identified National Socialists, how many of the clergy in Nauen, Pirna, and Ravensburg aligned themselves so closely with NSDAP? To answer that question, we must look to three sources of evidence: German Christian membership, NSDAP membership, and the presence of positive responses to political developments in Germany.

To be a member of the German Christian Movement was to be aligned with National Socialism. The core of German Christian belief was a fusion of National Socialist ideology and traditional Protestant belief, and the goal of the movement was to galvanize religious support for Hitler. As one of their leaders put it, "The church must enter completely into the Third Reich, it must be coordinated into the rhythm of the National Revolution, it must be fashioned by the ideas of Nazism, lest it remain a foreign body in the unified German Nazi community."[37]

Membership in the NSDAP itself or any number of the many party organizations would also seem to be an obvious alignment with Hitler and his ideology. Because many Germans joined the Nazi Party or its affiliate agencies for social or professional reasons, however, participation in the institutions of Nazism could have ambiguous meaning. For example, the National Socialist People's Welfare (*Nationalsozialistische Volkswohlfahrt*, or NSV) became the largest social agency in the Third Reich and took up many of the public welfare duties traditionally carried out by Protestant or Catholic parish organizations. Consequently, many clergy and church leaders joined the NSV so that they could maintain their previous involvement in social work. Even the Confessing Church recognized this and instructed its parish ministers to join the NSV, as Pastor Hermann Klemm of Burkhardswalde, Saxony, argued during the denazification process after the Second World War.[38] That said, when ministers acknowledged the importance of their party membership, as they often did, that membership was surely an indication that they had aligned themselves with National Socialism as a matter of principle.

A third way that clergy aligned themselves with National Socialism was by making affirmative statements about the political developments in Germany under Nazi rule. Which pastors praised radical measures undertaken by the Nazi Party, or defended the Führer as a man of faith, or spoke publicly about the need to work toward Nazi racial goals? Unfortunately, we do not really know, for it is precisely here that the evidence grows scarce, at least in the local church records of Nauen, Pirna, and Ravensburg. Save for a few comments pertaining to measures against the Jews, *none* of the following important national events is taken up with any significance in the official correspondence of district church records: the April 1, 1933, boycott of Jewish shops and stores; the book burnings of May 1933; the many decrees and laws concerning the coordination and centralization of German political, social, cultural, and economic life, especially in 1933 and 1934; the murder of SA leaders and other enemies of the regime on June 30, 1934; the March 16, 1935, reintroduction of universal military service; the September 15, 1935, Nuremberg racial laws; the March 8, 1936, reoccupation of the Rhineland; the 1936 implementation of the Four-Year Plan for economic autarky to prepare Germany for war; the November 9–10, 1938, Kristallnacht Pogrom; the September 1939 attack of Poland and launch of the Second World War; and the subsequent steps to the Holocaust.

This silence is troubling. One might have expected a pastoral word on some of these matters, but perhaps it was only that—a word, and not a personal letter or official church publication. The lack of information does not imply either the acceptance or rejection of National Socialism by Protestant clergy. It is only evidence that specific political opinions of any kind were generally left undocumented by Protestant parish clergy.

So what do German Christian membership and Nazi Party membership tell us about the extent to which parish clergy aligned themselves with National Socialism? In Nauen, of the thirty-one ministers in office between 1933 and 1935, fourteen belonged to the German Christian Movement.[39] It is not clear how many were members of the NSDAP.

In Pirna, Protestant clergy appear to have been overwhelmingly favorable to the Hitler regime. In a February 1934 letter to the Saxon bishop, Superintendent Max Zweynert declared, "All the pastors in my district are nationally reliable and loyal, even those who belong to the [Pastors'] Emergency League. There has not been the least bit reported to me that would cause complaint from the political point of view. There is no one who can speak of an attitude hostile to the state." As proof, Zweynert noted that even the church opposition in the Pastors' Emergency League included NSDAP members and supporters. Moreover, many local ministers were also participants in the Working Group of National Socialist Pastors and the German Christian Movement.[40] When the Pirna clergy were surveyed in 1937 and 1938 to find out who held positions in the NSDAP or its member organizations, the superintendent's office reported that at least sixteen ministers in the thirty-nine parishes had been Nazi Party members since 1933. Five others were applicants in waiting or previously unsuccessful applicants for party membership. Another five clergy were members of the German Christian Movement but not of the NSDAP.[41]

In Ravensburg, the record of the political convictions of Protestant clergy is murkier, in part because there were fewer public displays of nationalism among Protestants and fewer outbursts of church-political conflict than in Nauen and Pirna. Moreover, since the Württemberg Protestant Church had remained "intact," free from German Christian control at the highest levels, there was less made of the political allegiances of pastors than in Brandenburg or Saxony, where pro-Nazi church officials politicized the churches more thoroughly. In all, there were only five German Christian pastors in the eleven parishes of the Ravensburg district, and only Pastor Karl Steger of Friedrichshafen remained committed to the movement for the duration of the Third Reich. In sum, then, based on the level of participation in the German Christian Movement and NSDAP, we can estimate that not less than half of the clergy in Nauen, Pirna, and Ravensburg were political supporters of Adolf Hitler and the NSDAP, at least during the early years of the Third Reich.

## Church and Nation

How, then, did the existence of religious nationalism and NSDAP political support among Protestant pastors affect their approach to church ministry? For many, the answer was simple: their churches existed to serve their nation. Others, however, found that the nationalistic fervor aroused by the Nazi political takeover created a real sense of confusion between their spiritual and political loyalties. Already in 1933, one of the pastors from Nauen (very likely Superintendent Graßhoff himself) was struggling with the two duties he recognized in preaching: to proclaim the nation as a created order of God, and to proclaim the gospel message of personal salvation in Jesus Christ. In a letter to a senior churchman, the pastor expressed his fear that if he preached on the theme "nation is of God," then his parishioners would fail to see their need for personal choice for God. All the same, he confessed, he was reluctant to preach the inescapably unpopular formula "nation is of God, but nation is fallen," since it would mean a revival of "the old difficulty, that we degrade National Socialism insofar as it is without Christ." As he groped for the right psychological approach to his preaching and asked his correspondent for advice, it is clear that the Nauen pastor was grappling with a conflict between Nazi and Christian conceptions of human nature. In the end, after much soul searching, he decided to preach a rather cumbersome compromise. If anyone were to take up the National Socialist struggle in his own strength, boasting about his own exploits, he would be lost before God. That said, if anyone were to come to the crucified Christ, abandon his sinful nature, and enter the National Socialist struggle as a faithful Christian, he would be engaging in a holy struggle.[42]

Pastor Karl Partecke of Sebnitz, in the Pirna district, experienced the same difficulty. Caught between upholding the Nazi image of an exalted German nation and defending the Christian doctrine of original sin, his answer to this quandary was somewhat clearer than the fuzzy compromise proposed by the pastor from Nauen. In a March 1934 talk entitled "On the Question of Preaching in Keeping with the Times," Partecke defined the nation as "indivisible, encompassing the totality of blood and soil." Still, he clearly viewed his racial community as subject to the spiritual effects of the Fall. Gloomily, he portrayed the German nation as a mass of people trying to enter the narrow gate to heaven marching six abreast, an unsubtle reference to both the mob mentality and the tight formations popular with Nazi Party organizations. The German national community, Partecke concluded, was spiritually lost without God. The community of Christian believers could stand before God only on the basis of grace, not merely as the German nation. Renewal, he added, would come from a spiritual rebirth, not from a political transformation.[43] Here was a clear answer to the tension between spiritual and political loyalty generated by the Third Reich. Denying the alluring myth of Aryan racial supremacy, Partecke held firmly to the traditional Lutheran message of original sin and salvation in Jesus Christ and refused to allow his preaching to be swayed by Nazi ideology.

The tension between the claims of the nation and the claims of the Christian faith was a persistent problem for German Protestant clergy ministering in the Third Reich. In 1939, six years into Hitler's rule, Pastor Konrad Isleib of Hakenberg was still trying to work out the connection between his belief in the lofty destiny of the German nation and his convictions about the message of the Christian gospel. In a confused letter to his friend and colleague Nauen interim superintendent Ulrich Bettac, Isleib put forward his case for creating a unitary German Reich Church, five years after that quest had been abandoned by national church leaders! At any rate,

Isleib asserted not only that the Reich Church was vital for the well-being of the nation, but also that it was an expectation of the Führer. A member of the moderate wing of the German Christians, Isleib revealed his movement's utter inability to bridge the gap between the ultimate claims of both Christianity and National Socialism when he declared, "But for us, the Fatherland stands above everything, just as it always has been for us, even when for us, naturally, our conscience, bound to God and his Word, speaks the final word." The Fatherland stands above all, but the Scripture-guided conscience speaks the final word? Which, then, was the ultimate allegiance, nation or faith? If Isleib was unusually contradictory about his answer to the question, other pastors failed to even discern the potential for tension between Christian and Nazi worldviews. As Pastor Georg Gartenschläger of Bötzow asserted, his work as a German Christian pastor was all about "our great fighting goal, unity between nation and church."[44]

Not all ministers were so preoccupied with the need for some sort of fusion of Protestant Christianity and German nationalist ideology. Many simply proposed that the Protestant churches take on the simple duty of serving the German national community and therefore also the Nazi state. This is why so many clergy hailed the coming of a united Reich Church in 1933. They believed it would be an effective vehicle for German Protestants to contribute to the national renewal. Pastor Wacker of Leutkirch, near Ravensburg, anticipated in his parish newsletter that the coming Reich Church would be the culmination of four hundred years of Protestant history in Germany and exclaimed, "May God now bless its work in our nation."[45]

Three years later, the same theme of service came up in two special events in the Ravensburg district: a parish anniversary and a men's conference. In the case of the parish anniversary, Ravensburg superintendent Hermann Ströle equated Christian service with service to the German nation and argued that the Christian community was the "source of life" for the nation.[46] That desire to forge a close connection between church and nation or state often led Protestant clergy to ascribe Christian characteristics to the Nazi state. For example, Pastor Julius Eichler, head of the Württemberg Parish Service, explained the importance of love for one's neighbor to a Ravensburg men's conference and placed the discussion squarely within the realm of Nazi politics. As he put it, "It is a very gratifying fact that now, under the leadership of the state, the *whole* nation is presently participating in this duty of love." Eichler continued his discussion of Christian service, then summed up his message with a stirring injunction infused with National Socialist language: "A true Christian will always be a fighter [*Kämpfer*] in the service of his Lord."[47]

But what would the Protestant men of Ravensburg have taken away from Eichler's talk? By calling on them to participate in the social work of the Nazi state as a Christian activity, using militant National Socialist language to describe Christian service and locating Christian love solely in the context of the German national community, Eichler effectively blurred the lines between his Christian sermon and the Nazi propaganda the men were exposed to in their everyday lives. So, at the end of the day, the men basically learned that being good Christians and being good National Socialists were more or less the same thing.

The messages of both Ströle and Eichler illustrate the theological weakness of the German Protestant preoccupation with the idea of *nation* in the 1930s. Both men limited the scope of their message to the German racial community and to its human needs. It was an entirely national, political form of Christianity that they spoke for—a faith oriented around humanity rather than Christ. For instance, nowhere present was the uniquely Christian message of love for one's neighbor defined cross-culturally, as in the parable of the good Samaritan, the key biblical passage on the subject. Even more remote were the timeless Christian themes of human sinfulness and eternal salvation in the atoning death of Jesus.

This theme of Christian service to the national community was directed particularly at Protestant women. At the 1933 Nauen district church assembly, Pastor Cramer of Kremmen opened the women's meeting with the charge that it was the duty of every Protestant woman to live out the theme "Ready for Service" in this "fateful time for our nation." In a subsequent session, a visiting Berlin pastor traced the experiences of German mothers during the time of the First World War and through the weak and hopeless Weimar era. Now that the nation had experienced the joyous celebration of Hitler's rise to power, the pastor reminded his female audience that it was time to rebuild the German nation. German men would build the great German Fatherland, while German women would fashion the "cottage" of the Christian family: "No one else can do this holy, essential service for the nation but you, Protestant woman! . . . Be German, Protestant mothers ready for service for God, church and Fatherland!"[48]

Seven years later, during the tenth anniversary celebration of the Women's Aid in the Schwante parish, near Nauen, retired Pastor Daab gave the women of the parish yet another lesson on their domestic role in the Third Reich. Calling on the women to help build up the national community, he reminded them that their two realms of labor were the domain of the house and the domain of the heart. He urged each woman to make her *house* into a *home*, and her *home* into a *heaven*. Then, in order to drive his point home, he asked: "How shall the life of our nation be built up, if not from the house? Who shall perform this great service for our nation, which is fighting today for its freedom, if not the woman? She shall let the men know how happy it is for those who live in a house in which Christ rules in his goodness, in his love, and with his peace."[49]

If the church was to become the servant of the Nazi state, women would surely take the lead. In good times and bad, and especially in times of war, parish clergy depicted the domestic labor and spiritual character of Protestant women both as the will of God and as their vital service to the German nation. Gender roles were, it was assumed, divinely ordained. More generally, Christian service was understood only in the limited sense of service to the German national community, and not to fellow humans in general nor even to non-Christians outside the church.

These kinds of clerical attitudes about gender and the German nation reveal just how culturally bound Protestant clergy had grown, caught as they were in the net of the Third Reich's insular obsession with nation, blood, and race. Even if pastors were not directly aligned with the NSDAP, all their talk about the mystical connection between the Christian church and the German nation meant that they were ill prepared to preach the whole gospel, care for social outcasts, or see beyond their own political borders. For the parishioners among whom the clergy labored, the Protestant churches' preoccupation with nationalism, National Socialism, and Nazi language amounted to a compelling legitimization of the Hitler government and the Nazi Party.

## Skeptics and Critics

There were also ministers and other church leaders who were skeptical about the ability of the Protestant church to serve the German nation in such a grand way. Pastor Paul Schneider from the Pirna church district reached this conclusion in a July 1935 lecture entitled "The Question of Church and Nation in the Present Situation." Schneider bluntly pointed out to his fellow pastors that all the talk about the church serving the nation was misguided, since the German nation was not even asking the church for its service. Given the basic fact of general public disinterest in the message of the church, he suggested that pastors could do little but wait on the matter and continue to preach the gospel loyally and conscientiously in the private knowledge that the German people sorely needed it. They could only hope that, in time, the German state and society would perceive their vital need for the church and its services.[50]

Another mildly critical perspective on the relationship between the spiritual and political spheres comes from one of Schneider's colleagues in the Pirna district, Pastor Martin Rasch of Reinhardtsdorf. Like Schneider, Rasch recognized the gulf that separated overheated National Socialists and traditionally minded Lutherans. In a strange way, he embodied the problem he was grappling with, for he was both an applicant for Nazi Party membership and a supporter of the Young Reformation Movement, the unpopular opponents of the German Christians in the 1933 church election. As he explained in a letter to Superintendent Zweynert of Pirna in May 1933, Rasch intended to work hard for the National Socialist renewal of the German nation. But, in contrast to so many of his fellow pastors who had embraced the German Christian Movement, Rasch did not advocate a simplistic adaptation of the German Protestant churches to the demands of National Socialism. Rather, coming at things from the opposite direction, he wanted to bend the Nazi movement toward the values of a Protestantism that stood independent from the state, rooted in the authority of Scripture and the Reformation Confessions. As he related to Zweynert:

> I am writing to inform you that I have applied to become a member of the NSDAP. I anticipate my acceptance, in spite of the current ban [on new members].
>
> The basis for this decision is twofold:
>
> 1. I do not want to celebrate the successes of the [Nazi] freedom movement without making a sacrifice for it, and without actively promoting it.
>
> 2. I do not want my patriotism and my enthusiasm for the national revolution to be brought into question at all because of certain *ecclesiastical* decisions.
>
> Contrary to the views expressed in my presentation to the last district assembly, I have become convinced that the NSDAP is not such a firmly established organization that one can demand from it a definitive explanation of what is meant by "positive Christianity"! Rather, it is perhaps especially necessary that we pastors and theologians work with all our strength, so that National Socialism would affirm a church confession in the sense of the Young Reformation Movement and would place itself wholeheartedly under the gospel. It seems to me to be fully justified to hope for an acceptable solution to the as yet unresolved church-political issues.[51]

As it turned out, Rasch had good reason to fear the implications of his "*ecclesiastical* decisions.*" His adherence to Berlin pastor Martin Niemöller's Young Reformation Movement (which later grew into the Pastors' Emergency League and Confessing Church) landed him in trouble with the Saxon Lutheran church authorities several times throughout 1933 and 1934. His eventual solution (and that of two colleagues from neighboring parishes) was to abandon the Confessing Church for fear that his membership in it would divide his parish and undermine the "unity work" of the NSDAP in German society. It was a painful choice he made reluctantly.

Rasch's hopes for a dialogue between National Socialism and the biblical, confessional Christianity of the Young Reformers were soon dashed because of the dominance of the German Christian Movement, whose enthusiastic nationalism, racism, and disregard for church tradition made it politically attractive to Hitler. In the context of the clerical nationalism in Nauen, Pirna, and Ravensburg, however, Rasch's proposal was a unique attempt to shape Nazi ideology under the influence of confessional Christianity, and so to connect the national renewal and the spiritual renewal he and so many other ministers longed for.

Elsewhere in the three church districts, administrative irritations created by church-political conflict periodically provoked more fundamental criticisms of the National Socialist state. In Nauen, Interim Superintendent Bettac poured out his frustration over managing local church-political divisions among clergy to his colleague in Berlin. Angered by the radicalism of German Christians, Bettac wrote: "I cannot say it any other way—consciously or unconsciously, [the German Christians], on behalf of the state, are destroying the bothersome church."[52] Six months later, Bettac was openly skeptical about any possibility of unity between church and state in the Third Reich. In dialogue with a colleague, Bettac argued that the National Socialist state "is declaring that it is not and does not want to be Christian." In light of that fact, he wondered how *any* union of state and church could possibly be achieved, especially as long as the state kept advancing its totalitarian claims over everything, even the church.[53]

The most energetic critic of the union of nationalist ideology and Protestant belief among all the clergy in Nauen, Pirna, or Ravensburg was Pastor Herbert Posth of the Berge parish, near Nauen. Like other Confessing Church ministers around him, Posth was the subject of frequent ecclesiastical investigations and administrative harassment. In part, this was exacerbated by the fact that Posth was a cranky correspondent and never at a loss for words when discussing the relationship between the political and spiritual realms of life. In an article for a 1935 edition of his parish newsletter, Posth presented his most concise and compelling theological statement about the place of the church in the Nazi state. "One is *born* into the nation," he wrote, "one belongs to it through blood and race; one is *called* into the church by the Holy Spirit in the Word of God . . . independent of blood and race." Three years later, in the midst of a dispute with the Brandenburg church authorities, Posth reiterated this view, writing, "The opinion [that] the church should 'promote the life of faith of the members of the nation' contradicts the clear Word of God. . . . It amounts to disobedience against the Word of Christ to preach the gospel to *all* nations—the word *member of the nation* [*Volksgenosse*] is not a church word at all, but rather a political word."[54] This could hardly be clearer and reflects the fact that Posth's convictions were founded solely in Scripture and in confessional theology rather than in the politics of the day. Sadly, such clarity was the exception rather than the rule among the parish clergy of Hitler's Germany.

Four years later, in 1943, Posth worked with his Confessing Church colleague Günther Harder of Fehrbellin and others on a document condemning the violation of the Ten Commandments throughout the Third Reich, including the murder of non-Germans. Soon after that, in December 1943, Posth found himself fighting with the mayor and the schoolteacher in his parish town of Berge over the use of the Nazi salute, which they claimed he had forbidden his confirmation students to use during their classes. While he denied having done that, Posth did speak against the use of the Nazi salute within the realm of the church and against the interference of the mayor and teacher in what was purely church business.[55]

One of Posth's colleagues, Pastor Kurt Fritzsche of Groß Behnitz, also found himself under attack. In March of 1938, Fritzsche's parishioners exploded in anger over his membership in the Confessing Church, which they interpreted as an anti-national and anti-Nazi stance. This kind of accusation was what Confessing Church pastors both feared and found difficult to avoid. Fritzsche's parishioners argued that his teaching created division in the German national community, a serious charge in Nazi Germany. Recognizing the total claims of the Nazi state, they denied that "there could be some other law for a German church than there is for the German nation." Several times Fritzsche's enemies repeated the assertion that his church politics were un-German and illegal, and claimed that his Confessing Church was trying to set aside not only the authority of the Old Prussian Union Church government but also "the sovereignty of the state."[56]

Over in the Ravensburg district, there were also several pastors and church leaders who called both the ideology and the activities of the National Socialist regime into question. One was the Protestant theologian Helmut Thielicke, who served as a vicar in the parishes of Ravensburg and Langenargen for two years during the war. In his memoir, *Notes from a Wayfarer*, he described his beginnings as a "greenhorn vicar" in Upper Swabia, complete with his miscues, misadventures, and altercations with National Socialist opponents. One of these confrontations occurred at the funeral of a young judge in Ravensburg, a man who had joined the NSDAP and the SA at a very early stage but whose widow insisted had kept his Christian faith over the years. Thielicke opened the graveside service with some passages from an SS pamphlet describing death. He then turned the tables on his audience, using the Nazi propaganda he had just read to demonstrate the bankruptcy of the pagan, collectivist view of humanity at the core of Hitler's regime and to chastise the party faithful attending the funeral. Thielicke later recounted his funeral oration:

> We constantly hear in our country that the life of the individual is of no significance compared with the life of the nation. And when it comes to dying, we are told, then it's only as if a leaf had fallen from the tree of the nation. The living trunk, however, constantly brings forth new leaves in a process of creative renewal. I have a question with regard to this. 'Does any one of you gathered here today *dare* in front of this grave and in the presence of the widow, parents, and three children of the deceased to repeat this and to maintain *here* (not in the pub or at the safe distance of one's desk) that this man, loved as a husband and father by his family, is merely an interchangeable leaf on the tree of our nation?' I had said all this with a considerable vehemence and then used what I had said as the peg on which to hang a brief meditation on the infinite worth of the individual in the eyes of God.[57]

Thielicke also spoke out forcefully in confirmation classes, critiquing the Nazi ideology of his obstinate students and mocking its exaltation of strength and power.

In nearby Isny, Pastor Siegle used the occasion of his 1938 farewell sermon to make some pointed criticisms of his own concerning the effects of the National Socialist movement in his parish. He criticized the recent politically coerced resignations of his parish councilors, remembered battles with city officials over control of the prayer room in the local hospital, and lamented the withdrawal of his right to give religious instruction. Alluding to "difficulties with the current powers," Siegle went on to mourn the recent decline in the vitality of his parish: "Since National Socialism has been here, people have absolutely no sense for things Protestant, and the same circles which initially awoke such hopes in Isny and appeared as if they wanted to help the Protestant cause, have now so shamed the Protestant cause that I have often said: 'Indeed, they are only good for Catholicism.'"[58] The circles Siegle referred to were none other than local branches of the NSDAP and its auxiliary organizations. Siegle found that administrative frustrations and basic differences between National Socialist and Christian interests drove him to adopt a critical stance toward the regime as a whole. Ministers like Posth, Fritzsche, Thielicke, Bettac, and Siegle were not alone in their discovery that the early promise of National Socialist religious renewal was a false hope for German Protestantism. They were, however, part of what was only a small minority of clergy who were brave enough to express their disappointment and disagreement to their colleagues or parishioners.

## An Assessment

To conclude is to return to the initial questions posed in this chapter: Why did Protestant clergy in Nauen, Pirna, and Ravensburg identify so strongly with the national renewal unleashed by the National Socialist seizure of power? To what extent did their nationalism mark them as National Socialists? How did they understand the relationship between their ministry and the renewal of the German nation? And how did the nature and extent of clerical nationalism compare across the church districts of Nauen, Pirna, and Ravensburg?

In answer to the final question, there appears to have been very little difference in the tone and language of clergy among the three church districts, despite obvious differences in their political, geographic, and demographic contexts. Indeed, it made little difference to their religious nationalism whether their regional church government had been taken over by members of the German Christian Movement, as in Nauen (Brandenburg) and Pirna (Saxony), or whether it remained in the hands of theological and church-political moderates, as in Ravensburg (Württemberg). In all three districts, a great majority of ministers advocated that their churches support the National Socialist political revolution and its national and moral transformation of Germany, and they did so for similar reasons: the belief that the national renewal would bring with it a moral renewal of Germany; the belief that the Führer was calling them into a partnership to transform Germany; their approval of the Nazi campaign against atheistic communism; and their theological predispositions toward obedience to the state and the importance of created orders such as blood, soil, and authority.

Overall, while a handful of parish clergy in Nauen, Pirna, and Ravensburg questioned the close connection between German nationalism and their churches, the majority hoped and worked for a special role for Protestantism in the new Germany. By promoting the ideal of national or racial unity within the churches, they hoped to earn what they believed was their rightful place of leadership in Hitler's revitalized society. The stories of their ideas, careers, and struggles comprise some of the later chapters in this book, which seek to examine more fully the parish politics that shaped the Church Struggle in Nauen, Pirna, and Ravensburg.

# chapter two

## National Socialism as a Catalyst for German Protestant Renewal?

 **Hitler's rise to power in the first months of 1933** unleashed waves of patriotic exuberance across Germany. A new spirit of optimism was centered in the belief that Germany was undergoing a "national renewal" that would see the country shake off the defeatism, weakness, division, and moral chaos of the Weimer era. For many Germans, the national renewal stirred hopes for a restoration of the traditional values of the old imperial era: authority, order, family, nation, land, and church.

The year 1933 was a tumultuous one for Protestant clergy, who had to grapple with the social and theological ramifications of National Socialism and to sort out their church-political loyalties. More than a few pastors regarded the ascension of Hitler as a divine wonder. As the National Socialist Pastors' Association put it, "Every Protestant pastor should be deeply grateful that at last no atheists are at the head of the German people, but rather Christian men. . . . Hitler fought fourteen years for Christianity and church, misunderstood and opposed by many Christians. Next to God, the church and Christendom has the National Socialist leader Adolf Hitler to thank for its existence."[1] Pastors in Nauen, Pirna, and Ravensburg responded enthusiastically to the Nazi national renewal, caught up in the expectation that Hitler would lead Germany through a healthy moral renewal and grateful that the Führer had crushed Communism.

Just as German political life underwent a profound upheaval in 1933, Protestant church life was turned upside down by a revolution of its own. As quickly as the National Socialists rose to political power in Germany, members of the German Christian Movement seized control of the institutions of Protestantism by winning a national church election and overwhelming regional and national church synods with their majorities. Their champion and Hitler's advisor on Protestant church affairs, Ludwig Müller, was elected Reich bishop—head of what was supposed to become a united, centralized Protestant Reich Church.

This dual revolution was a whirlwind that stirred up German Protestants and reshaped both their political and religious landscape. But what day-to-day effect did all this have on ordinary Christians? How was parish life affected by the rise to power of Hitler and the NSDAP? In some parishes, little changed. Pastors and parishioners continued in their regular religious routines of Sunday worship, parish meetings, baptisms, confirmations, weddings, and funerals. In other parishes, local church life was turned upside down, as church-political tensions polarized communities.

## Nauen, Brandenburg

Of the three church districts that constitute this study, Nauen was closest to the center of German political power. Its proximity to Berlin brought Protestants from the Nauen area into direct contact with the storm center of the German Church Struggle. The resulting politicization of parish life was exhibited in the general commotion experienced by many of these otherwise quiet, rural Havelland parishes during the 1930s. This was true especially in 1933 and 1934, when the political ascent of Adolf Hitler and his National Socialists was accompanied by a surge of nationalism and an upswing in Protestant church activity. At its outset, this transformation appeared to be a godsend. District Superintendent Graßhoff and the other pastors in the district were stirred by the National Socialist seizure of power. They fundamentally agreed with Hitler's aspiration for a national rebirth, his campaign to destroy Communism, and his practice of authoritarian politics.

For those reasons, the May 1933 Nauen district church assembly revolved almost entirely around developments associated with the new National Socialist regime. [2] Setting the tone for the meetings, Superintendent Graßhoff interpreted the rise of Hitler as a great transformation through which "God has spoken to our German nation." Over the balance of his address, Graßhoff predicted massive and miraculous social and moral changes in Germany and called on local pastors and church members to help save Germany by cultivating a new, pure, national character. Other sessions at the assembly echoed the patriotic tone of Graßhoff's speech. Pastor Cramer of Kremmen urged the women's assembly to live up to the conference theme, "Ready for Service," especially "in this great moment of destiny for our nation." Another speaker praised Hitler's piety and commended the manner in which "the young chancellor of the nation openly professed his faith in God and promoted the work of the Christian churches." The Nauen women were instructed to cultivate pious lives, since "only such pious, German mothers provide the basis on which the young Germany can really thrive." Their duty as women was domestic: "Be German, Protestant mothers ready for service for God, church, and Fatherland." In yet another speech, Pastor Gerhard Schumann of Nauen continued to call attention to the interwoven duty of women to God and nation: "We need holy German mothers, mothers who bring their children to the savior of the world, who make their hearts warm for Jesus, the only one who can make them free for selfless, holy service for God and our beloved German nation."

If the women's assembly revolved around traditional themes of motherhood, Germanness, and piety, the Nauen men's assembly even more explicitly linked Protestant faith with the revolutionary events of 1933. Superintendent Graßhoff introduced Counselor Karl Schlabritzky from the Brandenburg Consistory, who spoke on the theme "The Church and the National Renewal." Asserting that Germany stood at a turning point in its history, Schlabritzky depicted the German past as a cycle of perpetual struggle: from first-century Hermann the Cherusci to nineteenth-century Otto von Bismarck, Germans had suffered defeat only when they had lost their fear of God and their brotherly love. The Weimar era had been an age of defeat, a time when honor and faith were scorned. But, he continued:

> Then the nation awoke. Faith and honor celebrated their resurrection on the Day of Potsdam, on National Labor Day. Just as Bismarck achieved the external unification of the German nation, so the current chancellor of the nation is achieving the inner unity of the Fatherland, the genuine national community that smashed Marxism. He wants to create this on a religious foundation, wants the assistance of the Christian churches. We hear this call with joy. We are ready to provide assistance.

As he concluded his talk, Schlabritzky discussed two kinds of assistance that the church could give the new Nazi state. First, he hoped that Protestants would be able to heed the call to create a unified Reich Church and not miss the opportunity, as they had at key national moments in the nineteenth century. Second, he hoped that Germans could create a genuine bond of community between church and nation.

General Superintendent Otto Dibelius, one of the most important church leaders in Germany, was the next to speak. He echoed the call for unity between the Protestant churches and the German people and challenged the church to carry out its new task, to work for the renewal of Germans and Germany:

> In the last fourteen years, this task appeared to be only a beautiful dream. Now it has become reality. . . . Concerning the Weimar state, there was only one option for the church: Dissociation! Utmost reserve! To the new German state that wants our assistance, we are intimately bound. . . . Therefore, the motto will now be: As the new state now calls on every citizen for active cooperation, so also must the church afford joyful assistance to all parishioners. Only then will the church be able to contribute its share to Germany's true renewal. Only then will God be able to bless our German nation along its new way.

These speeches elicited vigorous applause from the Nauen audience. Male parishioners, like their female counterparts, heard their leaders praise Adolf Hitler and his Nazi movement as the solution to years of division within German society. In particular, they heard that the churches were to be an important contributor to the reawakening and the reassertion of the German people. This message resonated strongly with Protestants during the spring and summer of 1933.

Pastors from the Nauen district witnessed all this firsthand, of course, and understood the impact that the new Nazi regime was having on their people. Superintendent Graßhoff knew it, too, and asked pastors from across the district to submit reports about the current conditions in their parishes. While some pastors noticed little change in church conditions, for many others 1933 was clearly a singular year.

The dominant theme of these pastoral reports was the rallying of the Protestant populace around the traditional values and institutions of national community, warmhearted piety, and the parish church. For instance, parishioners in Bötzow erected a memorial to commemorate the deaths of local soldiers in the First World War, an act that highlighted the importance of the Fatherland and created "an especially warm bond between family and church."[3]

Pastors were generally pleased about such developments because they were signs that the social and political atmosphere created by Hitler and National Socialism might help them win back estranged flocks. This is exactly what was happening in many parishes, based on the attendance reports they submitted to Superintendent Graßhoff. Pastor Günther Harder of Fehrbellin declared that attendance in his "unfortunately unchurchish parish" was higher than it had ever been since 1914. In late April of 1933, Harder was pleasantly surprised when he encountered 540 parishioners attending a service—over one-quarter of his entire parish population.[4]

No pastor in the Nauen district described the religious impact of the national renewal of 1933 as vividly as Pastor Lux of Groß Behnitz. Attendance at his church had surged, and Lux attributed it directly to National Socialism:

> The political movements of the last year and first months of this year have had a strong effect throughout our parishes. With them, everything has advanced in the greatest peace and order. On National Remembrance Day, for the first time, the swastika flag of the SA stood beside the flag of the military association in the church, and the members of the SA in Groß Behnitz, Klein Behnitz and from the neighboring towns took part in the Remembrance service *en masse*, in their brown uniforms.[5]

Ten days later, on March 21, there was an illuminated parade through the town. This was followed by a giant bonfire and speeches by local political leaders, who echoed the message of national political leaders that day, affirming the importance of the churches in the national revitalization of Germany. Similarly, on National Labor Day (May 1), Pastor Lux held special services in both Groß Behnitz and Klein Behnitz. Attendance at those services was the highest Lux had ever experienced during his fifteen years there. As he reported, "Every strata [of society] and every house was represented." Lux's sermons that day gave voice to the warm feelings of local Protestants for the rebirth of Germany under Hitler. In the afternoon, Lux's congregation listened to a radio speech by the Reich president then planted "Hitler linden" trees to mark the occasion. After dark, there were torchlight parades through town. In every way, the balance of the May Day celebrations in Groß Behnitz reinforced the centrality of the National Socialist political revolution.

As he reflected on these momentous events, Pastor Lux summed up his hopes for the coming months: "God grant," he wrote, "that the strong national movement may also be accompanied by an upturn of church life." Actually, that potential was already being realized across his parish. Parishioners were making enthusiastic inquiries about the Word of God; the Groß Behnitz volunteer fire department had asked if they could attend church en masse, and the local military association had inquired whether Lux would conduct a special church service for a jubilee they were going to celebrate.

In Flatow, Pastor Otto Schmidt also encountered newfound interest in the church among his people. Interpreting this as a product of the national renewal, Schmidt responded with church services that would foster the religious nationalism of local Protestants. Describing his aim as the "cultivation of the German-Christian cultural assets," Schmidt planned to hold camp services at the district military festival and at the district Stahlhelm veterans' festival. He also arranged a church ceremony on National Remembrance Day and hosted various discussion evenings on topics of national interest. Participants there could discuss the heroic Germans Albert Schweitzer and Richard Wagner, or reflect on the film Mother and Volk, with its traditional images of women. Finally, Schmidt also arranged special guest lectures on the relationship between faith and Fatherland by neighboring German Christian pastors. [6]

Other pastors echoed Harder, Lux, and Schmidt, and credited the German Christian Movement for turning the energy of the national renewal into the religious revitalization of their parishes. In the parish of Kremmen, interest in church matters had grown after local Protestants had founded a German Christian group. Two new German Christian parish councilors elected in the fall of 1932 had transformed the parish council through their "lively interest" in the affairs of the church. In Vehlefanz, Pastor Feder praised the National Socialist takeover as a positive ecclesiastical event and praised the stimulating effect of the German Christian Movement. Of particular significance was Feder's belief that the renewal of the church by the German Christians was an important *political* development in the Third Reich—a sign of his conviction about the connection between the Nazi seizure of power, the national renewal, and the new vibrancy of Protestant church life. Feder saw the German Christians as the key link between these developments. They were a rallying force within the church that he commended for bringing new men into local church leadership.[7]

Feder's point is important, for it illustrates the way in which the political momentum of National Socialism toward the unification of the German national community propelled a parallel movement (led by the German Christians) toward the unification of the Protestant regional churches. In short, patriotic pastors and church leaders who were enthusiastic about the political developments of early 1933 helped to translate the nationalistic political energy unleashed by the NSDAP into the realm of the church. And in this effort, German Christians led the way.

The general picture of religious renewal in Nauen was tempered by reports of pockets of disinterest and heterodoxy: some pastors lamented the indifference of parishioners, while others complained about rival religious movements. Still, the most striking responses of pastors from the Nauen district were celebrations of the Nazi seizure of power and the national renewal and calls for their Protestant church to devote itself to the quest for national unity and revitalization. Almost one-half of the pastors in the district translated that sentiment into concrete action by joining the unabashedly pro-Nazi German Christian Movement.

Indeed, the rapid rise of the German Christian Movement in Nauen was in itself an illustration of the great impact of the religious-national renewal both locally and across the Brandenburg Province of the Old Prussian Union Church. In the 1933 national church election, German Christians practically swept the table. In Nauen, forty-seven of the fifty-eight delegates elected to the district synod were German Christians, including twelve pastors. Alongside these elected representatives, seven of the eight teachers and church musicians who reported to the synod were German Christians too.[8]

Church statistics in Nauen confirm the anecdotal reports of Protestant renewal. A number of key indicators show that public religious observances were significantly higher in 1933 than they had been before or would be afterward. For instance, the number of people becoming new church members in the Nauen district jumped almost 350 percent between 1932 and 1933 (almost all of these new members had no other previous church affiliation). That soon tailed off, however, so that only one solitary new church membership was taken out across the entire district in 1939.[9] In complementary fashion, the number of people officially *withdrawing* from church membership fell by 54 percent from 1932 to 1933 but then began to climb again through the later 1930s, as enthusiasm for the Protestant church waned and people drifted away again.

Other statistics confirm this basic view. Just as more people from Nauen became members of the Old Prussian Union Church in 1933 and 1934 than either before or after that time, far fewer parishioners withdrew their church membership during that same period. Membership withdrawals dropped in half from 1932 to 1933, and then by another two-thirds in 1934. After 1934, however, the rate of withdrawal increased steadily, so that by 1938, the number of withdrawals from church members was 250 percent of what it had been in 1933. Given that these departing parishioners did not generally transfer their membership into another Christian church, it appears that the new interest in Protestantism generated by the national renewal in 1933 and 1934 waned and that many Nauen district Protestants who had been drawn to the church in those years became disenchanted and withdrew from organized religious life.

A similar rise and fall are discernible in other statistical categories. Participation in communion across the Nauen district increased about 7 percent between 1932 and 1933, though variations from parish to parish meant that in a few congregations the number of communicants rose between 41 and 83 percent in the first year of Hitler's rule. By 1938, however, participation in communion across the Nauen district had dropped by over 30 percent from the high point of 1933. Marriage statistics show a similar jump from 1932 to 1933, and then significant decline through the second half of the 1930s. One of the most telling church statistics in Nauen comes from baptismal records. While most families baptized their children as young babies, there were 112 children over the age of one baptized in Nauen district churches in 1933, and 124 in 1934. There can be little doubt that these were the children of the many people who had newly joined or at least reengaged with their parish churches in the first years of the Third Reich.

These statistical measurements conform to the other signs of parish vitality in 1933 and 1934: the pastoral reports of surging religious observance and national enthusiasm; the attraction of the clergy themselves to the national renewal; the rapid emergence of the German Christian Movement in Nauen and its dramatic victory in the 1933 church elections. Taken together, these developments strongly suggest that the temporary revitalization of public religious observance among Protestants in the Nauen district was largely a response to the national renewal promoted by the new National Socialist government. This effervescence soon passed, however, as the declining statistics for baptisms, church weddings, church membership, and participation in communion illustrate. So too did the pastors' own optimism about the potential for the Protestant churches to work hand in hand with the Nazi state. Over time, at least one-third of the clergy who served in the Nauen district became members or active supporters of the Confessing Church and worked to keep the German Christians, those torchbearers of religious nationalism, from controlling parish life.

## Pirna, Saxony

Developments in the Pirna church district during the early months of the Third Reich were similar to those in Nauen in three significant ways. Like Nauen, Pirna was bursting with religious national enthusiasm in 1933. And like Nauen, the 1933 district church assembly in Pirna proved to be a powerful outlet for these sentiments. Superintendent Max Zweynert captured the mood of the day when he pledged the support of his clergy for the new Hitler government and its renewal of the nation. Finally, as in Nauen, local church statistics confirm the anecdotal evidence for the connection of the political emergence of National Socialism and the revival of parish life. In the case of Pirna, however, parish statistics suggest an even more extraordinary surge in religious observance.[10] Simply put, Saxon Lutherans flocked to their churches. Across the district, the number of people who became new church members shot up almost 1,800 percent between 1932 and 1933, from 212 new members to 4,005. When another 1,150 new adults took out church membership in 1934, the two-year total rose to over five thousand new members! While impressive, 1933 and 1934 marked a high point that was followed by a progressive decline in new church memberships that lasted right into the war years. In 1940, for instance, only fifty-two adults in the Pirna district joined the Saxon Lutheran Church.

Complementing the wave of new church members in 1933, Lutherans in Pirna all but stopped withdrawing their church memberships during the same period. Membership withdrawals declined 74 percent from 1932 to 1933 and a further 86 percent from 1933 to 1934, when only thirty-one people officially quit the church. As in Nauen, however, Lutherans abandoned their church memberships in ever-increasing numbers between 1935 and 1939. While the increase was modest at first, withdrawals shot up to over one thousand in 1937 and almost 2,500 in 1939. Such astounding swings in church membership statistics imply a tremendous surge of public interest in the church in 1933 and 1934, followed by growing disinterest and antagonism later in the 1930s.

Indeed, the monthly breakdown of new church membership and membership withdrawal in 1932 and 1933 illustrates just how close the chronological connection was between the surge in new church membership, the abrupt end to membership withdrawals, and the National Socialist rise to power in Germany. It was during the months of March and April 1933, when the Hitler government consolidated its hold on power and began the reorganization of German society, that Pirna and area residents began to join the church in proportionately very large numbers. Similarly, Lutherans almost completely stopped withdrawing from church membership after those same two months (see tables 1 and 2).

Table 1. New Church Membership in the Pirna District, 1932 to 1933

| Month | Sep 1932 | Oct 1932 | Nov 1932 | Dec 1932 | Jan 1933 | Feb 1933 | Mar 1933 | Apr 1933 | May 1933 | Jun 1933 | Jul 1933 | Aug 1933 |
|---|---|---|---|---|---|---|---|---|---|---|---|---|
| Totals | 16 | 44 | 19 | 17 | 24 | 24 | 238 | 299 | 226 | 198 | 224 | 172 |

Table 2. Church Membership Withdrawals in the Pirna District, 1932 to 1933

| Month | Sep 1932 | Oct 1932 | Nov 1932 | Dec 1932 | Jan 1933 | Feb 1933 | Mar 1933 | Apr 1933 | May 1933 | Jun 1933 | Jul 1933 | Aug 1933 |
|---|---|---|---|---|---|---|---|---|---|---|---|---|
| Totals | 31 | 57 | 54 | 45 | 42 | 96 | 43 | 12 | 3 | 3 | 2 | 0 |

In keeping with the tremendous growth in church membership, participation in the sacrament of communion rose dramatically, with increases ranging from 10 to 80 percent in twenty-four of the forty-two parishes in the district. As in the case of church memberships, however, 1933 proved to be a high point. Thereafter, religious observance in the form of communion-taking declined substantially, though unevenly, across the district.

What generated such a wave of public religious participation in Pirna in 1933? As in Nauen, anecdotal evidence points to a strong correlation between the excitement surrounding the national renewal fueled by Hitler's new government and the fortunes of the local Lutheran parishes. The new wave of religious nationalism was propelled by the German Christian Movement. In the July 1933 church elections, German Christians swept to power in Pirna and the rest of Saxony. After that, the Saxon Lutheran church government reconstituted all the parish councils in Pirna and throughout Saxony, so that at least three out of every four parish councilors was a German Christian. This ensured that local church leaders would consistently support the National Socialist government and spur their churches on to participate in the national renewal.[11]

The attitudes and actions of the Pirna clergy both reflected these developments and contributed to them. Conservatively speaking, at least fourteen out of the thirty-one pastors and curates who served in the district during the first years of the Third Reich belonged to the German Christian Movement.[12] Many of these were among the sixteen local pastors who took out memberships in NSDAP, mostly in 1933. Motives for joining the party no doubt varied, but the explanation of Pastor Martin Rasch of Reinhardtsdorf corresponds to the mood of the day. He believed in the national renewal; he believed in the National Socialist movement; and he believed it was his duty to join in the party's efforts to revitalize the nation. Other Pirna district pastors may not have expressed themselves so forcefully, but all of them were reputed to be politically loyal to the National Socialist government as of 1934.

Like their parishioners, these pastors understood that the recent developments in local Protestant life were an outgrowth of the new political climate in Germany.

Community groups were attending church services *en masse;* many new and returning church members were flocking into churches; and interest in Lutheranism among the general populace was the highest it had been in years. In fact, a few pastors became alarmed over the dramatic changes, because they recognized that the renewal of their parish was not a genuine religious revival but rather an essentially political event. For instance, in early 1934, Pastor Karl Partecke of Sebnitz warned his colleagues about the danger of political fervor leading to religious activity and lamented the lack of genuine Christian devotion in Pirna. The notes from his talk are sparse but ominously clear:

> Real incorporation into the parish is not there; many external re-entries [into the church]; the national enthusiasm in its devotion for an ultimate greatness is at the same time a danger! Religious attitude and Christianity become confused. Beside the converted Marxists, the embittered and disappointed. Our time has a *political* character . . . the church in danger of becoming an organ of the state.[13]

If Partecke perceived the increasing shallowness of parish life in the Pirna district, so did one of his colleagues, who argued that the root of the problem was that large numbers of Saxons were attending church because of Hitler's encouragement, the urging of other National Socialist leaders, and the presence of many of the Nazi "old fighters" at church. This party support for Protestantism appears to have been very short-lived, however, because already in October 1933, a local mission campaign had collapsed because local Nazis had not participated as had been expected.[14]

Still, no matter how problematic the sudden surge of interest in the churches appeared to a few of the Pirna clergy, Saxon church leaders were triumphant in their assessment. No less a figure than Saxon bishop Friedrich Coch proudly embraced the new religious vitality of 1933 and 1934 as a product of the Nazi national renewal. In October of 1935, Coch told the Pirna district church assembly how the national reawakening of Germany was responsible for the spiritual revival of Protestant church life: "Are not the churches—everywhere grown out of the German soil and the German search [for Jesus]—the cathedrals and the village churches, gripping witnesses of this yearning and its fulfillment?" After Coch finished, Pirna district superintendent Zweynert delivered his annual report, reminding the district church assembly of the astounding growth in religious observance. In a section of the report entitled "Encouragement," Zweynert gratefully reviewed recent developments in Germany. First, he reflected on the "battle of the church against Marxism, free thinking and brutal terror in 1932 and on the liberation of Germany through Adolf Hitler." He went on to list the recent positive developments of Protestant life in Pirna: "growth in communion [participation] figures, increase in the baptisms and church weddings, belated confirmation of adults, five thousand [new church memberships], friendly cooperation with schoolteachers, a new singing movement, and so forth."[15]

By 1935, however, much of the nationalistically inspired religious fervor of 1933 had already begun to dissipate. Illustrative of this collapse was the debate in Pirna surrounding failure of the May Day church services that year. These services were scheduled by the Saxon church government and were intended to inject a Lutheran religious element into the May 1 National Labor Day celebrations. The services were so poorly attended, however, that Saxon church officials immediately requested reports from pastors throughout the state. After reviewing reports from his clergy, Pirna superintendent Max Zweynert concluded that the services had failed largely because the proliferation of political celebrations had allowed no time for any religious observances on the May 1 holiday. As a result, the Labor Day church services had been pushed back in some cases to the eve of the holiday, an embarrassing setback and clear evidence of the declining status of the Lutheran church in the eyes of Saxon state and party leaders.

Reports from local pastors confirmed Zweynert's assessment. Pastor Franz Häßner's May Day service in Eschdorf was "very poorly attended" because of a scheduling conflict with some political meetings. Pastor Heinrich Zweynert of Neustadt, son of Superintendent Maximilian Zweynert, was disgruntled because attendance at his May 1 service was the lowest of any that year, even though he had planned the event together with the local party leadership. He concluded that unless the NSDAP guaranteed the participation of its members, associations, and vocational groups in the May Day church services, there was no point in planning any: "No one is served and it is least beneficial of all for the reputation of the church."

In contrast, Pastor Arno Hesse of Stürza reported "good participation" in his parish. The NSDAP, the War Association, the Choral Society, the Volunteer Fire Service, the municipal and church representatives and the youth had all taken part in a service that was definitely the exception to the rule in the Pirna district. More in keeping with the overall trend was Pastor Siegfried Meier's experience in Sebnitz, where only fifty-eight parishioners showed up at his "relatively poorly attended" service. Not surprisingly, Meier discouraged future May Day church celebrations. In Porschdorf, Pastor Joachim Grießdorf had managed to hold a worship service at the usual Sunday service time, thanks to the cooperation of the local NSDAP leader. Even so, attendance was down from the previous year, when local party officials had made church attendance more or less mandatory for local Nazis. Over in Gottleuba, however, the local NSDAP had refused to attend any service at all in Pastor Friedrich's church. Even scheduling a service had been next to impossible, since public celebrations were scheduled in every conceivable time slot in the weekend. A frustrated Friedrich could only conclude bitterly that his membership in the Pastors' Emergency League had led to his banishment from the community celebrations. [16]

On the whole, Pirna clergy were quite upset with the 1935 May Day church service debacle, so much so that a number of them, led by Pastor Heinrich Zweynert of Neustadt, lodged a complaint with Saxon church officials. The depth of their frustration is telling, for it reveals their awareness that the May Day celebrations, which the NSDAP had taken full control of, were quickly turning into a new type of secular national holiday from which the Christian churches would be excluded. However, rather than tracing the root of the issue, which was the all-encompassing nature of Nazi rule, the pastors simply petitioned the Saxon Lutheran Church to extract guarantees from the political authorities that in future years the usual morning hours would be set aside for May Day church services.[17]

In any event, the misery of the pastors over the 1935 May Day holiday vividly illustrates how short-lived the era of religious-national excitement was in Pirna. Just as the statistical measurements of public religious observance dropped markedly after 1934, so too local clergy perceived the waning interest of their parishioners and the growing antipathy of Pirna NSDAP leaders.

Among the many signs of this problem was the growth of ideological challenges to the church from various German neo-pagan groups like the Tannenberg Union, the Ludendorff Union, and the Hasselbach Home Defense, all of which had organized political meetings in the Pirna area.[18] A far more substantial threat came from Jakob Wilhelm Hauer's German Faith Movement, the largest neo-pagan group in the Third Reich. Pirna superintendent Max Zweynert discussed this organization at a 1936 pastoral conference, warning area clergy of its dangerous claim "to bring the ultimate fulfillment and coronation of the National Socialist hope." Zweynert observed that it was very hard for ordinary Germans to distinguish between political and religious belief systems, particularly because of the confusion created by the overlapping ideologies of the neo-pagan German Faith Movement, the German Christian Movement, and the National Socialist Party itself. Though he labeled the German Faith Movement "pure anti-Christianity" and hoped that the public would reject it, he was forced to admit that it attracted nominal Lutherans who embraced the Nazi worldview. A particular problem was the growth of neo-paganism among young people, who were being swayed by their Nazi schoolteachers. Worse yet, public confusion was deepened by the vagueness of the Nazi's own terminology of *positive Christianity*.[19]

All this posed an almost impossible situation for Pirna pastors. If clergy tackled the problem of neo-paganism head-on and denounced its idolization of the German race as heresy, they would also find themselves denouncing the racial ideology of the NSDAP, a dangerous and unpopular strategy. Moreover, such a challenge would also undermine the religious national sentiment within their own churches, which had proven so attractive to Protestants back in 1933. Therefore, unwilling or unable to prevent the worship of Germanness in his corner of the Third Reich, Zweynert simply proposed to combat the growth of neo-paganism by encouraging the Saxon Lutheran Church to ensure that all important public holiday festivities opened with church services. It is not clear whether Zweynert planned to use these occasions to promote uniquely Christian values or simply to present Lutheranism as a component of true German identity. Either way, he did not believe the church was in a position to challenge its neo-pagan rivals directly.

Ongoing conflict between Lutheran pastors and Nazi officials was another serious problem that affected the Pirna district. Even before Hitler came to power, National Socialists in Porschdorf created a stir when they asked Pastor Dr. Gottfried Polster to consecrate their flag. A newspaper article under the headline "Nazi Flag in the Church!" described the visit of uniformed National Socialists to the Porschdorf church in mid-January 1933. The article was critical of Polster for performing the ceremony: "Even if the pastor believes he has to sympathize with the NSDAP, it is nonetheless unbelievable to most of the inhabitants of Porschdorf that someone can simply misuse the church for party-political activities."[20] The angry criticism of that newspaper article was prophetic, in that it anticipated how National Socialists would use the church as a tool for their own purposes, without regard for the traditional role that it played in German life. That was certainly the lesson that Pastor Rudolf Peter of Pirna learned in the first months of Nazi rule.[21]

Pastor Peter was an established member of the Pirna community, having ministered there since 1918. In early 1933, he was eager to learn about Nazi plans for the renewal of Germany. To that end, he decided to attend a National Socialist election rally on March 1, 1933, at which Reich Minister Hermann Göring was scheduled to speak. Peter was seriously considering voting National Socialist in the upcoming March 5 election and hoped to hear Göring address the important political issues of the day. Peter was even planning to ask some questions of his own, and so he waited seventy-five minutes for Göring to arrive, listening to music and enduring the repeated assurances of local NSDAP leaders that the Reich minister was indeed coming. Peter finally gave up and left. On his way out the door, he asked briskly, "Is this the honesty of the Third Reich?" and demanded a refund of his entrance fee. At the cash desk, an official told Peter to pick up his money at the local party office at a later date. When he did so, he was harangued by the head of the Pirna party office "as never before . . . in the sixty-three years of my life" and "above all with the words: '*It is a shame that pastors like you still stand in the pulpit!*'"

Soon after that, Peter found himself in deep trouble. On March 9, he was returning from the cemetery and passed by the office of the local newspaper, when a man called out to him: "Pastor, now the public bookshop is about to be occupied!" Peter looked around and quickly moved on, since it was not his intention to involve himself in the matter. Three houses past the newspaper office he heard shouting behind him: "Clear the street, close the windows, or you will be shot!" Not knowing whether to move on or duck into a house, Peter witnessed members of the NSDAP throwing books out of a local bookshop. The sight was such a shock that Peter said to a man standing near him: "Why are they throwing books on the street in so *rough a manner? Why don't the people get a truck and ship them away?"* After about two minutes, Peter remarked that he could not bear to watch any longer and continued on his way. As he walked on, he repeated his brief remarks to a shopkeeper he knew to be a friend of the NSDAP, and then again with a female teacher with right-wing sympathies. Peter was not meaning to be seditious. In fact, he had no idea what was going on and only learned about the Nazi campaign to burn the literary works of Jews and other politically or artistically suspect authors when he was talking with the schoolteacher.

That afternoon, however, as Pastor Peter was about to begin his confirmation class, three auxiliary policemen from the NSDAP appeared and summoned him. He replied that he would be at their disposal at the end of the confirmation hour. The police left then returned with the declaration that he was to accompany them immediately. Peter was placed under arrest, forced to leave his confirmation class, dismiss the students, and cancel his other classes.

Under the escort of the three National Socialists, one of whom carried a drawn handgun, Peter was led through the city "with people standing like a wall!" Scandalized by the public humiliation of his arrest, Peter was brought into the local newspaper office and detained together with six members of the Social Democratic Party—for a conservative like Peter, this was an additional insult! There he was held for four hours, until Superintendent Zweynert could obtain his release. According to local Nazi officials, Peter had allegedly declared that "cultural books" were being burned, which would have indicated sympathy with the authors the NSDAP regarded as enemies of the state. Peter flatly denied the allegation, pointing out that he had no knowledge of the plan to burn the books until well after the scene at the bookshop. Peter added that he too had heard words to that effect and suggested that someone else had probably made the statement. Superintendent Zweynert reported that Peter had used words like "outrageous, shameful . . . scandalous" but had not used the expression "That is a crime against culture," of which he was accused.

Peter was incensed at the defamation of his office and person, extremely offended that he was being made out to be the enemy of a right-wing party, and demanded a public apology from the auxiliary police. Further, he wrote to various officials, not least the Reich plenipotentiary for Saxony and Reich President Hindenburg, hoping for public rehabilitation. Peter defended himself vigorously:

> *For I stand entirely behind the national concern,* I have continually acted affirmatively and supportively to all things national and as a pastor to all things social, the more so as I am a former National-Liberal and from the earliest days of its founding until now as a *registered* and paying *member* of the *German National Party*. In addition, my actions described above were not directed against the national *government,* but against specific measures of the *Pirna NSDAP.*

In a letter to the Saxon Consistory, Peter explained that he had repeatedly tried to convince the Social Democrats he had met in the course of his pastoral duties that they could have achieved their social goals through the "National *Socialist* German *Workers* Party." He had tried to convince parishioners of the merits of the German Christian Movement and had preached on the two Sundays following his detainment (one was National Remembrance Day) in such a manner as to win the praise of patriotic parishioners, not least a schoolteacher who belonged to the NSDAP. Superintendent Zweynert also came to Pastor Peter's defense, noting that the arrest and public humiliation had "aroused indignation in the parish" and had been "met with public disapproval."

If Rudolf Peter's experiences were any indication, parishioners concerned about the well-being of their Pirna church had good reason to worry. Local police and party officials had rudely and maliciously defamed their parish pastor and had all but ignored the attempted intervention of Superintendent Zweynert. Fortunately for Peter, he was not forced to resign his pastoral position, as he had originally feared. Authorities in the Saxon Church Office did, however, force Peter to give up his roles as prison chaplain and deputy to Superintendent Zweynert, both of which were assigned to Pastor Paul Teichgräber, an NSDAP member and German Christian.[22]

More fundamentally, Peter's story demonstrates the ideological confusion generated in the early days of the Third Reich. Simply put, patriotic, nationally minded Germans did not yet understand that National Socialists who used national and social language would invest it with more radical, revolutionary meaning than traditional conservatives like Peter could ever imagine.

For Superintendent Zweynert, Peter's case was only the first of many times he was forced to appeal to local National Socialists to remember the rights of the Saxon Lutheran Church. In May 1933, the same month Rudolf Peter was undergoing his humiliation, Zweynert was compelled to write all the city councils and municipal authorities in the Pirna church district in order to urge them to support traditional Sunday observances. Zweynert reminded local politicians that Hitler and other Nazi leaders had affirmed the fundamental importance of Christianity in the Third Reich. For Christianity to fulfill its task in the national and moral renewal of Germany, Zweynert argued, "Sunday must really become a Lord's Day again." In order that the churches could engage in their proper spiritual labor, Zweynert requested that local political authorities ensure that the traditional Sunday service hours (from nine to eleven in the morning) remain free of other meetings.[23]

Protests like Zweynert's must have had some effect, since the regional NSDAP leadership subsequently ordered local Nazi officials not to interfere in parish church affairs. After 1936, however, once Hitler concluded that the churches could not manage their own affairs, he began to use police to control them. Beginning in March 1937, pastors in the Pirna district were required to register all church meetings in advance with the local police, no matter the purpose of the meetings or whether they were formal or informal in nature. Initially, the purpose of this measure was ostensibly to monitor the campaign for the national church election that Hitler had announced in February 1937, but which was never held. Over time, this policy was used to ensure the political reliability of all church meetings and, ultimately, to restrict all Confessing Church meetings in the district.[24]

Another ominous development took place in May 1938, when Saxon Lutheran authorities required all pastors to report the nature, history, location, and frequency of any Bible studies held outside official church facilities. The purpose of this order was to identify "difficulties" arising from Bible studies in privately owned venues. In reality, it enabled Lutheran authorities to detect politically suspect meetings of the Confessing Church.[25]

Conflict between Pirna clergy and Nazi officials over the education and care of German youth was yet another factor in the ongoing deterioration of church life. In May 1934, Pastor Max Knoch from Langenwolmsdorf explained how sharply the NSDAP had cut into the Saxon Lutheran Church's ability to reach its youth. Speaking at a pastoral conference near Pirna, Knoch complained that church authorities should work with Hitler Youth leaders, so that at least *one* Sunday each month could be kept free of all party youth activities, enabling the children to attend church. These conflicts were severest in the countryside, where the parish and the party often held their meetings in separate communities. Exacerbating the problem was the fact that lay leaders for church youth groups were increasingly hard to find and competition between different sets of adult leaders vying for the children's allegiance created high levels of tension and periodic public confrontations.[26]

In a similar manner, the busy schedule kept by the Hitler Youth and League of German Girls undermined the ministry of Pastor Scherffig of the Heidenau-Christus parish. Because Saturdays were regularly filled with party activities, the youth of Scherffig's parish were no longer available to serve in the children's choir that sang at weddings and funerals. Between school and party commitments, it was in fact becoming hard to schedule any meetings at all with the children, and so Scherffig asked Superintendent Max Zweynert to appeal to Lutheran officials to prevent the "additional restriction and disruption of parish life."[27]

In 1935, Pastor Lothar Ebert of Pirna also discovered that the local NSDAP was attacking his work. After confirmation class one day, some of the girls told him that their leader in the League of German Girls had forbidden them to sing Christmas carols in an upcoming public concert. In fact, she had scheduled party youth activities at the same time as the concert! Apparently, the League of German Girls leader was following the example of the local Hitler Youth leader, who had withdrawn his church membership and adopted the "Twenty-Four Guidelines" of the German Faith Movement as his religion. Ebert complained that these incidents had greatly upset his confirmation candidates, and he argued that the actions of the youth leaders had also contravened Article 24 of the NSDAP Program, the official religious policy of the Third Reich. As his colleagues had done, Ebert appealed to his district superintendent to inform the Saxon Church Office in order to get district and regional Nazi leaders to put a stop to this "anti-Christian demonstration" and the "anti-Christian agitation within the local League of German Girls and the local Hitler Youth."[28]

Contrary to the hopes of Pastors Knoch, Scherffig, and Ebert, relations with local party and civic leaders only deteriorated as time wore on. In November 1936, Pirna police forbade the distribution of church pamphlets at the local cemetery on the Sunday before Advent, when Protestants in Germany traditionally remembered their dead family members and friends. For the church, this was an important event at which to reach nominal Lutherans with literature designed to stir them to more active religious observance. Superintendent Zweynert was at a loss to understand how such evangelistic work to Germans could impinge on the state, and he lamented to Saxon Church authorities that the prohibition was a great blow to the parish, which had prepared four thousand leaflets for the occasion.[29]

By 1939, more trouble was surfacing. In Ottendorf, an NSDAP member told a party meeting that civil weddings were far nicer than church weddings and added, "What the pastor said, the papist man, that was all lies and deception." When the local pastor, Walter Börner, found out about the event (word of which had spread throughout the parish), he asked the district superintendent to pursue the problem with the appropriate party officials in Pirna. In another incident at Ottendorf, Pastor Börner's daughter borrowed a fellow student's notebook to catch up on missed schoolwork and found in it the sentence "The Bible is a Jewish Book," dictated by the schoolteacher, an NSDAP leader named Reuter. Börner was scandalized by the dictation, which he felt violated the National Socialist fundamentals of tolerance and freedom of conscience (?!). Quoting a recent Hitler speech to make his point, Börner complained that Reuter's statement unfairly set aside the New Testament, which "is also the fundamental historical document for the Positive Christianity on which the Party stands." In an ingenious if dubious argument, Börner concluded that Schoolteacher Reuter had actually attacked part of the NSDAP Program and asked Superintendent Heinrich Leichte to pursue the matter with church and school officials, so that Reuter might be put in his place.[30]

Pastor Lothar Ebert of Pirna reported yet another outrageous incident that same year. In Pirna, Nazi youth leader Lippold told some Lutheran youths: "Just as the synagogues are burning down now, one day the day will come when we burn down the churches." Lippold went on to berate one of his charges for helping to deliver the Pirna parish newsletter, declaring, "A Hitler Youth must not carry a parish newsletter." As Börner had done before him, Ebert complained that the statements of the Hitler Youth leader contravened the official platform of the NSDAP and stood in direct contrast to the public statements of Hitler and his representatives, who frequently proclaimed religious freedom. "They create justifiable indignation among the parents," he added, "and lead the children into very serious conflicts." Once again, Ebert requested that Pirna superintendent Heinrich Leichte speak with the local party youth leaders, so that such "brutal statements" would stop.[31] Leichte, an ardent National Socialist and a local party official himself, was probably the least likely person to intervene on behalf of frustrated pastors. His ascendancy to the position of superintendent brought a departure from the moderation of his predecessor, Dr. Max Zweynert, and led to a sharpening of conflicts between pastors and the NSDAP, as well as between Confessing Church pastors and his own office.

There is no evidence that relations between the Pirna churches and local National Socialists improved during the Second World War. Indeed, they likely got worse, judging from the 1940 annual report of Pastor Werner of Dohna. Werner predicted that the ongoing shortage of clergy would lead to dire consequences in local parishes, "particularly in this time, where so much work is secretly and publicly done against the church and all *religious instruction is eliminated from the schools.*" Werner went on to describe how the *"battle against the church"* had worsened in Dohna during the past year. At the city's nine-hundred-year anniversary celebrations, for instance, the district Nazi Party leader used his ninety-minute speech to launch a shocking attack on the church, making false accusations about the high incomes of clergy. Thankfully, according to Werner, "the effect of such basely anti-clerical propaganda was indeed a different one than the speaker had surely expected. A number of the visitors left the room during the speech. The speaker even had to endure, for example, the loud and clear answer 'No' to his rhetorical question." A few weeks later, the NSDAP Christmas celebration in Dohna was canceled when only sixteen people appeared, instead of the several hundred visitors that local party officials had expected. "The inhabitants of Dohna apparently feared similar gaffes as at the centennial anniversary," was Werner's assessment. Werner's report concluded with the deterioration of parish life in Dohna caused by local Nazi agitation: adult church attendance and children's church attendance had both dropped; confirmation instruction was growing more difficult; and the party campaign to get parishioners to withdraw from the church was on the increase again.[32]

Between 1933 and 1939, parish life in Pirna had been turned completely upside down. While the rise of the Nazis in 1933 produced a spectacular show of interest in local Lutheran churches, that interest soon waned and disgruntled parishioners abandoned the church almost as quickly as they had rushed in. If the prominence of the German Christian Movement, the interest of pastors in the NSDAP, and the testimony of Pirna clergy attest to the power of religious nationalism to enliven parish life at the outset of the Third Reich, then the growing frustration of Pirna clergy over the interference of the Nazi Party in local church life shows just how illusory their belief was that the NSDAP would actually contribute to a genuine moral renewal of German society. Though a few Pirna pastors maintained their faith in the compatibility of National Socialism and Lutheran Christianity, most of them eventually chose one of two nonconformist options: either they joined the Confessing Church or they joined a group promoting a compromise that steered away from the German Christian campaign to nazify the Saxon Lutheran Church.

## Ravensburg, Württemberg

In stark contrast to conditions in Nauen and Pirna, no great wave of Protestant nationalism swept through the eleven parishes of the Ravensburg church district in 1933. To be sure, there were outbursts of nationalist euphoria over Hitler's seizure of power, like the way District Superintendent Hermann Ströle praised the "miracle" of renewed German unity under National Socialism and predicted that a spiritual renewal would soon engulf the nation.[33] Similar remarks at a Protestant men's meeting that August indicate that the new National Socialist government was generally accepted among local Protestants. Pastor Theodor Bidlingmaier greeted the large gathering of men from around Ravensburg with a string of references to the sunny weather, the good harvest, the men's good health, and "the new discipline and order in our Fatherland." Police Inspector Seemüller, leader of the visiting Weingarten men's group, echoed Bidlingmaier's greeting. He commended the brotherly assembly gathered "in this time of great patriotic experiences" and added, "It is a great fortune, that the Führer, Adolf Hitler, has fought in such an earnest and far-sighted way for the deepest foundations of national life, Christian faith, and Christian morality. May God keep him healthy and strengthen him for his difficult task!"[34]

In February 1935, Protestant men in Friedrichshafen were still reflecting happily about Hitler's rise to power two years earlier. In a well-attended meeting, their leader, Konrad Kühlwein, spoke on the topic "Our Faith." Influenced by the political theology of the day and the propaganda of the Hitler regime, Kühlwein explained how various nations and races found their expression in different languages, and that he regarded each nation or race as a divine creation. In language local Nazis would understand clearly, he stated: "God has assigned the individual nations and races their boundaries. If these boundaries are often points of friction, then the nations have the right and duty to respect and to protect the boundaries assigned to them. Here begins the battle, the battle for existence." While he pointed out that Christian faith crossed those racial boundaries, Kühlwein immediately added that this should not offend or impinge upon the national community, because the national community was God's will. Kühlwein attacked various neo-pagan movements, emphasizing instead the cultivation of a combined community of the nation, of the faith, and of God. He described how God made world and German history and how, in divine foresight, God had appointed Hitler to transform Germany. He also explained that the Third Reich's emphasis on national unity and reawakening of love and sacrifice for one's neighbor were Christian concepts that Lutheran men ought to emphasize and respect.[35]

Aside from speeches like this, however, parish life in the Ravensburg district unfolded rather uneventfully in the 1930s. In contrast to the predominance of church-political concerns in Nauen and Pirna, the correspondence between Ravensburg clergy, their district superintendent, and higher church officials in Stuttgart revolved around everyday matters such as buying and selling land and managing property. Several parishes rented space in their parsonages or parish halls to the German military and party organizations such as the National Socialist Welfare, National Socialist Motor Club, and Hitler Youth, generally without complaint.[36] In several parishes, pastors and their parish councils were working with the Württemberg Protestant Church to plan and construct new facilities. In Fischbach-Manzell, a collection of villages in the parish of Friedrichshafen, the construction of a parish hall in the mid-1930s consumed much of the local curate's time and eventually led to the creation of an independent pastorate. Similarly, in Tettnang, pastors worked to advance plans to construct a chapel in Meckenbeuren and contemplated a new church in Tettnang itself. In Leutkirch and Langenargen, pastors and parish councils grappled with instructions from the regional church authorities to add another apartment to their parsonages. So did the Ravensburg parish council, which also investigated applying fire retardant to church buildings and executed a plan to improve the church's heating system. During the war, pastors and parish councils in Friedrichshafen, Isny, and Ravensburg all devised plans for bomb shelters and worked to save church bells from confiscation by the German military.[37]

In contrast to these mundane issues, one subject of deep concern to both clergy and laity in Ravensburg was the decision of the Württemberg Education Ministry to transform Protestant and Catholic confessional schools into secular community and national schools. For the Lutheran minority in the Ravensburg region, closing their small confessional schools meant that they would become increasingly marginalized alongside the Catholic majority and would have a harder and harder time maintaining the Protestant identity of their children. While pastors and parish councils all across the district pondered the impact of school secularization, practically speaking there was little that they could do about it except to ensure that at least one Protestant schoolteacher (or the local pastor) was always available to teach religious instruction in the new community schools. Equally difficult were the problems of finding new uses for vacant school buildings and negotiating new contractual agreements with teachers who rented apartments from the parish councils.[38]

The Ravensburg district was substantially affected by the decline of German fortunes during the Second World War. Pastoral workloads increased dramatically, though new opportunities emerged to minister to the fearful and discouraged German populace. In Leutkirch and Isny, local ministers and extra church workers sent by the church authorities in Stuttgart struggled to provide adequate religious instruction and pastoral care for hundreds of evacuated mothers and children from Friedrichshafen, Stuttgart, Duisburg, and Essen. In Leutkirch alone, Pastor Hilmar Schieber established seventeen temporary stations for worship services and religious instruction in the villages of his parish.[39] Adding to the difficulties, at least a dozen ministers from the Ravensburg district were called up for military service between 1939 and 1945, meaning that their colleagues left behind were constantly scrambling to conduct all the church services and religious instruction classes that fell to them. Pastor Duisberg, for example, served in at least six different pastorates *after* his retirement in 1939. In Langenargen, where Duisberg labored from 1940 to 1942, no fewer than four different ministers served the parish during the war years, while at least two others, Drs. Helmut Thielicke and Günther Dehn, made their residences in the parsonage but served in Ravensburg parishes, meaning that for several years there was no resident pastor in all Langenargen.[40]

Apart from the death of many local men, including Pastors Immanuel Spellenberg of Friedrichshafen and Gottfried Hoffmann of Waldsee, the Second World War impacted church life most dramatically in the physical destruction of the Ravensburg district, and Friedrichshafen in particular. An initial attack of Allied bombers swept over the town during the night of June 20–21, 1943. Far more destructive, however, was the giant air raid of April 27–28, 1944, when eight hundred to one thousand planes descended on Friedrichshafen, destroying the historic town center. Fire broke out in the main parsonage. Much of the landmark palace church was destroyed, as were other church facilities. As he assessed the damage, Friedrichshafen pastor Ludwig Schmidt lamented that no one yet knew how many wounded or dead there might be and added dismally that there were only a few undamaged houses in the whole town. In response to the disaster, the Württemberg church authorities transferred a large sum of money to the Friedrichshafen parish, equipping it to care for the parishioners most severely affected by the attack.[41]

In July 1944, two more air raids hit Manzell and Friedrichshafen, destroying the Zeppelin wharf and an engine factory. Although the parish halls and parsonages suffered some damage, miraculously (so the report said), they were not directly hit. During the first air raid on Manzell, Mrs. Spellenberg, the widow of the local pastor, who had only recently died in combat, comforted the inhabitants of a bomb shelter by reminding them that they were all in God's hand. After the attack passed, she led them in the Lord's Prayer, in thanksgiving for their survival. During a second attack two days later, Mrs. Spellenberg again comforted those in the bomb shelter, including the local NSDAP leader. She quoted from Psalm 20: "Some take pride in chariots, and some in horses, but our pride is in the name of the Lord our

God." Calming the crowd, she instructed them to pray rather than to murmur or argue. Quoting various biblical texts and explaining Jesus' care for everyone in the shelter, Spellenberg soothed the crowd and led them in the Lord's Prayer, as she had done before.[42] With her help, the parishioners of Friedrichshafen and Fischbach-Manzell survived the air raids, the worst crisis in the Ravensburg district during the National Socialist era.

Aside from the physical damage of the air raids, there is little anecdotal evidence to suggest that the National Socialist seizure of power and course of the Church Struggle in Württemberg greatly affected spiritual conditions in the Ravensburg district, either in 1933 or later. Rather, pastors and parish councils spent time discussing the ongoing problems of land, buildings, and education, and tried to cope as best they could with the social and physical displacement brought about by the war.

Statistical records from the Ravensburg district confirm this picture. Although some pastors and a few prominent parishioners grew excited about the potential for the new National Socialist state to ignite a renewal within their churches, neither district nor parish statistics from Ravensburg suggest that any of the mass excitement of Protestants in Nauen and Pirna found its way to Ravensburg. For instance, the absolute number of communicants in Ravensburg increased only 2 percent from 1932 to 1933, and the percentage of parishioners who participated in communion actually dropped slightly. So did the number of church weddings, baptisms, and the amount of voluntary church giving.[43]

None of these trends improved over the following years, and indeed the number of communicants declined until the middle of the Second World War, by which time the course of events might have convinced parishioners to cultivate their spiritual lives more ardently. Even then, however, males comprised an ever-smaller number of communicants in Ravensburg church services, accounting for fewer than one in three attendees after 1942, when many were away at war. Only in Friedrichshafen, where the passionate German Christian and National Socialist propagandist Dr. Karl Steger ministered, was there a significant jump of 14 percent in communion-taking between 1932 and 1933. Other statistical categories suggest virtually no significant change in the level of public religiosity.

One of the few measures that stood out was the noticeable increase in church membership withdrawals in the second half of the 1930s, from 37 across the district in 1936 steadily up to 255 in 1939. Most of the more than 500 parishioners who quit the church in those years joined the German Faith Movement, German Christian Movement, or Reich Minister Hermann Göring's *God-believers* or some other non-Christian religious movement. At the parish level, fully two-thirds of church membership withdrawals took place in the towns Friedrichshafen and in Ravensburg, while the other nine parishes in the district were only marginally affected. So while parish life in Nauen and Pirna was full of controversy during the Hitler era, in Ravensburg it was fairly calm.

In light of this, we might ask why there was such an absence of religious-national enthusiasm among Ravensburg Protestants. Certainly, there was no popular rush into the Protestant churches of Ravensburg, no surge of Lutheran nationalism as in Nauen and Pirna. That difference was in large part a product of the varied demographics of the three districts. Unlike Nauen and Pirna, where the population was roughly 90 percent Protestant, in Ravensburg it was only about 10 percent Protestant. Simply put, there were far fewer non-Catholics in the general population who were not already attached to the church. Another reason that public religiosity in Ravensburg did not show a significant statistical increase in 1933 was that Protestant participation was already a lot higher in Württemberg than it was in either Brandenburg or Saxony. District church statistics demonstrate this, and anecdotal evidence confirms it. For instance, the percentage of Ravensburg parishioners who took communion in 1933 was about 50 percent, while that ratio was only around 15 percent in the Nauen district and perhaps 20 percent in Pirna. Dr. Günther Dehn, a pastor in Ravensburg during the war, was astounded at the deep connection between south German Protestants and their churches. It was certainly something he had never experienced in his north German home.[44]

The fact that Ravensburg Protestants were a distinct minority in the region of Upper Swabia might also account for a lower level of religious nationalism in two other ways. First, there was generally far less enthusiasm for National Socialism in the Catholic south of Württemberg than in the Protestant regions of northern Germany. Voters in Upper Swabia remained solidly behind the Catholic Centre Party, which consistently dominated the NSDAP in free elections and even bested the National Socialists in the unfree election of March 5, 1933. Within this largely Catholic political milieu, Protestants in the Ravensburg district did not have the same freedom (or perhaps inclination) to articulate a Lutheran religious nationalism that majority Protestants in Nauen and Pirna did.[45]

Second, and related to the dominance of Roman Catholics in the Ravensburg area, any public political exuberance over National Socialism that occurred took place in a secular, public space and not in the minority Protestant or the reserved Catholic churches. Unlike conditions in Nauen and Pirna, Protestants and their pastors did not stand near the top of the Upper Swabian political elite. Without the same central position in the public life of their communities, there was little emphasis on the ceremonial importance of Protestant services and Protestant pastors—a vital factor in the linkage between Protestantism and nationalism in Nauen and Pirna. There is no evidence that church membership, church rites, or church sacraments were ever important to National Socialists in the Ravensburg area. Consequently, the external expressions of Lutheran religiosity in the Ravensburg district remained almost entirely untouched by the weighty political events of 1933. Only the gradual draining of participation in church life due to the constant demands of the NSDAP was a shared reality in Nauen, Pirna, and Ravensburg.

Ravensburg aside, if the experiences of Protestants in Nauen and Pirna are representative, the year 1933 was enormously significant to German Protestantism at the parish level. As ironic as it seems in hindsight, the National Socialist seizure of power unleashed a national renewal that generated a breathtaking, if illusory, revitalization of public interest in German Protestantism. Amid the political revolution of 1933 and the wave of enthusiasm sweeping through many Protestant parishes, it is understandable—though ultimately tragic—that so many Protestant pastors looked with awe and wonder upon Adolf Hitler as the savior of their Christian churches. As the NSDAP came to dominate German public life to an extent that the churches could not rival, it is not clear why is took so many of them so long to react to their growing marginalization in German society. One thing is sure: only the brightest and most influential pastors were capable of navigating their congregations through the surge of religious nationalism that swept over their communities and their churches and so avoid a disastrous collision with the anti-Christian elements in National Socialist ideology.

# chapter three

## Pastoral Appointments and the Local Church Struggle

**In parishes across Germany, no single factor shaped** the course of the Church Struggle more than the church-political views of clergy. Whether German Christians, neutrals, or members of the Confessing Church, pastors possessed a great deal of personal and positional authority. They administered the sacramental blessings of the church as they baptized, confirmed, married, and buried their parishioners. They taught children and young people, led Bible studies and prayer meetings, chaired parish council meetings, presided over public functions, visited homes, prisons, and hospitals, counseled troubled parishioners, edited parish newsletters, and preached sermons. Curates and vicars, who were ordained and unordained clergy in temporary positions, were generally less influential than pastors, though if they were especially energetic and had proven themselves over time, they too could attain a position of importance in their local communities.

Pastoral appointments were unpredictable events. Often they took place without incident, and new appointees sustained parish life just as their predecessors had. Periodically, however, pastoral appointments erupted into noisy battles between factions of parishioners, clergy, and regional church authorities. During the Nazi era, Protestants on both extremes of the church-political spectrum coveted the power to control pastoral appointments. For this reason, the appointment process provides an ideal window through which to view grassroots Protestantism in the Hitler era. Simply put, understanding pastoral appointments is vital to understanding the Church Struggle as a whole. Unfortunately, however, this aspect of church life has been largely overlooked in the history of the German Church Struggle, either because it was perceived to be too mundane to warrant exploration or simply because it was too far removed from the national and regional church politics to be noticed. But with participation from every level of the church from regional bishops to local laypeople, pastoral appointments illustrate the extent to which the factional struggles within the governing institutions of the German Protestant churches affected the everyday lives of German Protestants.

How exactly did the process of appointment work? Initially, regional church authorities determined whether a clerical vacancy would be filled by a new permanent pastor or by a temporary cleric—a vicar, curate, or retired pastor who would serve under the administrative supervision of a pastor from a neighboring parish. In the case of a new pastoral appointment, those same regional church authorities spoke the final word of approval for any hopeful candidate. In between those two ends of the process, however, district superintendents, supervising pastors, parish patrons, parish councils, district synods, and individual parishioners all had input into the process. They urged their superiors to authorize new pastoral appointments, campaigned for candidates of their choice, launched grievances against appointments they believed to be unjust, and when all else failed, resorted to blatant obstruction.

Though the process of appointments varied slightly between the Brandenburg Church Province of the Old Prussian Union Church, the Württemberg Protestant Church, and the Saxon Lutheran Church, most followed a series of common steps. In Brandenburg, vacancies were generally advertised in official church publications. Once a vacant position was advertised, officials in the Brandenburg Consistory, the administrative headquarters for the church province, usually suggested the names of potential candidates. Next, the parish patron (often a local aristocrat or the resident mayor) would then nominate the candidate of his or her choice, usually in consultation with some combination of the parish council, the district superintendent, the district synod executive, other pastors, and the consistory in Berlin. Next, a candidation visit would take place, during which the prospective pastor would lead a worship service, deliver a sermon, and perhaps give religious instruction to a group of children. Afterward, the parish council would consider the reactions of parishioners and other stakeholders and then vote on the appointment. Within a limited period of time, disgruntled parishioners were entitled to submit letters or petitions of protest, which were taken into account by the Brandenburg Consistory. Only afterward did the consistory ratify the appointment, arrange for moving expenses, and assign a start date for the new pastor.

In the Third Reich, the Nauen, Pirna, and Ravensburg districts all experienced a substantial turnover of pastors. Nauen suffered the greatest shortages of the three, with almost half of the pastorates vacant at the start of the Second World War. The vacancies in Pirna and Ravensburg were less problematic, since almost all of them were associate pastoral positions in multiple staff parishes. The Nauen vacancies were almost all solo pastorates responsible for entire parishes. In all three districts, the number of pastoral appointments in the prewar era was about one-half of the number of total pastorates in the district. In Pirna and Ravensburg, regional church authorities continued to make pastoral appointments during the Second World War. Not so in Nauen, where pastoral appointments tapered off after 1939, and none were made after July 1942. Vacant pastoral positions were not the only measure of the instability in Protestant parish ministry. The many retirements, deaths, and transfers of clergy from parish to parish resulted in a significant level of pastoral turnover. Here too Nauen fared worse than either Pirna or Ravensburg. Fewer than one-quarter of its pastors held the same position from 1933 to 1939, while about one-third of Pirna and Ravensburg pastors held stable positions in the prewar years of Nazi rule (see table 1 below).

| Table 1. Pastoral Vacancies and Appointments in the Nauen, Pirna, and Ravensburg Districts | | | |
| --- | --- | --- | --- |
| District | Nauen | Pirna | Ravensburg |
| Total Pastorates | 28 | 57 | 17 |
| Long-term Pastoral Vacancies (vacant from 1933-1939) | 3 | 9 | 0 |
| Pastorates Vacant as of September 1939 | 13 | 16 | 4 |
| Pastoral Appointments during the Prewar Era (1933–1939) | 15 | 32 | 9 |
| Pastoral Appointments during the Second World War (1939–1945) | 5 | 15 | 8 |
| Stable Pastorates (same pastor from 1933–1939) | 6 | 19 | 6 |

## Ravensburg, Württemberg

Curiously, in the district of Ravensburg, the clerical appointment most significant for the Church Struggle occurred in 1929, four years before the National Socialists came to power. That was the year Dr. Karl Steger was appointed to the associate pastorate of Friedrichshafen. Initially recommended by the Württemberg Superior Church Council, Steger was approved only after a thorough investigation by the Friedrichshafen parish council, which had several concerns about Steger: his health, his personal history, and, above all, his political attitudes. The Friedrichshafen parish was searching for a liberal pastor to complement their conservative senior pastor, and Steger appeared to be the exact opposite of what they were after. However, the Friedrichshafen parish councilors chose Steger after discussions with a range of contacts, including Theophil Wurm, who would soon rise to the position of bishop of the Württemberg regional church. An "outstanding" conservative pastor like Steger, they reasoned, was better than a mediocre liberal pastor.[1]

In hindsight, Steger's appointment in Friedrichshafen was probably a mistake, considering the heretical tendencies of his nationalist theology, his scandalous opposition to the Württemberg church authorities, and his continuously divisive presence in Friedrichshafen. Certainly, there was no other pastor in the district who caused so much trouble as Steger did between 1933 and 1945. For everyone who had to deal with him, from his parish council on up to Württemberg bishop Wurm, Steger embodied the theological and political excesses of the German Christian Movement at their worst. In the Nazi era, and particularly after the short-lived German Christian attempt to seize control of the Württemberg regional church in 1933 and 1934, Bishop Wurm and the Württemberg Superior Church Council ensured that they would not end up with another appointment like Steger's. To that end, they used their final authority over pastoral appointments to undercut German Christian activity in the Ravensburg district, by appointing important adherents of the Confessing Church to vacant positions and ensuring that all pastoral candidates upheld the traditional authority of Scripture and the Reformation Confessions of Faith.

Various examples bear this out. In August 1937, the Württemberg Superior Church Council appointed Pastor Gottfried Hoffmann in Bad Waldsee. Hoffmann came to the Ravensburg district after a turbulent history in Bad Liebenzell, west of Stuttgart. There the German Christians who briefly controlled the Württemberg Protestant Church had suspended Hoffmann for two months in 1934 for criticizing their unlawful takeover. When he refused to abide by his temporary banishment, the Bad Liebenzell police prohibited him from performing any official pastoral duties. Even after order was restored in the church and Hoffmann was reinstated, the local police and regional political authorities refused to allow Hoffmann to return to his position. For that reason, he was transferred to Bad Waldsee, near Ravensburg.[2] In Bad Waldsee, Hoffmann inherited a pastorate in which his predecessor had been fighting a long-running battle with a number of prominent families in the parish. After 1933, these families formed an aggressive German Christian group that harassed local clergy. From the perspective of the Württemberg church authorities, Hoffmann was an ideal candidate for Bad Waldsee. He was unafraid of ideological conflict, committed to the Confessing Church cause, and skilled enough to neutralize the German Christian opposition in the parish.[3]

In another church-politically strategic appointment, the Superior Church Council sent Pastor Eugen Schmid to the difficult parish of Friedrichshafen in October 1939, just after the outbreak of the Second World War.[4] The discussions leading up to Schmid's appointment illustrate the interaction between local and regional church leaders and underscore the primacy of the Württemberg Superior Church Council in matters of personnel. As a representative of the Superior Church Council and the Friedrichshafen parish council began talks, they quickly agreed that the recent influx of Protestant factory workers from across Germany into Friedrichshafen necessitated a new pastor who could reach out to new people effectively. The new residents were not making their way into the church, since "the church does not find its way to them." [5] Both the Superior Church Council and the Friedrichshafen parish council also agreed that the splintering of the parish made it vital that the new pastor care for the nucleus of lay leaders and their organizations. Referring to the divisive work of German Christian associate pastor Karl Steger, the Friedrichshafeners also requested that the new pastor "do justice to the inner longing of the parish to preach nothing but the pure gospel." Amid the social upheaval and ideological pressure of the Third Reich, the parish council asked for a strong leader (declining to put forward the names of any candidates themselves), essentially promising that parishioners would follow him and not cause any trouble. The Superior Church Council's answer was Eugen Schmid, an experienced pastor who soon earned the trust of the parish and kept associate pastor Steger in check.

In the case of another appointment two years later, Württemberg bishop Wurm got directly involved in the appointment process in order to place the young theologian Dr. Helmut Thielicke into a vacant pastorate in Ravensburg. Thielicke had grown unpopular with the Gestapo, who forced him from his position on the theological faculty of the University of Heidelberg in 1940. He endured a short stint in the army until a medical problem allowed him to return to civilian life. Unemployed and politically compromised by his earlier criticisms of National Socialism, Thielicke was rescued by Bishop Wurm, who gave him a quiet post in Upper Swabia so that he could devote time to preparing for his future role as a theologian and leader in the Württemberg Protestant Church. Thielicke pastored in Ravensburg from January 1941 until September 1942, when Wurm commissioned him to serve as his theological advisor and head up a new theological department in Stuttgart. [6]

After Thielicke left Ravensburg, the Superior Church Council sent another theological exile to take his place: Dr. Günther Dehn, a former professor at Halle University. [7] Dehn was already infamous across Germany for condemning the glorification of war and for demanding that the church advocate international peace and reconciliation. Those opinions aroused the fury of nationalists and National Socialists beginning in 1928, when Dehn first voiced them, and then again in 1931 and 1932, when the so-called Dehn Case erupted. A Berlin pastor at the time, Dehn was first offered and then driven out of theological professorships in Heidelberg and Halle. [8] Sheltered in the Württemberg regional church during the war, Dehn followed Thielicke to Ravensburg, pastoring there from late 1942 until 1946. Dehn enjoyed his time in Ravensburg, where the deep interest of parishioners in the affairs of their church impressed him. After 1945, Dehn's theological exile ended and he returned to his academic life in northern Germany, much to the disappointment of the Ravensburg parishioners. [9]

## Pirna, Saxony

In the district of Pirna, clerical appointments were made by a combination of the Saxon Lutheran authorities, the parish patron, and the parish council—at least that is how it had been done in the days before the First World War, when Superintendent Maximilian Zweynert began his pastoral career in Pirna.[10] By the 1930s, however, there was little evidence for the existence of any tradition of significant local input into pastoral appointments. In fact, in 1933, at the outset of the German Church Struggle, the Saxon church authorities surveyed local clergy about two proposals that would have given more power to the Saxon Lutheran bishop to appoint parish clergy and district superintendents. In both cases, pastors responded favorably to the idea, and by the mid-1930s, church authorities in Dresden were using their control over appointments to place German Christian pastors into vacant pastorates throughout the Saxon Lutheran Church.[11] In Pirna, this one-sided policy in favor of the German Christians destroyed the ecclesiastical peace that Superintendent Zweynert had worked so hard to establish at the outset of the Church Struggle in the early 1930s.

When Zweynert retired from ministry in June 1937, the appointment of his successor demonstrated both the authority of Saxon church officials in Dresden and their willingness to use it for the political advantage of the German Christian Movement. At first, the Saxon Church Committee designated Pastor Martin Meinel of Bad Schandau as interim superintendent for Pirna. Meinel was one of the senior pastors in the district and had also been Zweynert's standing substitute during some of the former superintendent's absences.[12] Despite his obvious credentials, Meinel lasted only four months in his new post. First, the local National Socialist leader expelled Meinel from the party. Then the district court opened an investigation against him. Finally, authorities in the Saxon Church Office and its finance department suspended Meinel from his position and gave it to Pastor Heinrich Leichte from Königstein.[13] Meinel briefly resisted his ouster, refusing to hand over the keys to the superintendent's office on November 18, 1937. By the following day, however, a circular letter to the Pirna pastors had been sent out under Leichte's signature, indicating that he had taken over from Meinel after all.[14]

Local clergy were fully aware that Leichte's appointment was politically motivated. An outspoken German Christian and National Socialist, Leichte was already working for the NSDAP before Hitler came to power. He joined the party in 1933 and was a leader at the local level.[15] Among local pastors, however, Leichte was something of an outcast because of his unremitting German Christian agitation and his well-known lack of collegiality.

Leichte's installation service reflected his commitment to the twin movements of National Socialism and German Christianity. His guest list included more than seventy-five officials from the Nazi Party, various levels of government, and the school system, but only nine local church leaders, two of whom were radical German Christians.[16] One notable omission was Leichte's predecessor, retired Superintendent Max Zweynert, who sent Leichte a congratulatory postcard almost a year later, when he first found out about Leichte's appointment.[17]

Leichte's appointment illustrates the extent to which the Saxon bishop and his administration controlled pastoral appointments in Pirna. There is no suggestion that any local opposition tried to block the process, even though it was so obviously influenced by Leichte's Nazi political loyalties. Nor is there any record of controversy surrounding any of the forty-six other pastoral appointments in Pirna between 1933 and 1942, this despite the fact that there were over a dozen dissident clergy in the Confessing Church who generated all kinds of church-political conflict over many other issues in the district. Normally, circular letters from Superintendents Zweynert and Leichte simply noted new pastoral appointments and rarely commented on the process at all.[18]

# Nauen, Brandenburg

In the Brandenburg church district of Nauen, both the administration of vacant parishes and the process of appointing new pastors generated infinitely more controversy than in either Ravensburg or Pirna. With so many parishes left vacant throughout the 1930s and 1940s, providing adequate pastoral care became a constant challenge. Church-political rivalry greatly complicated what was already a pressing problem and resulted in a flood of administrative proposals from local clergy and Brandenburg church officials, with everyone competing to influence vacant pastorates toward either the German Christian Movement or the Confessing Church.

## Complex Problems and Complicated Plans

Because the number of vacant pastorates was so high in Nauen, attempts to justify new appointments usually involved juggling issues of economics, geography, and personality over multiple parishes in one or another corner of the church district. A good example of the complexity of these problems and the complicated nature of the plans advanced to solve them comes from the parishes of Groß Behnitz, Retzow, and Ribbeck, all of which lay southwest of Nauen. The Brandenburg Consistory, interim superintendents, and local pastors all submitted plans to redistribute pastoral work and justify new pastoral appointments for these parishes. Despite these efforts, Groß Behnitz remained vacant for over two years following the retirement of Pastor Lux in October 1935. Retzow remained vacant for one and a half years following the retirement of Pastor Koch in December 1935, and Ribbeck remained vacant from early 1934 until after the end of the Second World War.

In Ribbeck, the retirement of Pastor Werner left parish patron Erich von Ribbeck scrambling to find a neighboring pastor to help care for his parishioners. However, the two closest clerics, Pastors Koch of Retzow and Lux of Groß Behnitz, were both close to retirement, and neither felt able to take on the extra work of serving the Ribbeck parish. Reluctantly, Pastor Herbert Posth of Berge agreed to take on the responsibility.[19] In addition to his primary duties in Berge and his temporary assistance in Ribbeck, Posth soon ended up as the temporary pastor in Groß Behnitz too, after Pastor Lux fell ill in the months prior to his retirement. Overburdened by performing triple duty, Posth requested that the consistory quickly appoint a pastor in vacant Groß Behnitz. If it were necessary to combine several parishes to generate enough income to pay for a pastor, he suggested that the consistory consider joining Groß Behnitz together with the vacant Markau parish and even Retzow parish, if necessary.

Posth did not know it yet, but officials in the consistory were already considering other options. In July 1935, they advanced a plan to link Groß and Klein Behnitz and their one thousand parishioners with tiny Riewend and Bagow (450 parishioners in total), which were both filial churches[20] from the Päwesien parish in the neighboring Brandenburg-Dom church district.[21]

A third plan for Groß Behnitz was advanced in January 1936, this time by Interim Superintendent Otto Schmidt. Schmidt's idea was to combine the parishes of Groß Behnitz, Markau, and Retzow. This plan was virtually identical to Herbert Posth's original proposal, except that Schmidt now advocated appointing the new pastor to the Markau parish, not to Groß Behnitz, as Posth had suggested. Six months later, Schmidt changed his mind and suggested linking Groß Behnitz and Retzow. As usual, Schmidt's aim was to accumulate a significant number of parishioners (and therefore parish income) to pay for a pastor.[22]

This was now the fourth proposal over the course of a year for providing pastoral care to the vacant parishes of Groß Behnitz, Ribbeck, and Retzow. It too failed to find support. When Pastor Ulrich Bettac replaced Schmidt as the interim superintendent, Bettac argued against linking Groß Behnitz and Ribbeck, on account of the poor roads that linked them. Moreover, as Bettac pointed out, the Groß Behnitz-Ribbeck combination would still require extra funding from the consistory, a death knell to any proposal put forward during the 1930s, because of fiscal shortages in Berlin.

Bettac considered a new combination—Groß Behnitz, Retzow, and Pessin, with a total of fifteen hundred parishioners and plenty of parish income to pay for a pastor—but he later decided that Schmidt's plan to link Groß Behnitz and Ribbeck was a good idea after all, since it would permit the combination of Retzow and Pessin into another viable pastorate.[23]

In this merry-go-round of local church politics, Bettac's ideas were promptly scuttled by the opposition of Herbert Posth, who was still the temporary pastor for the two key vacant parishes, Ribbeck and Groß Behnitz. As much as Posth wanted a settlement—he complained that he could not physically manage the extra work much longer—Bettac's plan made little sense to him. Fortunately, Posth had an alternative to suggest, having just finished a detailed analysis of the various vacant parishes and the factors that would influence the appointment of new pastors and the provision of adequate care for parishes with no pastor: numbers of parishioners, church incomes generated, and distances between the parishes. He submitted his proposal to the consistory in December of 1936. It was easily the most thorough and ambitious plan for the area to date.

In brief, Posth asserted that neither of two combinations of parishes (Groß Behnitz and Ribbeck or Groß Behnitz and Retzow) would work. In both cases, poor roads meant that the distance between the parishes was just too great, since each trip could reasonably be accomplished only by detouring through Nauen. Moreover, both combinations would have created as many problems as they would have solved, since the ripple effect would have left adjacent parishes without adequate pastoral care.

Instead, Posth proposed linking Ribbeck with Retzow, and Groß Behnitz with two filial churches (Riewend and Bagow) from the neighboring Brandenburg-Dom district. Posth's calculations were so complicated that his plan also had to include linking together two other churches, Päwesien and Wachow, neither of which was even in the Nauen district.[24]

To drive home his point, Posth wrote to the consistory again one week later. After explaining how he had been overworked for four years while caring for neighboring parishes along with his own congregations, Posth let it be known that if the consistory could not arrive at a settlement within one month, he was going to resign his temporary supervision over Groß Behnitz. Interim Superintendent Bettac advocated for Posth's plan before both the consistory and the Nauen district synod, whose opinion also counted in these matters.[25]

Posth's threat was probably a bluff, but perhaps it worked, because Brandenburg church authorities finally woke up to the necessity of appointing a new pastor in Groß Behnitz. In March 1937, they adopted part of Posth's plan, advocating the combination of Groß Behnitz, Bagow, and Riewend. At the same time, they proposed to create a conglomerate position out of congregations in Retzow, Ribbeck, and filial church Möthlow, an idea that Interim Superintendent Bettac and the Nauen district synod executive both supported. As ever, these plans aimed to accumulate enough people and income to justify new appointments.[26]

Ultimately, all this work went for naught, or so it seemed. In mid-1937, more than two years after the problem of pastoral care in this part of the Nauen district had surfaced, the Brandenburg Consistory finally appointed Pastor Walter Pachali in Retzow, but did so without announcing how the neighboring parishes would be cared for. Not that it mattered terribly, for soon Pachali was the nominal supervisor of vacant parishes in Pessin, Ribbeck, and even Groß Behnitz, where parishioners were awaiting the final approval for the appointment of their new pastor, Kurt Fritzsche. But when church-political infighting delayed that appointment too, desperate parish councils from Groß Behnitz and Päwesien (in the Brandenburg-Dom district) submitted a joint request for action to the consistory.[27] Two months later, in March of 1938, Fritzsche was finally appointed and promptly succeeded Pastor Pachali of Retzow as the temporary pastor for the unfortunate Ribbeck parish, which was the biggest loser in this game of ecclesiastical musical chairs. Ribbeck had been vacant since 1934 and would remain so right through the time of the Third Reich.

For all the planning of local and provincial church officials, the ever-expanding needs of vacant parishes repeatedly forced pastors who were in office to take on burdensome duties in any number of vacant locales around them, whether convenient or not. The resulting fatigue, frustration, and administrative gridlock undermined effective pastoral ministry across the Nauen district, creating conditions far more destructive to Protestant life than in either Pirna or Ravensburg. Moreover, if the problem of justifying new appointments and providing pastoral care for parishes with no pastor wasn't hard enough, church-political competition for control of these vacant pastorates made the situation even worse. The case study of Markau illustrates this problem, revealing how German Christians in the Brandenburg Consistory and the Nauen district cooperated to advance the interests of their movement at the parish level, and how Confessing Church clergy and laypeople worked to block German Christian appointments.

### Case Study: Markau

Located south of Nauen, the Markau parish suffered badly following the death of Pastor Ideler in January 1935. A series of four young clergy served the 950 parishioners of Markau very poorly, generating frustration and disinterest with their brief, inept stints in ministry. Two vicars, Klundt and Dreves, were accused of stealing. Klundt also angered parishioners with his German Christian views, so much so that seventy-five parishioners signed a petition to fire him. While this was no mass protest, it did represent a greater number of parishioners than took communion in 1935. In fact, the low number of communicants in Markau during the mid-1930s indicates that people there reacted to the typically poor pastoral care chiefly by staying away from church rather than complaining to officials in the Brandenburg Consistory.

Klundt's successor, Vicar Dreves, failed to complete some extra accounting work he was paid to do, creating such confusion in the church tax records that the parish could not collect church taxes properly during the 1936 harvest. When Dreves moved on to another parish without having completed that work, the neighboring pastor responsible for Markau, Pastor Ernst Höft of Zeestow, hounded the consistory to force Dreves to pay back his unearned wages. Yet another young cleric, Vicar Bolle, was soon sent away after subverting the authority of his supervisor, Pastor Höft.

In the wake of these incompetent and corrupt vicars, both Pastor Höft and Interim Superintendent Schmidt of Flatow implored the consistory not to send any more temporary clergy to Markau. Höft claimed there was so much opposition in the parish that any new vicar would be forced to live in Nauen and not Markau, because the parish was so "enormously embittered." Schmidt described Markau as a "dying parish" in which only four to six people regularly attended the Sunday worship service—in some weeks, no one came at all![28]

While Höft, Schmidt, and the Markau parish council called for the appointment of a new permanent pastor who could put an end to the two-year vacancy and win back the parishioners to their church, no steps to that end were taken by the consistory. With the parish languishing, plans for providing temporary pastoral care to Markau began to multiply. To a great extent, these plans were components of the larger proposals for facilitating new pastoral appointments in Groß Behnitz and Retzow, where caretaker pastor Herbert Posth was working to find permanent pastors who would care for the Confessing Church communities there.

In contrast to Herbert Posth, Interim Superintendent Schmidt of Flatow initiated a plan in early 1936 to unite the parishes of Groß Behnitz, Markau, and Retzow. Schmidt's goal appears to have been to further his own interests as much as anything else, for he hoped to transfer the headquarters of the district superintendent from Nauen to Markau, and to fill the new position himself. This was a grand strategy that required the cooperation of no fewer than five parish patrons, five parish councils, several of Schmidt's fellow pastors, and the Brandenburg Consistory. With so many competing interests, opposition was inevitable. In the end, even the patron in Markau, a friend of Schmidt, rejected his plan as a dissolution of pastoral care in his domain.[29]

Schmidt's plan did not die, however, because both the Markau patron and officials in the consistory supported his basic plan to move the district superintendency from Nauen to Markau. That they would pursue such a transfer despite the weak condition of the Markau parish underscores the church-political roots of the plan. Because Schmidt was loyal to the Brandenburg provincial church government and antagonistic toward the Confessing Church, Consistorial Councilor Hermann of Berlin began to promote Schmidt's plan among officials in Berlin. Hermann hoped to undermine the strength of the Confessing Church in Nauen by appointing a German Christian superintendent in Markau, whether it was Schmidt or someone else. Nothing came of this in 1936 or 1937. In the meantime, Schmidt suddenly quit as interim superintendent, a move that "really irritated [officials] in the consistory" and eliminated any possibility that Schmidt could ever become the permanent superintendent in the Nauen district.[30]

It was then that Pastor Ulrich Bettac of Beetz became the new interim superintendent. By early 1938, Bettac was working closely with the Brandenburg Confessing Church to convince both a sympathetic official in the consistory and the Markau patron, General Director Schoch, to appoint the current Confessing Church curate in Markau as pastor.[31] Arguing that the Markau parish needed more care than a new superintendent stationed there would be able to give, Bettac appealed to the Markau patron's concern for his own parish, but without success. In 1939, Bettac tried and failed once more to convince Patron Schoch to press for the permanent appointment of a local Confessing Church curate. As before, Bettac's objective was to undermine Councilor Hermann's plan to place a German Christian superintendent in Markau, an idea that both the consistory and the Markau patron were still considering.[32]

For all these false starts on both sides, even in 1940 the possibility remained that a new German Christian superintendent might be appointed to Markau. At that time, Bettac was forced to resign his interim superintendency as a result of his wife's infidelity and his collapsing marriage. A rumor began to spread that one of the former German Christian pastors in the district was going to become the new superintendent. Hearing this, outspoken Confessing Church pastor Posth wrote in panic to Bettac: "We must *immediately* react energetically against it, before it is too late!" But there was little Bettac could do. As he explained to Posth, the only thing he knew about the future of the superintendency was that Consistorial Councilor Hermann was still trying to place a German Christian in the position and to move it to Markau. Two months later, in December 1940, Bettac learned that the consistory had chosen Superintendent Simon, a moderate German Christian from the neighboring district of Oranienburg, to take over the interim superintendency, and that a new permanent superintendent might eventually be coming to Nauen from the Danzig region. As it turned out, Simon served an uneventful term as interim superintendent from 1941 until his death in early 1944. After that, Bettac returned to his former role as interim superintendent for the final year of the war, and no German Christian was ever permanently appointed in Nauen.[33]

In the meantime, however, Markau had become an ecclesiastical mess. For five whole years, German Christians had been threatening to place one of their own in the influential position of superintendent of the Nauen church district, and to move the district headquarters to Markau. While the efforts of Interim Superintendent Ulrich Bettac and others helped avert this, the cost to the Markau parishioners was seven and a half years of life in pastoral no-man's-land, from 1935 to 1942. Neither the church-political strife nor the consequent lack of proper pastoral care during this period improved the health of the parish, and parishioners continued to avoid their church. Only after the appointment of Pastor Glockner did conditions improve, but even that was not accomplished until after the parish council was forced to block Patron Schoch's nomination of yet another unwelcome candidate.[34]

## German Christian Frustration

The saga in Markau is but one example of the church-political turbulence surrounding pastoral appointments in the Nauen district. It does reveal, however, the surprising limitations of German Christian church politics. Simply put, German Christian influence in Nauen pastoral appointments came largely from the strength of the movement in the Brandenburg Consistory and Old Prussian Union Church offices in Berlin, and not from local supporters. As Interim Superintendent Bettac confirmed in a letter to his colleague Pastor Konrad Isleib of Hakenberg, while most requests for new appointments sat for two or three months on the desks of the Superior Church Council in Berlin, in the case of German Christian appointments, "it happens in twenty-four hours."[35] In Markau, the ongoing involvement of Berlin Consistorial Councilor Hermann meant that there was always the possibility of that sort of sudden appointment of a new German Christian pastor or even district superintendent.

That said, the Markau case also demonstrates the narrow limits of German Christian influence over pastoral appointments. Pastor (and sometime Interim Superintendent) Schmidt of Flatow and Consistorial Councilor Hermann in Berlin were unable to achieve their goal of appointing a German Christian superintendent in Markau, simply because they faced concerted, effective opposition from a variety of local actors: Interim Superintendent Bettac; the parish pastors who served as administrative supervisors for vacant pastorates, and the Markau parish council. In many cases, these opponents were members or supporters of the Confessing Church, who used their local networks to block German Christian parish politics.

Nowhere is the efficiency of grassroots opposition as plainly illustrated as in the confidential instructions that Bettac gave to a woman parishioner from Vehlefanz, Mrs. Eichler. Discussing a new curate named Klähn who was about to come to Mrs. Eichler's parish, Bettac admitted that he did not know the man's church-political convictions, then added:

> If I may give you advice *confidentially*, it is this: As soon as Herr Pastor Klähn is there, establish his church-political position by asking him openly. If he is not a "German Christian," I would ask you to work with him, but if he is a "German Christian," reject him and turn to me again, so that we can get another temporary pastor in there.[36]

Bettac understood that Prussian church authorities were simply unwilling to place either temporary or permanent clergy in positions in which they were manifestly unwelcome by local parishioners. Together with the Confessing Church pastors from Nauen, he exploited this fact to keep new German Christians out of Markau, Vehlefanz, and other pastorates across the Nauen district. This was accomplished wherever there were enough parishioners committed to the Confessing Church to create a considerable fuss for consistorial officials and wherever Bettac and the Confessing Church pastors could convince other decision-makers, such as parish patrons and councils, to demand that pastoral candidates base their ministry solely on the Bible and the Reformation Confessions of Faith.

Even Interim Superintendent Ulrich Bettac's own situation demonstrated the limits to German Christian influence over pastoral appointments. As much as German Christians in the consistory might have wanted to place one of their own in the Nauen superintendency, as long as that position remained a temporary one, it was normally assigned to one of the senior pastors of the district. Thus it was that Bettac held the position from 1936 to 1940, even though he openly supported the Confessing Church and opposed the German Christians, and was restored to the position from 1944 to 1945, even when the collapse of his marriage might have provided the consistory with grounds to pass him over.[37]

### Case Study: Confessing Church Success in Groß Behnitz

If German Christians were largely unsuccessful in their attempts to influence pastoral appointments in the Nauen district, the Confessing Church proved surprisingly adept at the task, by placing member pastors or friendly supporters in at least seven parishes during the mid-1930s. Groß Behnitz serves as a good example. There the parish patron, Dr. Ernst von Borsig, nominated Confessing Church member Kurt Fritzsche for the vacant pastorate in 1937, after the parish had endured several years without a full-time pastor. Controversies generated by two Confessing Church vicars in late 1937 and early 1938 delayed the appointment process for a time, but eventually the Groß Behnitz parish council elected Fritzsche as their pastor in early March 1938. All that remained was the final approval of the Brandenburg Consistory.[38]

Alas, complications soon set in. On March 7, 1938, the mayors and teachers of Groß and Klein Behnitz and 101 other parishioners filed a complaint with church authorities in Berlin, hoping to overturn Fritzsche's appointment. Comprising roughly one-tenth of the parish population and including two members of the parish council (one of them the mayor of Groß Behnitz), the complainants were infuriated because Fritzsche belonged to the Confessing Church: "For the sake of our German nation . . . we can make no allowance for teaching which tears apart the national community." They argued that when Fritzsche had taken out membership in the Confessing Church, he had united himself with "un-Lutheran and un-German teaching." Describing their pastor elect as a dangerous "lawbreaker from conviction," they demanded he either resign from the Confessing Church or leave the Old Prussian Union Church. In the meantime, they demanded that the consistory appoint German Christian Pastor Friedrich Siems of Nauen to supervise their parish until another pastoral candidate could be found.[39]

This belated grievance—it was submitted after the period for parish petitions against the appointment had closed—was answered two days later by two petitions in support of Fritzsche's appointment, containing a total of 392 parishioners from Groß and Klein Behnitz, including the patron and five other parish councilors. Signed by almost 40 percent of the parish population, these petitions demanded the speedy investiture of Pastor Fritzsche. They argued correctly that no protests against the appointment had been submitted within the allotted time frame.[40]

On March 14, 1938, on the heels of the petitions in favor of the Fritzsche appointment, parish patron Dr. von Borsig weighed in on behalf of his candidate. Von Borsig complained to the consistory that the news he was promised confirming Fritzsche's appointment had not yet reached him, and he surmised that "the petitions of irresponsible parishioners" had delayed it. While "a host of younger curates [and] vicars" had ministered in Groß Behnitz since the retirement of former Pastor Lux in late 1935, von Borsig argued that they had failed to win the trust of the parish "on account of their youth" and the frequency with which they had been transferred in and out of the parish. Von Borsig pointed out that the Groß and Klein Behnitz parishes were among the most devoted to the Old Prussian Union Church in the entire Havelland, and he reminded the consistory that there was no legal basis for putting off the appointment any longer, because Fritzsche had been called to the parish according to protocol and no complaint had been filed during the prescribed period. Furthermore, von Borsig explained that there had been no "deception of the parish," since the parishioners were well aware that Fritzsche was a member of the Confessing Church. He had, after all, read a pulpit notice from the Confessing Church during his candidation visit. Describing the consistory's refusal to confirm the appointment of Fritzsche as a "serious attack on my rights as patron," von Borsig explained that he had chosen Fritzsche from among forty to fifty candidates not simply because he was a member of the Confessing Church, but because of Fritzsche's strong letter of application, a handwriting expert's opinion about Fritzsche's temperament, Fritzsche's preaching, von Borsig's personal impression, and a four-hour interview in which Fritzsche's "calm, serene, determined and very loving manner" set him apart as "the most suitable candidate."[41]

The fact that Fritzsche had won the favor of the majority of parishioners was a bonus for von Borsig, who described "the most awful demagogic manner" in which signatures were gathered by Fritzsche's opponents. Describing his own hasty efforts to launch a counterpetition, von Borsig asserted that roughly 75 percent of adult parishioners from Klein Behnitz and 80 percent from Groß Behnitz had signed the petitions on behalf of Fritzsche. "There could hardly be a more impressive number," claimed the patron, who added that between forty and fifty signatures on the petition for Fritzsche were those of parishioners who had renounced their signatures on earlier protest against his appointment. In contrast to that, von Borsig depicted the vast majority of the complainants against Fritzsche as participants in "efforts hostile to Christianity" and as people "who have never had any time for Christianity and the church."

Patron von Borsig's letter moved consistory officials to ratify Fritzsche's appointment, even though they shared the concerns of Fritzsche's opponents in Groß Behnitz. In part, they were assured by Fritzsche himself, who declared his readiness to work with the church authorities in the consistory, a move they hoped would be the first of many steps away from the Confessing Church. Consistorial officials might not have thought that way if they had known that the Groß Behnitz parish council had already voted back in May 1937 to formally join the Confessing Church, under the direction of their temporary pastor, Herbert Posth. None of Fritzsche's enemies had mentioned that fact, however, and the consistory learned about the membership of the Groß Behnitz parish council in the Confessing Church only in July 1938, over a year later and too late to change anything about Fritzsche's appointment.[42]

## Internal Tensions within the Confessing Church Movement

Ironically, conflict between the German Christian Movement and the Confessing Church over pastoral appointments was often overshadowed by significant divisions within the Confessing Church camp itself. At the heart of these disagreements were fundamental differences of opinion about the relationship of the Confessing Church to the Brandenburg Consistory and, more generally, the Old Prussian Union Church. Full-fledged *members* of the Confessing Church who followed the rule of their leader, Martin Niemöller, and the decisions of the various Confessing synods refused to recognize the spiritual leadership, legal authority, or administrative control of the Old Prussian Union Church. Warmhearted *supporters* of the movement agreed with the theological arguments of the Confessing Church and its opposition to the German Christian Movement, but believed that it was more effective to pursue those goals by cooperating with consistorial officials and working from within the structure of the Old Prussian Union Church.

For the most part, when locked in battle against German Christians, these two branches of the Confessing Church in Nauen worked hand in hand. Interim Superintendent Ulrich Bettac regularly negotiated to supply parishes with Confessing Church vicars and curates, as he had done in parishes like Markau and Vehlefanz. In Pessin, for instance, he consulted with the Brandenburg Confessing Church Council to find out what they knew about the church-political positions of potential vicars and pastoral candidates, and supported the appointment of a neutral pastor who was supportive of the Confessing Church.[43]

In Linum, Bettac worked with the local patron to achieve the same goal, where the retirement of radical German Christian Pastor Herbert Kahle created an ideal opportunity to change the church-political orientation of the parish.

Bettac was convinced that a competent Confessing Church curate could "build a nest" in Linum, since the parishioners there had been "radically cured from the German Christians by Kahle." The parish patron in Linum, Magistrate Demuth, also wanted to appoint either a neutral or Confessing Church pastor, a position Bettac encouraged.[44] When the time came for Demuth to nominate a candidate, Bettac gave him a list of applicants, along with some advice. From a total of sixteen names, Bettac pointed out three German Christians, knowing already that the patron would reject them. He then suggested four others who would be good choices and three who might be suitable, noting that he had no knowledge of the other six. Bettac appreciated that Demuth would choose a candidate who adhered to the Bible and Reformation Confessions, which turned out to be a man who supported the Confessing Church but still recognized and cooperated with the Prussian Church authorities.[45]

When Bettac managed pastoral appointments in this way, it ensured that German Christians would be shut out of Nauen parishes, as long as there was sufficient local sympathy for the Confessing Church from parish councilors and patrons. That did not mean, however, that Nauen pastors who were *members* of the Confessing Church agreed with Bettac's policy. They still believed that the Brandenburg Consistory and the rest of the Old Prussian Union Church leadership were fundamentally heretical and illegitimate and refused to cooperate with them.

This philosophical difference between *members* and *supporters* of the Confessing Church is best captured in the ongoing debate between Confessing pastor Posth of Berge and Interim Superintendent Bettac. Their divergent views about the legitimacy of the Old Prussian Union Church first emerged in the context of the administrative supervision and pastoral care in Ribbeck.

Vacant since before 1933, the Ribbeck pastorate was without adequate supervision, a fact that its patron, estate owner Erich von Ribbeck, made clear to authorities in Berlin. Von Ribbeck argued that none of the neighboring pastors was able to care for Ribbeck: Berge parish pastor Posth's health was poor, and Pastors Koch in Retzow and Lux in Groß Behnitz were simply too old and sick to come any longer. After a face-to-face meeting with officials from the consistory, Ribbeck had to settle for the continuation of temporary pastoral care. Pastor Posth of Berge was saddled with the supervision of the Ribbeck parish, despite his suspect health. Almost immediately, both Pastor Posth and Patron Ribbeck petitioned the consistory to assign a curate for the Ribbeck parish.[46]

Ironically, although Posth was initially reluctant to take up the supervisory work in Ribbeck, his church-political convictions impelled him to continue in his role long after the consistory tried to relieve him of the burden. Posth and Patron von Ribbeck worked with the Ribbeck parish council to shepherd the parish into the fold of the Confessing Church, and Posth kept a tight hand on the parish administration throughout the balance of the 1930s. In 1937, the

Brandenburg Consistory and Interim Superintendent Bettac attempted to transfer the administrative responsibility for Ribbeck to Walter Pachali, who was the new curate (and later pastor) in neighboring Retzow and a supporter of the Confessing Church. The Ribbeckers refused, and Posth declined to hand over the supervision of Ribbeck because Pachali was not a formal member of the Confessing Church.[47]

In fact, Posth had already opposed Pachali's appointment in Retzow itself. Posth argued that it would be best to dispel antagonism against the Confessing Church in Retzow through a competent new Confessing pastor. Rather this than to allow the unjust accusations of radical German Christians against the Confessing Church to remain unchallenged under the leadership of a neutral pastor. Posth was firm about the matter: there could *never* be a situation in which a neutral pastoral candidate ought to be preferred over a Confessing Church pastoral candidate. Any compromise on that point would undermine the claim that Posth and the other Confessing Church pastors stood by, namely, that the Confessing Church's Provisional Church Leadership was the uniquely legitimate authority in the Old Prussian Church.[48]

As a result, from October 1937 to January 1941, Pachali was the *de jure* administrative supervisor of the Ribbeck parish, while Posth remained the *de facto* chairman of the parish council. Interim Superintendent Bettac did not approve of this anomalous situation but admitted that he had no ability to change it. Posth was in a strong position, enjoying the support of Patron von Ribbeck and the local parish council. To his credit, Bettac treated his friend Posth with benevolence, as did Pachali, who was averse to pressing his rights by force.

With the appointment of Kurt Fritzsche in Groß Behnitz in 1938, Posth decided he had found a suitable replacement as supervisor for Ribbeck. Fritzsche met Posth's primary condition for giving up control of the Ribbeck parish, in that he was a full-fledged member of the Confessing Church. Posth made a spirited case to the consistory on behalf of Fritzsche and against Pachali, and argued that Ribbeck should be linked with Groß Behnitz (and not Retzow, Pachali's parish) for no fewer than six reasons: Fritzsche no longer needed to supervise Riewend and Bagow (filial churches of the newly filled Päwesien parish); Fritzsche owned his own car and could manage the distances involved; Ribbeck was in a poor location vis-à-vis the Retzow parish; the Retzow pastor would probably soon have to care for a new filial church in Möthlow; Ribbeck parishioners preferred Pastor Fritzsche to Pastor Pachali because Fritzsche was a member of the Confessing Church; and connecting Ribbeck to Groß Behnitz would be cheaper than attaching it to Retzow.[49]

While Pastor Posth put forward a convincing case, nothing came of his offer for a whole year. Only after Pachali was called up into the military in April 1940 was Fritzsche the only other logical choice as supervisor, and so Posth finally consented to give up administrative control over the ever-vacant Ribbeck parish.[50] Posth had made his point. More than three years after he should have given Ribbeck over to Pachali, Posth's tenacity and the support of the Ribbeck patron enabled the Confessing Church to maintain its hold on the vacant Ribbeck parish.

Meanwhile, in Retzow, Posth and Bettac had to find a replacement for Pachali, who was off fighting in the war. Not surprisingly, they soon fell back into their disagreement over support versus membership in the Confessing Church. As before, Posth argued that Bettac ought to summon a full Confessing Church member to take over for Pachali. Bettac pointed out the difficulties of Posth's demand, most obviously the fact that the officials in the consistory would only assign replacement clergy who would recognize their authority. Mixing his biblical metaphors, Bettac outlined his practical view of the situation:

> Herein lies the whole difficulty, to find a place for the Confessing Church brothers, and on this basis, I have taken and do take the view that the Confessing Church hurts itself through its isolation. What does it matter if the brothers get themselves legalized? Indeed, they would then enter into regular pastorates and we could work through the whole church like leaven, until the extremely patched up German Christian wineskin bursts.[51]

In the end, these were relatively minor disagreements and did not prevent Confessing Church pastors like Herbert Posth from working closely and effectively with neutral but supportive pastors and superintendents like Bettac. Indeed, despite the powerful rhetoric employed by the Confessing Church clergy who denied the legitimacy of the Old Prussian Union Church, it is highly doubtful that they would have achieved very much at all in districts like Nauen without the patient and understanding cooperation of Confessing Church supporters who worked with the Brandenburg Consistory and remained subject to the conventional church authorities. By agreeing to work together, however, Confessing Church members and supporters like Posth and Bettac kept the German Christian influence out of much of the Nauen district, which in turn suggests that German Christian rule in the Old Prussian Union Church may have been far more superficial than has been previously assumed.

### Case Study: The Battle for Nauen

All the elements that made up the complex and often emotional nature of parish appointments during the National Socialist era are clearly visible in the most heated and drawn-out conflict over any clerical appointment in the Nauen district, the battle over the appointment of a new associate pastor in the Nauen parish. Nauen was not only the seat of the district superintendency but also the largest parish in the district and the home of the NSDAP district leadership. The contest over the appointment in Nauen from 1937 to 1943 illustrates how important local personalities and circumstances were in shaping the course of the Church Struggle in communities across the Third Reich.

The problems in Nauen began in 1935, when Pastor Gerhard Schumann, a moderate conservative and one-time member of the German Christian Movement, was joined by a more radical German Christian pastor, Friedrich Siems. By 1937 Schumann had retired and Siems had become the senior pastor in Nauen. Siems was a political activist—and not only within the church. He was a longtime NSDAP member, served as a local party official, and had married the daughter of the deputy mayor. Indeed, one of his colleagues was convinced that it was those factors that had earned Siems his appointment to the coveted senior pastorate in Nauen.[52]

The first wave of open conflict swept through the parish in the spring of 1939, when Pastor Werner Andrich from the neighboring parish of Vehlefanz was nominated for the vacant associate pastorate. Like Pastor Siems, Andrich belonged to the racial Thuringian wing of the German Christian Movement. Reviving old quarrels, Confessing Church parishioners in Nauen launched a grievance against the election of Andrich, based largely on the argument that Pastor Siems was already serving the German Christian minority in the Nauen parish and that the appointment of a second German Christian pastor would be unfair. The protesters argued that *they* represented the majority in the parish, the ones who stood by the "old faith," and they appealed to an Old Prussian Union Church precedent: in divided parishes, multiple appointments were to be divided between rival church-political groups.

On top of this basic charge, they piled on other grievances: Andrich had managed his parish finances irregularly in Vehlefanz and was under investigation there; his clothes were unclean; he baptized children born to parents who had formally withdrawn from the church; he conducted funerals for people who had abandoned their church membership; he had played with his confirmation students while dressed in his bathing suit; he called the parish Women's Aid a coffee club; and, finally, his own parish found him unbearable and the elders in Vehlefanz said that he was not always truthful. If some of these claims were trivial, taken together they represented a concerted effort by a majority of active parishioners in Nauen to thwart the appointment of Pastor Andrich.[53]

Other grievances soon followed and were more substantial, taking issue with Andrich's teaching and ministry. Complainants cited seven errors, including Andrich's failure to employ a trinitarian invocation during church services, his elevation of the Führer as a model of Christian piety, and his exaltation of the religious unity of the German nation under National Socialism above the Word of God. Apparently, Andrich had claimed that Jesus Christ gave Christians the power to fulfill the divinely created order of National Socialism, and he had added that it was his highest aim as a preacher to spur his congregation on to deeper and more devoted service to the Nazi movement. In response, the protesters argued that there was no single form of government approved by God above all others and that seeking God's kingdom and righteousness was the Christian's highest duty. They charged Andrich with blurring the critical distinction between Christians and non-Christians in his quest for the religious unity of the German nation.[54]

Despite this list of grievances, Interim Superintendent Bettac remained pessimistic about the chances of overturning the appointment of the Andrich. Bettac suspected that the Brandenburg Consistory in Berlin would use the appointment in Nauen for two purposes: first, to rescue Andrich from the uncomfortable circumstances of his current parish, since it appeared that the baby Andrich and his new wife were expecting was going to be a "seven-month child," and, second, to set a German Christian superintendent in Andrich's old parish, in the place of Interim Superintendent Bettac, a firm opponent of the German Christian Movement.

Bettac tried to prevent Brandenburg church officials from interfering by appealing to the head of the local Women's Aid, Mrs. Krüger. He hoped she could convince the patron of the parish, Mayor Urban of Nauen, to withdraw Andrich's nomination. Bettac bemoaned the fact that Urban had not consulted with his counterpart in Vehlefanz about Andrich, nor with the neighboring pastor in Velten, nor with Bettac himself. As interim superintendent, Bettac had already initiated two complaints against Andrich and was well placed to assess his character and skills. For instance, when complainants in Nauen protested that Andrich lacked any semblance of pastoral dignity, Bettac was already aware that prominent parishioners in Vehlefanz had described Andrich as a "harlequin." Frustrated with the lack of disciplinary action against Andrich, Bettac vented his anger over the "scandal" of the consistory's continual protection of German Christian clergy.

Mrs. Krüger tried to help by enlightening the mayor about the long history of conflict between her 170-member organization and the German Christian pastor Friedrich Siems. She made it clear that the Women's Aid steered clear of church politics and expected at least a neutral pastor, if not a member of the Confessing Church—in other words, a pastor who would lead theologically orthodox services and cooperate with the women of the parish.

Thanks to these and other efforts, Andrich's appointment was scuttled and the Nauen parish was saved from a second German Christian pastor. However, the saga of the associate pastorate resurfaced the following year, 1940, when church officials restarted the process to appoint a new associate pastor. Once again, local members of the Confessing Church demanded a new pastor who would support their neglected church-political orientation. And so a new candidate came to Nauen, a preacher by the name of Gustav Gille. He preached a candidacy sermon from Luke 16:10: "Whoever is faithful in a very little is faithful also in much; and whoever is dishonest in a very little is dishonest also in much." Gille interpreted the passage to mean that Nauen parishioners ought to be politically loyal to a fault. Otherwise, he essentially urged them to imitate God's faithfulness. He employed the normal formula of service, including the trinitarian version of the invocation and the Apostles' Creed. Since he appeared to be a theologically orthodox young pastor, the Nauen parish council supported his appointment.

Then came the explosion. It soon came to light that Pastor Gille was in fact from the extreme racial wing of the German Christians. He had in the past regularly deviated from the Apostles' Creed because he did not fully subscribe to it and generally conducted syncretistic German Christian religious celebrations rather than the prescribed services of the Old Prussian Union Church.

Immediately, Nauen parishioners began circulating petitions. One accused Gille of neglecting to preach about Jesus Christ, of belittling God by conflating divine and human faithfulness, and of emphasizing human obedience as the way to God rather than Jesus' atoning death and resurrection. The other stated simply that parishioners wanted an associate pastor who would preach on the basis of the Bible and the traditional Confessions of Faith. Both petitions were spearheaded by the Nauen Women's Aid.

When these initial petitions were rebuffed by officials in the consistory, protestors from Nauen wrote many angry letters to the Brandenburg church authorities, reiterating their grievances and adding a few other allegations, namely, that Gille had portrayed Jesus only as a model teacher and not as the Savior too, and that Gille had led the children of the parish into a renewal of Old Testament legalism and works, rather than pointing them toward Christ.

Curate Gille and Pastor Siems tried to rebut these accusations, as did Mayor Urban of Nauen. In fact, Urban informed the Brandenburg Consistory that no matter what happened in the case of Gustav Gille, as parish patron he would continue to nominate German Christian candidates for the Nauen pastorate. Unfortunately for him, Gille did not help his cause with several significant lapses into unprofessionalism. Early in the controversy in Nauen, he had insulted Mrs. Krüger of the Women's Aid on her barrenness and described his church-political opponents as a clique of academics, officials, and small business owners.

Throughout the conflict, both the Confessing Church and the German Christians tried to present themselves as the legitimate voice of the parish. Curate Gille claimed the support of a three-hundred-member German Christian group and argued that the parish associations who opposed him constituted only a vocal minority who did not have the greater interests of the parish at heart. Against him, the parishioners who initiated the grievances against Gille's appointment claimed to speak for a group of almost three hundred themselves, including 170 in the Women's Association, sixty-nine in the Protestant Union, and fifty-one in the Christian Fellowship. Moreover, according to the synod executive, which did represent legitimate authority in the parish, the German Christian group consisted of only a few faithful parishioners and many marginal Protestants, while those in opposition to the appointment included the leading parishioners who were most committed to the church.

Ultimately, the Nauen district synod executive supported the grievances against Gille and urged the Brandenburg Consistory to overturn his appointment. The synod executive argued that Gille had fraudulently employed the full trinitarian invocation and the Apostles' Creed in his candidacy sermon in order to deceive parishioners about his true theological position. Further, they understood that Gille had tricked the parish with the full connivance of senior pastor Siems. They also added the mundane complaint that Gille had preached his candidacy sermon without looking at the congregation in Nauen, and (more significantly) they introduced a recent discovery of theirs, that Gille had a prior record of German Christian agitation in his old parish.

By the time the Nauen district synod executive had rendered its judgment, Gille had returned to his former parish in Saxony-Anhalt and to his position as an officer in the German army. Nonetheless, his supporters continued to agitate on his behalf. Pastor Siems was incensed at the Nauen district synod executive for its rejection of Gille. Although he was serving in the army in the east, he sent a letter criticizing the Women's Aid for exploiting the older women of the parish and for adopting "parliamentary methods from a democratic past." Rather than listen to the "small circle" of complainants, Siems argued that the consistory ought to look to "people capable of judgment, who really stand in the contemporary, pulsating life of the Third Reich." He contended that the Women's Aid had separated itself from parish life by refusing to work with him when he was present in Nauen and suggested that Patron Mayor Urban was looking to the interests of the majority of the twelve thousand people in the Nauen parish when he nominated Gille, whom Siems praised for his "manly" attitude in the face of hateful opponents.

Mayor Urban also defended Gille and castigated the consistory's treatment of the National Socialists in the Nauen parish as "a snubbing and a clear violation." He was incensed that they had abandoned his candidate Gille, "a front soldier since the beginning of the war!!!" and reminded the Consistory about a 1940 regulation that recommended the appointment of veterans to pastoral positions. Attacking his Confessing Church opponents, Mayor Urban pointed out that they could only gather about 120 signatures, which he described as "a storm in a water glass!" and "a Marxist maneuver."

Although Urban pursued his nomination of Gille until June 1941, he finally gave up trying and nominated another war veteran, a disabled military chaplain named Erich Schröder. Schröder, who had served as a vicar in Nauen from 1939 to 1940, was posted with the army in the east and could not get leave for a candidation visit in Nauen until mid-1943, a year after his nomination. Faced with the prospect of yet another round of protests from the Confessing Church in Nauen, Schröder explained to local church leaders that he had no interest at all in any church-political movement. Describing his many experiences as a soldier and military chaplain, Schröder made it clear that his constant exposure to mortal danger had driven him to the simple message of salvation in Christ, which he preached as he ministered from the Word of God and the Reformation Confessions of Faith. This was enough to satisfy both sides of the church-political conflict, and so Schröder was called to Nauen in May 1943. At last the four-year struggle to appoint an associate pastor in Nauen had come to an end.

The events in Nauen are a reminder that both clergy and laypeople did have a meaningful influence on parish life in the Third Reich. They possessed a significant range of freedom in which to act, as is evident not only from the success of the noisy, emotional complaints that the Confessing Church made against German Christian appointments but also from the fundamental nature of those grievances. Parishioners periodically articulated their aversion to the application of National Socialist values within their Protestant churches, and they usually based these challenges explicitly on the authority of the Bible and the Reformation Confessions of Faith that defined Protestantism in Germany. In the Nauen parish, Protestants opposed clergy whose preoccupation with National Socialism made them poor servants of the church. In other parishes around the district, popular opinion was mobilized for a variety of reasons, such as pastoral negligence and church-political radicalism. Moreover, in all these controversies, there were few signs that direct opposition to the imposition of National Socialist ideology in these parishes resulted in brutal police retaliation or even censure from the local Nazi Party. Within the limits of communal life, they were relatively free to direct their own ecclesiastical affairs.

The lack of similar upheaval in Ravensburg and Pirna is a sign of the greater centralizing power in the Württemberg and Saxon regional churches, whose bishops—though on opposite sides of the Church Struggle—both appealed to the Führer principle to take on powers previously held by synodal or administrative bodies. Both Bishops Wurm of Württemberg and Coch of Saxony used their personal power to pull their respective regional churches in the direction of their theological, confessional, and political convictions. Although they did not have the ability to suppress all of their opponents, Wurm and Coch largely controlled new pastoral appointments, especially compared to their counterpart, President Werner of the Old Prussian Union Church. Over time, that power of appointment enabled Wurm and Coch to place a cadre of loyal clergy in the parishes of their regional churches. Thus, the relatively peaceful pastoral transitions between pastors in Ravensburg and Pirna stand in stark contrast to the fractious and fruitless effort to appoint new German Christian clergy in Nauen.

Thus, the issue of pastoral appointments reaffirms the diversity of local conditions in the German churches of Hitler's Germany. Whether it was the strength of the Confessing Church at the grass-roots level in Nauen or the importance of parish pastors for setting the tone of church life in all three districts, parish politics was never more intense or unpredictable than when it came time to choose the new pastor.

# chapter four

## Clerical Responses to Euthanasia and Anti-Semitism

 **Blood and race were the obsessions around which** National Socialism revolved. Armed with his pseudo-scientific Social Darwinism, Hitler preached the superiority of the so-called Aryan race, to which the Germans supposedly belonged.[1] For the many party leaders, civil servants, doctors, police, and army officers who served the Führer, the mission to purify German blood justified a host of evil policies: the sterilization and euthanization of physically and mentally handicapped Germans; the persecution of Gypsies, homosexuals, and other so-called asocials; and the persecution and annihilation of European Jews. If the appointment of clergy was the most important local issue in the Church Struggle, Nazi racial policy was the most important national issue faced by German Protestants.

The story of the Nazi persecution and ultimate annihilation of the Jews began with Hitler's anti-Semitic oratory and the thuggery of the SA, which paved the way for the legalized persecution of Jews following the Nazi seizure of power in 1933. After an abortive attempt to boycott Jewish businesses across Germany, the National Socialists promulgated a series of decrees and laws that cut Jews off from public and higher education and from careers in the civil administration, education and culture, and the legal, medical, and financial professions. Alongside this social marginalization, National Socialists pursued the darker and deadlier quest of purifying German blood from "alien influences." In July 1933, a sterilization law was passed, legalizing the "voluntary" sterilization of those with "incurable" and inheritable mental and physical diseases. In September 1935, the infamous Nuremberg Laws redefined citizenship on the basis of blood, stripping Jews of German citizenship, redefining them as alien subjects, and prohibiting sexual relations between Jews and Aryan Germans. In 1936, Reich SS leader Heinrich Himmler established the "Fount of Life" program to promote a higher birth rate among the SS, the supposed racial elite. Himmler flouted traditional marriage laws, arguing that military triumphs would be empty without a corresponding reproductive victory over the enemy.[2]

For Jews, the horizon darkened in 1938, the year they were publicly segregated and forced to add the names Israel or Sara to their existing names, if their given names were not identifiably Jewish. Then, on the pretext of the murder of a German embassy official in Paris by a young Jew, Himmler and other SS leaders launched the "Kristallnacht" Pogrom of November 9–10, 1938, during which thousands of Jewish homes, businesses, and synagogues were smashed, looted, and burned. Over ninety Jews were killed, while twenty-six thousand Jewish men were interned in concentration camps across the Reich.

With the onset of war in 1939, Nazi racial policy evolved along two fronts. Within greater Germany itself, the SS established a special office at Tiergarten 4 in Berlin to administrate the so-called euthanasia program, whereby thousands of handicapped Germans were murdered. Selected patients were generally transferred to one of six main killing centers to be gassed and cremated: Grafeneck in Württemberg, Brandenburg near Berlin, Sonnenstein in Saxony, Bernburg in Saxony-Anhalt, Hadamar in Hesse, and Hartheim in Austria. Between 1939 and 1941, over seventy thousand patients were killed at these centers, along with tens of thousands more in the "wild euthanasia" program that continued in health-care institutions across the country, even after Hitler officially put a halt to the euthanasia program in August 1941.[3]

In conquered Poland, SS units began rounding up Jews and concentrating them in ghettos. Two years later, in the wake of the invasion of the Soviet Union, four SS *Einsatzgruppen* (special action units) were unleashed in a murderous sweep through the east, killing up to two million Jews and other victims. A wide network of concentration, work, and death camps was established, where another three to four million Jews and other victims were brutally worked, beaten, starved, tortured, shot, gassed, or marched to death between 1942 and 1945.

German Protestant pastors lived and worked in this wider context. While most were not exposed to the murderous rampages in Eastern Europe, they were well aware of the anti-Semitic propaganda and policies of persecution that were ubiquitous throughout the Third Reich, including the boycotts, segregation, Nuremberg Laws, and Kristallnacht Pogrom. How, then, did the anti-Semitism of the Third Reich affect the German churches? Many pastors were enthusiastic about the emergence of Hitler as a national leader in 1933 and sympathetic to the nationalistic aspirations of the Nazi movement. Did that also mean they supported the National Socialist racial policy? How did Protestant clergy view German Jews? Did they accept or reject the anti-Semitic legislation of the early 1930s? How did they react to the Nuremberg citizenship laws and the bureaucratic measures to determine the so-called Aryan ancestry of public servants and Nazi Party members? How did they view the Kristallnacht Pogrom of November 1938? Did they accept or reject the euthanasia program, or have anything to say about the genocidal policy of their government?

## Pastors and Jews

The unfortunate answer to these questions is that there is no evidence from the correspondence, publications, or actions of Protestant clergy in Nauen, Pirna, and Ravensburg to suggest that they were significantly affected by or preoccupied with the euthanasia crisis or the "Jewish question." As Wolfgang Gerlach found in his probing study of the relationship between the Confessing Church and the persecution of the Jews, pastors and church leaders were either too conflicted, too preoccupied, or too afraid to defend persecuted Jews.[4] They were too conflicted because so many of them had so earnestly welcomed Hitler and National Socialism as a providential salvation for Germany and for their own Protestant churches. They believed in Hitler's mission to reform and revitalize German society and actively supported that mission by participating in public events that contributed to Nazi rule. Even when many clergy frowned on the violent or intolerant facets of Nazism, they still affirmed other aspects of the Third Reich, such as the new emphasis on order or Hitler's tough foreign policy. During the Second World War, loyalty to the Fatherland overrode any thoughts of criticizing the Nazi regime.

Protestant pastors were also too preoccupied to defend German Jews. Theological battles against aggressive German Christians put the Confessing Church on the defensive for much of the Third Reich, reasserting the authority of the traditional confessions of faith and struggling to free their churches from state or party influence. Too often they debated the content of theological statements, skirting the very real needs of the physically or mentally handicapped Germans or the German Jews who were suffering all around them.

Finally, pastors were too afraid to defend Jews or other enemies of the Third Reich. Even Julius von Jan, the Württemberg pastor whose sermon condemning the Kristallnacht Pogrom earned him a severe beating, home invasion, arrest, and imprisonment remarked, "We were afraid to touch this sensitive spot of the regime."[5]

As we have already seen, pastors in Nauen, Pirna, and Ravensburg were enthusiastic supporters of the "national renewal" of 1933. They believed the National Socialist revitalization of Germany would also usher in a profound moral renewal that would reawaken Protestant spiritual life. Furthermore, they believed Hitler was calling them to assist him in his mission to Germany, and they praised the Nazi leader for his successful defeat of godless Communism. As a result, clergy in the three districts were obsessed with the relationship between their churches and their faith, on the one hand, and the German nation and National Socialist movement, on the other. And all this was founded theologically on the conviction that the nation, race, family, state, and soil were sacred orders of life created by God and worthy of special status on earth. Indeed, many theologians and pastors regarded racial purity as a divine mandate. All of this led Protestant clergy quite naturally into a positive stance toward National Socialism and meant that, at best, they were too conflicted to be anything but ambivalent about the fate of the Jews.

This conflicted attitude was apparent in the sermons of District Superintendent Hermann Ströle in Ravensburg. Even before the Nazi seizure of power, Ströle asserted that the German national community would be saved by Christian piety and devotion. In his message titled "The Life of Our Nation in the Light of the Bible," he stated, "National character, in its totality, is and remains the basis of our common development and work, according to God's creative order."[6] That said, Ströle took pains to affirm the equality of all races in a September 1933 missionary sermon. The very act of preaching from a text like Romans 1:16 ("For I am not ashamed of the gospel; it is the power of God for salvation to everyone who has faith, to the Jew first and also to the Greek") must have spoken volumes to his congregation, coming as it did in the midst of the first wave of Nazi anti-Semitism. Just to make sure his parishioners were getting the message, he explained that the gospel was given without differentiation to all races of the earth, according to the will of God.[7] Two months later, however, Ströle was once more caught up in the euphoria of 1933, praising the "new recognition of our identity as a nation" as "a miracle of God."[8]

Caught up in the nationalism of the Third Reich, some pastors ventured beyond the general excitement over the rebirth of Germany and the desire to forge a strong relationship between church and nation. They began to encourage the pursuit of German blood purity as a religious mission, using language that mirrored the propaganda of the NSDAP. In November of 1934, Pastor Ernst Ranft of Helmsdorf addressed his colleagues in the Pirna district with a message titled "The Importance of Race Research for Religion and Christianity." Significantly, the starting point for Ranft's talk was neither theological nor scriptural but rather ideological—he began by explaining the fundamental importance of race in the National Socialist worldview. When Ranft eventually turned to the connection between race and religion, it was only so that he could affirm his conviction that religions were racially specific in nature and that there were definite limits to the universality of any religion. Ranft *did* state that the revelation of Christ was God's answer for all humanity and added that the demand to tailor Christian preaching to specific racial preferences could not be allowed to reduce the content of the gospel. Indeed, Ranft explained how Christian preaching for a particular race must be "a loving entrance into the special certainties of the life of a nation and a race, not least into the failures and peculiarities attached to it." The Christian sermon must always be a call to repentance, though the outworking of preaching in the practices of faith and piety "should and ought to be thoroughly racially specific." According to Ranft, the life application of the preaching of the Word of God demanded the serious efforts of German Protestant clergy in order that it might produce a renewed Christian-German community.[9] What Ranft *failed* to mention was that most of the new racially specific preaching that he and other Lutheran pastors were engaged in neglected to point out any of the failures of the German nation. Rather, their sermons exalted Germany and its Lutheran legacy, conflating Protestant piety and German patriotism.

In an example of this confusion about how the cultivation of blood purity connected with the message of the Bible, Pastor Adolf Wertz of Isny declared, "National uniformity of the blood, national character is God-willed." Wertz made this statement in the context of a 1936 message to his fellow Ravensburg pastors entitled "State and Church." His comments were based on an interpretation of Noah's family tree and the belief that Genesis 10 accounted for the existence of the three main racial branches of humanity.[10] Wertz's belief in the cultivation of German blood purity adds a deeper racial tone to his nationalism. His colleague in the parish of Friedrichshafen, Pastor Karl Steger, had similar beliefs about the demands of the German racial community, making his simple slogan "One God, one Christ, one Nation" into a call for biological purity.[11]

Other pastors sent confusing messages to their parishioners by attempting to hold together the traditional Protestant belief that the historic and spiritual roots of Christianity lay in Judaism and the contemporary Nazi belief that a pernicious Jewish influence in Germany needed to be stopped. Two instances illustrate this quandary. First, in January 1936, Vicar Priester of Lietzow, in the Nauen district, found himself in trouble for agitating against the Prussian church authorities in a sermon. Priester, a protégé of radical Confessing Church pastor Herbert Posth of Berge, criticized the attempt to impose racial criteria on Protestant clergy through the application of the Aryan Paragraph, and then took up the broader subject of the relationship between Jews and Aryans. According to one report, Priester called belief in the racial superiority of Aryans arrogant and selfish, then declared that everyone in his congregation was Abraham's seed and that the belittling of "the chosen people" before God was wrong. These comments incensed the local schoolteacher and the local NSDAP leader, who accused Priester of using confirmation classes and Sunday services to undermine the educational work they were doing at school and in the Hitler Youth.

As he explained the situation to Pastor Posth, his supervisor, Priester insisted he was *not* agitating against the National Socialist state. No doubt he hoped to avoid any charges of treason under the Insidiousness Law of 1934, which made open criticism of the state a crime punishable by death. Priester did admit, however, his frustration that the neo-pagan worldview of Nazi leader Alfred Rosenberg's *Myth of the Twentieth Century* was presented time and again in public as the only route to happiness for the German people, and that religion was regularly portrayed as bad for Germans. In bold language, Priester asserted: "If the warning and guiding word of the church is interpreted as agitation against the state, if the church is suspected and defamed as an enemy of the state in its care for the souls of the nation, then it must suffer this reproach, but out of truthfulness towards its Lord must not be silent."[12]

When forced to make a public statement about his sermon, however, Priester was more concerned to point out his political loyalty: "I have spoken out expressly for the solution of the racial question in the National Socialist sense." He continued, trying to account for his sermon on Galatians 3:26–29: "For in Christ Jesus you are all children of God through faith. As many of you as were baptized into Christ have clothed yourselves with Christ. There is no longer Jew or Greek, there is no longer slave or free, there is no longer male and female; for all of you are one in Christ Jesus. And if you belong to Christ, then you are Abraham's offspring, heirs according to the promise."

First, Priester admitted that the passage "sounds strange in a time which shows us the importance of the difference between races, their various character attributes." Claiming that the apostle Paul was not trying "to blur these differences" or "to speak the word of international brotherhood," Priester interpreted the passage so as to evade any practical application of the biblical depiction of the unity of believers under Christ: "The differences of the races, of the estates and occupations, the differences of the genders, they remain and must be respected, as long as this earth stands. Where the disregard, the suspension of this ordinance leads—that our nation has had to experience itself. We cannot arbitrarily bring about the unity and equality of which Paul speaks. It is realized, it is valid only in the living community of the church." In other words, Priester believed in the principle of the spiritual unity of all Christians but not the practice of their social or political unity.

With respect to the biblical description of shared family identity of Christians and Jews through faith in Christ, Priester asserted that the meaning of his sermon was only that "we may say that we do not stand nearer to God than others based on earthly merits or qualities, rather only on account of his grace and love for him as our father." As for the assertion that everyone in his congregation was Abraham's offspring, Priester explained that this connection to Abraham was only a spiritual identification through faith in God, not a physical connection. So, while Priester challenged his congregation to consider both the Jewish roots of Christianity and the supraracial implications of membership in God's family, he also affirmed the exclusionary orientation of National Socialist racial policy in Germany. When he was called to account, his preoccupation with theological precision was a means to evade the full implications of his teaching on the Jews.

Like Priester, Curate Immanuel Spellenberg of Friedrichshafen, near Ravensburg, sent conflicting messages about the Jews. Spellenberg's backround seemed solid enough—as an SA man, he had conducted a propaganda tour of Romania in 1936, and earlier still, as a student, he had conducted research on the life of the nineteenth-century nationalist Ernst Moritz Arndt. Still, in January 1939, for reasons that are not clear, Spellenberg felt compelled to issue a written clarification about his views on Jews and the Old Testament. On the one hand, Spellenberg affirmed how, as a National Socialist and old SA leader, he had always taught children about the destructive influence of godless Judaism and about the judgments of the Old Testament prophets against the Jews. In the same way, he declared his determination to continue teaching the Old Testament so that "the moral sensitivities of the German race are not hindered."[13] On the other hand,

Spellenberg tempered his condemnation of Jewish influence in Germany by arguing that because of his belief in the New Testament, he could not completely reject the Old Testament. Since Jesus Christ had taught from the Old Testament and had proclaimed the fulfillment and not abolition of the Old Testament law, Spellenberg refused to part completely with the Hebrew Scriptures. His statement cut to the core of the predicament faced by Christians in National Socialist Germany. As much as they might agree with the anti-Semitic ideology of the NSDAP, they could never escape the charges of party extremists that Christianity was a Jewish religion. To do so would amount to the abandonment of the historical foundation of the Christian faith and the denial of the essential Jewishness of Jesus.

If pastors like Priester and Spellenberg were unwilling to deny the essential connection between Judaism and Christianity, several of the most radical German Christian pastors in Nauen, Pirna, and Ravensburg were willing to cross that theological threshold in their attempt to expunge Jews and Judaism from German Protestantism. In Nauen, Pastor Friedrich Siems inveighed against "Judaism and its fearfully destructive influence," attacking them both as communists and capitalists. He denied any substantial connection between Judaism and Christianity, even doubting that Jesus was Jewish: "As German Christians, we have discerned that the founder of Christianity had nothing, really nothing at all to do with the Jewish people, rather they were always his sharpest opponents. . . . The personality of Christ is too great and too holy for us to bring it into connection with [Jews, who have] become a curse for the whole world."[14] In fact, because Siems believed German blood purity was a divine order of creation, the presence of Jews posed not only a risk to the German racial community but also an obstacle to the fulfillment of God's law. In other words, it was an act of faith to eliminate both Judaism from Christianity and Jews from Germany.

In Pirna, Pastor Paul Teichgräber of Eschdorf denigrated Jews and Judaism in the course of a 1934 report about the activities of the local Seventh-day Adventist sect. Above all else, Teichgräber judged the Adventists harshly for their political subversion and their Jewish practices. He claimed that the sect followed "Jewish teaching and tendencies" even more closely than the outlawed Jehovah's Witnesses and supported his contention with examples of "Sabbath-keeping, tithing, a materialistic view of salvation and law-keeping, and the *exaltation of the Jewish people as the people of God*." Teichgräber denied the idea that the Jews were the means God used to bring the message of salvation to earth, or that the experiences of Old Testament Israel foreshadowed either Christ or Christianity. He rejected the assertion that Old Testament sacrifices were similar to Jesus' death, or that the Passover feast and Christian sacrament of communion were essentially comparable.[15]

Another Pirna pastor, Dr. Ernst Rothe, also analyzed the relationship between Christianity, National Socialism, and racial questions in an October 1935 lecture on "The Christian and the Burning Questions of the Present." Rothe's talk is important because he delivered it to local pastors and church leaders at the annual district church assembly and because he was the pastor at the chapel attached to Sonnenstein, the large special care institution in Pirna. As the pastor with the best vantage point from which to understand the outworking of Nazi racial policy, Rothe identified three pressing issues for his colleagues to consider: the sterilization law, which protected the blood of the German nation from contamination by the hereditarily diseased blood of "deviant" Germans; the Jewish question in Germany; and the objectives of the National Socialist worldview.[16]

First, Rothe asserted that advocating sterilization was not contrary to Christian love. There was just no other way to hinder those who were hereditarily diseased, capable of reproduction, and therefore a danger to the strength of the German racial stock. In addition, he argued that even the Inner Mission, the national organization responsible for managing many Protestant special care institutions, recognized this fact and supported the sterilization program.

Second, with respect to the Jewish question, Rothe discussed the recent passage of the Nuremberg Citizenship Law and the Law for the Protection of German Blood and Honor, which stripped Jews of their German citizenship and forbade them from having sexual relations with Aryans. Here too Rothe argued that Nazi measures to protect the German race were consistent with the Christian duty of love, the goal of which was to build God's kingdom and preserve life. Significantly, however, these goals of loving others, building the kingdom of God, and preserving life applied only to healthy Germans. For Rothe and so many other Protestants who shared his Nazi ideology, the condition of Jews, Gypsies, or the physically or mentally handicapped was simply irrelevant. They were, in the Nazi vernacular, "lives unworthy of life." Any practical responsibility to these people that might have existed for Protestants who thought as Rothe did dissolved in their spiritualization of Christian unity and mind-numbing insistence on the irrevocable demands of the mystical German racial community. By placing Jews outside the community of Germans, Rothe consigned them to a space in which Christian love did not apply.

Third, Rothe outlined the goals of the National Socialist worldview and reiterated the old Nazi demand that the common interests of the nation had to come before anyone's individual interests. Rothe described this concept as similar to the ethical requirements of Christianity and then asserted that both great worldviews (National Socialism and Christianity) ought to advance together. The National Socialist worldview was practical in its approach, argued Rothe, and was not bothered with the ultimate questions of existence that concerned the Christian faith. Correspondingly, in the practical realm of this earth, the Christian worldview would direct Germans toward their duty to the Fatherland, as defined by National Socialism.

Unfortunately, there is no record of how the pastors or laypeople in attendance at the district church assembly received Rothe's message, nor any subsequent account of Rothe's response to the escalation of National Socialist racial policy at the Sonnenstein institution, where the facilities were turned into a euthanasia killing center from 1939 to 1941. There is no public record that would suggest that there was ever any attempt by Lutherans to help either the handicapped or the Jews in the Pirna region.

Along with Pastors Siems, Teichgräber, and Rothe, Pastor Dr. Karl Steger of Friedrichshafen also tried to expunge Jews and Judaism from German Protestantism. Steger used the parish newsletter he edited to advertise his anti-Semitic views to local Protestants. In the May 1936 edition, he reported on a speech he had recently given to Friedrichshafen German Christians on the theme "Was Jesus Jewish?"[17] In his speech, Steger introduced a series of specious arguments designed to create doubt about Jesus' ethnic roots. First, Steger evaded the very question he posed by asserting that Jesus' racial identity was less important than the subjective question of faith: "What is Jesus *to you?*" Steger then compared Christian salvation through Jesus to medical cures adapted from other nations. German doctors would never reject a remedy because it was not German, but would always use any cure that worked, regardless of its origin. For Steger, the same logic held true for human salvation: "Are we supposed to reject Christ, because perhaps his ancestry is not racially unambiguous?" Steger contended that the enemies of Christ were simply using anti-Semitic attacks on Christianity as a way to avoid the challenging claim of Christ on their lives; he lumped them together with "extreme Talmud Jews," whose ongoing purpose was to make Christ look inferior.

Steger then turned to Houston Stewart Chamberlain, "the precursor of the National Socialist world of thought . . . for whom Christ was an Aryan," since Chamberlain's writings spoke directly to "all this filth and trash that is heaped up over Christ by these spiteful opponents of Christianity." Steger quoted Chamberlain's argument that it was naïve to believe that Christ was a mythological figure or an inferior Jew. Science would clear up the uncertainty around Christ's racial identity just as it had cleared up all kinds of other religious questions. Denouncing the Jewish world press for its campaign to dig up anything to discredit Christianity, he explained Chamberlain's view that Christ had been raised as a Jew but was probably not racially one, since he came from the racially mixed region of Galilee and since his opposition to Judaism and consequent death on a cross made it seem unlikely he could be Jewish himself.

Steger buttressed his argument further with words from President Ernst Graf Reventlow of the pagan German Faith Movement, whom he described as an honorable opponent of Christ, a thoroughly decent intellectual, and even a pious man. Like Chamberlain, Reventlow asserted that Christ was so different from Jews that he could not possibly be Jewish. Where Jews were materialistic, Christ was spiritual and heavenly minded. Where Christ proclaimed the kingdom of God as an attitude of the soul, Jews believed in an earthly kingdom. Where Christ rejected money, it ran counter to the Jewish mentality. Where Jews focused on a holy, Old Testament law, Christ was indifferent to the law. Where Christ preached love for others, Jews could not grasp it. Steger finished his talk (and article) by pronouncing his verdict on the question. Not surprisingly, Steger considered the notion that Jesus was a Jew to be "very problematic," a conclusion greeted with applause by Steger's German Christian audience.

## Sympathetic Clergy

In contrast to these evasions of the Jewish roots of Christianity, a few pastors spoke and acted in ways that suggested they might be sympathetic to Jews. In all cases, they were members of the Confessing Church, primarily from the Nauen church district. From the beginning of his tenure in Groß Behnitz, Pastor Kurt Fritzsche found himself in trouble with parishioners whose racial ideology did not correspond to his. One of them was Groß Behnitz school principal Lehmann, who accused Fritzsche of possessing the attitude of "an enemy of the state," largely on account of Fritzsche's loyalty to the Confessing Church. On November 11, 1938, one day after the Kristallnacht Pogrom, Fritzsche spoke to his confirmation students on behalf of Jewish Christians, perhaps even for Jews as Jews, as he discussed the question of Jewish responsibility for the pogrom. His students reported him to local authorities and quoted him as having uttered the comments, "Jews are also people like us," "The Jews of [Bible times] are not the Jews of today," and, "The Jew from Paris is only one criminal." [18] When his students argued back, blaming other Jews too, Fritzsche exclaimed: "*That is not true!*" One of the students quoted Principal Lehmann, Fritzsche's enemy, who had said that anyone who helped a Jew was not German, while others shouted out around Fritzsche: "He is a Jew too!" As a result of Fritzsche's outburst and the spectacle that followed, Lehmann forbade Fritzsche from using the school for any further confirmation instruction. In addition, local Gestapo agents and officials from the Superior Church Council in Berlin both censured Fritzsche, though no further action was taken against him. [19]

Two other clergy from the Nauen district took a stand on the question of baptizing Jews who converted to Christianity. In 1936, Pastor Günther Harder of Fehrbellin baptized a Jewish woman, the wife of a Protestant. When Reich Minister for Church Affairs Hans Kerrl found out about the event, he wrote an angry letter to the Berlin church authorities, complaining that the baptism had aroused "great exasperation" in the local population: "Harder deemed it necessary to announce the baptism of this Jewish woman from the pulpit on Sunday, 19 July." Furthermore, as Kerrl pointed out, Harder had the temerity to permit the couple's half-Jewish children to sing in the church choir. Kerrl was particularly frustrated that Harder had not kept the baptism "as inconspicuous as possible," since he knew full well the "extremely detrimental experiences with the baptism of Jews." As a result, Harder received a letter of censure from the Reich Church Committee then governing the Old Prussian Union Church. [20] Subsequently, his colleague Confessing Church Vicar

Heidrich of Groß Behnitz was temporarily expelled from the NSDAP in 1937, not because he was jailed for ten weeks for refusing to turn in voluntary church collections to the Brandenburg Consistory, but because he stated he was ready to baptize Jews too. Upon appeal, a regional NSDAP court overturned Heidrich's expulsion.[21]

Heidrich's supervisor, Pastor Herbert Posth of Berge, was one of several clergy whose complaints to Prussian church authorities over filling out Proofs of Aryan Ancestry may have stemmed from more fundamental disagreements with the anti-Semitic policy that lay behind them. German pastors were regularly called on to research the baptismal records on which Nazi racial identity was based, in order to provide Proofs of Aryan Ancestry for any civil servants, party members, or other Germans who needed to assure authorities of their Aryan identity. Pastor Posth was the only pastor in either Nauen or Pirna who voiced any substantial complaint about the work, grumbling to a member of the Brandenburg Consistory that filling out forms and undertaking background checks by telephone was a waste of his time: "the pastor is not bound to employ his time for the care of souls and parish visitation in this unheard-of way, for paper work that has nothing to do with the parish office." Still, there's no evidence that Posth or any other pastor refused to perform this vital service for the German Reich. Posth's colleagues in the Confessing Church, Pastor Günther Harder and Ms. Hebe Kohlbrugge, also filled out Proofs of Aryan Ancestry, though they claimed there was never a case in which the parishioner in question had non-Aryan grandparents.[22]

In Pirna, several pastors neglected to submit their own Proofs of Aryan Ancestry after the Saxon Church Office had requested the information in June 1939. When Superintendent Heinrich Leichte of Pirna repeated the demand over two years later, nine pastors and two vicars still had not filled out their forms. At least six of the nine pastors were members of the Confessing Church. Even after Leichte set a new deadline of October 15, 1941, for the submission of the outstanding paperwork, some of the pastors had still not submitted their forms as of November 10.[23] Though antipathy to National Socialist racial policy is only one of several possible reasons for their reticence to fill out the Proofs of Aryan Ancestry, at the very least, one can assume that these nine pastors were not eager to comply with the administrative burdens created by their government's racial policy.

## Sonnenstein and the "Euthanasia" Killings

Over the following years, the Saxon church officials corresponded periodically with pastors over racial and eugenic issues. In 1935, they sent out application forms for the local chapter of the German Society for Racial Hygiene, led by Dr. Hermann Paul Nitsche, the chief physician from Sonnenstein, who went on to practice forced sterilizations and then to oversee the transformation of Sonnenstein into a killing center in 1939. Five months later, they requested information about requests for baptism from Jews or about actual baptisms of Jews. In 1939, they ordered all clergy to report whether they and their spouses possessed German or alien blood, and to report the presence of Old Testament symbols, figures, pictures, emblems, scriptural texts, or other items in their churches. There is no record of pastoral response to any of these requests.[24] In July 1940, Leichte repeated his request for information on Old Testament symbols in local churches. He noted that pastors had portrayed his initial request as "an attack on religious faith and confession." Leichte called upon the pastors to take stock of the situation, argued that the request for information did not revolve around their religious faith and confession, and warned that the Saxon church authorities would take judicial action against pastors who continued to refuse to answer. Despite this warning, there is no record of any response.[25] The following year, higher church officials asked for information on Jews themselves, not just Jewish symbols. The Saxon Church Office wanted to know how many Jews had joined the Lutheran Church in the Pirna district since 1934.[26] Though this request did not yet touch on the baptism of Protestant children from racially mixed marriages, it clearly implied that the churches were to aid the National Socialist regime in identifying racial Jews in their midst.

While church authorities continued to send racial inquiries to Superintendent Leichte and Pirna clergy, a government policy of murder directed at German citizens, including Protestant parishioners from the Pirna church district, was implemented right on Leichte's doorstep. Only a short walk up the hill from the offices of the Pirna church district and city parish stood Sonnenstein, the special care institution for the mentally ill and mentally handicapped. A prominent landmark in almost every view of Pirna, Sonnenstein overlooked both the Elbe River and Pirna city center from atop its stately perch.[27]

The institution changed radically in 1939, however, when it was remade into a euthanasia killing center. Under the National Socialist euthanasia program *Aktion T4*, named after its office address, Tiergarten 4 in Berlin, Sonnenstein became one of six main killing centers in which mentally ill and mentally handicapped men, women, and children were gassed to death and then cremated. Between June 1939 and August 1941, at least 13,720 Germans (many from the surrounding region) were killed in a horrible realization of National Socialist racial policy. During the height of the euthanasia action in July 1941, 2,537 patients were killed, over one hundred per working day.[28]

The euthanasia system at Sonnenstein operated essentially as follows. Patient records from all German special care institutions were sent to the central office in Berlin. Based on a cursory glance at each record, medical doctors in the employ of the SS selected the patients for euthanasia. Generally, these patients were transferred to a holding institution, then transferred again to the killing institution—in part to make it more difficult for families to trace records or to intervene on behalf of their loved ones. In the case of Sonnenstein, four institutions served as collection points for patients selected for killing: Arnsdorf, Großschweidnitz, Waldheim, and Zschadrass. The transports in which victims rode were generally special gray buses with blacked out windows, which both the mental patients and general public came to know by sight.

When the patients arrived at Sonnenstein or any other killing center, their records were verified. They were then told to undress for a shower, checked over (those with gold fillings got a cross marked on their chests), and sent into a shower room that was really a gas chamber. Some of the dead were used for pseudo-scientific experiments. Those corpses with the cross on their chests had the gold fillings broken out of their mouths; then they were thrown into the cremation ovens with the other dead. Families of the patients were informed that their relatives had succumbed to infectious diseases of one sort or another and that their bodies had been cremated out of necessity, to prevent the spread of disease. Urns were filled with ashes from the ovens, which were then sent to the families of the euthanized patients when requested.

As death rates at special care institutions like Sonnenstein skyrocketed and vague death notices became a commonplace in newspapers, the German public became increasingly aware of the nature of the euthanasia program, and protests from relatives and others prompted Hitler to order the official termination of *Aktion T4* in late August of 1941. In Sonnenstein and elsewhere, however, the killing continued even after this, with malnourishment and intentional overdoses of medication taking the place of the gas chamber. In Saxony, much of this subsequent killing was perpetrated not at Sonnenstein itself but at holding institutions like Großschweidnitz, where 5,717 patients were murdered between September 1939 and May 1945, and Waldheim, where another eight hundred patients died between 1940 and 1945.[29] Meanwhile, in November 1941, SS leaders, doctors, and assistants met at Sonnenstein to plan the transfer of personnel and technology east to Belzec (and later Sobibor and Treblinka), where euthanasia teams were set to work in death camps for European Jews.[30]

Shrouded in secrecy, the story of Sonnenstein and other euthanasia centers has taken decades to emerge fully from the shadows. No record of the events at Sonnenstein exists in the local church records, or for that matter in the local press or civic archives.[31] This is so, despite the fact that those living in the city center saw the buses and the thick black smoke over Sonnenstein, smelled the foul stench from the incinerators, and understood that people were being killed in the institution. Older residents of the city have admitted so, as have personnel who worked in Sonnenstein but refused to participate in the killing action. A former nurse at Sonnenstein, Dora Schumann, reported how her husband, a nurse, was offered a position on the special commando that handled the patients as they came to be killed. Friends of theirs told them about the construction of the crematorium at Sonnenstein, about the patients in the blacked-out buses waiting to enter, and about the starvations and overdoses of the wild euthanasia at Großschweidnitz. According to Schumann, on one occasion great flames shot out of the chimney at Sonnenstein, but when the fire department rushed out there, no one would let them onto the grounds. Because the air smelled of burning flesh, it was obvious to people in the community that patients were being murdered and cremated there. Although "it smelled like hair and like bones" and "the commotion was great," Schumann recalls that no one was allowed to ask anyone about what was going on.[32] As far as the Lutheran Church was concerned, Sonnenstein and its chapel were part of the Pirna parish until the institution was changed into a killing center and the chapel was closed.

This silence about Sonnenstein both demands and defies explanation, given that there must have been hundreds of handicapped Lutherans from Pirna and around the district who were killed at Sonnenstein and other smaller euthanasia centers in Saxony. One case has been recorded: a forty-three-year old Lutheran mother from the parish of Ottendorf was murdered in November 1940, although she only suffered from depression due to overwork. Because the death notice had been sent from the Hartheim killing center in Linz, the woman's daughter did not discover until 1991 that her mother had been killed at Sonnenstein.[33]

## Euthanasia in Württemberg

In the Ravensburg church district, the state psychiatric hospital at Weissenau also suffered the trauma of the euthanasia process. Located in a village on the outskirts of Ravensburg, the chapel at Weissenau was regularly served by one of the associate pastors from town. In October 1939, doctors at the hospital were surprised to receive a stack of forms to complete concerning their patients, which they were told were for the purpose of facilitating wartime economy measures. No word of the confiscation and transformation of the special care institution in Grafeneck had yet reached the doctors at Weissenau. In November 1939, Dr. Egon Stähle of the Württemberg Health Authority in the Ministry of the Interior began issuing orders to transfer large numbers of patients from various psychiatric hospitals, Weissenau included, accompanied only by the vague justification of the "current situation." From late 1939 on, regular lists of seventy-five names arrived at psychiatric hospitals, with instructions to prepare the selected patients for transport to an "unknown destination," which proved to be Zweifalten, the holding institution from which patients would be forwarded to Grafeneck to die.[34]

Director Sorg of the Weissenau institution was slow to understand what was happening to the mental health system, even when the first shipments left from Weissenau. Only when the driver of the transport shrugged off Sorg's warning about seventeen patients who were permanently contagious with typhus did Sorg begin to wonder if something unusual was going on. When the driver told Sorg, "It doesn't matter to us," Sorg began to ponder the situation, but was "unable to realize the underlying significance of his words." Gradually, however, rumors began to circulate through the public and the patient populations that many people were dying at Grafeneck, and from strange causes. Through rumors circulating in the general public, both patients and staff at Weissenau gradually learned about the euthanasia program, which affected their work substantially. As one doctor explained:

> Shock therapy was almost impossible, as the patients and their relatives suspected each injection of being the "death injection." Not one patient or relative believed anything we said any longer. We were embarrassed to face the relatives and it was seldom possible to create even the vaguest basis of trust.

He went on to describe the horrible effect that the knowledge of their destiny had on patients being transported to Grafeneck:

> Patients who slowly began to realize what was happening were led to the buses pale and shaking. I remember in this context the schizophrenics in Weissenau who awoke from their lethargy when they were collected and bade the other patients farewell with a pathos of which no-one would have thought them capable, as the condemned going to their deaths. These were fortunately few. Most of the acutely ill did not outwardly react. In hospitals which were confessionally bound the patients were religiously prepared for death the night before their collections were made. In state institutions this was forbidden.

Of the roughly fifteen thousand patients killed in Grafeneck, 691 came in eleven different transports from Weissenau, between May 1940 and March 1941.

Even as they became aware of the crimes with which they were implicated, doctors and other medical staff at Weissenau and other hospitals generally chose to collaborate with the euthanasia program. *Aktion T4* officials often implicated the director of Weissenau by sending lists of more than seventy-five patients (the quota for each transport), forcing him to choose which patients to keep back. After keeping back two patients who were good workers, the Weissenau director later suggested to the Württemberg Ministry of the Interior that they be included in the next shipment, since their condition had deteriorated. In this way, doctors at Weissenau accepted the elimination of psychiatric illnesses through murder "alarmingly freely." They accepted the Nazi ideology that measured worthiness to live based on productivity, as well as the supposed necessity of eliminating their inferior patients for the greater good of the German nation.

Weissenau was not the only institution in the Ravensburg church district from which mentally ill or handicapped patients were transported to Grafeneck. In February 1940, thirteen patients were taken from the epileptic asylum Pfingstweide, near Tettnang. They were simply chosen by officials from outside the institution from the names on the Pfingstweide patient list that began with the letters *B* through *H* and included veterans of the First World War who had suffered physical and psychological damage. When officials at Pfingstweide learned of the deaths of their patients, they protested to the Württemberg Interior Ministry and the Württemberg headquarters of the Inner Mission, the Protestant agency responsible for Pfingstweide. [35]

Despite these protests, another transportation was planned for October 1940, when fifteen more patients were selected to be killed. Knowing that the Pfingstweide doctors opposed the transfer, representatives from the Württemberg Interior Ministry and doctors from Berlin came to Pfingstweide in person to ensure the success of the transport. For four hours, the transport bus waited outside Pfingstweide while doctors tried to persuade officials from the Württemberg Interior Ministry to allow the patients to remain at Pfingstweide. Their efforts were partially successful: four men, two of them Jewish, were left behind. The other eleven were transported to their deaths. In order to prevent further transports, doctors from Pfingstweide informed the families of patients about the danger and appealed to high-ranking officials to secure the safety of the patients. Still, in March 1941, five more patients were transported from the asylum to the state institution at Weinsberg, where they were murdered in spite of protests from the Pfingstweide doctors. Of the seventy-five patients in the asylum, twenty-nine were murdered in 1940 and 1941.

The Ziegler Institution at Wilhelmsdorf, an asylum for the deaf, mute, and other special-needs patients, faced similar pressures. In August 1940, doctors there received word of planned transports. In response, Inspector Hermann, head of the Ziegler Institution, wrote a firm letter of protest: "I know the purpose of this systematic requisition. I know of the many death notices . . . I cannot in good conscience remain silent about that and take part . . . I simply have the conviction, that *the authorities are committing an injustice with the killing of certain patients.* We humans do not have the right to the annihilation of life other than as the expiation for certain crimes or in war." Warning that God would avenge the blood of those murdered by their fellow men, Inspector Hermann quoted 2 Samuel 14:14 as the basis for his decision:

> "But God will not take away a life; he will devise plans so as not to keep an outcast banished for ever from his presence."—No family is sure that one of its children will not become mentally handicapped through sickness or an accident. With the annihilation of such an ill or simply abnormal family member or patient, we are acting against God's will. That is why I cannot take part in this affair. I am sorry, but a person must obey God rather than man. I am prepared to accept the consequences of this my disobedience.

Inspector Hermann followed up his words with concrete actions. When the Württemberg Interior Ministry demanded a list of patients from the Ziegler

Institution, Hermann sent in forty-five patient names instead of all 110 and then informed the families of patients so they could take them home. Hermann also received help from an unexpected source. During the inspection of patients, a member of the medical commission from the Württemberg Interior Ministry tore up three patients' forms so that they would not be taken. This was an act of kindness for which Inspector Hermann was extremely grateful but not satisfied. In his letter of thanks to the medical commission, he appealed for the lives of his other patients as well. As in the case of Pfingstweide, success at the Ziegler Institution was only partial. In March 1941, eighteen more patients were transported from the Wilhelmsdorf asylum and murdered. Through his efforts, though, Hermann had managed to save ninety-two patients. He was certainly more successful than doctors at the Roman Catholic hospital in Liebenau, near Tettnang, where 270 patients were transported to Grafeneck.[36]

As in Pirna, church records in Ravensburg are eerily silent about euthanasia. The one mention of the subject was a memorandum from the Württemberg Superior Church Council to the district superintendents, noting the unrest among the populace in areas where mentally ill, mentally handicapped, and epileptic patients had been killed in asylums. The note explained that Württemberg bishop Wurm had written a long letter to the Reich Interior Minister, explaining "why these measures must be judged as disastrous from the human and the Christian standpoint," and had encouraged pastors and family members of affected inmates to contact the Reich Interior Ministry themselves. There is no record that Ravensburgers ever responded to that request.[37]

## Euthanasia in Brandenburg

The same holds true for the Nauen church district, where pastors were far more likely to be caught up in controversies surrounding pastoral appointments. There is one notable exception to this, however. Günther Harder of Fehrbellin advocated for Christians of Jewish descent in Brandenburg by trying to rouse fellow pastors to protest the so-called Fürle decree of December 1941, issued by top officials in the Old Prussian Union Church. That decree was a response to the increasingly brutal treatment of Jews and Jewish Christians in Nazi Germany and its occupied territories and called upon the government to legislate the exclusion of Jewish Christians from the Protestant churches. Recalling his protest against this decree, Harder believed the efforts of Confessing Church pastors may have helped prevent the German government from acting on the wishes of the Berlin church leaders.[38]

As a member of the Confessing Church Council in Brandenburg, Harder was party to the letter of protest that the Confessing Church Provisional Church Government wrote against the Fürle decree in February of 1942:

Together with all Christians in Germany who stand on the ground of the
Scripture and the Confession, we are compelled to declare that this request from
the Church Chancellery is incompatible with the confession of the church. . . .

By what right do we desire to exclude, for racial reasons, Christian non-
Aryans from our worship services? Do we want to be like the Pharisees, who
renounced communion with the "tax collectors and sinners" in the worship
service and, because of this, reaped Christ's judgment?"

Noting that Christ and the apostles were Jewish, the Provisional Church
Government wondered whether they would be expelled from Protestant
church services as well. Despite the clarity and force of this protest letter, the
Confessing Church leaders still managed to send conflicting messages about Jews
and Jewish Christians. Despite their determination to treat baptized Jews as "our
brethren in Christ," they never challenged the authority of the state to pass a law
excluding Jewish Christians from the Protestant churches. Nor did they make
a clean break with anti-Semitism when they tacitly acknowledged the state's
"certain measures against the Jews" and praised Martin Luther's "legitimate
wrath against the Jews, who defame the Christian church and undermine the
morals of the Christian people."[39]

Again that August, Harder took up the cause of Christians of Jewish descent, as
the chair of a committee comprised of Dietrich Bonhoeffer and four other Confessing
Church theologians, in conjunction with the Eleventh Prussian Confessing Church
Synod. As Harder later recalled, he and his colleagues took up the Jewish question
and instructed the churches: "The exclusion of non-Aryan Christians from church
fellowship violates Holy Scripture and the Confession and is therefore unacceptable
under church law. We exhort pastors and parishes, for Christ's sake, to maintain
church fellowship with them." On top of that, Harder and others gathered money
and food ration cards for Jewish Christians and "helped to hide not a few of the same
in our parishes." Indeed, Harder's secretary, Mrs. Jacobi, herself part Jewish, was
sentenced to eighteen months incarceration for her role in the scheme.

Then, in October 1943, at the Twelfth Prussian Confessing Church
Synod, both Pastors Günther Harder of Fehrbellin and Herbert Posth of Berge
collaborated on the committee that wrote the "Word of the Church" concerning
the Ten Commandments. Intended for use in church services on the annual Day
of Repentance and Prayer, the document began: "Throughout our nation and
even throughout our Protestant parishes and Christian families passes a great,
ever-growing insecurity about whether the holy Ten Commandments are still in
effect." The declaration went on to address the Fifth Commandment, "You shall not
murder," and condemned the state for its misuse of power and its disdain for human
life: "Concepts like 'elimination,' 'liquidation' and 'worthless lives' are unknown in
God's order." Continuing, it read:

Woe to us and to our nation, when God-given life is despised and the person, created in the image of God, is valued solely according to his utility; when it is considered justified to kill people because they are considered unworthy of life or belong to another race, when hate and mercilessness parade about. Then God speaks: "You shall not murder."

Harder later remarked at the many warnings he had received against reading out the "Word of the Church" in his parish church. When he did so and faced no judicial consequences, he attributed it to the distraction of the bombing in Berlin.[40]

## Conclusions

In light of the initiatives of Günther Harder, Herbert Posth, and the heads of Pfingstweide and Ziegler special care institutions, the general lack of response among pastors in Nauen, Pirna, and Ravensburg to the euthanasia program and the persecution of Jews is disheartening. Returning to Wolfgang Gerlach's assessment of the Confessing Church, we have already seen how conflicted Protestant clergy were in their views of Jews and handicapped people. While at times affirming the inherent dignity of these victims of Nazi racial policy, pastors sent mixed messages by exalting the German racial community as divinely ordained and calling on Protestants to support the renewing work of the National Socialist regime. Pastors were also very often too preoccupied with their own struggle to preserve the independence of their church institutions and to defend theological truth that they neglected to challenge the social and political attitudes of the Third Reich, or to aid the victims of Nazi persecution. Certainly we can also add that fear must have played an important role. While those pastors and leaders who did speak out in Nauen and Ravensburg did not, for the most part, suffer significantly for their actions, no one could be sure when opposition to church leaders or state officials might result in harassment, beatings, imprisonment, or worse. Dora Schumann's memory of the way that public turmoil over euthanasia at Sonnenstein was shrouded in a cloak of silence provides a window through which to see how Lutherans in Pirna might have responded to the murders and murderers in their midst by withdrawing in fear. Certainly, there were other times where local clergy despaired of conditions in their parishes and felt helpless to struggle against National Socialism. Still, the willingness of Confessing Church clergy to defy the Brandenburg and Saxon church governments and to engage in all manner of illegal activity on behalf of their local churches raises the question of why they did not do the same for the victims of euthanasia and the Holocaust. Surely this is the blackest stain upon their record. It is a testimony to the force of their sociopolitical environment and the weakness of their theological and ethical training that they were either so ideologically maladjusted or psychologically intimidated that they could no longer respond to the divine injunction: "Give justice to the weak and the orphan; maintain the right of the lowly and the destitute. Rescue the weak and the needy; deliver them from the hand of the wicked" (Psalm 82:3-4).

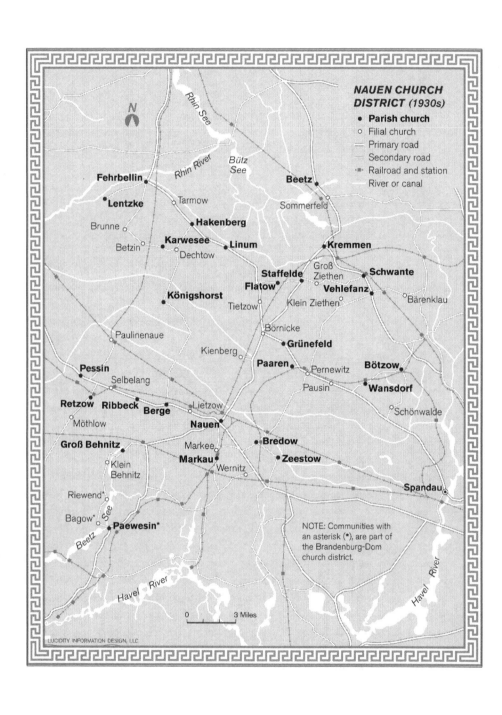

**NAUEN CHURCH DISTRICT (1930s)**

- Parish church
- Filial church
- Primary road
- Secondary road
- Railroad and station
- River or canal

NOTE: Communities with an asterisk (*), are part of the Brandenburg-Dom church district.

Fehrbellin
Lentzke
Brunne
Betzin
Tarmow
Hakenberg
Karwesee
Dechtow
Linum
Königshorst
Tietzow
Staffelde
Flatow
Groß Ziethen
Klein Ziethen
Vehlefanz
Schwante
Bärenklau
Kremmen
Sommerfeld
Beetz
Börnicke
Grünefeld
Paulinenaue
Kienberg
Paaren
Pernewitz
Pausin
Bötzow
Wansdorf
Pessin
Selbelang
Retzow
Ribbeck
Berge
Möthlow
Nauen
Lietzow
Schönwalde
Groß Behnitz
Klein Behnitz
Markee
Markau
Wernitz
Bredow
Zeestow
Spandau
Riewend*
Bagow*
Paewesin*

*Rhin See*
*Bütz See*
*Rhin River*
*Beelz See*
*Havel River*
*Havel River*

N

0   3 Miles

LUCIDITY INFORMATION DESIGN, LLC

# chapter five

# The Church Struggle in Nauen, Brandenburg

 The extensive conflict surrounding pastoral appointments in the Nauen district and the single-mindedness with which the Saxon and Württemberg church governments guarded their authority over personnel decisions illustrate the critical importance of parish clergy in the local Church Struggle. At the center of a web of relationships between parishioners, church patrons, local political leaders, clerical colleagues, and the higher church officials, parish clergy had the power to shape the fundamental course of parish life during the Nazi era. They normally set the church-political tone for their parishes, though they were periodically vulnerable to the noisy protests of their parishioners and the ill-treatment of their ecclesiastical superiors.

The next three chapters examine the Church Struggle in the three districts of Nauen, Pirna, and Ravensburg. Each one will address three large questions about Protestant parish life in the Third Reich. First, to what extent did the tensions and issues of the Church Struggle in Berlin, Dresden, and Stuttgart filter down into the parishes of Nauen, Pirna, and Ravensburg? Second, in what ways did Protestant pastors initiate or engage in church-political conflict? Were the issues that concerned them local, regional, or national in nature? Third, how were clergy affected by opposition or assistance from parishioners, fellow pastors, district superintendents, local National Socialists, or their regional church governments?

In the Nauen district, the politicization and polarization of church life placed an immense strain on the relationships of area pastors. The two large church parties that dominated German Protestantism in the Third Reich, the German Christian Movement, and the Confessing Church, turned sleepy, rural parishes into battlegrounds for hearts and souls. As we have already seen in the analysis of pastoral appointments in the Nauen district, the noisy victory of German Christians in the

July 1933 church elections and their resultant seizure of power in the Brandenburg Church Province did not necessarily translate into either administrative control or spiritual leadership at the parish level. In the Nauen district, this was largely due to the moderating influence of two key district leaders, Superintendent Graßhoff (1932–1935) and Interim Superintendent Ulrich Bettac (1936–1940, 1944–1945). Both men shunned the excesses of church-political radicals and worked to unite parish clergy in the face of increasingly tense church conditions.

This policy of moderation was not an easy one to sustain. No ecclesiastical position demanded more wisdom and tact during the Church Struggle than that of the district superintendent. As officials of the Old Prussian Union Church government under the authority of the Brandenburg Consistory, Nauen superintendents transmitted information and instructions from Prussian church authorities to their parish pastors and acted as the executive arm of the church government in their districts. They participated in pastoral appointments, enforced church legislation, mediated parish disputes, and presided over the district synod and various other church associations. As pastors to the pastors in their districts, superintendents mentored young clergy, oversaw the continuing education of pastors, and worked to create harmonious relations among local clergy. Finally, since they were also parish pastors, superintendents continued to preach, teach, and perform other pastoral functions in their own parishes. In all these roles, superintendents found themselves caught up in church-political controversy, whether in the parishes, among feuding clergy, or between local pastors and Prussian church authorities.

In Nauen, the challenges inherent in the position of superintendent were compounded by the fact that there was no permanent superintendent for ten of the twelve years of National Socialist rule. Superintendent Graßhoff served from 1932 until only April 1935, when a chronic stomach disorder forced him to retire prematurely.[1] After two other pastors served as interim superintendents, Pastor Ulrich Bettac from Beetz took up the position in 1936 and remained interim superintendent until the end of 1940, when the collapse of his marriage made it necessary for him to resign. Superintendent Simon from the neighboring district of Oranienburg was appointed interim superintendent in Nauen in 1941, but after his untimely death in March 1944, the consistory turned again to Bettac to oversee the Nauen district.[2] This procession of local leaders did little to strengthen the hand of the Brandenburg Consistory in Nauen and opened the door for the successful careers of dissident clergy across the district. In fact, one of the chief characteristics of the Church Struggle in Nauen was the lack of close connection between ecclesiastical events in Berlin and those in the rural parishes of the district. One reads little in the local correspondence about the German Christian seizure of power in the Old Prussian Union Church or of Pastor Martin Niemöller and the events leading up to the creation of his Pastors' Emergency League. For the most part, ecclesiastical conflicts in Nauen between 1933 and 1945 were largely local affairs, influenced by larger events only insofar as Confessing Church pastors participated in the widespread disobedience to the Prussian church authorities, withholding collections and reading unauthorized pulpit declarations. One factor in this relative isolation may have been the reduced status of interim superintendents, whose transitory role did not gain them entrance into higher church politics in Berlin.

Nauen superintendent Graßhoff and the interim superintendents who succeeded him faced two major obstacles to the fulfillment of their duties. One was the church-political radicalism of Confessing Church pastors, who refused to recognize either the spiritual or administrative authority of the Brandenburg Consistory. The other problem was the resulting conflict among local pastors, which was often exacerbated by the unreasonable demands of local German Christian clergy. In the Nauen district, pastors were almost evenly divided between members and supporters of the German Christian Movement and members and supporters of the Confessing Church. A remnant of neutrals tended to oppose radicalism from either end of the church-political spectrum. Among the junior clergy of Nauen whose church-political stance is known, however, there were over six times as many members and supporters of the Confessing Church as there were German Christians, evidence of the success of the Confessing Church in controlling local personnel decisions.

| Church-Political Orientation among Nauen clergy[3] | | | | |
|---|---|---|---|---|
| Church-Political Status | Pastors | (%) | Vicars/ Curates | (%) |
| German Christians | 14 | 33 | 3 | 8 |
| German Christian Supporters | 3 | 7 | 0 | 0 |
| Neutrals | 6 | 14 | 2 | 5 |
| Confessing Church Supporters | 7 | 17 | 1 | 3 |
| Confessing Church Members | 8 | 19 | 12 | 32 |
| Unknown | 4 | 10 | 19 | 51 |
| Total | 42 | | 37 | |

In light of this division, the local Church Struggle is best understood through the careers of a handful of leading pastors: two from the Confessing Church, Pastors Günther Harder and Herbert Posth; one moderate interim superintendent, Pastor Ulrich Bettac; and the energetic German Christian organizer in Nauen, Pastor Friedrich Siems. Each of these was a prominent churchman who was active in the controversies that shaped the Church Struggle in Nauen.

The two leaders of the Confessing Church in the district, Harder and Posth, both stand out for their willingness to defy the Prussian church authorities and disrupt the flow of information between their parishes and the Brandenburg Consistory. Guided by the Brandenburg Confessing Church Council, the two men boldly led their parishes into rebellion against the Brandenburg Consistory, which they regarded as illegitimate, on account of its embrace of German Christianity. For this stance, they endured the criticism of fellow pastors, the scorn of local political leaders, and the disciplinary measures of the Old Prussian Union Church.

Both Harder and Posth were also active in the leadership of the Brandenburg Confessing Church. Harder served as a New Testament professor in the Kirchliche Hochschule (seminary) in Berlin from 1936 to 1972. In this capacity, he examined illegal Confessing Church theological candidates for ordination during the Nazi era. In addition, he sat on the Brandenburg Confessing Church Council and, after 1943, on the Old Prussian Union Confessing Church Council as well. On May 9, 1937, at the Fourth Prussian Confessing Church Synod, he gave the opening sermon, in which he lamented the growing disinterest of German society in Christianity: "the world simply doesn't want to know anything of the church, of its service, of its message, of the truth to which it testifies." In August 1942, Harder chaired a committee comprised of Dietrich Bonhoeffer and four other Confessing Church theologians, whose purpose was to formulate a public statement for the Eleventh Prussian Confessing Church Synod concerning the organized murder of disabled people and Jews by the Nazi state. Finally, in October 1943, both Harder and Posth worked on the Confessing Church committee that wrote the "Word of the Church" concerning the widespread violation of the Ten Commandments in preparation for the Twelfth Prussian Confessing Church Synod.[4]

Günther Harder was the Confessing Church district pastor for the Nauen district, as well as for two other districts in Brandenburg.[5] As such, he presided over a cadre of Confessing Church pastors who committed themselves to conducting their pastoral ministry according to the teaching of the Word of God and the Reformation Confessions of Faith, as they had promised in the vows of ordination they had sworn at the outset of their ministry. Along with Harder and Herbert Posth of Berge, the group included Pastors Johannes Engelke of Königshorst, Kurt Fritzsche of Groß Behnitz, Martin Lehmann of Karwesee, Max Oestreich of Lentzke, Bogumil Rocha of Pessin, and Pastor Wiese of Zeestow. Since they believed that the German Christian domination of the Old Prussian Union Church government violated that biblical standard in both principle and practice, these pastors refused to submit to the authority of the Brandenburg Consistory, the ecclesiastical body to which they were responsible.[6]

Harder pastored in Fehrbellin, a parish in the northwestern corner of the Nauen district that grew from roughly two thousand to thirty-five hundred parishioners during the years of National Socialist rule. Only twenty-seven years old when he was appointed in 1929, Harder reliably guided both his own parish and the Confessing Church party in the Nauen district throughout the Church Struggle, defying political, ecclesiastical, and police authorities, frequently at great cost to himself and his parishioners.[7]

It did not take Harder long to become a stubborn opponent of the German Christian attempt to reorder the Old Prussian Union Church along National Socialist lines. Indeed, he reacted sharply to the early events in the Berlin Church Struggle, where the Prussian educational minister appointed District Court Councilor Dr. August Jäger as an administrative commissar in the Old Prussian Union Church in August 1933. Jäger immediately purged the Prussian church administration, suspended the general superintendents, and placed loyal German Christians in positions of authority in the Old Prussian Superior Church Council and in the various provincial administrative bodies, including the Brandenburg Consistory. In response to this event, Joachim Hossenfelder, who had just been appointed commissarial bishop of Brandenburg and general superintendent for the Kurmark region, announced plans for celebratory worship services to be held on July 2, 1933. Hossenfelder intended, of course, for pastors and parishioners in Nauen and other districts in the Kurmark to express their gratitude for this German Christian "reform" of the church. Harder was away from his office during the time of these events and returned home to learn about plans for the celebratory service in the local newspaper. Shocked that no one had bothered to ask him whether such a service ought to be held in Fehrbellin, Harder took strong action, transforming the intended celebration into a service of mourning and repentance. Refusing to read the prescribed celebratory message from Brandenburg bishop and German Christian leader Hossenfelder, Harder chose instead to read out prohibited messages from ousted general superintendent Otto Dibelius and former Reich bishop Dr. Friedrich Bodelschwingh, who had resigned in protest against Jäger's measures. Harder also preached a sermon based on Ephesians 4:3-15, which emphasized the importance of Christian unity, peace, love, the supremacy of Christ, and the need for wisdom and maturity to overcome the storms of life. In doing so, he shocked a delegation of local NSDAP leaders who had expected a more triumphal word from their resident pastor.[8]

Harder's resolute adherence to the Confessing Church meant that he also ran afoul of the Prussian interior ministry, which led to altercations with local police. Initially, Harder aroused the attention of police when he read the denunciation of the neo-pagan German Faith Movement issued by the Second Prussian Confessing Church Synod of Dahlem in March 1935. Based on the first commandment, the Synod rebuked those who were setting up lesser gods of blood and race and raising racially inspired notions of honor and freedom above the Lord God of the Bible. Because this critical declaration obliquely attacked Hitler and the NSDAP, the Prussian interior ministry forbade the public reading of the text, which Confessing Church leaders had planned for March 17, 1935. At first, the threat of house arrest made Harder insecure, and he told police that he would not read the declaration. After a sleepless night, however, he changed his mind and informed local officers of his intention. Local police responded to Harder's change of heart by sealing the doors of the church and refusing to allow the Sunday service to take place, a first for Fehrbellin. Since that Sunday was Repentance Day, a prominent church holiday, news of the canceled service raced "like a wildfire through the town." The result, ironically, was the general arousal of interest in the wording of the banned declaration, so that even some traveling salesmen staying at the local inn heard about the commotion and took a copy with them on their way.[9]

Harder was not alone in his decision to proclaim the message of the Second Prussian Confessing Church Synod. In spite of the threat of arrest and the pressure to celebrate the reintroduction of military service in Germany announced the day before, at least five other Confessing Church pastors in the Nauen district read the same declaration as Harder in their services: Pastors Bettac of Beetz and Posth of Berge and Curates Rehfeld of Kremmen, Lehmann of Karwesee, and Fritzsche of Groß Behnitz. As part of a roundup of over seven hundred Confessing Church clergy in the Old Prussian Union Church, Harder and the other five were placed under arrest, though they were soon released, after Confessing Church leaders assured Prussian authorities that the declaration was directed solely against the neo-pagan German Faith Movement and not National Socialism itself. As part of the broader Confessing Church opposition to the authority of the Old Prussian Union Church, it was not the last time that Harder and his colleagues would suffer legal consequences for their actions.[10]

Indeed, Harder and his fellow Confessing Church clergy endured another round of arrests two years later, in August and September 1937, during their struggle with Prussian church authorities over control of voluntary church collections. Harder was detained for three weeks for refusing to submit his church collections to the Brandenburg Consistory, but was sustained by the loyalty of his Fehrbellin parishioners. As he later recalled: "They had learned in those years to sacrifice. They had learned that the collection is a real offering of thanks, and until 1945, not once was an offering of thanks from the parish handed over to the consistory and [its] Finance Department."[11]

Other Confessing Church clergy also were incarcerated for their refusal to surrender their church collections to the Brandenburg Consistory. Vicar Krause, who worked under Harder in Fehrbellin, was jailed for a month during the fall of 1937, not only because of the collection but also on account of provocative statements he made in a sermon. Pastor Posth of Berge spent almost a month in jail too, until he was amnestied by ecclesiastical authorities. Curate Fritzsche in Groß Behnitz was in custody for only two days before he was amnestied, but Curate Mickley of Königshorst spent three weeks in jail and Vicar Heidrich of Groß Behnitz was incarcerated for ten weeks.

The ecclesiastical struggles between Harder and the Prussian Church continued unabated. In 1939, the Brandenburg Consistory withheld Harder's salary for eight months because he supported a special intercessory liturgy issued by the Confessing Church in September 1938, amid widespread fear that a new war was about to break out. The liturgy confessed the Third Reich's repeated attacks against traditional values and institutions and described the coming war as a form of divine judgment on Germany. Outlawed by the Prussian church authorities, the liturgy remained controversial, even after the Munich Agreement dampened the fear that war was imminent. During the time of Harder's punishment, his parishioners helped him with gifts and food, encouraged that Harder would serve them whether he was paid or not. Thanks to the intercession of Interim Superintendent Bettac, Harder's salary was finally restored after the Brandenburg Consistory amnestied him.[12]

In 1941, Harder was incarcerated yet again, this time from May to December. During that time, other Confessing Church pastors and vicars provided spiritual care in Fehrbellin, particularly Pastor Lehmann from Karwesee. Looking back on the event, Harder credited his wife for watching closely over the parish to ensure that no "false shepherds" appeared to lead parishioners away from their Confessing Church orientation. Harder also found that the experience drew his parish much more closely together: "Never before or since were more tears of emotion and joy shed in a Christmas service of the parish as on that December 24, 1941, as Harder—released the day before from jail, even if now as an ex-convict—held the Christmas Eve service." Harder's final incarceration lasted from January to April 1945, by which point the war was nearing an end and the Fehrbellin parish was well prepared to endure his temporary absence.[13]

With the help of his Confessing Church colleagues and parishioners, Harder was able to survive the serious consequences of his refusal to recognize the jurisdiction of the German Christian church authorities in Berlin. His participation in a series of Confessing Church illegalities shaped the Church Struggle in Fehrbellin, which revolved not around external attacks on his ministry but rather around his attempt to establish his parish as a center of Confessing Church faithfulness to Scripture and the Reformation Confessions. Still, his choices cost him months of freedom and lost salary, not to mention the disfavor of local Nazi officials and the stigma of a criminal record.

Though Günther Harder was the district pastor for the Confessing Church, there was no character in the Nauen district who generated so much annoyance in the Brandenburg Consistory or so many headaches for Nauen district superintendents as Pastor Herbert Posth of Berge. Just as certainly, there was no one in the district who was more principled in his refusal to tolerate National Socialist values or terminology within the church. Posth criticized the religious nationalism that so many of his fellow pastors succumbed to, and fought more stubbornly than anyone else in the district to ensure that Confessing Church pastors and vicars served in the parishes he supervised. Like Günther Harder and others, Herbert Posth was briefly arrested after reading the outlawed Confessing Church pulpit declaration from the Second Prussian Confessing Church Synod in March 1935.

The Berge parish pastor demonstrated the same resolve in reading a subsequent Confessing Church pulpit declaration on August 23, 1936. After the Brandenburg Provincial Church Committee issued a ban against reading the declaration, Interim Superintendent Otto Schmidt from Flatow immediately telegrammed ten Confessing Church pastors across the district to warn them. However, as the organist in Lietzow reported, Pastor Posth read out the prohibited pulpit declaration in church anyway and also neglected to intercede for the Führer during the closing prayer.[14] Posth was jailed once more in 1937—this time for almost a month—for failing to turn over church collections to the Prussian church authorities.

Posth's perseverance in the face of Prussian Church pressure was best illustrated by his exploitation of the administrative authority he exercised in the vacant Ribbeck parish, which he turned into a bastion for the Confessing Church. In Ribbeck, Posth enjoyed the support of the majority of parishioners and the church patron, Erich von Ribbeck, who was himself a member of the Confessing Church. An important product of these close relationships was the May 1937 decision of the Ribbeck parish council to lead their parish into membership in the Confessing Church. As the parish councilors discussed and then accepted Posth's seven-point decision paper, they found themselves in agreement with several of his Confessing Church assertions. They agreed that the Old Prussian Union Church had adopted un-Protestant teaching and practices in 1933, that the Protestants who opposed the teachings and practices that contradicted the Bible and Reformation Confessions had congregated as the Confessing Church, and that the Confessing Church was the only legitimate church leadership. In response, they pledged to support Confessing Church institutions with their finances. While their decision did not bind Ribbeck parishioners as individuals, the parish council never could have acted without the support of the patron and a significant portion of the local church community behind them.[15]

Although Posth and his Confessing Church influence in Ribbeck irritated officials in the Brandenburg Consistory, the personnel shortage in the Nauen district ensured that they had little choice but to leave him in charge of Ribbeck. That changed in 1937, however, when Walter Pachali was appointed pastor in nearby Retzow. Pachali supported the Confessing Church but did not become a formal member because he preferred to remain under the authority of the Old Prussian Union Church government. As the consistory attempted to transfer authority in Ribbeck from Posth to Pachali, a protracted war of wills began.

This contest started when the Brandenburg Consistory demanded that Posth give up control of the Ribbeck parish by the end of September 1938, a demand they repeated in mid-October after Posth refused to comply. It was then that Mayor Stackebrandt from the neighboring town of Groß Behnitz entered the fray. An enemy of the Confessing Church, Stackebrandt filed a complaint against the illegal decision of the Ribbeck parish to join the Confessing Church. The consistory agreed with Stackebrandt and declared that the confessional mandate of pastors did not give them freedom to set aside the legal authority of the Old Prussian Union Church. Posth's pastoral freedom of conscience applied only to his preaching, they argued, which they agreed ought to be based on the Bible and Reformation Confessions.[16]

As in so many of the conflicts between German Christian church authorities and Confessing Church pastors, Prussian church officials persistently distinguished between the external ecclesiastical administration, which could be altered, they argued, and the internal spiritual life of the church, which should not be violated. This was a bifurcation of the church that Posth and other Confessing Church pastors fundamentally rejected. Unrelenting in his commitment, Posth refused to give up his administrative control of the Ribbeck parish. His reply to the consistory's agreement with Stackebrandt's complaint was a full-scale essay explicating Posth's most fundamental church-political positions, a blistering attack on the theology and practices of the Old Prussian Union Church government.

Posth rejected the view that Ribbeck's membership in the Confessing Church was "unconstitutional and legally inoperative." Turning the matter on its head, he argued that it was the Confessing Church that upheld law and order in the church, unlike the unlawful and heterodox German Christians in charge of the Old Prussian Union Church. He stood on the Confessing Church's Barmen Declaration of 1934, challenging consistorial officials to explain what was unconstitutional about it. And he based his refusal to give up control of the Ribbeck parish on the decision of the Sixth Prussian Confessing Church Synod, which forbade returning authority for the administration of parishes to an ecclesiastical bureaucracy not bound to the Reformation confessions. To do so, Posth argued, would amount to a breach of his vow of ordination, in which he pledged to uphold the Bible and Reformation Confessions. Posth acknowledged that the Bible did not legislate the external shape of the church, but argued that both the Bible and the confessions provided boundaries defining what could and could not be done in the church. With that in mind, Posth pointed to Article 28 of the Augsburg Confession, which mandated disobedience as a response to any episcopal teaching or action that violated the gospel, an idea reiterated in the Reformation-era Schmalkaldic Articles. For Posth, the Bible and Reformation Confessions remained the measure of church leadership, and his judgment that the Prussian church authorities had departed from them constituted legitimate grounds to disobey their orders to hand the administration in Ribbeck over to Pastor Pachali of Retzow.[17]

Posth also criticized the consistory's use of political force to compel obedience within the church. This he based on Matthew 20:25-26, where Christ contrasted selfish worldly leadership with selfless spiritual leadership. Posth also added a reference to Article 15 of the Augsburg Confession, which teaches that human traditions are unnecessary and potentially dangerous additions to the gospel. If that wasn't enough, he cited the formulas for pastors' and elders' oaths in the 1922 and

1933 church constitutions, in order to reiterate that the Bible and Reformation Confessions formed the basis for not only the teaching but also the work and the community life of the church—in other words, for all conduct within the church. For Posth, political methods were simply not welcome in the ecclesiastical realm.

Posth continued his diatribe against his critics in the consistory by pointing out that it was the duty of church leaders to ensure the preaching of the pure gospel. Falling back once more on the Schmalkaldic Articles, Posth affirmed the principle of establishing new church leadership where the existing one failed to provide for the preaching of the gospel, and he cited the injunction to ordain "capable" people for church offices. As Posth pointed out, these same historic confessions formed the basis for the Barmen and Dahlem Declarations of 1934, as well as all subsequent Confessing Church declarations. Citing Article 7 of the Augsburg Confession, he contended that that pure teaching would unite the church and that it was the duty of every church leader, from the highest authorities down to the local pastors and parish councilors, to keep watch over that purity of teaching. "Precisely here, the church leadership today is failing at all levels," he judged. As proof, he reminded the consistory of its angry denunciation of a decision he had made one time to block the visit of a pastor who "speaks openly against the confession of the church—thus against the gospel."

Rooted in this understanding of church as the outgrowth of the pure preaching of the Bible under the guidance of the Reformation Confessions, Posth launched into a fundamental critique of the German Christian concept of a German national church.

> The opinion (that) the church should "promote the life of faith of the members of the nation" contradicts the clear Word of God in a dual sense. It amounts to disobedience against the Word of Christ to preach the gospel to *all* nations—the word *member of the nation* [*Volksgenosse*] is not a church word at all, but rather a political word—and to all races. It would also show an infinite lack of love towards all the people for whom the Lord has also shed his blood.

In other words, scriptural and confessional integrity demanded the application of Christ's atonement for all people, not only Germans.

Posth identified a second sense in which the idea of a national church was a violation of the Bible, based on the apostle Paul's teaching in 1 Corinthians 2 that the natural person does not understand the Spirit of God. Since people could not come to true faith in God through nature—in other words, through their national or racial identity—Posth argued that the consistory was adopting an unacceptable hybrid of faith in Germanness and faith in God:

> The gospel is no psychological "help" for a naturally pious feeling, but rather is the preaching of the *judgment* of the holy God over an entire sinful nature—that means the cross of Christ too!—and of *grace* for the sake of Christ. It

is unintelligible to me how a church authority can say that the gospel says nothing about what is good and evil, just and unjust. If human reason alone has to determine order in the church, then I am justified without the appeal to the Scripture and confession! Then with what right can the church authorities punish disobedience—unjustified as well? Then everyone has a right; that leads to the destruction of *all* order whatsoever.

Simply put, Posth was arguing that if the Bible and confessions alone were not the basis for human salvation and the life in church, then no basis existed at all, and every decision was arbitrary and the church would devolve into nothing more than a chaos based on raw power.

Posth's final objection to handing over administrative authority in Ribbeck to the Brandenburg Consistory stemmed from this aversion to political power in the church. He asserted that the state must not be allowed to decide religious truth for the church, for that would violate Article 28 of the Augsburg Confession, which asserts that ecclesiastical authority comes solely through the preaching of Scripture and the administration of the sacraments, and that the civil power has no authority to interpret Christian truth from the Word of God. He also noted that political interference in the church would contradict the words of political leaders in the period after 1918, when they had given up control of the German Protestant regional churches.

Given Posth's principled opposition to the Brandenburg Consistory, relations between the Ribbeck parish and ecclesiastical authorities in Berlin had grown quite tense, since Posth would not give up his administrative authority and the consistory would not recognize him. Interim Superintendent Ulrich Bettac was caught in the middle of what Posth bemoaned as "a real juridical curiosity!" As Posth complained to Bettac, "I am supposed to respond, but my statement is of no legal consequence; the parish council is supposed to respond, but it is invalid without the chairmanship of [Pastor] Pachali. What now? I see absolutely no juridical possibility!"[18]

Still, Posth continued to argue for a fundamental settlement of the Ribbeck administrative deadlock. While he was in no mood to compromise, the struggle weighed on him, cost him hundreds of hours of time, and led to repeated confrontations with his ecclesiastical superiors: "I am forever disheartened for the sake of our church! How long will it still last, until this demon is overcome. It is all pointless, if no one takes a good look at the question of *truth*, as we see it." As frustrated as he was about his poor relations with Prussian church authorities, however, Posth refused to compromise his belief in the truth of the Confessing Church cause.

In 1939, the Brandenburg Consistory adopted a new approach to the intransigence of Posth and other Confessing Church clergy. Hoping to avoid long arguments over the relationship between the Bible, the Reformation Confessions, and Prussian church policy, it appointed an official from its finance department, Gustav-Adolf Hoppe, as financial plenipotentiary for Ribbeck. Hoppe immediately

informed the Ribbeck parish treasurer that Pastor Posth was prohibited from any
further financial management in Ribbeck and was not even allowed to receive
information about the state of the accounts.[19]

Hoping to prevent the transfer of authority in Ribbeck from the Confessing
Church to the German Christians in the Brandenburg Consistory, Posth countered
with a proposal to place his Confessing Church colleague, Pastor Kurt Fritzsche
of Groß Behnitz, in charge of Ribbeck. Financial Plenipotentiary Hoppe declared
himself "completely uninterested" in the idea. Refusing to give up, Posth entered
into a war of wills with Hoppe for control of the Ribbeck parish finances, which
lasted from May 1939 until April 1940. Hoppe demanded that Posth hand over all
the records, submit receipts for every disbursement, cease using the pastoral bank
account to finance a local print mission project, and (most contentiously) submit
the weekly church collections. Posth refused. Over time, relations between Posth
and Hoppe deteriorated so badly that the finance department of the Brandenburg
Consistory formally requested that the political authorities in Potsdam provide
a law enforcement officer to force Posth to hand over the Ribbeck finances. To
strengthen their case against Posth, the consistory noted that he had already been
jailed once before "for statements hostile to the state."[20]

Once again Posth justified his resistance to Hoppe's authority, this time in a long
letter on July 8, 1939, in which he advanced three main arguments. First, he leaned
on the support he had from the elders and patron in Ribbeck, who had collectively
decided to follow the Confessing Church collection plan and to use the surplus funds
in the pastoral account to fund an outreach program for women and children.

Second, Posth appealed to the principle of freedom of conscience. He argued
that both the Bible and his vow of ordination prohibited him from complying with
Hoppe and the rest of the finance department of the consistory:

> When the state attacks [the vow of ordination], we must go to jail for the sake
> of this vow! But I consider it a bit much, when the *church* authorities want to
> cause the pastor to break his vow of ordination. It would be unheard of, if they
> were to coerce him to do that through the threat of force. How am I going to
> stand in the pulpit then! Either I keep my vow, which I have sworn before God
> and the parish—as long as God gives me the strength to take upon myself all the
> trouble that results from that too—or I must resign my pastorate. At this point,
> things revolve around the ultimate tie of conscience in our office! A threat from
> the church authorities does not release me from my vow![21]

By reducing the church-political issues to their theological roots, Posth was
able to employ the argument of conscience to deny Hoppe's demands.

Third, Posth defended himself by attacking Hoppe's actions as un-Christian:
"The parish and every church member are also bound by God's Word! We all,

even *you* as a Protestant Christian, are *bound*. We have no freedom *against* God's Word!" Posth went on to argue that Hoppe's obedience to his superiors in the finance department was governed by the teaching of the Bible as defined by Article 29 of the Augsburg Confession, which commanded disobedience to ecclesiastical demands that violated the Word of God. Boldly, Posth argued that Hoppe was just as responsible for the proper use of church collections as any pastor or congregation.

In making his case, Posth leaned on the support of the Ribbeck parish: "The *parishioners* have learned well in the collection war that they may only give their gifts for the likes of the *real* gospel." Posth informed Hoppe that his parishioners had decided to give "not a penny of collection!" for official church offerings. The fact that Posth had such strong support from his parishioners meant that if Hoppe pressed the matter, the collections would simply stop. By regularly referring back to his parish council, his patron, and his parishioners, Posth reminded the Prussian church authorities that he was not simply acting of his own accord. His strategy illustrates the way in which pastors could afford to sever their relationships with the Old Prussian Union Church government, as long as they maintained their support base in the local church community.

And so the standoff between Posth and Hoppe continued. For every new argument Hoppe raised, Posth was ready with a principled theological answer. When Hoppe warned Posth about the potential consequences of his defiance, Posth retorted, "A pastor does not act according to any kind of consequences, but according to his vow of ordination! I have considered all the consequences, but I *must* not act in any other way, as I must act in *commitment* to *God's Word!*" Decrying the use of state power within the church, Posth even dared to criticize Dr. Friedrich Werner, the German Christian president of the Old Prussian Union Church, whose policies Posth described as "against *God's law*" and "ecclesiastically intolerable." Posth noted that Werner might get his way, with the help of the state, but reiterated that his policies "destroy the church and . . . build nothing!"

By this point, Posth had whipped himself into a real fury. He declared to Hoppe that if the present policy continued, the Protestant church would die in Germany within the year. The consistory, he explained, "seems not to have the faintest idea . . . what a terrible crisis of conscience now lies upon individual parishioners!!!" Dazzled by political power and lost in its "ignorance," the consistory was plunging "daggers into the *consciences* of the *parishioners*!!!" The result, argued Posth, would be the falling away of many shaken parishioners, while the small band of loyal parishioners left over would survive the removal of churches, parsonages, property—even the absence of pastors. Posth stated, "We shake our heads [in disbelief] over the illusion that people still ought to accept such measures as positive for the future of the church." Again, Posth was able to press his case because he was confident of the support of his parishioners. Ultimately, he believed that the faithful Christians of Ribbeck would withdraw completely from the Old Prussian Union Church if its leaders continued to oppose the law of God.

By the middle of August 1939, the dispute between Pastor Posth and Financial Plenipotentiary Hoppe had deteriorated to the point where Posth hid the parish records and began actively to disrupt Hoppe's work. Ironically, although Posth had previously condemned the use of political force in the church, he now informed Hoppe that political force would be the only way the consistory would ever obtain the Ribbeck records and added that the consistory would "surely forfeit any respect" in the parishes of Brandenburg if it coerced its pastors to violate their vows of ordination by collecting offerings for a heretical Prussian church government. When the Second World War began in September 1939, Hoppe and his colleagues in the consistory had still not achieved a solution to the dilemma in Ribbeck. Hoppe continued to accuse Posth of insubordination, of neglecting parish work, of siphoning funds from Ribbeck for the use of the Confessing Church, of squandering money, and of violating the prohibition on church services during wartime blackouts. For his part, Posth rejected all these accusations, calling them "stupid," "rash," and "terribly stupid." In his rebuttal, Posth compared Hoppe's demand to that of some NSDAP local group leader collecting money for the party and then using some of it for the Communist cause. As he asked Hoppe, "Shall we really use our money for the enemy of our Protestant faith, for the German Christians?" Ultimately, as Posth made explicit, he and the parishioners at Ribbeck "call ourselves a Confessing Church, because we want to remain subordinate to the confession."[22]

Frustrated by Posth's intransigence, Hoppe filed a report with the finance department of the Brandenburg Consistory in April 1940, in which he reminded his superiors once more that Posth had been investigated once before by the Gestapo, with the implication that it might be appropriate to do so again.[23] On the other side, Posth's allies were also growing weary of the increasingly bizarre church-political battle over Ribbeck. The Brandenburg Confessing Church Council encouraged Posth to settle the financial controversy in Ribbeck, hoping that one of the young Confessing Church pastors could be appointed in Ribbeck and bring peace to the parish.[24] Ultimately, however, Posth persevered and got his way. Until 1941, Posth continued in his role of supervising pastor in Ribbeck, at which time he passed the administrative authority over to Pastor Kurt Fritzsche of Groß Behnitz, *his* choice. For all Posth's insubordination, there is no local record of any disciplinary action against him in this matter. Through sheer stubbornness and the support of the patron and parishioners in Berge and Ribbeck, Herbert Posth had managed to overcome the administrative pressure of the Brandenburg ecclesiastical authorities for much of the 1930s.

Günther Harder and Herbert Posth both displayed the strength of character (and in Posth's case at least, the mulishness) to refuse to compromise their biblical, theological, and church-political convictions, even when that meant running afoul of the Brandenburg Consistory. Others in the Nauen district were not so willing to break with the Prussian church authorities, because they believed that they could accomplish more by working *within* the existing church government, even if it was corrupt and misdirected. Ulrich Bettac, pastor in Beetz and twice interim superintendent in Nauen, was the leading proponent of this church-political orientation. More interested in settling disputes than in creating them, Bettac worked to smooth over the ruffled relations between pastors like Harder and Posth and the Brandenburg Consistory. For the most part, Bettac was successful and increasingly won the trust of clergy from both the Confessing Church and the neutral camp in Nauen, albeit at the cost of separating himself from German Christians, who wanted no part of Confessing Church "illegalities." It is no exaggeration to conclude that without Bettac's aid, Harder and Posth would not have been able to hold their parishes so effectively for the Confessing Church. In short, Bettac's mediation consistently created the space for the radical Confessing Church clergy to function effectively.

Initially, Bettac's choice as interim superintendent in 1936 was a curious one, because he came from the ranks of the Confessing Church. An early member of the ecclesiastical opposition, Bettac was even jailed briefly in March 1935 for refusing to submit some church collections to the consistory. As time went on, however, Bettac consciously placed himself in the church-political center, allying himself not only with the Confessing Church but also with neutrals who stayed in the Old Prussian Union Church.[25]

If his rejection of church-political extremism kept Bettac from full-fledged membership in the Confessing Church, his demand for theological orthodoxy and ecclesiastical independence drove him to support local Confessing Church pastors in their struggle to thwart a German Christian takeover of the Nauen district. This he accomplished in three ways: by advancing pastoral candidates who would support the Confessing Church in their parishes, by transforming the divisive monthly pastoral conferences into informal "brotherly get-togethers" which drew in neutral and Confessing Church clergy, and by opposing German Christian clergy in interpersonal conflicts among pastors in the Nauen district.

As interim superintendent, Ulrich Bettac played a key role in all pastoral appointments in the Nauen district between 1936 and 1940, and again after 1943. In no fewer than six parishes, he actively supported pastoral candidates who would defend the theological positions of the Confessing Church while continuing to recognize the administrative authority of the Prussian church authorities. In other parishes, including Nauen itself, he opposed German Christian pastoral candidates for vacant positions.

The second means by which Bettac undermined German Christian interests in the Nauen church district was his authority over the monthly pastoral conferences of district clergy. He repeatedly invited alienated Confessing Church pastors, despite the fact that they rejected the authority of the Prussian Church government, including his own authority as interim superintendent. When Confessing Church pastors refused to attend the official pastoral convent, however, Bettac created an unofficial meeting called the "brotherly get-together." Excluding the radical German Christians, who he felt were not working for the good of the church, Bettac invited all moderates and members of the Confessing Church to the get-togethers, which became far more successful than the old conferences had been, notwithstanding the protests of local German Christians.

In his effort to unite local clergy, Bettac openly confessed his own church-political standpoint and did not shy away from broaching the subject with others. For instance, in his invitation to Vicar Böck, a newcomer to the Staffelde parish, Bettac explained that the brotherly get-together (for Böck, he called it a "Confessing Church convent") was meant for both members and friends of the Confessing Church, as well as neutral clergy. Bettac added that he hoped that Böck was not leaning toward the German Christians and that he would join the other pastors and vicars who met under Bettac. Explaining his own position, Bettac wrote: "Openly, I would like to inform you that I belong to the mild Confessing Church orientation, and for that reason I also take part in the [official Old Prussian Union Church] and take the position that we all must build a common front against the German Christians, in order to save our church. I would be delighted if you stood the same way."[26]

Finally, Bettac advanced the cause of the Confessing Church by opposing the German Christian Movement and taking up conflicts against German Christian clergy. In the midst of the period in which he strove to shut out German Christian pastoral candidates throughout the Nauen district, Bettac became increasingly frustrated with the political methods of the movement. Writing to a colleague in a nearby parish, Bettac argued that the German Christians were destroying the church on behalf of the state. On another occasion, in late 1938, Bettac tried to convince Pastor Herbert Posth, a key member of the Confessing Church in the Nauen district, that it was a lesser evil for Posth and the Confessing Church pastors to recognize the legality of the district synod by nominating new members than to allow the German Christians to take over the district synod through inaction. Such a withdrawal from the system would only give the German Christians "the desired opportunity to destroy the church." It was better, Bettac reasoned, to use the local superiority of the Confessing Church in the Nauen district to control the official church organs than to let them be controlled by a minority of German Christian opponents. It was this pragmatic approach to the Church Struggle that made Bettac an effective interim superintendent and allowed him to maintain good relations with most of those around him, save for the radical German Christians, who denounced his willingness to deal with the Confessing Church.[27]

In fact, during his time as interim superintendent, Bettac opposed any change in church practice that he felt was church-politically motivated. He was reticent to swear an oath of allegiance to Hitler and opposed the regulations that banned confessional meetings outside churches. Further, when the consistory suggested that superintendents in Brandenburg should consider working to make their parish councils younger, Bettac was quick to voice the mistrust of his constituency. He suggested that the consistorial proposal was probably another element of interference connected to the Church Struggle, since older parish councilors were more immune to German Christian innovations. Bettac noted that one of the reasons there were few younger men committed to the churches was the ruling opinion among members of the NSDAP, including German Christians, that the church was a relic institution filled with old people out of step with the National Socialist movement.[28]

By 1938, relations between local clergy from the German Christian and Confessing Church camps had grown decidedly cool, and Bettac found it increasingly difficult to hold the middle ground of compromise in the Church Struggle. Under attack from German Christians, he began to side more and more openly with the Confessing Church. Ardent German Christians grew frustrated with this and lumped Bettac in with the Confessing Church pastors accused of insufficient loyalty to the Old Prussian Union Church. In February 1938, for instance, German Christian pastor Georg Gartenschläger of Bötzow took Bettac to task for failing to encourage the district synod to approve Gartenschläger's recent request for funds. He accused Bettac of undermining his application for funds by not speaking directly enough in his favor. Such a petty objection is understandable in light of earlier unsuccessful attempts by Gartenschläger to get funding from Bettac and the Nauen district synod, both of whom were cool to his German Christian extremism.

Gartenschläger then raised another complaint, which cut straight to the heart of the German Christian frustration with Confessing Church clergy. It came in the context of Gartenschläger's opposition to a request for funds for youth work submitted by Pastor Herbert Posth of Berge:

> As far as I know, Pastor Posth does not support the legal church government. The attitude of Pastor Posth gives rise to the suspicion that he carries on youth work, in a way that creates difficulties with the political authorities. As the responsible district youth pastor, I must therefore object to a financial contribution to him.[29]

Similarly, Posth's request for aid for a kindergarten in Ribbeck raised the ire of Gartenschläger. He asked whether Posth was authorized to sign such a request, since "according to the information of the consistory, Pastor Posth is not responsible for Ribbeck." Rather than work with the Confessing Church pastors and accept their refusal to work with the Prussian church authorities unless it suited them, Gartenschläger and other German Christians simply dismissed their Confessing Church colleagues as lawbreakers.

Even among colleagues with whom he was on good terms, Interim Superintendent Bettac found it difficult to navigate the stormy church-political waters of the later 1930s. Early in 1939, for instance, Bettac's concern over religious conditions in Germany surfaced in an exchange of letters with his friend and colleague Pastor Konrad Isleib of Hakenberg. Their debate reveals much about the turmoil within the Church Struggle, since the two pastors could not even agree on what the most important issues facing German Protestants were. For Isleib, recent experiences in Berlin led him to believe that the most pressing question for the church was unity. The "essential aim," he explained, was "to establish a unifying band which encompasses the individual church groups, in order to have a Protestant church for our nation which is at least externally united, and to a great extent [internally] unified, a church that our nation and Fatherland need and that our Führer expects from us." Isleib believed his day was a time in which the German church would either "bend or break," and it pained him that so many pastors failed to see this truth. He argued that his colleagues should greet any step toward unity no matter where it came from, then negotiate any matters of conscience that divided Protestants from one another, particularly if the divisions were related to the external aspects of the church, where the state had an interest in change. Isleib argued that many so-called matters of conscience did not even touch on personal faith concerns, and he felt they could be set aside, especially in the wake of a mass movement of pastors toward such a "unifying, powerful, and clearly and joyfully decisive deed" as the creation of a German Reich Church. In sum, nothing mattered more to Isleib than uniting the divided German Protestant church, and not least for political reasons: "The civil war and the disunity must be overcome. We must come out of the paralyzing ecclesiastical discord and fruitless battle of groups; we must come to a clear relationship between church and state."[30]

While Bettac agreed with Isleib's desire to come together "under a common roof with the various church groups," he refused to work with the radical Thuringian German Christians, whether they were local pastors or officials in the Berlin church administration. Bettac argued that Isleib did not see the kernel of the situation clearly enough: "The state wants to sharply divide the spiritual leadership and the administration of the church, as the [church] finance department demonstrates." Bettac then perceptively outlined for Isleib two situations in which a state-controlled church administration could easily interfere with the spiritual leadership that Isleib believed was a separate realm: first, if the Brandenburg Consistory decided to send a curate to a desperate rural parish but the financial department refused to grant the funds for some reason or other; and, second, if local political authorities decided to sell the land that generated the income for the organist and instead pay the organist out of pocket, it would not be in their interest to see many extra worship services, given the extra expense. Bettac insisted that the spiritual leadership of the church needed to control the church administration or else it would be powerless. Explaining that "the finance department, in other words the state," was already enmeshed in the church, Bettac then bemoaned, "This state declares that it is not and does not want to be Christian." He went on to ask how a union of state and church could possibly be achieved, as long as the state kept advancing its totalitarian claims over everything, the church included. Reflecting on these problems, Bettac lamented: "Here lies the enormous difficulty, and not in the questions of faith. God help us and our church!"[31]

In his desire for a middle ground between the outlawed Confessing Church and the destructive German Christians, Bettac was willing to cooperate with the Brandenburg Consistory, local neutrals, and even moderate German Christians, as long as the result served the ministry of the church according to its traditional basis of Scripture and the Reformation Confessions, so that Protestants in the Havelland suffered as little disruption to parish life as possible. Though he was successful most of the time, he often found himself under attack from the radical Thuringian German Christians of Nauen and their leader, Pastor Friedrich Siems.

As a German Christian leader and NSDAP member, Pastor Friedrich Siems was a fervent nationalist, anti-Bolshevik, and anti-Semite, as evidenced by his speeches, sermons, and correspondence. In Nauen, much of his energy was expended in the vain attempt to win the appointment of a second German Christian pastor in the Nauen parish. Siems was a contentious character who often exasperated his colleagues in the Nauen district and stirred church-political passions with his radical German Christian ideology. In October 1937, for instance, Siems rashly filed a grievance against Interim Superintendent Bettac over a dispute in a pastoral conference. The disagreement started after Vicar Stehmann offered an effective, theologically complex rejoinder to a lecture by German Christian pastor Werner Andrich on the essence and mission of Christianity in the old German Reich. The younger Siems plunged into a debate with the older Stehmann, whereupon Stehmann asked Siems how he could reconcile his ideas with his vow of ordination. Siems angrily packed his bag and left, uttering some kind of retort to Stehmann. That very day, Siems filed an official complaint against Bettac for not censuring Stehmann during the debate.[32]

Interim Superintendent Bettac was highly critical of both Siems's outburst at the pastoral conference and the hasty letter of complaint that followed. Calling the grievance "laughable" and "grotesque," Bettac pointed out that Siems should have known to wait twenty-four hours before writing up such a complaint and added that if anyone had acted so as to justify a grievance, it was Siems himself, for walking out on the pastoral conference without justification. The other pastors in the conference agreed with Bettac, and even Curate Wallmann of Bötzow, who also left the conference in support of Siems, could not understand why the Nauen pastor had lost his temper.

Siems's combative nature led him into another dispute with Bettac in 1939, in which he again filed a complaint against the interim superintendent. This time, Siems took offense at Bettac, who had accused Siems of failing to book an organist for a church service Bettac held for the Nauen Women's Aid and then lying about it. Siems lashed out at Bettac and also accused Mrs. Krüger, leader of the Women's Aid, of spreading rumors about him around the parish. After Bettac repeated his assertion that Nauen pastor Siems was not telling the truth over the matter of the organist, Siems filed a complaint with the Brandenburg Consistory (again, on the same day that the insult had reached him). In response to inquiries from Berlin, Bettac simply explained that Siems had lied about arranging for an organist and that the organist had confirmed that fact in the presence of witnesses. Bettac also tried to convince the consistory to demand that Siems change his behavior and drop the matter, which Siems had since brought before a civil arbitrator. In turn, Siems accused Bettac of more misunderstandings and wrote two more letters of protest to the consistory in Berlin. By this time, two months after the original events, the dispute had devolved into a series of mutual insults and slander that completely soured what was left of the relationship between Siems and Bettac. There is no record that the consistory ever decided the affair, and the two men carried their argument across into the struggle over the appointment of new clergy in Nauen.[33]

In that context, Siems lost his temper once more in January 1940, when he wrote a nasty letter replying to a complaint filed by Carl Quehl of the Nauen district synod executive against the election of German Christian pastoral candidate Gustav Gille in Nauen. Siems accused Quehl of waiting until he was away from Nauen (at the battlefront) to send the complaint to the Brandenburg Consistory. He also took exception to Interim Superintendent Bettac's recent complaint that German Christian curate Erich Schröder was regularly referred to as "Pastor Schröder" in the newspaper, although *pastor* was not a rank that he had reached. Siems ranted that Bettac ought not to waste his precious time on details if he wished to promote the welfare of the Nauen Protestant church. Threatening further action in the future, Siems instructed Bettac, "It would be better for you and the future of the church if you would change your methods."[34]

Carl Quehl wrote a forceful reply to Siems, mocking Siems's notion that he was intimidated by the young pastor's presence and waited to file his complaint against Gille. Quehl reminded Siems that he expected an objective response to his grievance from Siems. He then opined that Siems lacked the ability to deal objectively with matters and had to resort to "laughable threats" instead. After commenting, "always the same methods," Quehl reminded Siems how he had failed to answer Vicar Stehmann objectively in the Nauen pastoral conference (three years earlier!). Recalling Siems's complaint that Interim Superintendent Bettac had not protected him in the debate against the vicar, Quehl corrected Siems: "No, you should have protected yourself and your own affairs!" Reopening the old wound, Quehl asserted that Siems had left the pastoral conference only because he had been unable to answer Stehmann in the debate.[35]

Returning to the current controversy, Quehl attacked Siems's pretensions and lack of pastoral ability. In response to Siems's reference to "my parish,"

Quehl suggested that Siems consider the poor attendance at his services so he could understand whether or not he had a parish. Quehl also criticized the large advertisements Siems took out in the local newspaper. Finally, he stated that parishioners were demanding to hear the gospel, that they were not interested in Siems's substitute—indeed, 90 percent of the parishioners had already rejected Siems as a pastor. Wrapping up his attack, Quehl turned Siems's own threat on its head, suggesting that Siems change his approach and concentrate on serving the Nauen parish more effectively rather than fighting with his church-political opponents. This Siems refused to do. Rather, he continued to promote the German Christian cause and fight for the appointment of a like-minded pastor in Nauen, even from his post in the German army on the Eastern Front during the Second World War.

## Other Clergy in Nauen

Other pastors in the Nauen district were not as active in the local Church Struggle as Harder, Posth, Bettac, or Siems but still found themselves in trouble with NSDAP officials and higher church authorities. The three cases of Pastors Ewald Rehfeldt of Kremmen, Friedrich Rumpf of Schwante, and Martin Lehmann of Karwesee demonstrate the high level of political tension in rural Brandenburg and the ease with which clergy could fall in and out of political controversy.

Pastor Ewald Rehfeldt of Kremmen was accused of praising England during a confirmation class in May 1940, even though the class took place before the Battle of Britain had begun. Attacked by the Gestapo for "breaking the resolve for war," Rehfeldt made light of the affair in a letter to Interim Superintendent Bettac. Even so, the experience of appearing before the Gestapo had shaken him, and he commented soberly, "Woe to those who must go to Potsdam!" For six hours he had waited behind the iron doors, "tired, worn out, without food or cigars, with a hang-dog feeling in his chest," until the matter was settled. From that point on, declared Rehfeldt, he would only wish such a trip to Potsdam on his enemies.[36]

If Rehfeldt assumed the matter was closed, he was wrong. In fact, the National Socialist paper *Das Schwarze Korps* published a defamatory article against him on September 12, 1940. Entitled "St. Halifax and the Cubs," the article quoted Rehfeldt and then slammed him as a British lackey and a "sixth column of prayer." Only then was the story of Rehfeldt's action told: Rehfeldt had been teaching his confirmation candidates about merit and had reiterated that humans do not merit anything from God, just like "thirty-three generations of pastors" before him. Unfortunately, at that point Rehfeldt had chosen to use the war with England as an analogy. First, he got his students to affirm that they thought Germany merited a victory against England, and he asked them if they thought it was true that the English were scoundrels and that the Germans were the only good people. Having reminded his students of their stereotypes of superior Germans and inferior English, Rehfeldt went on to describe how the English could buy Bibles at newspaper kiosks, how there were Bibles on all English hotel night tables, and how trains in London stopped running during church services. Having stunned his students, Rehfeldt concluded briskly: "Now no Pharisaism, as if we are better. Before God, no one deserves the victory, not us and not them."[37]

The *Schwarze Korps* blasted Rehfeldt for assuming that he knew what the outcome of God's grace was and mocked him as a "motorcycle pray-er." Finally, it declared that Rehfeldt was the only one, the English included, who took British "pseudo-piety" seriously and mocked: "the Bible [as a cover for] the chamber pot, the Bible beside the smutty romance at the train station kiosk, the Bible in Chamberlain's hand."

Rehfeldt was understandably shaken and offended by the article, although it is hard to understand why he would have chosen to employ an analogy that exalted England, whose government had declared war on Germany. The Brandenburg Consistory excused Rehfeldt as a "simple country pastor" with a common faith, who had never given cause for complaint. It added, "We may assume that he has drawn from this incident the relevant lesson for his life."[38]

Another pastor whose words landed him in legal trouble was Friedrich Rumpf of Schwante. Sometime during and after October 1943, Rumpf twice criticized the National Socialist religious and military policies. Charged with defeatism, he was placed in custody, brought before the Special Court of Berlin on August 10, 1944, and sentenced to four years in prison. Fortunately for Rumpf, the court took into account his weak constitution and his tendency to utter emotional statements—both the result of combat in the First World War—and declined to issue the normal sentence for his crime, which was death. As a result of his conviction, Rumpf was dismissed from his pastorate and denied his pension. His wife received only a small monthly allowance in order to survive during his imprisonment.[39]

Along with Pastors Rehfeldt and Rumpf, Pastor Martin Lehmann of Karwesee was twice forced to answer for his words and actions in various Sunday services in Karwesee. First, in August 1937, Otto Bellin of Karwesee filed an official complaint against Lehmann with the Brandenburg Consistory, accusing his parish pastor of undermining National Socialist racial policy and attacking the state. Bellin charged Lehmann with deviating from the Nazi racial worldview and thereby making himself unfit to be a pastor, simply for stating, "Abraham is the father of our faith." Lehmann replied that Bellin had taken the statement entirely out of context and failed to comprehend that he was preaching about the distant past, not current racial policy. The legal committee in the Brandenburg Consistory agreed with Lehmann's explanation and also dismissed Bellin's accusation that Lehmann had not preached suitable sermons on particular church holidays over the two previous years.[40]

The legal committee did take Lehmann to task, however, for reading out lists of names of Confessing Church pastors who had been persecuted, imprisoned, or oppressed. Bellin had accused Lehmann of calling the affected clergy "martyrs," a term Lehmann denied using. Even so, the legal committee argued that the public reading of intercessory lists of imprisoned clergy, which was outlawed, came dangerously close to attacking the state. In a surprising twist of logic, however, the legal committee decided that since many Confessing Church pastors read outlawed lists of clergy for intercessory prayer and faced no disciplinary measures, neither should Lehmann. With that, they dismissed Bellin's grievance and Lehmann continued to read his lists of suspended or imprisoned Confessing Church clergy.

Suddenly, on September 12, 1941, the Gestapo detained Lehmann over the same issue of his public reading of intercessory lists of suspended and arrested Confessing Church clergy.[41] No formal charges were pressed against him, however, and he returned to work for the Confessing Church in Karwesee.

In conclusion, Nauen clergy from across the church-political spectrum participated passionately in a wide range of local ecclesiastical conflicts, from Confessing Church violations of Old Prussian Union Church authority to petty squabbles over personal insults. Invariably, these conflicts strained or severed relations between parish clergy, with church superiors, or with lay opponents within the parishes of the Nauen district. Nauen district pastors, curates, and vicars were not simply responding to the events of the Church Struggle in Berlin, events that are often never mentioned in local church correspondence. For Confessing Church pastors, engagement in the local Church Struggle was a matter of conviction and personal choice, although their vulnerability to church discipline or judicial persecution was also ameliorated by the support they enjoyed from patrons and parishioners. For German Christians, early success gave way to a frustrating marginalization within the parishes of the Brandenburg Church Province that they were supposed to control. That reality points to the most interesting conclusion about the participation of Protestant clergy from the Nauen district in their local version of the Church Struggle: Prussian Church authority was difficult to translate into local strength, and even the support of the local chapter of the NSDAP did not gain them power in the church. For local influence, they required the support of the committed Christians at the parish level, an asset they frequently lacked.

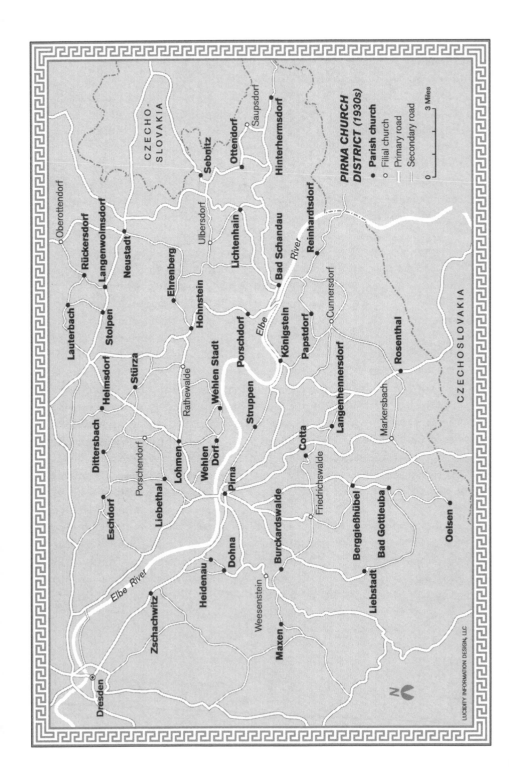

**PIRNA CHURCH DISTRICT (1930s)**

- Parish church
- Filial church
- Primary road
- Secondary road

0 — 3 Miles

CZECHO-SLOVAKIA

CZECHOSLOVAKIA

Oberottendorf
Rückersdorf
Langenwolmsdorf
Neustadt
Lauterbach
Stolpen
Helmsdorf
Stürza
Dittersbach
Eschdorf
Liebethal
Porschendorf
Lohmen
Wehlen Dorf
Rathewalde
Ehrenberg
Hohnstein
Wehlen Stadt
Porschdorf
Struppen
Pirna
Cotta
Friedrichswalde
Langenhennersdorf
Markersbach
Rosenthal
Cunnersdorf
Papstdorf
Königstein
Reinhardtsdorf
Bad Schandau
Lichtenhain
Ulbersdorf
Sebnitz
Ottendorf
Saupsdorf
Hinterhermsdorf
Elbe River
Heidenau
Zschachwitz
Dohna
Weesenstein
Maxen
Burckardswalde
Liebstadt
Bad Gottleuba
Berggießhübel
Oelsen
Dresden

Elbe River

N

LUCIDITY INFORMATION DESIGN, LLC

# chapter six

# The Church Struggle in Pirna, Saxony

 **In contrast to the rather localized Church Struggle in** the Nauen district in Brandenburg, events in the Pirna district were intimately tied to larger conflicts at the highest levels of the Saxon Lutheran Church. In May 1933, Maximilian Zweynert, the Pirna district superintendent, placed the question of church–state relations at the top of the local church agenda, announcing to the annual district church assembly that area pastors would work to the utmost of their ability to assist the "responsible work" of the new Nazi state toward the moral and national renewal of the German nation. As Zweynert explained, the Lutheran pastors would contribute by reviving Protestant church life in Saxony and helping to build a united Reich Church.[1]

In actual fact, however, by the time the Pirna superintendent spoke those words, the campaign to renew the Saxon Church was already well under way. The retirement of Lutheran bishop Ludwig Ihmels opened the door for radical Thuringian German Christians to demand immediate church elections for a new Saxon Synod. They expected a German Christian victory, which would pave the way for their candidate, Pastor Friedrich Coch, to become the new bishop and to lead the Saxon Lutheran Church boldly forward into the Third Reich. A new church-political group, the Association for Luther's Church in Saxony and in the Reich, backed this call for new church elections and committed itself to supporting Hitler's government by assembling all German Christians in a united, nationalist, Lutheran, and anti-Bolshevik church. An opposing group, the Positive Volk Church Union, argued that there was no need for a new church election, and that the existing Saxon Synod should choose Bishop Ihmels's successor. Saxon Nazis rejected this idea as antiquated and out of step with the new Germany: "Who, then, is the church?" asked the writers of their paper, the *Freiheitskampf*. "The church is not the 'consistory,' not the old Synod, not the pastors, not the 'Young Reformation Movement,' not the 'Association for a Lutheran Church,' not this association and not that union within the church, rather we, we *National Socialists* who belong to the nation and to the parish, we are the church."[2]

Such a public attempt to nazify the church was hard for Saxon Lutheran clergy to ignore, particularly since the NSDAP could mobilize masses of Protestants to vote for the German Christian Movement in a new church election. Not that Pirna pastors were unsympathetic to the Nazi point of view. Several of them were already party members by the time that Pastor Martin Rasch of Reinhardtsdorf made the decision to join the NSDAP in May 1933. Rasch hoped to make his Nazi loyalties clear and to support the party for its dramatic revival of German national spirit. Recognizing that the NSDAP doctrine of *positive Christianity* was at best unorthodox, he hoped to moderate the party by bringing Nazis into closer contact with Protestants who upheld traditional church confessions and stood wholly for the gospel. By joining the NSDAP, he believed he had found the path toward a "good solution to the unresolved church-political questions."[3]

Rasch and his colleagues around the Pirna district were deeply concerned about the growing church-political storm in Dresden, about which they received regular updates from Superintendent Zweynert. Indeed, tensions rose in the Saxon Church as National Socialists and German Christians took hold of the levers of power in the spring of 1933. National Socialist clergy were often the first to hear about the newest developments in the church crisis. In late June 1933, for instance, Pastors Paul Teichgräber of Pirna, Heinrich Leichte of Königstein, and Walter Börner of Ottendorf were all summoned to Dresden, together with about fifty other pastors from the National Socialist Pastors' League in Saxony. They met with Friedrich Coch and other leaders in the National Socialist Pastors' League, learning that Coch would soon be appointed as emergency bishop of Saxony—all this before any word about that eventuality had been transmitted through official church channels.[4]

And so it was. On June 30, Saxon interior minister Fritsch issued a Decree for the Removal of the State of Emergency in the Saxon Lutheran Church, which announced Coch as the Saxon Lutheran bishop and granted him emergency powers that combined the authority of the Saxon bishop, consistory, Church Committee, and Standing Synodal Committee—in short, complete legislative and executive power over the Saxon Lutheran Church. Almost immediately, Coch suspended most of the Saxon Consistory and several district superintendents, introducing a new set of executive assistants before an assembly of all Saxon clergymen, on July 6, 1933.

That same month, Coch began to formalize the radical centralization of ecclesiastical authority represented in his emergency powers. Pastors in Pirna and throughout Saxony were surveyed about proposed constitutional revisions designed to bring the Saxon Lutheran Church closer to the hierarchical, authoritarian administrative style favored in National Socialist Germany and captured in the term

*Führer principle*. Superintendent Zweynert asked Pirna clergy to consider simplifying local church elections, diminishing the powers of local synods, freeing higher church authorities to appoint new clergy with little or no local participation, centralizing church finances, and increasing the power of the Saxon bishop. While some pastors questioned these significant alterations to Protestant church polity, at least as many supported the proposals. German Christian pastor Ernst Ranft of Helmsdorf argued that the "strongest emphasis of the Führer principle is necessary, on account of the absence of insight in the broader church community," while Pastor Dr. Walter Leonard of Stolpen even argued that the Saxon bishop ought to be empowered to appoint new superintendents without any participation from the district church governing bodies.[5]

News of Coch's rise to power in the Saxon regional church unleashed a frenzy of celebratory newspaper articles and church services. The subsequent success of the German Christian candidates in the July 23 national church elections confirmed Coch's triumph. Three quarters of the delegates "elected" to Saxon parish councils through prearranged unity lists were National Socialists committed to following Coch. In turn, these parish leaders chose representatives to sit on the Saxon Synod, giving an overwhelming majority to members of the Association of National Socialist Pastors and the German Christian Movement. Despite this show of support, Bishop Coch never allowed the new Saxon Synod to meet. Rather, on August 8, Coch overrode the Saxon church constitution and began to rule personally and directly, according to the Führer principle.[6]

## Church-Political Conflict in Pirna

Coch's opponents in the Saxon Lutheran Church grew increasingly upset with his arbitrary rule. As a result, in late 1933 and early 1934, two new church-political organizations emerged in Saxony. The first of these was the Pastors' Emergency League, Martin Niemöller's national association committed to upholding the authority of the Bible and Reformation Confessions within the church. If necessary, its members were prepared to reject the authority of church leaders they believed to be heretical, men like Coch and German Reich bishop Ludwig Müller. The second organization was unique to Saxony. Unnamed at first but later known as the *Middle*, it united moderate Lutherans who rejected both the ultranationalist agitation of German Christians and the refusal of the Emergency League and Confessing Church to operate under the authority of the existing Saxon regional church government.[7]

Before long, the dramatic developments at the summit of the Saxon Lutheran Church reverberated down into the Pirna church district. By November 1933, clergy from around the district began to join the Pastors' Emergency League. Sharply critical of Bishop Coch and his administration, local members of the League also condemned the illegal, immoral, and coercive measures of German Christian leaders in the Reich Church government in Berlin.

The first official complaint about National Socialist influence within the church was filed by Walter Schumann of Hohnstein. Disgusted by the radicalism of the Berlin German Christians at the infamous Sport Palace rally of November 13, Schumann informed Superintendent Zweynert that he was refusing to display the Saxon regional church poster "With Luther and Hitler for Faith and Nationality" on his church door. The poster, Schumann explained, referred to an illegal application of racial criteria within the church, which he could not accept "in good conscience." Likewise, Pastor Gustav Carl of Cotta refused to display the offending poster, declaring that it invoked "the confession-violating Aryan Paragraph," which exiled non-Aryan pastors from Protestant churches.[8] In a tangible expression of his disapproval of the German Christian Movement, Schumann prohibited all its activities in his parish of Hohnstein. This decision sparked an immediate conflict with a neighboring pastor, Heinrich Leichte of Königstein, who served as a resource and leader for the German Christians in Schumann's parish. When Schumann heard that Leichte had protested to Superintendent Zweynert, he warned Leichte that any involvement with local German Christians would be interpreted as "an attack on the peace" in Hohnstein.

Zweynert replied to both Pastors Schumann and Carl, explaining that it was his duty to report their poster protest to the Saxon Church Office in Dresden, which would in turn lead to disciplinary measures. He added, however, that he would not immediately inform the ecclesiastical authorities about their letters, so that the two pastors had time to think about how they might avoid suspensions. In this important communication, Zweynert set the tone for his future dealings with these pastors and their colleagues in both the Pastors' Emergency League and the Confessing Church. Time and again, Zweynert turned a blind eye to the demands of Saxon church law, patiently tolerating disruptions and challenges to his authority. His aim was to give time and space for dissenting pastors to moderate their positions and abandon their unlawful defiance of higher church authorities. While he waited, Zweynert protected his dissidents from hostile German Christian officials in Dresden by delaying his responses to official correspondence and then, when forced to account for his pastors, by defending their character and downplaying their disobedience.

In the case of Schumann and Carl, Zweynert went so far as to advise the two pastors not to officially inform him of their decision but to direct their protests to the Saxon Church Office via the Pastors' Emergency League in Saxony, a more circuitous route that would delay consequences and enable Zweynert to avoid the kinds of direct confrontations that would only upset the church peace and force him to punish his pastors. This approach worked wonders in Pirna, keeping open the lines of communication between Zweynert and dissenting clergy. It was also perilously close to subversion and placed Zweynert in a very delicate position with his German Christian superiors.[9]

Indeed, Zweynert himself was starting to grow disenchanted with Bishop Coch, in part because Coch regularly accused opponents of disloyalty to the church, hatred of National Socialism, and insincerity toward Hitler and the Third Reich. In addition, Coch derided the appeal of churchmen to their consciences as the last vestige of an undesirable individualism, castigated opponents of the German Christians for overreacting to the Sport Palace speeches of November 1933, and accused his enemies of trying to thwart the creation of a German national church. Such harshness offended Zweynert, who was working hard to combine loyalty to the Nazi regime with faithfulness to the traditional teachings of Saxon Lutheranism.[10]

But traditional Lutheranism was not what Coch had in mind. Rather, Coch proclaimed an ecclesiastical revolution when he published his *28 Theses of the Saxon Volk Church for the Inner Establishment of the German Evangelical Church* as guidelines for the Saxon Lutheran Church. Lauded by the German Christians, the *28 Theses* attempted to unite Christianity and National Socialism by declaring that the German Protestant church stood *in* the state, as a national church (*Volkskirche*). Moreover, this national church understood race as the creation of God, professed its belief in German blood, and declared that only members of the racial community could be members. While the *28 Theses* called for the preaching of the gospel of Jesus, it also affirmed the divine authority of certain orders of life: family, nation, and state, all of which found their expression in the total claim of the National Socialist state. Though the foundation for this new national church was supposed to be the Bible and Reformation Confessions, the *28 Theses* did not regard the Old Testament as being equal to the New Testament in value. Rather, the Old Testament served as a warning of the way in which a people could continually wander from God, in spite of his repeated revelation. The Jews, it claimed, had committed the sin of falling away from God, a betrayal that culminated in the crucifixion of Jesus. Neither did the *28 Theses* accept the Reformation Confessions as absolute, but rather noted that they were historically bound up in the peculiar questions posed in the time of their writing: "Not back to the faith of our fathers, but forward *in* the faith of our fathers!"[11]

Disenchanted with Bishop Coch's *28 Theses* and his harsh response to the growing conflict in the Saxon Lutheran Church, Pirna superintendent Zweynert canceled his membership in both the Working Group of National Socialist Pastors and the National Missionary Movement of the German Christians. In letters to both organizations, he reiterated his support for Hitler's new political regime in Germany but rejected the National Socialist Pastors' slander of their opponents in the Pastors' Emergency League and denounced the refusal of German Christian leaders to distance themselves from the radicalism of the Berlin Sport Palace speeches of November 1933.[12]

More important still was the step Zweynert took in late December, when he wrote directly to Bishop Coch to tell him that Pirna pastors felt "depressed, joyless, and pessimistic" about church conditions in Saxony. Zweynert made it clear that this pessimism was not the result of any political disloyalty. Indeed, the superintendent felt that the negativity of Pirna clergy toward Coch's church government was "all the more distressing and critical because, as far as I know, all the clergy of the district deliberately and gladly profess themselves for the National Socialist state, and since the ablest and most zealous pastors are seized by this mood, and even Party members enter into it." Zweynert added that there was so much mistrust among local clergy, "that an open discussion of the unresolved problems within the community of pastors is virtually impossible."That Zweynert continued to harbor doubts about the politicization of the church by German Christians is clear from a letter written to one of his fellow superintendents, in which he bemoaned a decree banning the use of the name Church of the Atonement: "This decree has shaken me and filled me with great concern. If Church of the Atonement is no longer suited to the times, will Redeemer Church and Church of the Cross suffer the same fate, which logic would say they must suffer? Can anyone still answer for that in good conscience?"[13]

By the end of 1933, relations between parish clergy in the Confessing Church and the German Christian Movement were rapidly disintegrating. Pastor Martin Meinel of Bad Schandau bemoaned the inability of local pastors to fellowship together, even as he informed Superintendent Zweynert that he would not be coming to the year-end family get-together. Pastor Gotthelf Müller of Heidenau notified Zweynert that he was so offended by the German Christian Sport Palace assembly in Berlin that he had withdrawn from the movement. After a fruitless discussion with Saxon bishop Coch, Müller had promptly joined the Pastors' Emergency League.[14]

In his 1934 New Year's message to the Pirna pastors, Superintendent Zweynert confessed that the church-political situation in both Pirna and Saxony was confused and unclear. He called on God to direct the pastors and to lead the deeply divided group back together again into a trusting brotherhood. His next announcement betrayed the extent to which relationships among local pastors had soured: the usual Christmas pastoral conference was canceled "on account of the acute differences among the clergymen in the way they assessed the church-political situation." Sebnitz pastors Siegfried Meier and Karl Partecke replied to Zweynert's message, respecting his decision but asserting that Pirna clergy "must hold a [monthly district pastoral] conference immediately, so that we can come to a sense of community in spite of the opposing attitudes of individuals."[15]

Unfortunately, the sense of community that Meier and Partecke were looking for was nowhere to be found. Clergy in Pirna remained deeply divided both in 1934 and throughout the National Socialist era. A primary consequence of this division was the frequent cancellation of monthly pastoral conferences around the district from 1933 through 1936. The situation in Bad Schandau is illustrative: after positive meetings in November and December 1934, the Schandau conference was rocked in early 1935 by the decision of Pastor Heinrich Leichte of Königstein to file a formal complaint with the local NSDAP leadership against his colleague Pastor Walter Schumann of Hohnstein, a member of the Pastors' Emergency League. Leichte alleged that Schumann had uttered statements hostile to the state during the course of one of the monthly conference discussions. Adding insult to injury, Leichte acted long after the discussion in question had taken place and after he had shaken hands with Schumann and welcomed the Hohnstein pastor back from an earlier disciplinary suspension. By taking his complaint to a third party and making it public, Leichte had not only slandered Schumann but had also created the impression that the Bad Schandau conference was the source of "a reactionary mentality." As a result, the January 1935 Bad Schandau pastoral conference was canceled, and when the pastors met again in February, they did so as an unofficial gathering of clergymen. That way, the Emergency League pastors would come and Leichte would not have to be invited. "In this way we managed," explained Pastor Martin Meinel, "so that pastors in our circle did not lose contact with one another."[16]

In the meantime, Maximilian Zweynert and over a dozen of his fellow Lutheran superintendents were growing increasingly outspoken in their opposition to Saxon bishop Coch, demanding the reinstatement of two of their suspended colleagues, the withdrawal of legal measures and defamatory statements against the Pastors' Emergency League, and the repeal of the controversial 28 Theses. As Zweynert embraced the moderate path in Saxon church politics, he repeatedly shielded members of the Pastors' Emergency League from the disciplinary actions of the Saxon Church Office and tried to convince Pirna pastors from both church-political extremes to adopt his moderate stance.[17] He regularly added heartfelt personal messages to the ever-harsher orders he was forced to convey from Saxon Lutheran authorities to the parish clergy, urging his pastors to make peace with the official church. This was not only for the sake of the pastors but also to free the church from "the suspicion of having a fundamental attitude that is reactionary and hostile to the state, which currently hangs over it and hinders its effectiveness." Citing the need for personal sacrifices in the interest of ecclesiastical and national unity, Zweynert asked the pastors to end their program of opposition to the Saxon church government, either by working for the dissolution of the Pastors' Emergency League in Saxony or by withdrawing from it. While Zweynert's patient and personal approach did not persuade pastors to abandon the Emergency League—indeed, by April 1934 no fewer than eighteen area pastors were active in it—it did salvage the strained relationships among his clergy. Pastors' Emergency League members reminded Zweynert that they too "yearned most ardently for peace in the church," but explained that they felt compelled "to stand up for the cause of the gospel." In contrast to Zweynert's policy of compromise for the sake of peace, they reminded him that "there can only be peace and order which is rooted in truthfulness and in the spirit of the church."[18]

Around this same time, at the beginning of 1934, local police and political authorities began to intervene in Pirna parish life for the first time since several

Pirna SA members had arrested and humiliated Pastor Rudolf Peter in March of 1933. In January 1934, Pirna authorities prohibited Pastor Carl of Cotta from holding a church meeting they felt would disrupt the community—it is likely that Carl was organizing on behalf of the Pastors' Emergency League.[19] But while Nazi officials were disrupting parish life, local pastors did not seem to want to blame Hitler himself for their problems. For example, Pastor Walter Plotz wrote to the Saxon Church Office in January 1934, urging church leaders to intervene against a one-hundred-thousand-man march the SA was planning to hold in Pirna on Palm Sunday. Not only the beginning of the Easter week, Palm Sunday was also a confirmation Sunday, one of the most important and well-attended services of the entire church year. Plotz complained that Lutheran clergy had already given up the November 1933 Luther anniversary celebrations "for the sake of Germany, out of devotion to our Reich Chancellor Adolf Hitler [and with] hearts not wholly light." He did not want to see another important liturgical moment lost to political celebrations, especially when the church was supposed to be "the guardian of the Protestant cause and of Christian morals." Plotz demanded that Saxon Lutheran authorities act: "The more earnestly and truthfully I struggle each day for the blessing of God upon Hitler and his work, the more my right grows to not have my Protestant conscience and my evangelical sensibility shaken by his assistants."[20]

Pirna clergymen who belonged to the Pastors' Emergency League faced their first significant test that January 8, when they had to choose whether or not to read a prohibited pulpit declaration. The declaration criticized the Reich bishop for failing to denounce German Christian clergy for their scandalous Sport Palace assembly in Berlin the previous November. When Superintendent Zweynert requested reports from pastors who had read or posted the Emergency League declaration, seventeen pastors replied. Most had read out the pulpit declaration in their churches, though some had read out only parts or had added their own explanations to their parishioners.

Rather than immediately reporting these dissidents to his superiors, Superintendent Zweynert sent them an emotional appeal to abandon the Pastors' Emergency League, even as he acknowledged their criticisms of the Saxon regional church government. Several pastors replied to Zweynert in a similarly personal form, revealing their motives for participating in the Emergency League. Pastor Gotthelf Müller of Heidenau explained how his journey into the Emergency League began when he attended an NSDAP meeting that was held in conjunction with a church outreach project in the Pirna area. Müller went along to the Party event because he did not want to appear guilty of disunity but was dismayed at the answers that Protestant Nazis gave to the fundamental confessional question: "revelation in Christ or revelation in blood and race." Müller took direct aim at radical German Christians, arguing that they, not the Emergency League, were causing the unrest within the Saxon Lutheran Church. Franz Ploedterll responded similarly, arguing that even the lofty goal of German national unity was not more important than maintaining the purity of the gospel. He criticized the German Christians and their church government for preaching blood, race, and Germanic religion, for introducing the Aryan Paragraph to create an artificial, heretical racial segregation in the church, and for implementing the radical *28 Theses* in the Saxon Church. Pastor Klemm of Burkhardswalde employed similar language when he explained that he could not leave the Emergency League, because "we must, in purity and truth, seek to go the way that God leads us."[21]

To drive home the force of these individual replies, seventeen members of the Pastors' Emergency League from around the Pirna district signed a joint letter to Superintendent Zweynert on April 17, 1934. They thanked him for his recent letter and praised his sense of responsibility for the condition of the church, but countered with five reasons why they could not "*abandon the cause of the Pastors' Emergency League, for the sake of the church.*" Knowing that no one would believe that they had undergone a change of heart even if they quit the Emergency League, the pastors declared their intention to continue to work against the German Christians. Convinced that there could never be "'peace at any price' in the church, if it comes at the cost of truth and the confessions," they felt a duty from God to support their fellow Confessing Church pastors across Germany. Moreover, they believed that God was working for them, through the Reich Church Law of April 14, 1934, which prohibited new legal measures against members of the Pastors' Emergency League and instigated a review of all earlier judgments against them.[22]

By late April, however, the growing extremism of the Pastors' Emergency League was beginning to worry three of its member pastors from the southeast corner of the Pirna district: Pastors Martin Meinel of Bad Schandau, Martin Rasch of Reinhardtsdorf, and Gerhard Zweynert of Papstdorf, son of Superintendent Maximilian Zweynert. In an informal conversation with Superintendent Zweynert, they expressed their concern that their membership in the Emergency League would divide their congregations. In a subsequent letter to the three, the superintendent agreed with their concerns and added his own worry that it would also dishonor the church in the eyes of a growing majority of Germans. Zweynert warned the pastors about reports that reactionary laypeople were using the Emergency League as a cover for their opposition to the National Socialist state and urged them to withdraw from the Emergency League.[23]

Superintendent Zweynert's letter struck a chord with Pastors Meinel, Rasch, and Gerhard Zweynert, driving them back into discussions with one another and provoking them to question their Saxon Emergency League leader, Superintendent Hugo Hahn of Dresden. Their crisis of conscience was exacerbated by the fact that the Pastors' Emergency League was entering a new, more radical phase. Under the leadership of Lutheran bishops Hans Meiser of Bavaria, August Marahrens of Hanover, and Theophil Wurm of Württemberg, leading Protestant dissidents from the Emergency League met in the city of Ulm on April 22, 1934, and founded the Confessing Church as the "legal Protestant church of Germany."[24] One month later, on May 29 and 30, Reformed and Lutheran delegates met at the First Synod of the Confessing Church, at Barmen in Westphalia. There they approved the Barmen Declaration, rejecting the leadership of Reich Bishop Müller and the theological heresy of the German Christians.

In Pirna, the formation of the Confessing Church and its founding principle of rejecting the legitimacy of the existing church governments across Germany created a split among pastors who had belonged to the Emergency League. Most willingly joined the Confessing Church, but a few, including Pastors Meinel, Rasch, and Gerhard Zweynert were unwilling to make a complete break with the Saxon Lutheran Church and began to consider joining Superintendent Zweynert's growing group of church-political moderates.

Another significant event affecting local church conditions in Pirna was the May 4, 1934, decision of the Saxon Synod to integrate Saxony into the German Reich Church, under Reich bishop Ludwig Müller. The fledgling Confessing Church in Saxony immediately attacked this decision, arguing that the synod did not have the authority to make such a decision and insisting that the external structure of the church could not be changed without altering its internal confessional reality and therefore its spiritual vitality. In light of this opposition, Saxon bishop Coch made appointments to speak with Confessing Church clergy from each district, but the Confessing Church pastors from Pirna and seven other districts stood their ground and refused to speak with Coch, who they did not believe would honestly consider their concerns.[25]

The polarization of the Saxon Church made Pastor Martin Meinel of Bad Schandau so distraught that he published an open letter to all Lutheran clergy in Saxony, which he subtitled "What do we do now?"[26] In it, Meinel lamented the disunity among Protestants and challenged his colleagues to consider how they could minister to one another as "brothers," quickly adding, "and this word *must really not be a farce!!*" He contrasted the community spirit of early Christians, who were known for their love for one another, with the contentious relationship among the current "shepherds" of the Saxon Church. Prodding his colleagues to set aside their division, Meinel reminded them of all they had in common—not least their shared experience as soldiers in the Great War and their campaign against the red flag of Bolshevism during the 1918 revolution. Appealing to their sense of national community, he urged them to stand in the gap between the two sides of the Church Struggle, to care for one another, and to care for Saxon Lutherans. Wary that his fellow clergy might think of him as a political reactionary, Meinel let them know that he was a member of the NSDAP.

Meinel urged pastors to build themselves into a spiritual dwelling place for God, based on the principle "that Jesus Christ is the cornerstone." He set forth a four-point plan for peace in the Saxon Church, based on the centrality of the Bible and the Reformation Confessions, with monthly district pastors' conferences, a brotherly gathering of Saxon clergy under the spiritual ministry of Bishop Coch, the reinstatement of suspended clergy, and the withdrawal of all defamatory statements against church-political opponents. As he put it, "There can be no valuation of brothers in ministry as second-class Christians and second-class Germans." Meinel admitted that his ideas were only a beginning but confessed that he felt himself constrained by the Spirit of God to act. He argued forcefully for making unity and the restoration of Christian love the starting point for the settlement of the conflict in the Saxon Church, based on the message of Galatians 5:13: "Serve one another in love."

Meinel's open letter signaled a substantial shift in his church-political position and was soon followed by his resignation from the Pastors' Emergency League in July 1934. "After many inner struggles and after repeated discussions," Meinel and his two closest colleagues in ministry, Martin Rasch of Reinhardtsdorf and Gerhard Zweynert of Papstdorf, joined the growing *Middle* movement in the Saxon Church. Even so, both Meinel and Rasch feared that their decision would not improve conditions in the church significantly, and Rasch made it clear that "the concern for our church weighs heavy on our hearts, even as before." In his letter of withdrawal from the Emergency League, Rasch reiterated the predicament the three pastors found themselves in: "For months, we have found ourselves in an unbearable tension, because this [Emergency League] parish movement that leads to schism contradicts our National Socialist will for the unity of the nation."[27] Eventually, that tension overcame them, and they chose to pursue unity within the established church and harmony with their National Socialist political values, even at the cost of tolerating the infidelity of their ecclesiastical superiors to the Bible and Lutheran Confession of Faith.

If Pastors Meinel, Rasch, and Zweynert hoped to avoid church-political conflict for the sake of peace in their parishes, such was not the will of the other Emergency League pastors, who were growing increasingly determined in their opposition to the church governments of Saxon bishop Coch and Reich bishop Müller. In October 1934, Pastor Klemm of Burkhardswalde notified Superintendent Zweynert that local members of the Pastors' Emergency League would no longer recognize the authority of either the Reich or Saxon church governments, serving notice that these clergy had now become full-fledged members of the Confessing Church. In doing so, they were subscribing to the argument of the Confessing Church's Dahlem Synod of October 1934, which declared that the national church administration had acted illegally and had therefore set itself out of existence. The Dahlem Synod attempted to establish a new church government and called on German Protestants to completely cease recognizing the official church, as Klemm and his colleagues in Pirna were doing. Moving from words to deeds, the Emergency League pastors from Pirna followed up their letter by refusing to attend the monthly pastoral conferences in their district.[28]

In response to these developments, Superintendent Zweynert sent a letter to the Pirna clergy on November 5, demanding to know within three days whether or not individual pastors were going to submit themselves to the Saxon Lutheran authorities. Attached was a nine-point questionnaire in which pastors were to provide details about their church-political memberships, activities, writings, and declarations. Zweynert appealed to the ordination oaths of pastors and urged them not to disrupt the church peace in Saxony any more than they already had.[29]

For a number of pastors in the Pirna area, Zweynert's intervention and the collapse of Reich bishop Müller's campaign forcibly to incorporate the south German churches into his Reich Church were enough to drive them from the Emergency League. For example, Pastor Rudolf Peter notified Zweynert that he was no longer in the Emergency League, in large part because of the removal of Prussian Church Commissar August Jäger and the restoration of a secure legal basis for the churches. Peter did not take this step without mixed emotions. In a letter to Confessing Church District Pastor Hermann Klemm of Burkhardswalde, Peter argued that he could not yet agree to the establishment of a rival church and declared that even when the official church employed "un-Christian methods," it was still "the church." As he surveyed the church-political landscape, however, Peter had been pondering the question "whether it was not God's will, that now as before the Reformation, the church is supposed to exist for a time under un-Christian superiors. I believe that in this God has the intention to force us to work absolutely and solely internally, on the spiritual, and to silently put up with all that is external in the church, even when it is totally un-Christian, as a yoke imposed by him."[30] Peter suggested that God would allow the present political reality, with the Führer principle and "the un-Christian church government" to continue "ad absurdum." He argued, "As before the Reformation, the time will come when the majority of the nation will understand the un-Christian [nature] of the German Christian church government." As for the Confessing Church, Peter asserted that "we should learn to wait here," and not establish a rival church. Clearly, although Peter was abandoning the Confessing Church and its unlawful course of action, he was no less critical of the official Reich and regional church governments than any of his colleagues, and more disposed than most to speak about German church politics in terms of a spiritual conflict between the forces of good and evil.

Along with Pastor Peter, Pastor Kurt Hellner of Dohna also agreed to obey the Saxon church authorities as long as he was not hindered in his preaching, and Franz Ploedterll of Königstein informed Zweynert that he would too, as long as his conscience allowed him to and as long as the church followed the first commandment "to fear, love and trust God above all things." Herbert Dittmann of Ehrenberg was another pastor skeptical about the official church, though his great personal attachment to Superintendent Zweynert induced him to agree to obey the Saxon Lutheran authorities. Dittmann was also put off by the radical approach of the Confessing Church and argued that its leaders had gone too far when they proclaimed, "Obedience to the church government is disobedience to God."[31]

Others retained their membership in the Confessing Church, even if they felt uncomfortable with the radical implications of their decision. Pastor Johannes Herz of Berggießhübel wrote a note affirming his deep personal respect for and attachment to Superintendent Zweynert and asked Zweynert not to take his membership in the Confessing Church personally.[32] Herz remained with the Confessing Church but lamented the breach it forced between his district superintendent and himself.

By November 1934, then, the division between the Confessing Church and the Saxon Lutheran Church was more or less complete. Bishop Coch sent out a stern warning about the Confessing Church's call to "open rebellion" and professed a new desire for unity in the Saxon Church. Other voices called for moderation. Pastor Martin Rasch of Reinhardtsdorf sent a circular letter to all his colleagues across the district, expressing hope for a new church peace and asking his fellow clergy to consider supporting suffering Emergency League pastors with financial assistance or establishing a new group of pastors "standing between the fronts" in the event of a renewed conflict.[33]

In fact, all across Saxony, hundreds of clergy were joining the *Middle*, hoping to end the Church Struggle and to restore peace in the Saxon Lutheran Church. The group called for the reinstatement of suspended clergymen, the abandonment of the use of force by the Saxon Church Office, the dissolution of the German Christian Movement, a financial audit of the Saxon regional church's books, a return to the Saxon church tradition, and the withdrawal of the NSDAP from internal church business. Until those conditions were met, the *Middle* pledged to support the Confessing Church in Saxony. In Pirna, Superintendent Zweynert stood firmly behind this new movement and heartily recommended it to his pastors. In fact, Zweynert put forward a multipoint plan of his own designed to bridge the gap between the *Middle* and Bishop Coch's government.[34]

While the development of the *Middle* was a positive step on the path toward peace in the Saxon Lutheran Church, pastors in the Pirna district were growing exhausted by the struggle. In December 1934, Pastor Karl Partecke replied sharply to one of a long line of official church inquiries from Superintendent Zweynert: "If only this foolish necessity for letters would ever let up and we could take pleasure in our [pastoral] offices again." Even those who most earnestly supported the *Middle* were discouraged. In late November 1934, Pastor Meinel of Bad Schandau asked Superintendent Zweynert for clarification about what was really going on in the Saxon regional church, then shared his frustration: "As with me, so it is with very nearly all the pastors of our district, this awful waiting for what will happen, it wears us down. Confidence in the present church government is almost completely gone; and yet we clergymen . . . want an orderly development. . . . The nervousness, frustration, and bitterness are great."[35]

If conditions were discouraging for members of the *Middle* in the Pirna district, they were growing worse for pastors who remained in the Confessing Church. At the close of 1934, the Saxon Church Office demanded yet another confirmation of the clergy who were members in the Confessing Church, and Superintendent Zweynert predicted a new round of disciplinary measures in early 1935. In truth, he did not even have to wait that long, for on the final day of 1934 the Saxon Church Office launched an inquiry into the withholding of voluntary church collections by members of the Confessing Church. Zweynert informed the Saxon Church Office that eleven pastors from the Confessing Church in Pirna had refused to hand in voluntary collections. In June, ten of those same pastors refused to hand in annual reports, once again earning the censure of the Saxon Lutheran authorities.[36] While over a dozen Pirna pastors faced disciplinary measures of one kind or another, three stand out for the outspokenness of their opposition to church authorities, the level of disruption in their parishes and the extent of the consequences they faced: Walter Schumann of Hohnstein, Gustav Carl of Cotta, and Hermann Klemm of Burkhardswalde. Their stories are richly illustrative of the nature of the Saxon Church Struggle at the level of the Pirna district and its parishes, particularly during the tumultuous years of 1934 to 1936.

## Pastor Walter Schumann of Hohnstein

As a member of both the Pastors' Emergency League and the Confessing Church, Walter Schumann of Hohnstein regularly defied his ecclesiastical superiors. His ability to survive in office through the most heated phase of the Church Struggle was directly attributable to the strength of his character, the authenticity of his ministry and consequent support of local Lutherans, and the extent to which Pirna district superintendent Zweynert was willing to go to stand up for Schumann and other members of the Confessing Church in his district, even when they were obviously operating outside the law.

It did not take Pastor Schumann of Hohnstein long to find his way into conflict with the NSDAP leadership in his community. On December 19, 1933, the NSDAP in Pirna filed a complaint with the Saxon Church Office in Dresden, on the grounds that Schumann had recently failed to read a message from Saxon bishop Coch to the Rathewalde congregation. As District Party Leader Sterzing noted in the complaint, this was not the first time that Schumann was alleged to have taken a strong stance against Coch, a fact that Sterzing regarded as "a very great insubordination" and a disruption in Schumann's parish, "since it stands united and full of devotion behind the leader of the Saxon church government." As a consequence of Sterzing's protest, Schumann met with Superintendent Zweynert of Pirna, where he rejected the accusations of insubordination and insurrection and declared that he had not spoken one word against Coch.[37]

Within a week of his statement, however, Schumann read an outlawed pulpit declaration of the Pastors' Emergency League and found himself in trouble once more. The declaration was both a criticism and a violation of the January 4 Emergency Decree of the Reich Bishop Concerning the Restoration of Orderly Conditions in the German Evangelical Church, the so-called Muzzling Decree. Recognizing that many parishioners felt confused about the unrest in their churches since the summer of 1933, the pulpit declaration Schumann read blamed the popular press for failing to explain the true meaning of the German Christian mass assembly at the Berlin Sport Palace, where in November 1933 "men who call themselves Christians" repudiated the divine revelation of parts of the Holy Scripture and advocated setting aside the "offense of the cross." The declaration also attacked Reich bishop Müller for endangering the unity of the church and for threatening to coerce those whose consciences impelled them to speak out against threats to the church: "Every attempt to intimidate consciences through external force is an apostasy from the spirit of the Reformation." As one who had read this declaration, Schumann was charged with subverting the authority of the church government and misusing his pulpit. On February 6, 1934, he was suspended from his pastorate and reduced to half his normal wages.[38]

In response, Pirna superintendent Zweynert wrote to Bishop Coch, defending Schumann and other pastors in his district who belonged to the Pastors' Emergency League. Zweynert argued against the police investigations and the coercive measures of the Saxon Church government against men like Schumann and assured the Saxon bishop that the Hohnstein pastor had read the Emergency League declaration only "out of the best, most noble motives, because he believed that the confession of the church, and thereby its existence, was threatened." Zweynert did not believe that this action deserved the damning suspension from office, when compared to the continual disobedience and neglect shown by other pastors. He asked Coch to reinstate Schumann and described him as "an uncommonly diligent, inwardly profound, honest, pious man" who had greatly promoted the ecclesiastical life of Hohnstein and Rathewalde. Zweynert pointed out how beloved Schumann was in his parish and asserted that politically, Schumann stood wholeheartedly behind the new state and worked to serve the Third Reich through his preaching and leadership of parish organizations. In what can only be described as a generous interpretation of Schumann's actions, Zweynert declared, "There can be no better representative of the new Reich in deed than him, and one could not quote a word of his speaking about which anyone could take offence."

More broadly, Zweynert protested the numerous police investigations of local pastors, pointing out that they generally caused parishioners to wonder whether their pastors were hostile to the state. In contrast to this notion, Zweynert made it abundantly clear to Coch "that all pastors in my district are nationally reliable and loyal, even those who belong to the Emergency League. There has not been the least bit reported to me that would cause complaint from the political point of view.

There is no one who can speak of an attitude hostile to the state." In support of his assertion, Zweynert noted that various members of the Emergency League in Pirna were members of or contributors to the NSDAP, members of the Working Group of National Socialist Pastors, and members of the German Christian Movement.[39]

In reply to Zweynert's entreaty, Consistorial Councilor Adolf Müller, Coch's assistant, suggested that the Emergency League might not be so politically benign as Zweynert believed. Müller described Emergency League leader Martin Niemöller's character as subversive and used the example of the contentious January 1934 meeting between Niemöller and Hitler as proof. As for police investigations, Councilor Müller explained that the Saxon bishop had nothing to do with them. When it came to disciplinary measures, however, Müller reminded Zweynert that pastors were not only bound to uphold the Scripture and the Confessions in their vows of ordination, but also to maintain proper submission to higher church authorities in the administration of their offices.[40]

Locally, however, it was Schumann and not Bishop Coch who was loved and supported by the parishioners in Hohnstein and Rathewalde. First, the youth group testified that Schumann was an upright leader in word and deed, who "also stands in Adolf Hitler's Reich with a joyful heart." Signing with a "*Sieg Heil*," the youth asked the Saxon Church Office to reinstate Schumann. Soon there followed a series of petitions. From the Rathewalde church, 180 parishioners requested the cessation of Pastor Schumann's suspension, describing how he had won their hearts over the course of his three years of service: "Nearly every member of the parish hangs with love on Pastor Schumann," they wrote, then explained how he was always ready to help his parishioners. They too asserted that Schumann was politically loyal, noting how "for several years, [he] has actively advocated the Hitler movement." Losing Schumann would be, they argued, "one of the most painful losses for every individual member of the parish." The Rathewalde Women's Aid and the grandmothers of the Rathewalde congregation also weighed in with their forty signatures on behalf of Schumann, citing his pure, honorable character, his powerful preaching, and his care for the elderly. As the grandmothers reported, "Adolf Hitler has in [Schumann] a loyal follower, who participates affirmatively in the Third Reich and loyally in the restoration in his parish." Finally, parish councilor and landlord von Zeschnig from Hohnstein added his word, echoing the pleas of the other parishioners. Noting the great affection that Schumann enjoyed in his parish, von Zeschnig wrote: "There is no one among the great and small, the poor and the rich, who does not appreciate and love and highly respect him." In fact, he added, Schumann's ministry had filled the empty church again and built bridges to the hostile elements in the parish—the elderly, poor, and ill all received support and daily gifts from Schumann, often out of his own means. Summing up the case, von Zeschnig declared that "the whole parish stands behind us, and if it were desired, we could bring the signatures of nearly all the parishioners."[41]

Another group wishing Schumann could return to work was the team of pastors substituting for him in Hohnstein and Rathewalde. By Easter, these pastors were beginning to tire of their extra workload and the frustrated hostility of Hohnstein parishioners, who only wanted Schumann back. Pastor Dittmann of Ehrenberg lamented the extra work, adding that he felt like he was the one being punished.[42] When Superintendent Zweynert complained to the Saxon Church Office for more help (hoping for a reinstatement of Schumann), the church office only called his bluff and offered to send theologians from Dresden to help cover services in Hohnstein.[43]

In spite of the outpouring of affection in Hohnstein and the frustration of his temporary replacements, Schumann remained suspended, perhaps in part because of his own stubborn actions. He refused to sign a declaration of loyalty presented to him by the Saxon bishop, and he also held unauthorized, private religious meetings with groups of his parishioners. Consequently, the Saxon Church Office increased its pressure on Schumann by transferring him to the parish of Großolbersdorf, in the Marienberg district, and declaring him replaced by Pastor Michael of Merschwitz. When Schumann refused to obey the transfer, the Saxon Church Office simply charged him with disobedience and docked his income another 10 percent.[44]

By late July 1934, however, Schumann's mind was apparently changed. According to Superintendent Zweynert, Schumann no longer objected to a transfer to another pastorate, but only wanted to hold a proper farewell service in Hohnstein. This, however, was a misunderstanding. Schumann soon let it be known that he intended to return to Hohnstein unless the parishioners there no longer wanted him. Schumann explained to Zweynert that he did not want to be seen to be running away from the consequences of his convictions: "That I cannot do. I have not acted in my own interests; I know myself bound in my actions to Scripture and confession and dare not act against my conscience. About that I am certainly glad, that the Lord of our church will help me in the hour of doubt and distress."[45]

As if to emphasize his determination, Schumann prepared a four-page, typewritten defense of his ministry, an answer to the question, "Why can I not abandon my parish Hohnstein?" In it, he raised six arguments: his legal and binding election by the Hohnstein parish, which no one save a few disturbers had asked him to renounce; the fundamental right of the parish to elect its pastor and the fundamental freedom of the pastor within his office; the faithfulness shown him by the parish during the first months of his suspension, offering him time, energy, and money; the emergence of a gradual spiritual awakening in the parish over the past year; a cryptic, unexplained obligation to "the blood of martyrs"; and last, the honor of his person and position, both of which would be sullied if he left after six years without a proper farewell sermon.[46]

Two months later, in September 1934, after a conversation with an official from the Saxon Superior Church Council, Saxon bishop Coch informed both Pastor Walter Schumann and Superintendent Zweynert that Schumann could finally return to his position in Hohnstein. Coch explained to Schumann that he expected him to keep the peace in Hohnstein, based on Schumann's declaration to that effect. Schumann and his wife, Maria, returned that same month, thankful for the love and care shown them during Schumann's suspension and confident that they enjoyed the support of many, if not most, in the Hohnstein and Rathewalde congregations. Over the next six months, Schumann's parish was at peace, and religion blossomed. As Schumann reported, attendance at church doubled, Bible study times were especially blessed, and people's doors were open to him.[47]

Schumann's sanguine perspective masked a new round of controversy that erupted after he led his parish into membership in the Confessing Church. This act alienated not only the Saxon Lutheran authorities over him but also some of the parish councilors and parishioners among whom he ministered, who did not condone this unlawful action. As a result, like other Confessing Church pastors in the Pirna district who refused to submit voluntary church collections to the Saxon Church Office, Schumann faced a new round of church discipline and was fined in both January and August 1935.[48]

Schumann's position was imperiled until, quite unexpectedly, conditions in the German Protestant churches changed in late 1935. The repeated judicial defeats of Reich bishop Müller brought the attempt to forcibly create a unitary Reich Church to an abrupt end, ushering in an era of appeasement in the Church Struggle. Church committees were created at the Reich and regional levels, pulling together neutrals and moderates from both the German Christians and Confessing Church in an attempt to settle the conflicts of 1934 and 1935. Church leaders hoped to create a new sense of order by maintaining a careful balance between the interests of pastors from the two main church-political parties. In the Pirna district, one of the effects of this new policy was the cessation of the judicial persecution of pastors in the Confessing Church. Thus, quite suddenly, Schumann's fines were repaid and his name cleared.[49]

In Hohnstein itself, however, Schumann's membership in the Confessing Church split the parish council. In February 1935, the mayor of Hohnstein and chairman of the parish council notified Superintendent Zweynert that he refused to recognize or invite all but two of the other parish councilors to any more parish council meetings, since the others supported Schumann and thus made it clear "that they no longer recognized the Saxon Church Office." The church office also took action against Schumann and his parish. In May, the ecclesiastical authorities refused to grant the customary transfer of funds to cover the budgetary shortfall in Hohnstein. Schumann complained to the Saxon ministry of the interior that the church government had no right to withhold the transfer payment, since church taxes had been regularly and correctly paid to Dresden, but had a difficult time arguing that the church government he refused to recognize should fund his outlaw parish. Little had changed by August 1935, when the Saxon Church Office threatened to dissolve the rebellious Hohnstein parish council and to appoint a new one.[50]

During this period, complaints against Schumann reveal not only the deep divisions within his parish but also his high level of popularity in the community at large and his efforts to achieve peace in the community. For instance, when Mrs. Marschner of Hohnstein repeatedly pressed the Saxon Church Office to take action against Schumann, the chief result was a sharp increase in her own unpopularity within the community. According to Schumann's report to Superintendent Zweynert, Marschner had once belonged to the Adventists and the Vandsburg Fellowship, then a Saxon Lutheran church fellowship, "until her conversion to National Socialism suddenly destroyed all her religious interest."[51] Without cause, she became "a furious opponent of the pastor," even though Schumann had often visited her Bible study group and her home and had gone so far as to lend her family two hundred reichmarks to help their struggling business, only part of which had been repaid. That she repaid this kindness with attacks was a serious enough matter in Hohnstein, but when her sixteen-year-old daughter gave birth to a child, fathered by a member of the SA, the family lost all respect among local Lutherans.

Relations between the Marschners and local Lutherans grew even more bitter when Mrs. Marschner and others sent roughly twenty anti-Schumann telegrams to the Saxon Church Office in April 1934, just before Schumann's earlier suspension was to have been lifted. As a result, Schumann remained suspended for another five months. "The indignation in the city was naturally great," explained Schumann, and when a list of the people who had intervened to extend his suspension was posted around the town, parishioners loyal to Schumann began to boycott certain stores, including the Marschners' bakery. In an attempt to overcome these deep divisions, Maria Schumann deliberately broke the boycott, choosing to buy bread and pastries at the Marschners in an effort to reach out to the family and set a good example for her husband's parishioners. "Even when I do not approve of the behavior of the Hohnsteiners," wrote Walter Schumann, "I can still fully understand their indignation. I can only say, in conclusion, that I feel sorry in my heart for the poor Marschner family and I pray to God that they will not remain in bitterness and hiding, but will find their way back to the steps of the church."

If the complaints of Mrs. Marschner and others—there was a complaint over Schumann's use of a special chapel for a girls' communion service—were essentially frivolous, the concerns of Schumann's neighboring colleague, Pastor Rosenthal of Lohmen, were far more serious. Although Rosenthal did not want to file a formal complaint, in May 1936 he notified Superintendent Zweynert that Schumann had been holding Bible studies and church-political talks for a group of his parishioners—generally eight to ten women in Lohmen—who were interested in the Confessing Church.[52] Though Rosenthal was worried about the divisive potential of such meetings, nothing came of them, because Schumann soon left Hohnstein. Whether he did so of his own choosing or under pressure from the

Saxon Church Office is not clear, but in June 1936, Schumann was appointed to the pastorate of Großrückerswalde in the Mauersberg district and a Pastor Beyerlein of Ramsdorf was placed as a vicar in Hohnstein to replace Schumann.[53]

With Schumann's departure, members of the Confessing Church in the Pirna district lost one of their first leaders, the pastor who had initially given direction to the Pastors' Emergency League in the district. A devout character, Schumann remained respectful throughout his conflict with his church superiors. He consistently provided meaningful spiritual care, both in office and during his suspension, actions that earned him the devotion of his parishioners. Such could not be said for his colleague in the Cotta parish, Pastor Gustav Carl.

## Pastor Gustav Carl of Cotta

Gustav Carl was another of the early members of the Pastors' Emergency League in Pirna and would prove to be an unwavering member of the Confessing Church after its inception in 1934. Like Pastor Schumann of Hohnstein, Gustav Carl defied the authority of the Saxon Church government and consequently struggled to retain his position. While Schumann left the Pirna district in 1936, Carl kept his post for the duration of the Church Struggle and did so at far lower odds. Tenacious in his defense of his fundamental rights as a pastor, Carl proved astonishingly staunch in his rejection of the Saxon Church Office's demands to submit to its authority.

Pastor Carl's ability to create division in Cotta came to the attention of Superintendent Zweynert in November 1933, when Carl's long-standing predecessor in Cotta, retired pastor Walter Eichenberg, informed Zweynert that Carl had publicly prayed for three Lutheran pastors suspended for protesting against the radical statements made by German Christians at the mass rally of November 13, 1933, at the Berlin Sport Palace. Angered that Carl had placed parishioners in a crisis of conscience between the convictions of their pastor and the decisions of the Saxon Church government, Eichenberg quoted several passages of Scripture to support his contention that Carl had erred: "Love your enemies. . . . Submit to the authorities who have power over you. . . . Give to Caesar what is Caesar's and to God what is God's."[54]

Though Eichenberg did not want to file a formal complaint against Carl, he was upset that his successor had used the house of God in Cotta for "a demonstration against the German Christians." Eichenberg asked Superintendent Zweynert to convince Carl "of the impossibility of his fight against the inner union of our *Volk*" and argued at length against Carl's supposed antipathy toward National Socialism and the conflict it was generating in Cotta. Eichenberg was insistent that Carl needed to understand the fundamental importance of state laws pertaining to Aryan ancestry, which Eichenberg believed were necessary for the spiritual cleansing of Germany. Here the retired pastor was implying that Carl was antipathetic to either the racial laws themselves or the extra work created by many requests for baptismal records, which were used to establish his parishioners' supposed blood purity. Lamenting Carl's inability to see the fundamental value of the German Christian Movement and his preoccupation with what Eichenberg saw as the senseless words of a few extremists, Eichenberg portrayed Carl's attitude as insolent. This stemmed from an angry exchange between the two over the nature of the emerging Church Struggle. When Carl described the growing tension as a *Kulturkampf*—a clear reference to inappropriate state interference in German religious life—and complained about a growing apostasy from the pure preaching of the Word of God in the Saxon Lutheran Church, Eichenberg retorted, "Is it really so un-Christian in our state?" Carl then replied, accusing Eichenberg of being one of the German Christians carrying out "the demolition of the church."

Though Eichenberg was deeply frustrated with Carl's attitude, his refusal to file a formal complaint was evidence of his desire to see Superintendent Zweynert persuade Carl informally to change his mind. Unfortunately for Eichenberg, these hopes were misplaced. Carl remained unshakable in his conviction of the justice of the Emergency League cause and continued to tolerate and, indeed, to create division within his Cotta parish as the cost of pursuing scriptural and confessional truth.

Among the parishioners displeased with Gustav Carl's church politics was the parish patroness, Mrs. Dora von Eschwege. Between December 1933 and February 1934, she wrote four long letters of complaint to Superintendent Zweynert, asking him to convince Pastor Carl to cease his church-political agitation in Cotta. First, von Eschwege echoed Eichenberg's complaint that Carl had used the Sunday service to pray for three pastors suspended by the church government. She added, however, that some members of the parish had distributed pamphlets (presumably from the Pastors' Emergency League) informing parishioners about current events in the church. Finally, she complained that Pastor Carl had not prayed for either Reich president Hindenburg or Reich Chancellor Hitler by name.[55]

Conditions in Cotta deteriorated after Carl read out a Pastors' Emergency League pulpit declaration on January 7, 1934. Von Eschwege reported how the declaration had accused the Reich bishop of false teaching, had announced that the Emergency League pastors like Carl would refuse to recognize the authority of the Reich Church, and had appealed to the Augsburg Confession for the justification to disobey the governing authorities in the church. "Such words," wrote the patroness, "must certainly drive away from the church many of those previously devoted to it; for [the words] produce strife in many [parishioners] who want to seek their God in the peace of the house of God but do not want to participate in church-political or theological conflicts." As if the pulpit declaration had not been enough, Carl had completely neglected (again!) to pray for either Reich President Hindenburg or Reich Chancellor Hitler. Superintendent Zweynert spoke with Carl about von Eschwege's complaints, but Carl argued back that he was only appealing to his conscience because he believed the foundation of the church to be threatened.[56]

Patroness von Eschwege continued to demand that Pastor Carl quit making outrageous church-political statements, and she continued to be disappointed by the reality that her pastor was a stout opponent determined to thwart any introduction of Nazi or German Christian ideology into the Saxon Lutheran Church. Carl consistently upheld fellow members of the Pastors' Emergency League in his Sunday prayers, on one occasion interceding for twenty-five suspended pastors "who suffer for the sake of their faith."[57] Extremely upset by this action, von Eschwege accused Carl of disturbing the peace in the Cotta parish and of subverting the unity of the German nation. Angry that Carl showed no respect for her opinion, she turned again to Superintendent Zweynert, asserting that the Emergency League pastors had been suspended not for their faith but for their refusal to obey the higher church authorities and for their openly divisive activities. Putting an explanation on her frustration, the patroness informed Zweynert that if Carl did not formally declare his intention to stop his agitation, she would file an official complaint with the Saxon Lutheran authorities.

Since Carl refused to do the bidding of his patroness, Superintendent Zweynert was forced to pass along her complaint to the Saxon Church Office.[58] Surprisingly, though, nothing came of von Eschwege's complaint, and nothing changed in Cotta either. Pastor Gustav Carl continued to agitate on behalf of the Pastors' Emergency League, despite being warned in May 1934 by the political authorities in Pirna to quit holding church-political meetings in his house. That August, he was still finding ways to preserve the independence of his church, opting to fly only religious flags from his parish buildings, and not the customary national political flags too.

Tired of Pastor Carl's subversive behavior and the division he was creating in the parish and on the parish council, the Saxon Church Office declared its intention to transfer Carl to a different parish.[59] Asked for his view on the matter, Superintendent Zweynert wrote a lengthy reply to the church office, admitting that Carl was "one of the most spirited members of the Pastors' Emergency League," but defending him as hardworking, conscientious, and blameless in the conduct of his duties and in his family life. Though NSDAP officials in Cotta made Carl out to be an enemy, Zweynert had nothing to report that would suggest that Carl was engaged in any opposition against the state. In fact, despite attacks against him, attendance at services in Cotta had doubled or tripled. Zweynert went on to clear up some of the misunderstandings about Carl's recent activities and concluded by recommending against any pastoral transfer, adding that many parishioners blamed Carl's enemies for the unrest in Cotta.[60]

Though Zweynert's support saved Carl's position in Cotta, it did nothing to change Carl's approach to church ministry. In fact, a few months later, Carl led his parish into membership in the Confessing Church, aided by sympathetic members of the parish council. After November 1934, then, Carl refused to invite the ten parish councilors who opposed the Confessing Church to any more meetings of the Cotta parish council, and he even passed an important business decision the following month without a quorum of parish councilors. At that point, the Saxon Church Office intervened, threatening to appoint a new parish council to work with Carl.[61] In April, the church office finally acted, stripping Carl of his position as chairman of the parish council and handing it over to his unlucky deputy, Martin Mühlbach, a farmer from Cotta.

Gustav Carl responded with a stern letter directed to Mühlbach and the nine other parish councilors who opposed both his pastoral leadership and his membership in the Confessing Church. Carl explained to them how recent court decisions in favor of the Confessing Church affirmed its legality, as opposed to "the unlawful church government of Coch." Because of that, Carl explained, he was not about to obey the order of the Saxon Church Office and hand over control of the parish council. Making good on his declarations, Carl refused to hand over the parish stamp, seal, and church keys to Mühlbach, who could only stand back and ask the Saxon Church Office for advice about what to do. Without the stamp, Mühlbach and his colleagues could not access the parish bank account, making it impossible for him to administer the parish.[62]

In the midst of these conflicts, the Saxon Church Office twice convicted and fined Carl for failing to submit voluntary church collections, though in both cases the fines were later overturned and refunded by the Saxon Church Committee in 1935. Even when the Saxon Church Office appointed five new parish councilors to replace Carl's allies in the Confessing Church, Carl still refused to hand over the stamp, seal, and church keys to Mühlbach and the official parish council.[63]

More troubling yet for the Cotta congregation was the fact that the standoff between Carl and Mühlbach left the parish without an organist from the middle of 1935 until sometime in 1936. Initially, this problem was the result of the resignation of Cantor Bortenreuter in June 1935, on the basis of his opposition to Pastor Carl and the Confessing Church, which Bortenreuter considered a danger to the peace at the local school where he taught. This vacancy came just at the time when the Saxon Church Office was reorganizing the Cotta parish council and led to a curious administrative quandary. Because Carl had been demoted from his position as chairman of the parish council, he was technically not responsible for the fact that all the church services were being conducted without organ music. However, Martin Mühlbach, *de jure* chairman of the parish council, had no access to parish funds with which to hire a replacement cantor until Patroness Dora von Eschwege gave him 187.50 RM to open a new bank account for the parish. When Mühlbach eventually appointed a new cantor in September 1935, Pastor Carl refused to give him the keys to either the church or the organ, speciously claiming that it was the pastor's job to find a new cantor.[64]

Surprisingly, parish records show little evidence of this divisive state of affairs. From 1933 to 1935, the number of church members grew modestly, and participation in communion remained steady at just under a quarter of all parishioners. Still, in autumn 1935, a group of Cotta parishioners were growing frustrated with the constant upheaval in their church life. At least ten of them wrote letters threatening to withhold their church taxes until the situation in Cotta settled down and a new pastor was appointed.

But Pastor Carl was not replaced. Like his colleague Walter Schumann, he was saved by the sudden creation of the Saxon Church Committee, which announced a cessation of the disciplinary measures against Carl and his recognition again as the chairman of the Cotta parish council. His fines were repaid and, ironically, he was even entrusted with the money Patroness von Eschwege had donated to establish a new church account when he had refused to hand over control of the parish finances.[65]

As with earlier attempts to pacify Carl, the decisions of the Saxon Church Committee did nothing to moderate his church-political attitudes. If anything, Carl became increasingly high-handed and rude in his triumph, launching a campaign of harassment against former parish council chairman Martin Mühlbach as he searched for information about Mühlbach's interim administration of the Cotta parish. When Mühlbach's wife wrote Carl to defend her husband as a good Christian man and to ask Carl to show consideration for his heart condition—a product of the stress in the Cotta church—Carl responded callously. He encouraged Mühlbach's wife to keep her husband out of parish work, questioned the authenticity of the Mühlbach's faith, and asserted that where Mühlbach thought he was doing his Christian duty, he had actually "*collaborated a great deal with the opponents of Christendom.*" Shockingly, Carl reminded Mühlbach's wife that he had often suggested in Bible studies that heaven and hell battled one another within her husband. Now Carl told her he hoped for the victory of light in her husband's life, a not so subtle suggestion that Mühlbach might have been serving the forces of darkness. The following day, Carl again wrote the Mühlbachs about unfinished parish business. Brusquely, Carl requested a host of details from Martin Mühlbach: copies of two contracts and thirty letters for the parish archives, plus reports about receipts and expenditures from the new accounts Mühlbach had opened and more reports about four telephone conversations between Mühlbach and church officials, including Superintendent Zweynert.[66]

Carl's harassment of the Mühlbachs and the fact that he had still not provided for organ music during Cotta church services provoked Patroness Dora von Eschwege to write a scathing letter to Superintendent Zweynert. She explained at length how Carl had ruined parish life in Cotta with unrest and division, and then she demanded his removal from the pastorate. Von Eschwege herself had long since broken with Carl and refused to attend church in Cotta. Recounting Carl's many misdeeds, and particularly the accusatory letter he wrote to Mrs. Mühlbach, the patroness argued that his attitude created "the impression, as if Pastor Carl considered all those who stand unreservedly behind the new movement [of National Socialism] and the Führer as opponents of Christendom." Von Eschwege observed that Carl had lost the confidence of everyone in the parish who stood loyally for the Führer, whether or not they were members of the party, then repeated twice more her accusation that Carl's attitude was hostile to the government and National Socialist movement.[67] Superintendent Zweynert passed von Eschwege's letter on to the Saxon Church Committee along with his own observations and urgently pleaded for it to appoint a new cantor and to force Carl to apologize for his accusations against the Mühlbachs.[68] Zweynert, however, did not call for Carl's dismissal.

Whether Carl ever apologized is unclear, but contrary to Superintendent Zweynert's pleas, he continued to wreak havoc in Cotta. In February and April, Carl withheld voluntary church contributions from the district office, choosing to send them to the Confessing Church administrators instead. Also in April, Carl twice fought with parishioners requesting permission to have their children baptized in a neighboring parish. Most ominous of all was a dispute over statements Carl made about the German army. In February 1936, he announced in a confirmation class that 80 percent of the soldiers in the Dresden garrison were believers in the pagan German Faith Movement. When the daughter of Farmer Heschel, the former head of the Cotta Military Association, reported Carl's statements to her father, Carl was forced to withdraw his claims as unfounded. As he argued with Heschel about the religious orientation of German military personnel, however, Carl very nearly confirmed Patroness von Eschwege's suspicion that he was an outright opponent of the National Socialist regime. "I consider it my duty," he wrote, "to instruct my parishioners to the best of my ability about the current worldview situation within the German nation and the widely held standpoint of rejection of Christianity." This resolve to abide by his conscience lasted, as did his career, well into the Second World War. True to his contrarian ways, in November 1941 Carl had still not submitted his "Proof of Aryan Ancestry" form, due in mid-1939, to the Saxon Church Office.[69]

In retrospect, the career of Pastor Gustav Carl, the most outspoken critic among Pirna pastors of the anti-Christian aspects of National Socialism, provides a curious and at times unsettling example of how stubbornness and conviction could enable a pastor to survive in office against heavy odds. In Carl's case, the parish patroness, most of the Cotta parish council, and the local NSDAP leaders were all firmly against him, while Superintendent Zweynert was only hesitantly and partially supportive. Still, he held on to his position in Cotta and defied the German Christian ecclesiastical authorities in Dresden throughout the course of the Third Reich.

## Pastor Hermann Klemm of Burkhardswalde

The third important member of the Pirna Pastors' Emergency League and Confessing Church was Dr. Hermann Klemm, pastor of the Burkhardswalde parish since 1929. Identified with the initial group of Emergency League pastors in April 1934, by October 1934 he had become their spokesman, declaring that he and his colleagues in the Emergency League would henceforth refuse to obey the Saxon Lutheran authorities. Moreover, after the Dahlem Synod of the Confessing Church, Klemm and others declared that they no longer recognized the legitimacy or authority of the German Christian church governments in either Berlin or Dresden.[70] It was that fundamental church-political decision that shaped Klemm's career in Burkhardswalde, guided him through the complications of the Church Struggle in the Pirna district, and enabled him to endure the sacrifices he was forced to make for his cause. Klemm's career illustrates the ability of Pirna pastors, buoyed by the unstinting cooperation of their parishioners, to frustrate the administrative initiatives of higher church offices. It also reveals how exasperating Confessing Church clergy could be to their law-abiding colleagues, who were forced to take on the burden of substituting in hostile parishes for pastors with whom they could not agree.

Along with other clergy, including Pastors Schumann of Hohnstein and Carl of Cotta, Pastor Hermann Klemm was disciplined in January 1935 for refusing to submit voluntary church collections to the Saxon regional church. Until then, his participation in the Confessing Church had not landed him in legal trouble. This changed on April 19, 1935, when the Pirna Gestapo arrested him for undisclosed reasons, sending Superintendent Zweynert scrambling to find a substitute for Klemm's parish. After Pastor Adolf Voigtländer of Maxen declared himself too ill, Pastor Werner of Dohna agreed to administer Burkhardswalde and Weesenstein temporarily on behalf of Klemm.[71]

It was only after May 4 that Zweynert found out from the Saxon Church Office that the Gestapo had arrested Klemm for reading a Confessing Church pulpit declaration and engaging in an intercessory prayer for incarcerated clergy on April 7, in spite of the prohibition of the political authorities. As usual, the church office requested a report from Pirna superintendent Zweynert. Zweynert was more restrained in his support of Klemm than he had been in the cases of Pastors Schumann and Carl. The superintendent explained to the church office that while Klemm was an academically gifted theologian whose family life and ministry were blameless, since Klemm's November 1934 decision to stop recognizing the authority of the Saxon church government, their relationship had collapsed. As chairman of the Confessing Church district council, Klemm functioned as a shadow superintendent. He received voluntary church collections, granted holidays, and even compiled annual reports for the Confessing Church parishes. Although Klemm refused to engage in official correspondence with Zweynert, the superintendent had learned from private sources that Klemm was more moderate in outlook than other Confessing Church pastors in the district and that the Burkhardswalde parish council was united behind Klemm.[72]

Superintendent Zweynert gained more reliable information from Pastor Werner of Dohna, after Werner met with both cantors and councils in Burkhardswalde and its filial church, Weesenstein. In Weesenstein, the parish council had agreed to work with Werner, and so he had put the local administration in order, even completing the budget. In contrast, only some of the Burkhardswalde parish councilors had come to the meeting with Werner, and their loyalty was sharply divided between the Confessing Church and the Saxon regional church. Klemm's wife exacerbated this split by refusing to hand over the Burkhardswalde parish records to Werner unless the parish council voted to work with Werner and the Saxon Lutheran authorities.[73]

A second meeting four days later determined that the Burkhardswalde parish council would not work with Werner. Ten of the eleven councilors attended the meeting, but only four voted to remain loyal to the Saxon regional church. As for the others, some were committed to the Confessing Church cause, while others were simply reluctant to decide "against Pastor Klemm." As a result, a disgruntled Pastor Werner was forced to concede his inability to assume temporary administrative oversight of the Burkhardswalde parish. Frustrated, Werner blamed the irresolution of the Saxon Church Office for his troubles:

> As long as the Saxon church leadership is not ultimately able to bring itself to a decisive resolution of the Church Struggle, it will be impossible for the lesser authorities to be responsible for an orderly provision [of spiritual care] in the parishes. Moreover, the parish councilors are so confused by this indecisive attitude of the ecclesiastical authorities that they no longer know, with the best will in the world, where justice and duty lay for them.[74]

Werner was no doubt frustrated by the ongoing refusal of Klemm's wife and the obstinate parish councilors to hand over either the necessary official documents or the parish stamp, seal, and church keys. This spirit of noncompliance, which Werner attributed to confusion, was the chief characteristic of the Burkhardswalde parish leadership throughout 1935, as local Lutherans drew courage for their subversion from Klemm's release from detention in early June.[75]

Although Klemm was free again, the Reich governor had forbidden pastors released from detention from serving in their pastorates again. Thus, Superintendent Zweynert instructed Klemm that Pastor Werner of Dohna would continue to substitute for him in Burkhardswalde and Weesenstein. Within two days, however, the Saxon Confessing Church council intervened, informing Superintendent Zweynert that there was no such order from the Reich governor that prohibited pastors who had been detained from preaching and ministering sacraments.[76]

News that the Confessing Church leaders supported Klemm's return to work initiated a month of utter chaos for substituting pastors in Burkhardswalde and

Weesenstein. On the first Sunday of Pentecost, June 9, 1935, Pastor Paul Teichgräber of Pirna was supposed to hold a service in Burkhardswalde at 8:30 in the
morning. At 6:45 A.M., Mayor Heyne of Burkhardswalde telephoned Teichgräber to
inform him that Pastor Klemm had planned a rival service for 8:00 that morning.
Teichgräber rushed out to Burkhardswalde and surprised Klemm in the church at
7:45. Klemm told Teichgräber to go on home, since Superintendent Hugo Hahn
from Dresden, leader of the Confessing Church forces in Saxony, was going to
preach. Instead, Teichgräber phoned Superintendent Zweynert and then proceeded
to the sacristy, where Klemm and Hahn were preparing for the service. A lively
exchange followed, after which Superintendent Hahn agreed to hold a separate
service at the parsonage.[77]

When Teichgräber announced to the congregation that he was the official substitute and would be holding a service shortly, Klemm stood up and told the row of
confirmation candidates: "Come with me over to the parsonage—there is nothing
for you here!" They left, as did the adults who were seated there. Outside were
other parishioners waiting to come in for the service. When they sat down, Parish
Councilor Wünsche began calling them out of the pews, row by row. By the time he
was finished, there were only twenty-five adults and ten children left. Teichgräber
quickly signaled the cantor to begin playing the prelude on the organ, and Teichgräber went on to conduct the official service. Outside, someone had been posted
to direct any latecomers to the Confessing Church service in the parsonage, further confusing innocent parishioners. Throughout Teichgräber's service, loud hymn
singing from the parsonage and the bustling of gawkers popping in and out of the
service (including local members of the pagan German Faith Movement) created a
frightful distraction.

Teichgräber was furious at Klemm and the Burkhardswalders for the embarrassing spectacle and demanded the dismissal of Parish Councilor Wünsche for
having the effrontery to summon parishioners out of Teichgräber's official church
service. In addition, Teichgräber called for the replacement of the Confessing
Church members on the parish council with "men who are proven Christians and
likewise well-disposed to National Socialism."[78]

Next it was Pastor Werner's turn again. The pastor from nearby Dohna came
during the following week to conduct a funeral in Burkhardswalde. There the bell
ringer refused to cooperate with him and the cantor sent the children's choir home,
saying they were not allowed to sing. Pastor Klemm stopped the children on the way
and managed to bring about half of them back to sing for the funeral, but Werner
was furious all the same. Werner demanded that if Superintendent Zweynert could
not put a stop to Klemm's antics, he should intervene immediately and energetically with higher church authorities to put a stop to events in Burkhardswalde: "It is
irresponsible and at present wholly unacceptable for children to be placed in such a
dilemma between two authorities. . . . If insubordination in the church continues to

be managed in the hitherto usual lax manner, the damage will be incalculable." Pastor Werner added that, in his opinion, there could be no solution to the problems in Burkhardswalde as long as Klemm remained there. [79]

When Werner returned to Burkhardswalde some days later to hold a confirmation class, only the children from Weesenstein appeared. Werner was surprised, because he had informed the parents that he would be the official instructor for their children, and that only the children who came to him could be confirmed the following year. Three days later, however, a Confessing Church pastor from Dresden informed the same parents that he had official permission to conduct the confirmation classes. Once more, Werner was incensed and lashed out at the Lutheran authorities for their neglect:

What the Saxon regional church lets take place in Burkhardswalde beggars description. I am of the standpoint that immediate assistance must be applied for from the state. Should it not be granted, then the Saxon regional church should leave Burkhardswalde. . . . In the end, there will be absolutely no one left that listens anymore. No one can expect of the little man that he endlessly makes a fool of himself, while far above him people only shuffle paper! [80]

Meanwhile, the day before, Pastor Walter Börner of Ottendorf had come to Burkhardswalde to substitute for Klemm on the Second Sunday in Pentecost. Only three women, two confirmation candidates, the cantor, and the choir were present at the service, and no preparations had been made for him. There was no order of service, no Bible, and not even any other service books, conditions Börner felt bordered on theft. Needless to say, Börner was extremely upset and suggested that Klemm's actions went beyond mere ecclesiastical mischief: "The conditions in Burkhardswalde cry to the heavens, not only with respect to the church but also in relation to the political state." [81]

In Burkhardswalde before the service, Börner had happened upon his colleague, Kurt Hellner, the associate pastor in Dohna. Hellner, a member of the Confessing Church, informed Börner that Pastor Klemm had already arranged for his own Confessing Church service. Börner rejected this idea, replying sharply that it was up to Pastor Werner of Dohna, the temporary legal administrator of the parish, to make arrangements for Burckhardswalde. Just then, local parish councilor Wünsche came by and insolently told Börner that the Burkhardswalders were not interested in his ministry. Börner could hardly believe Wünsche's behavior. In his report about the incident, he asked Werner, "How is it that this man is on the parish council at all?" Meanwhile, Klemm had indeed arranged for a rival church service in Burkhardswalde, to be held by retired pastor Lieschke of Dresden in the parsonage. While only five parishioners attended Börner's official service, sixty parishioners filled the parsonage to hear Lieschke.

After Börner had finished his very small, official service, he started to prepare for a scheduled church wedding. When the couple came, they turned out to be devotees of Pastor Klemm and declared that they would rather forgo the church wedding than be married by Börner. Just then Pastor Lieschke of the Confessing Church came along and told Börner that the couple had arranged for him to marry them.

While Pastor Börner was angry at the Burkhardswalders, he was also frustrated with the Saxon church authorities. In bold type, Börner wrote Werner asking how neither the Saxon Lutheran Church nor the Saxon state did anything to stop the unauthorized, rival church services that were now the rule in Burkhardswalde. Börner wanted to make an example of Klemm by stripping him of his position, salary, and pension if he would not stop his "crass *disobedience*." Adding insult to injury, Klemm's parishioners had maligned Börner's official church service as "pagan," which deeply offended him. Börner concluded, "A weak government is a misfortune for a people—a strong government is a blessing," and he described Burkhardswalde as a source of danger for the National Socialist regime.

The following week, Pastor Werner returned once again to Burkhardswalde in order to minister to the congregation there, but only three local women, two children, and Werner's own wife were in attendance. As Werner approached the church, he saw a posted notice advertising a religious celebration in the cemetery next to the church. Assuming it was for the following day, he began to prepare for his own service. Soon it became apparent that Pastor Klemm had organized a rival church service immediately outside the church, where parishioners sat on stools that had been set up. As the morning went on, the singing outside was so loud that Werner's sermon was hard to hear, all the more so because someone had opened the windows that stood directly between the two services. By the end of the service, Werner could be heard practically shouting out the closing prayer. Feeling "well and truly sunk" by the complete lack of support from Saxon Lutheran authorities, Werner resigned as substitute pastor for Burkhardswalde, though not before pressing charges against Klemm for the "*transparently and systematically planned disruption of a church service.*"[82]

The next Sunday, June 30, 1935, was just as grim. Confessing Church pastor Lieschke stared down the cantor until he shut the organ and left. Klemm himself took over the service inside the church. When Pastor Werner came by in the afternoon to perform a baptism, he discovered that no preparations had been made, and he had to send his son running to get water in a metal can.[83] Having reached the limit of his patience, Werner gave up trying to fight against Klemm and began negotiating permission from the Saxon Church Office for an interim settlement in Burkhardswalde. Under the agreement, Klemm was not permitted to resume his duties officially—he was not technically suspended, only prohibited from working in the wake of his temporary arrest by the Gestapo in April 1935—but he would not face any attempts to stop him from holding unofficial services. If parishioners in Burkhardswalde wanted a legal pastor for any official duties, one would be sent. Otherwise, they were on their own with the rebel Klemm. Eventually, the Lutheran authorities planned to discipline Klemm. In the meantime, however, Superintendent Zweynert and the Saxon church government had decided to heed Pastor Werner's warning not to try to appoint a vicar in Burkhardswalde, because Werner was convinced that nothing would change in the parish until Klemm was forced out of town.[84]

While news that Hermann Klemm could work informally as pastor was greeted with joy in Burkhardswalde, in neighboring Weesenstein it elicited an angry letter of protest from Mayor Erich Schmidt. In total contrast to the parishioners in Burkhardswalde, the congregation in Weesenstein wanted nothing to do with Klemm. On his first Sunday back there, only 6 of the 450 residents of the town came to the service![85]

Mayor Schmidt did not have to wait long for the Lutheran authorities to act. On July 30, 1935, the Saxon Church Office launched formal disciplinary action against Pastor Klemm for withholding church collections, distributing an unauthorized parish newsletter, and disrupting the authorized church services of Pastors Teichgräber, Werner, and Börner. After suspending Klemm and reducing him to 40 percent of his salary, the church office dissolved the parish council at Burkhardswalde and appointed a new and politically reliable group of leaders. More than ever, though, Superintendent Zweynert had a difficult time finding substitute clergymen for Burkhardswalde, despite assurances that the mayor would diligently work to forestall any interference from Klemm. As a result, Zweynert began to plead with Saxon Lutheran authorities to transfer Klemm out of Burkhardswalde, asserting that it was the only path to a lasting settlement of the Church Struggle in the parish. Mayor Schmidt of Weesenstein, recently made head of the parish council there, echoed Zweynert and appealed to keep politics out of the church: "If Klemm felt himself called to be a politician, then he should have known this already earlier and not only after he climbed up into the pulpit as a minister to souls." In fact, the new parish council in Weesenstein voted never again to let Klemm or his Confessing Church vicar enter any of the church facilities in their town.[86]

Ironically, after Saxon church authorities had gone to all the work of suspending Klemm and rebuilding the parish councils in Burkhardswalde and Weesenstein, the introduction of the Saxon Church Committee with its mandate to heal conflict-ridden parishes undid everything, which promptly reignited the church-political quarrel surrounding Klemm. On October 23, 1935, Saxon bishop Coch reinstated Klemm, and the Saxon Church Committee soon followed suit, overturning all prior legal judgments against him. Once more the Burkhardswalde parish council was reshuffled, this time with new members loyal to the Confessing Church replacing Klemm's opponents who had only just been appointed.[87]

The sudden reversal of fortunes must have left those hostile to the Confessing Church reeling. Almost immediately, they restarted their attacks against Klemm. In mid-November, the Pirna district school councilor wrote to Superintendent Zweynert about Klemm's influence in Burkhardswalde. Having recently visited the school in Klemm's parish, the councilor noted that only six children there were members of the state youth groups, such as the Hitler Youth and League of German Girls, attributing this fact to the open opposition of Pastor Klemm and his allies:

> Apart from the fact that personally I can spare no understanding for the fact that a pastor who has been detained in custody—after serving a sentence in jail—would return to his former place of service and again perform his duties, I can now say that as a National Socialist, I cannot tolerate our work here being sabotaged from the side of the church; for it is sabotage, when the body of educators, parents and students are hindered in their positions from fulfilling the duty that their Führer has received from destiny and passed on to them.[88]

The district school councilor warned Zweynert that the NSDAP in Pirna had authorized him to write, and he demanded that the churches obey the mandates of National Socialism.

On the heels of this letter, the mayors of Burkhardswalde and Weesenstein and the district leadership of the NSDAP successfully agitated for the Saxon Church Committee to revisit Klemm's case. Although the Saxon Church Committee had recently amnestied Klemm, its members now informed Superintendent Zweynert that they had agreed to hear the complaints of the two mayors and the NSDAP. Zweynert attended the hearing and recorded no fewer than ten accusations against Klemm. Among other things, the mayors and party leaders described the pastor as a disturber of the peace in the two communities of Burkhardswalde and Weesenstein, a saboteur of the NSDAP district leadership, and an enemy of the state who had made statements hostile to the Third Reich. In reply, Klemm denied that his ecclesiastical conduct was hostile to the state and argued that church and state were to be kept separate. Zweynert's notes catch the essence of Klemm's argument in his question to those gathered at his hearing: "Is the church there for God or for the *Volk*?" In the end, Klemm provided his own emphatic answer: "For God!"[89]

The Saxon Church Committee proceeded to appoint a three-member clerical committee to investigate church conditions in Burkhardswalde and Weesenstein. The result, however, was not the expulsion of Klemm but his victory over his local ecclesiastical and political opponents. The resistant Weesenstein parish council was reshuffled, ridding it of Klemm's enemies. This surprising decision effectively ended the threat to Pastor Klemm's position. For instance, when Burkhardswalde NSDAP leader Heine protested the dismissal of politically reliable (i.e., National Socialist) members of the Weesenstein parish council, Superintendent Zweynert simply replied that he had nothing to do with the decision and informed Heine that he would pass his complaint on up to the Saxon Church Committee.[90] With that, the matter was settled. Pastor Klemm had survived arrest by the Gestapo as well as the opposition of a host of opponents: local and district National Socialist leaders from Burkhardswalde, Weesenstein, and Pirna; school officials; two mayors; numerous parish councilors and parishioners; and even Superintendent Zweynert and three pastors who substituted in his parish.

Klemm had three factors going for him in his struggle to maintain control of his parish and guide it faithfully in the way of the Confessing Church. For one, the Confessing Church and its local members supported Klemm. Superintendent Zweynert had a difficult time finding substitute clergymen for Burkhardswalde in part because Klemm's neighboring pastors, including Gustav Carl of Cotta and Kurt Hellner of Dohna, also belonged to the Confessing Church. In Weesenstein, Cantor Theodor Aehnelt had refused to work when substitute clergymen came, asking for holidays instead.[91] In addition, retired pastor Lieschke and a few laypeople had regularly traveled from Dresden to hold unauthorized services, and other Confessing Church pastors and congregations had no doubt prayed for him during his arrest and suspension, as was their practice.

Second, Klemm's parish council and parishioners in Burkhardswalde remained steadfastly committed to his person and the cause of the Confessing Church. While Klemm was arrested, the parish councilors voted not to recognize the substitute authority of Pastor Werner of Dohna, and when Pastors Teichgräber of Pirna, Werner of Dohna, and Börner of Ottendorf came to conduct services in Burkhardswalde, parishioners stayed away *en masse*, choosing instead to attend the illegal Confessing Church services in the parsonage or churchyard.

Finally, Klemm had good timing on his side. In late 1935, after he was suspended and his allies on the parish council ousted, the emergence of the moderate Saxon Church Committee in Dresden brought an end to plans in the Saxon Church Office to be rid of Klemm. Judicial measures were overturned and Klemm and his allies restored to their positions of leadership.

All this says much about the vagaries of church-political conflict in the Pirna district during the Third Reich. The careers of Pastors Walter Schumann of Hohnstein, Gustav Carl of Cotta, and Hermann Klemm of Burkhardswalde demonstrate that a determined resistance to the German Christian church leadership—even of the radical variety, as in Saxony—*was* possible. Grassroots support was a key factor in the survival of Schumann and Klemm, though less so in Gustav Carl's case. The patience of Superintendent Zweynert was also an important factor in the early years of the Church Struggle in Pirna. Zweynert was willing to endure the complications of life with Confessing Church pastors as long they advanced his goal of church peace in Pirna. That Zweynert was less supportive of Klemm than of other Confessing Church pastors probably stems from Klemm's leading role among Confessing Church pastors in the district.

In the end, however, personal force of character played as great a role as any other factor. Only clergy with strong characters were willing to endure arrest, suspension, docking of pay, tense confrontations with church-political opponents, and the harassment of local political leaders. Only pastors with courage were likely to stand up to the growing infiltration of National Socialist ideology into the churches in Pirna or in other regions in which the party was particularly anticlerical or the higher church authorities particularly determined to root out the Confessing Church.

During the Nazi era in Pirna, Pastors Schumann, Carl, and Klemm were not alone in their conflict with the Saxon Lutheran authorities or the NSDAP. Pastor Friedrich Hagar of Rosenthal, a National Socialist Party member, was arrested for calling Reich youth leader Baldur von Schirach a danger to the youth. Upon his release, he fought a running battle with the local schoolteacher and with National Socialists in the Women's Aid. Pastor Siegfried Meier fought with his parish council over the distribution of Confessing Church newsletters and the collection of voluntary contributions for the Confessing Church. In Wehlen Stadt, Pastor Otto Scriba was fined for subversive comments about the official church government, and for refusing to hand in collections to the Saxon Church Office. In Heidenau, Curate Scherffig took an unauthorized holiday granted by Pastor Klemm, who acted as a shadow superintendent for the Confessing Church. Pastor Johannes Herz of Berggießhübel fought with his neighbor, Pastor Walter Börner of Ottendorf, over Confessing Church and German Christian confirmation practices, and he, too, was fined for refusing to submit voluntary church collections. Pastor Georg von Schmidt of Langenhennersdorf and Gotthelf Müller of Heidenau were both fined for noncompliance over church collections and nonrecognition of the Saxon Church Office. Finally, Pastors Martin Vorwerk of Liebstadt, Kurt Hellner of Dohna, and Johann Friedrich of Gottleuba all landed in legal trouble for refusing to submit voluntary church collections, as well as for disputes about funerals, unauthorized holidays, and outlawed parish newsletters.[92]

## Deteriorating Conditions

With conditions like these, even moderate pastors remained stuck in disillusionment and bitterness over the actions of German Christians in their parishes and in the Saxon church government. The extent of the problem became clearer as time wore on. By 1937, pastors expressed their discouragement and skepticism more openly. For instance, after Saxon police prohibited a range of benign-sounding parish meetings—children's church outings, churchwomen's outings to non-church facilities such as gardening exhibits, parish trips into the country, and other women's meetings in nonchurch facilities—for the second time in a six-month period, Pastor Martin Meinel of Bad Schandau bemoaned the state of affairs in his parish. Even though he had withdrawn from the Pastors' Emergency League in 1934 in order to avert a split in his parish, he still faced a wave of German Christian agitation in Bad Schandau in 1937. The chief cause of this conflict was a new radical German Christian curate, Pastor Spielmann, who broke a promise to abstain from church politics soon after his arrival in Bad Schandau. Rather, Spielmann helped plan a German Christian assembly in February 1937, highlighted by a speech by Saxon bishop Coch. About 160 people came to the event hosted by Spielmann in a local hotel, since Meinel refused to allow the German Christians to use his parish church. The young curate proclaimed that soon Bad Schandau would have its own German Christian group; then he introduced Bishop Coch. Discussing the theme "One *Volk*, One Faith," Coch looked forward to a time when National Socialism would subsume the church and there would no longer be any need for pastors or Sunday services. In a mocking, "pseudo-Jewish" tone of voice, Coch slandered the apostle Paul and then interpreted Jesus' word to "Give to Caesar what is Caesar's and to God what is God's" as if Jesus had elevated secular political authority over the commandments of God. Rejecting the Old Testament and deriding pastors, professors, and intellectuals, Coch advocated changing the forms of the sacraments and ceremonies of the church in anticipation of a future when no one would care about confessional differences between Protestants and Catholics.[93]

Unfortunately for Pastor Meinel, who had to suffer through Coch's heretical speech, his experience was only a taste of things to come in the Pirna district. In November 1937, the Saxon Church Office installed Heinrich Leichte, the ardent National Socialist and German Christian pastor from Königstein, as the new district superintendent. Leichte, who was already unpopular among his colleagues, completely abandoned former superintendent Zweynert's conciliatory leadership style, aggressively promoting the interests of the German Christian Movement throughout the district. Church disciplinary measures were taken against Confessing Church clergy. For instance, in February 1938, Pastors Georg von Schmidt, Johann Friedrich of Gottleuba, and Joachim Grießdorf of Porschdorf were all fined two hundred reichmarks by the Saxon Church Office for reading or distributing a Confessing Church pulpit declaration refusing obedience to the Saxon church government. Three months later, Pastors von Schmidt and Klemm were both fined three hundred reichmarks for refusing to answer official church correspondence.[94]

Leichte's burning ambition as superintendent of the Pirna district was to force open the church doors of neutral and Confessing Church parishes for radical Thuringian German Christian meetings, religious celebrations, church services, confirmation instruction, baptisms, and other events. From December 1937 to October 1939, Leichte and the Saxon Lutheran authorities employed their legal right of access to Saxon parish churches by sending out well over one hundred notices to Pirna pastors and parish councils from the Confessing Church or the

*Middle* group. In some cases, local clergy or church leaders attempted to block these German Christian meetings. In Sebnitz, Pastor Gerhard Bahrmann complained to Superintendent Leichte that the date chosen for a German Christian assembly conflicted with a Women's Aid meeting that had been planned four weeks before the German Christians intervened. When he could not stop Leichte's plan, he denounced the introduction of church-political division in his parish in a declaration to his congregation. In Dohna and Heidenau, parish councils tried to charge the German Christians a fee, arguing it would cost more than they could afford to heat and light the church for an unofficial, church-political event. Saxon church officials in Dresden also brushed that objection aside.[95]

In Liebstadt, Pastor Martin Vorwerk filed a formal complaint with the Reich Minister for Church Affairs over the "distasteful" attempt by German Christians to work their way into his parish. Vorwerk described how a first attempt to hold a German Christian meeting only drew three or four people, none of whom was a regular parishioner. German Christians then employed people who had withdrawn from the Lutheran church to distribute eight hundred leaflets, in preparation for a second meeting. Only thirty-five or so came to the meeting, many of whom Vorwerk knew had no interest at all in the welfare of the church. Vorwerk also protested the sale of German Christian pamphlets outside the church and complained that when Saxon bishop Coch came to conduct a German Christian church service, he failed to turn in any church collection to the parish. Once again, Superintendent Leichte rejected these charges, asserting that sixty or seventy had attended the German Christian meeting and explaining that his goal was to establish monthly German Christian meetings in Vorwerk's parish.[96]

This newly intensified Church Struggle in Pirna, in which Superintendent Leichte himself spearheaded the German Christian attack on neutral and Confessing Church parishes, stood in stark contrast to the patience and reserve employed by Superintendent Zweynert for so many years. For pastors who had hoped to find the middle road to peace in their parishes, Leichte's aggressive promotion of German Christian interests must have hurt deeply. For pastors in the Confessing Church, Leichte's aggression elicited an intransigence that clearly irritated the Pirna superintendent, as his response of November 1940 suggests: at the close of a circular letter containing instructions for local clergy, Leichte implored: "I ask [you] *just once* to observe this regulation."[97]

## War and the Collapse of the Third Reich

The beginning of the Second World War brought new problems for clergy in the Pirna district and elsewhere in the Saxon Lutheran Church, not least personnel shortages owing to the enlistment and conscription of many pastors and vicars into the German army. These shortages and the continuation of conflicts between pastors and local schoolteachers and NSDAP leaders made pastoral ministry during the war extremely difficult. In 1941, Pastor Dr. Brunner of Heidenau reported how religious instruction had not been given in Heidenau schools for two years. Pressure from the NSDAP meant that the number of parishioners withdrawing from the church continued as before, only now even people who used to stand very near the church were leaving too. Conflicts over confirmation instruction had sharpened, thanks in no small part to the demands of the Nazi Party on local youth. The sad fact is that Pastor Dr. Brunner had little time to address any of these problems, for he was the sole pastor left in a parish of around ten thousand souls.[98]

In Neustadt, no fewer than seven different pastors, curates, and vicars provided spiritual care during the turbulent year of 1940. Relations were also poor with local political leaders, who refused to grant the pastors access to municipal records so that they might keep track of the changes in the local Protestant population. In Dohna, Pastor Werner complained bitterly that the local schools no longer provided religious instruction to students, and wondered why the Saxon Church did not call on retired clergymen to come back and help with the overload of work faced by pastors. Local Nazi leaders continued their public attacks on the church, and although public reaction was often negative, party organizations continued to demand the time of Dohna children, so that children's church attendance had shrunk to one-third of what it had been in 1932.[99] Indeed, by the latter part of the war, church attendance throughout the district had plummeted to less than one-half of what it had been in the early years of the Third Reich. Still, as the war progressed, fewer and fewer people withdrew from church membership, and slightly higher numbers of Lutherans took out church memberships between 1939 and 1945.

Within the Lutheran clergy of Pirna, the initial success of the German military campaigns was reflected in the positive prayer of Superintendent Leichte in both 1939 and 1940: "God keep and bless our Führer; may he grant our nation victory and peace."[100] As the war progressed, however, the tone of official church correspondence grew increasingly tense. With the downturn in the eastern campaign, the launch of a second front by the Western Allies in France, and the regular procession of air raids on German cities, 1944 brought with it new crises for the churches in the Pirna district as well. In September 1944, Superintendent Leichte reported to his clergymen that the Saxon Lutheran Church had—like the rest of Germany—been summoned to "total war."[101] To this end, Lutheran authorities severely curtailed the number of associations, meetings, and church services in the parishes of the Pirna district, canceling virtually all public lectures, special celebrations, annual assemblies, and the like for the duration of the war. Pastors were increasingly left to their own devices, as all nonessential correspondence was discouraged. By early 1945, they were instructed not to burn candles in church services, in order to save supplies and reduce the risk of sighting by enemy bombers. Pastors were also instructed to compile war chronicles for their parishes, preserving at least a local record of important events. Reiterating the importance of following every ordinance sent by authorities in Dresden, Superintendent Leichte added, "As soldiers of the homeland, we do not want to grouse about this, but rather to stand in formation and also undertake our administration loyally and conscientiously, even as before."[102]

The physical destruction of Dresden in the massive air raids of February 13 and 14, 1945, left churchmen demoralized and communications in disarray. Leichte's circular letter that month focused almost entirely on the destruction of Dresden and its implications for ecclesiastical administration and record keeping:

> Through the terrible air raid on Dresden, the city center and even some suburbs were as much as completely destroyed. This fate has overtaken the Saxon Church Office, district church office and both superintendents' offices, as well as almost all the churches. For the Church Office, an emergency work place has now been opened in the apartment of [Superior Church Council] President Klotzsche . . . for the *most urgent* and *most important* matters.

Leichte went on to list several other emergency quarters established by the higher church authorities in Dresden and instructed clergy on what to do in the event they were forced to abandon their homes or offices:

> I ask for the greatest possible accommodation. If additional confiscation/impounding of office space is ordered [by military authorities], then parish business must be transferred to the parsonage or sacristy of the church. It must be left to the pastor to proceed charitably and resourcefully. All bureaucracy must now be fundamentally excluded.

Leichte concluded his circular letter with a prayer of hope and a challenge amid the collapse of the Third Reich he had so zealously worked for and believed in: "May the Lord God prevent additional disaster and grant us daily strength to hold out and persevere until the sun of his favor shines on us again. Everyone do his Christian duty to the utmost."[103]

No such salvation was forthcoming, however, and as the Third Reich collapsed under the weight of military defeat, pastors were left on their own to survive and minister as best they could. By July 1945, however, the Saxon Lutheran Church was beginning to reorganize itself. In Pirna, Pastor Martin Meinel of Bad Schandau had taken over the superintendency and had begun to invite local pastors to make appointments with him to discuss the affairs of their churches.[104]

Meinel and his colleagues set about to figure out how they could come together again in collegial fellowship. To be sure, it would not be around the mission to glorify the German nation. As Pastor Karl Partecke of Sebnitz argued, Hitler had been the fulfillment of Nietzsche's prophecy, the result of which was the prostration of the German nation, its future resting solely in God's hands. "Faith alone" would serve as the new foundation for the Christians in Germany, for, "it is clear to all thinking people that the old Party slogans now no longer say anything to us. . . . Today, all politics must stand before God. For God alone is now the hope of the German nation." Meinel himself summed it up best in a letter written in August 1945, when he repeated his desire that God would help the pastors "so that the church is really built upon the one foundation that remains: Jesus Christ."[105]

Meinel continued the difficult task of overseeing the Pirna district during the chaotic transition through the surrender, political dissolution, and Allied occupation of Germany, until Pastor Hermann Klemm of Burkhardswalde was appointed superintendent in Pirna in November 1945. Klemm had been district pastor of the Confessing Church throughout the National Socialist era, and his oppositional stance then won him the position of successor to the ardent National Socialist, Superintendent Leichte. Klemm had never been a member of the NSDAP and only belonged to the National Socialist People's Welfare (NSV), a membership that had been ordered by the Saxon Church Office and expressly approved by the Saxon Confessing Church Council.[106]

The assumption of leadership in the Pirna district by men like Superintendent Hermann Klemm and Pastors Martin Meinel of Bad Schandau and Karl Partecke of Sebnitz marked the victory of both the Confessing Church and *Middle* in Pirna. Preaching and teaching were once more based exclusively on the Bible and Reformation Confessions of Faith. Stable administration by spiritually mature church leaders was reestablished, and the influence of synods was restored. That victory, however, had come at great cost. A dozen years of church-political conflict had left many of the Pirna parishes divided, many parishioners distanced from the church, and many deep rifts between pastoral colleagues. Half a dozen years of war had left church buildings damaged, parish associations atrophied, administrative links with Dresden scrambled, and at least one colleague, Pastor Schulze of Dohna, fallen in battle.[107]

More worrisome still was the future, though Superintendent Klemm probably had little time to ponder it amid the chaos and ruin of 1945. After surviving twelve years of National Socialist Church Struggle, he might have despaired had he realized that Communist Party secretaries would soon replace National Socialist führers, that the Saxon Lutheran Church would once again be challenged by radical political ideology, and that Pirna archive files marked "Confessing Church" would not end in 1945 but would continue into the 1970s.

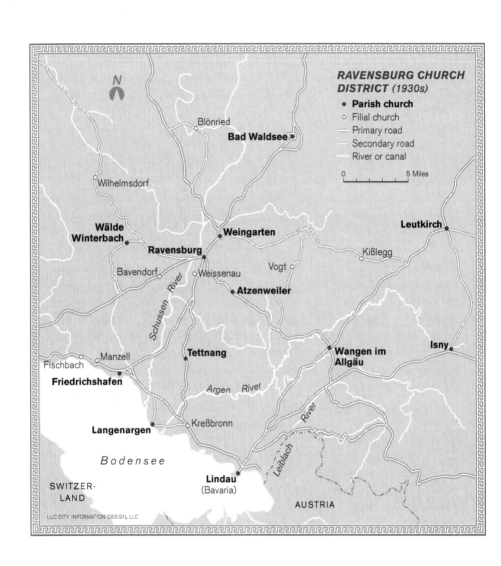

**RAVENSBURG CHURCH
DISTRICT** *(1930s)*

- ● **Parish church**
- ○ Filial church
- — Primary road
- — Secondary road
- — River or canal

0          5 Miles

N

Blönried

**Bad Waldsee**

Wilhelmsdorf

**Wälde
Winterbach**

**Weingarten**

**Leutkirch**

**Ravensburg**

Kißlegg

Bavendorf

Weissenau

Vogt

**Atzenweiler**

Schussen River

Manzell

**Tettnang**

**Wangen im
Allgäu**

**Isny**

Fischbach

**Friedrichshafen**

Argen River

**Langenargen**

Kreßbronn

Leiblach River

*B o d e n s e e*

**Lindau**
(Bavaria)

**SWITZER-
LAND**

**AUSTRIA**

LUCIDITY INFORMATION DESIGN, LLC

# chapter seven

## The Church Struggle
## in Ravensburg, Württemberg

**Parish life in Ravensburg during the Third Reich** was significantly more peaceful than in either Nauen or Pirna, where ideological division and church-political conflict gave the concept Church Struggle real meaning. Three factors contributed to the milder response of Ravensburg Protestants to the National Socialist political transformation. First and foremost, Lutherans were only a small minority in south Württemberg, a region in which the Roman Catholic Church and the Catholic Center Party set the religious and political tone for society. Lutheran pastors and Lutheran churches were not important for public ceremonies or holiday celebrations, as they were in Protestant northern Germany. The result was that institutional Protestantism was only loosely connected to the Nazi state, and there was far less ideological conflict in Ravensburg parishes than in Nauen or Pirna.

A second factor that set the church-political tone in Ravensburg was geography. Protestants were sparsely scattered in Upper Swabia, meaning that the Ravensburg district was at one and the same time geographically larger and numerically smaller than either the Nauen or Pirna districts. With only eleven parishes and seventeen pastorates, there were simply fewer opportunities for church-political conflict. Moreover, Ravensburg was located far away from the centers of political or ecclesiastical power, unlike Nauen and Pirna, which were immediately adjacent to Berlin and Dresden. Situated at the edge of both the Württemberg Protestant Church and the German Reich, Ravensburg was farther away from Stuttgart than any other church or political district in all of Württemberg.

The third factor that set Ravensburg apart from Nauen and Pirna was the stability of the Protestant church throughout Württemberg and in Ravensburg itself. This was largely the product of the steady leadership of Württemberg bishop

Theophil Wurm and his church administration in Stuttgart. In contrast to the German Christian takeovers of the Brandenburg and Saxon regional churches, which radically transformed the theological, administrative, and legal foundations of church life, Bishop Wurm successfully opposed the attempt of German Christian Reich bishop Ludwig Müller to seize control of the Württemberg Church, impose National Socialist political forms, and incorporate it into the German Protestant Reich Church. Because the Württemberg Protestant Church remained "intact" under Wurm, there was very little reason for church-political conflict between pastors and higher church authorities. Wurm ensured that the Bible and the traditional Reformation Confessions remained the rule of faith in his church, creating a stability that not only limited conflict in Ravensburg parishes but also meant that *German Christians*, and not members of the Confessing Church, were the church-political minority. In Ravensburg itself, there was little turnover among parish clergy during the Nazi era, and contemporaries reported that the pastors of the district were of a high quality. Bishop Wurm was a former pastor from the Ravensburg district. He understood the dynamics of parish life in the Protestant hinterland and found competent pastoral candidates to serve in both temporary and permanent positions—not least the two university theologians Helmut Thielicke and Günther Dehn. This institutional stability, together with the minority status of Protestants and the geographical distance of the district from Stuttgart, created a much more placid Protestant church culture in Ravensburg than in either Nauen or Pirna. It also gives us an opportunity to examine the Church Struggle in a context where the church-political roles were reversed.

This role reversal did not mean, however, that there were no dissident clergy in Ravensburg. Nothing could be further from the truth, for the most important local character throughout the entire Hitler era was Pastor Dr. Karl Steger of Friedrichshafen, an ardent German Christian and National Socialist. The only significant local opponent of the Wurm administration, Steger created by far the most church-political controversy in Ravensburg. Because he stands out so conspicuously from the other parish clergy, Steger and his story serve as the foundation for assessing both the possibilities and the limitations of pastoral influence in the local Church Struggle in Ravensburg.

## Karl Steger

When Karl Steger came to the Friedrichshafen parish in 1929, he was in mid-career, having already served as a parish pastor for thirteen years. He was also an academic and had developed radical right-wing political views during the course of his doctoral work on political nationalism in the 1848 German revolutions. Like so many academics in his day, Steger's research complemented his deep commitment to authoritarian nationalism as the means to Germany's political recovery. Just as in 1848, he argued, international enemies were seeking to weaken and divide the Germany of his day. This time, he contended, they must be stopped.[1]

Thus, in 1924, Steger entered the public forum, winning a seat in the Württemberg parliament as a member of the "*Völkisch*-Social Bloc," also known as the National Socialist Freedom Party. This pastors' movement attacked the Versailles Treaty "as a violation of 'the spirit of Christian love and justice.'" In addition, its members "swore fealty to Luther in his most militant guise, proclaimed 'honesty' and Christian charity as the essence of a genuine social policy, and, predictably, declared war on the alleged Jewish influences as inimical to true religion and a threat to the 'purity and rectitude of the German soul.'"[2] In keeping with these political views, Steger used a 1925 parliamentary debate to protest the decision of civil authorities in Stuttgart to prohibit Hitler from addressing a public rally in the city. Over the next two years, he campaigned for the movement and served as party secretary until the Bloc merged with the NSDAP in 1927. After that, Steger crossed over to the Citizens' Party until his parliamentary term ended and he began to focus exclusively on his ecclesiastical career.[3]

Steger's deep-seated political nationalism emerged as a stumbling block at the very outset of his relationship with the Friedrichshafen parish in 1929, when he was interviewed for the associate pastor position there. Tensions rose when two members of the Friedrichshafen parish council who were interviewing Steger informed him that they were searching for a politically liberal pastor to complement the conservative minister they already had. Steger promptly told them that liberalism was a failed movement lacking any "inner light," and then added that he was the most extreme right-wing pastor in all of Württemberg and would not compromise on that.

In spite of this rather stark difference of opinion, Steger was appointed to the Friedrichshafen position, based in large part on the recommendation of Prelate Theophil Wurm, who would later become the Württemberg bishop. From Friedrichshafen, the new pastor quickly immersed himself in Württemberg church politics on behalf of the German Christians, whose political convictions he shared. From 1933 until 1935, Steger held the position of *sponsor* for Württemberg German Christians, responsible for relations between German Christian pastors and the Württemberg church government. During the same period, he was also the leader of the German Christians in the southern district of Württemberg, which included the church district of Ravensburg. A natural outgrowth of this activity was Steger's election as the Ravensburg delegate to the Württemberg Synod in July 1933. When it met, the German Christians, who held a narrow majority, selected Steger to serve as synod president, a testament to his status among them. Church press reports confirm the contested nature of the selection—while the German Christian *Deutsche Sonntag* praised Steger's leadership as calm and skillful, the editor of the *Evangelische Kirchenblatt für Württemberg* depicted Steger's language as hurtful and hollow. As synod president, a position he held from 1933 to 1945, Steger chaired the executive Standing Committee of the synod and also sat on the powerful Württemberg Church Committee, a three-member body that oversaw personnel decisions, comprised of Bishop Wurm, Steger, and another German Christian delegate.[4]

Like his German Christian colleagues, Steger hoped to mobilize the spiritual resources of German Protestantism on behalf of the National Socialist renewal of Germany. Institutional Protestantism would have to march in step with the political centralization and authoritarian leadership of the National Socialist movement. To achieve such a close integration of church and state would take the unification of the twenty-eight Protestant regional churches (and ultimately the Roman Catholic Church too) into a centralized Reich church led by a powerful Reich bishop. These core convictions animated Steger's career during the Third Reich, whether he participated in Württemberg church leadership, parish ministry, or German Christian activism. But if Steger's objectives remained consistent, his strategy differed greatly depending on whether he was in Stuttgart or Ravensburg. Within the Württemberg church administration, Steger worked as an influential member of the inner circle, using his position on leading committees to provoke crisis and undermine Bishop Wurm's leadership. Within the Ravensburg church district, however, Steger was an outsider, ostracized by the other Lutheran clergy for his German Christian radicalism and contentious behavior. Forced to act independently, he used the local parish newsletter, confirmation instruction, and other pastoral functions to propagate his German Christian and National Socialist ideas.

### Karl Steger and Württemberg Church Politics

As president of the Württemberg Synod and so-called Protector of the Württemberg German Christians, Steger received many opportunities to address groups of German Christians. In 1933 and 1934, Steger spoke in cities such as Reutlingen, Göppingen, and Heilbronn, rallying local German Christians around his objectives. In his speeches, he called for church and state to cooperate in the upbringing of children and advocated the mobilization of German youth under Hitler's leadership. He presented Hitler as the answer to the state of crisis in German politics, comparing him to Luther and Bismarck. Under Hitler's guidance, Steger asserted, Germans were rediscovering their inner life of faith, in which their belief in God was lived out through a uniquely German form of Christianity rooted in a revived German national community.[5]

Also during the early part of the Third Reich, Steger participated in the preparation of a German Christian reform program for Württemberg. As a matter of course, the program advocated the incorporation of the Württemberg Protestant Church into the new German Reich Church. It also called for the creation of a German national biblical reader, comprised of parts of the Old Testament that were "un-Jewish" and therefore relevant to German Christianity, as well as the entire New Testament, a short history of Christianity in Germany, character portraits of the early church fathers, and the spiritual journeys of great Christian men, including various German Protestants. The program explicitly endorsed the new Nazi state and vilified Germany's supposed enemies: Marxist materialism, theological liberalism, divisive sects, the "inherited German defects" of subjectivism, particularism, and egoism, and, lastly, all other enemies of the Reformation heritage. It concluded with a proposal to reorganize the Württemberg Church along National Socialist lines, by eliminating class distinctions and creating a living community under authoritarian leaders.

As one of the few concrete products of German Christian theology, the reform program illustrates the way in which Steger and his colleagues hoped the Protestant church would martial its spiritual resources on behalf of the Third Reich, partnering with the Nazi state in the campaign to renew and unite the nation. In a subsequent communication, Steger and other German Christian leaders appealed to the entire Württemberg clergy to unite together under Hitler, whose coming they described as the product of divine Providence.[6]

Steger was nothing if not consistent in his work as a theologian, ideologue, and activist. Already in September 1933, he rallied a group of dissident pastors to challenge the authority of Bishop Wurm. This bid to stir up opposition in Stuttgart failed miserably, however, after speakers at a massive Berlin German Christian rally scandalized Protestants across the Third Reich. The incident took place on November 13, 1933, when twenty thousand German Christians gathered in the Berlin Sport Palace. There they heard Dr. Reinhold Krause, the regional leader for the German Christians in Berlin, call for the creation of a nonconfessional German people's church purged of all Jewishness, including the entire Old Testament and the New Testament teachings of the "Rabbi Paul."[7] For many traditional conservatives in the German Christian Movement, Krause's speech was a massive shock, revealing how easily radicals in the movement could slip into heresy in the interests of promoting German racial nationalism.

In Württemberg, the reaction was immediate and profound. Hundreds of clergy abandoned the German Christian Movement and pledged allegiance to Bishop Wurm. Up to eight hundred pastors joined Martin Niemöller's Pastors' Emergency League, devoting themselves to opposing the application of Nazi racial policy within German Protestant churches. In the Württemberg Synod, a secession of close to 150 delegates from the German Christian faction left only thirty hardliners who refused to submit to Wurm (among them, Steger). The secession fundamentally altered the balance of power in the Württemberg Church, because it eliminated the German Christian majority in the Württemberg Synod, jeopardizing the German Christians' control of two key executive committees: the Synod Standing Committee and the Württemberg Church Committee. Any new plenary meeting of the Württemberg Synod would surely include a vote leading to the dismissal of Steger and other German Christians from these two committees. This, in turn, would bring about the total collapse of the German Christian plan to incorporate the Württemberg Church into the German Protestant Reich Church.

During this period, Steger was on very bad terms with other Württemberg church leaders, some of whom considered him an unsavory character who never should have been elected to the Württemberg Synod in the first place.[8] Things went from bad to worse when Steger and his fellow German Christians broke a January 1934 agreement to respect the leadership of Bishop Wurm. Combative as ever, Steger complained that the Württemberg Church was too mistrustful and too slow to enter the unified Reich Church. As a German Christian, he explained how he yearned to deepen and spiritualize the Third Reich through the gospel and to elevate the National Socialist worldview by connecting it with German Christian values:

> Not as a subservient slave should the Protestant church fulfil its tasks in today's state, but in the free realization that our Führer's mission is God-willed and thereby deserves total dedication. If the Protestant church does not seize this task, then it will stand on the outside and its circle of activity will dwindle more and more, that is, it will ultimately ruin itself.[9]

Indeed, Steger believed the church had already lost its traditional roles in youth work, social welfare, and education because it had wasted so much time on endless internal negotiations, rather than rushing to join a centralized, supraconfessional German church.

If Steger's dream of a single German church would run roughshod over the traditional independence of the twenty-eight Protestant regional churches, it also contained a strong dose of anti-Catholicism. He made it clear that Protestants ought to prepare for "the final battle against Rome," and he warned that if German Protestantism would not subdue Catholicism, then the National Socialist state would take measures against both confessions. In light of these convictions, Steger accused Bishop Wurm of wasting a valuable opportunity to attract Catholics and unite Protestants through an aggressive church campaign based on the ideas of the German Christians:

> My experience in the Catholic Oberland, my own work in Friedrichshafen in miniature is for me proof that our way is the right one. My struggle from 1924 to 1927 as a National Socialist representative, where I have also spoken in the Oberland, has shown me in dozens of cases that the souls of our Catholic fellow citizens are largely open for [German Christian] beliefs; this realization was not the least of the reasons why I went as pastor to Friedrichshafen.

Steger's diatribe against Wurm underscored their theological as well as church-political differences. Steger argued that "faith and life" were the two poles around which the church and its ministry ought to revolve and glossed over the fact that this could easily carry the church away from its fidelity to Scripture and the Reformation Confessions of Faith. Moreover, by setting National Socialist values up as the benchmark for Christianity, Steger ignored the real possibility of a clash between Hitler's worldview and the traditional teachings of the church.

One month later, Steger's opposition to Wurm's church government moved from words to actions when he participated in the attempt of Reich Bishop Müller to seize control of the Württemberg Church and to incorporate it into the Reich Church. Steger and the other German Christians on the Standing Committee used their majority to exploit a deadlock in the debate over a new Württemberg church budget. At issue was funding for the Protestant Parish Service, which the German Christians viewed as an unhealthy competitor with the NSDAP in the realm of social work. Steger and his colleagues insisted that a German Christian be placed in charge of the Parish Service, and also that German Christians be given a majority on the Württemberg Superior Church Council. These were outrageous demands and were immediately rejected by Wurm, the Superior Church Council, and most members of the Württemberg Synod, who accused Steger and the other German Christians of playing a dangerous game of church politics.[10]

It was then that Steger and his German Christian colleague on the Standing Committee appealed to Reich Bishop Müller to intervene in the governance of the Württemberg Church, based on claims that Wurm thought only of Württemberg, opposed the Reich Church, and acted subversively toward the Reich bishop. Steger was put forward as a potential emergency caretaker over the Württemberg Church, to prepare the way for Reich Bishop Müller's annexation of the Württemberg Church.

Steger's actions provoked Bishop Wurm to schedule a plenary session of the Württemberg Synod for April 16, in order to settle the budget impasse once and for all. To prevent Wurm from using the Synod to oust Steger and the other German Christians from their powerful executive positions, Reich Bishop Müller intervened by calling a meeting of the Standing Committee for April 15, where Müller's assistant, Prussian ministerial secretary August Jäger, produced an emergency decree for the regulation of church conditions in Württemberg. The decree, which had already been predated and prepublished as Reich Church law when Jäger pulled it from his briefcase, gave Reich Bishop Müller sole power to summon or dismiss the Württemberg Synod, on account of the "emergency situation." With control of the Synod wrested from Wurm's hands, the plenary meeting scheduled for the following day was canceled, and Steger and the other German Christians on both the Standing Committee and the Württemberg Church Committee were once again secure in their executive positions.

Though this capricious intervention on behalf of the German Christian Movement offended Württemberg clergy deeply, Steger defended the action in two circular letters sent to Württemberg Lutheran pastors. Depicting Wurm as a rebellious bishop, Steger portrayed himself as a desperate counselor trying in vain to avert a crisis. As before, he argued, "Only a united, uniform Reich Church can fulfil great duties for our nation," and he insisted that the incorporation of Württemberg into the Reich Church would alter only its external structure, not its internal confessional nature: "To this day, I have not understood what this entire complex of questions has to do with the gospel of Jesus Christ." He continued to attack Bishop Wurm, criticizing Wurm's "Württemberg eccentricity" and implying that the bishop lacked statesmanship. Finally, Steger warned that Wurm would soon be unfit to hold his high office unless he calmed the church-political storms in Württemberg, began to support the Reich bishop, and quit pursuing his own separatist church-political agenda: "The unitary Reich Church is a requirement of the hour; our Führer knows and wants that too."[11]

Steger's account of events was sharply rejected by other members of the Württemberg Synod, who published two declarations in defense of Wurm. District superintendents also weighed in against Steger, as did the Superior Church Council, which condemned the hasty, arbitrary, and illegal methods of the Reich Church intervention. The council also took issue with Steger's artificial division between the external structure and the internal teachings of the church, noting that the principle of the priesthood of all believers mandated the participation of parish representatives at every level of church government and adding that the sharp opposition of the theological faculties (with their many committed National Socialists) demonstrated that there was more at stake than just the church's external structure.[12]

Despite these critiques, Steger's version of the April events found favor with the Württemberg state government, the Reich Ministry of the Interior, and the Reich bishop himself. As a result, Steger was quickly elevated to the highest levels of German church leadership. Invited by Reich Bishop Müller to participate in the Reich Church Constitutional Committee, Steger was also one of fifty-nine delegates nominated by the Reich Church Office to attend the Second Reich Synod in Berlin in August 1934.[13]

Meanwhile, the crisis in Württemberg was reaching a breaking point. On September 3, 1934, the Reich bishop dissolved the Württemberg Protestant Church and converted the region into an administrative province in the Reich Church. Five days later, officials from Müller's office together with Württemberg German Christian leaders, Steger included, forcibly occupied the headquarters of the Württemberg Superior Church Council, seizing control from Bishop Wurm and his associates. Members of the Superior Church Council allied with the Confessing Church were summarily dismissed from their positions, while Bishop Wurm was suspended, pending a final decision on his fate. In their place, German Christian commissars were appointed to manage the Württemberg Church Province. Karl Steger was directly involved in these actions as an assistant to one of the two top commissars and as a member of the reconstituted Superior Church Council, now dominated by German Christian servants of the Reich bishop. Later, he was also appointed to another commissarial role, as a regional superintendent over church districts in southern Württemberg.[14]

As for the Württemberg Synod, it too was reorganized under German Christian control, with Steger retaining his position as president. In October 1934, it met to debate the fate of Bishop Wurm. Steger argued vigorously and successfully for Wurm's outright dismissal, asserting that brute force was necessary to decide the leadership issue in the Württemberg Church. In words described as "cynical and malicious," he asserted that the Württemberg Church would not regain the confidence of parishioners until the insidious poison of Wurm was removed. As Steger summed it up, Wurm was simply "too small" a character for the crisis at hand.

Despite the initial success of the Reich bishop's takeover of the Württemberg Church, Karl Steger remained frustrated by the persistence of popular support for Wurm, lambasting the growing division between German Christians and the Confessing Church ("Psychosis!"). His worries would soon be justified. By the end of October, pressure from the German public and British church leaders convinced Hitler to order the reinstatement of Wurm and other suspended church leaders. Soon after that, a Stuttgart court ruled that the occupation of the Württemberg Superior Church Council offices by Reich Bishop Müller's officials had been illegal. As a result, all actions associated with Müller's seizure of power in Württemberg were repealed: the Württemberg Synod and Superior Church Council were reconstituted in their previous forms, Bishop Wurm resumed his authority over the church, and Steger and the other German Christian church commissars were dismissed. Steger even faced a criminal charge of slander, stemming from a speech he made at a German Christian meeting in Ravensburg. The charge was eventually dropped, but Steger's dramatic days in the center of Württemberg church politics were clearly at an end. Though he continued to sit as the president of the Württemberg Synod and maintained his role as a German Christian leader, Steger turned his attention after 1935 to working on behalf of the German Christian cause in Friedrichshafen and throughout the Ravensburg district.[15]

### Karl Steger as Pastor in Friedrichshafen

With Bishop Wurm firmly in control of the Württemberg Protestant Church again, Württemberg German Christians fell from their position as the dominant church party and took on a kind of pariah status, not unlike that of the Confessing Church clergy in the Old Prussian Union Church. For Karl Steger, this new reality meant that he was largely shunned by his fellow pastors in the Ravensburg district. Steger's participation in the ouster of Bishop Wurm was very badly received by other pastors in Ravensburg, who had refused to deal with Reich Bishop Müller's German Christian regime in Stuttgart. Indeed, as Superintendent Ströle stated repeatedly, following Wurm meant remaining faithful to the gospel of Christ, while following the German Christian commissars who served the Reich bishop meant compromising that fundamental commitment to Scripture and the Reformation Confessions of Faith.[16]

In response, Steger continued to defend both his German Christian commitment and his actions in the Württemberg Church Struggle. In a speech to the Protestant Men's Association in Friedrichshafen, he underscored his primary goal to establish a single Reich Church, denied the accusation that the Reich bishop and his German Christian allies planned to do away with the traditional church confessions, and lamented the portrayal of German Christians as heretics and fanatics. Invoking Protestant reformer Martin Luther as a German patriot, Steger summed up the German Christian campaign with the slogan: "One God, one Christ, one Nation."[17]

After the Reich bishop's unlawful incorporation of the Württemberg Protestant Church collapsed, pastors in Ravensburg gathered to discuss Steger and other German Christian clergy in their midst. As adherents of the Confessing Church in Württemberg, Superintendent Ströle and the other clergy of Ravensburg were angered by the participation of Steger and other local pastors in the German Christian Movement and the anti-Wurm campaign. Originally, five pastors from the Ravensburg district had joined the German Christians, though two of them had abandoned the movement after the Sport Palace scandal and another had subsequently declared himself for Wurm. Ströle and the other Ravensburg clergy agreed to work together with all of the former German Christians except for Steger, whom they unanimously refused to readmit into their circle of fellowship. Describing his attitude as overbearing and disrespectful, they declared Steger's church politics combative, dishonorable, irresponsible, and contrary to the spirit of the church. They concluded that Steger would continue to support what they saw as the fraudulent and dictatorial church government of the Reich bishop and decided that he was so insincere that any further confidence in him was impossible. Damning as those words were, they reflected not only the pastors' disapproval of Steger's church politics but also their judgment about his character.[18] For the next eleven years, this remained the situation between Steger and the rest of the Ravensburg clergy. According to Steger, Superintendent Ströle instructed him to keep his distance from all pastoral meetings and district church assemblies, because the other pastors rejected his church politics and refused to tolerate his presence. Steger was not invited to any district events, and no one would discuss his ostracization with him.[19]

Steger was also opposed by the Friedrichshafen chapter of the Protestant Men's Association, which held monthly lectures and discussions. Although the Men's Association was conservative and nationalistic in nature, its leaders consistently affirmed the eternal Scriptures as the witness of Jesus Christ and placed salvation through Christ alone, complete with the hope of eternal life, ahead of the pressing demand for service to the nation and state.[20]

Steger was not entirely alone, however, for he commanded a significant following among local German Christians. Friedrichshafen German Christians also held monthly meetings, often attracting over 250 people. Steger was their patron, though not officially their leader. He often made speeches in their meetings and arranged for prominent German Christians to visit.

One of Steger's most significant local speeches was a May 1935 consideration of the work, prospects, and goals of the German Christian Movement. He began defensively, with a denial that German Christians were in combat against either the Roman Catholic or Protestant churches. Instead, he claimed that German Christians were struggling solely to deepen and enliven the National Socialist German nation through a union of Germanism and Christianity.[21] In order to achieve their goal, German Christians strove to be faithful to the Fatherland, faithful in their parish work, ready to explain their work, objective, cooperative, and honorable. While the blessings of the German Christian efforts might not be visible at the time, Steger concluded, it was enough to know that they were serving their nation and Fatherland—the German soul—just as Christ had done. With a threefold *Sieg-Heil* to the Führer and the Reich bishop, Steger concluded his speech and invited his audience to sign up for the German Christian Movement.

Under Steger's care, the local branch of German Christians in Friedrichshafen grew into a zealous outpost for the movement in South Württemberg. In 1935, the group drafted its own theological statement, following Steger's conversion to a more radical, racial German Christian ideology. The resulting *Oberlandprogramm* hailed Hitler in the highest style, thanking God for the divine miracle of the German national renewal and extolling the miracle year of 1933, when God had sent the Führer to Germany.[22] The growing radicalism of Friedrichshafen German Christians manifested itself in new attacks on the Wurm church administration. In April 1937, a Friedrichshafen German Christian circular letter dismissed the "Confessing Front" as a collection of "popish orthodoxy, literalistic Christians, political reactionaries, Jews, and associates of Jews."[23]

Steger stirred up other controversies in his local work for the German Christians in Friedrichshafen. In the spring of 1935, Steger organized a speaking tour of Württemberg for Reich Bishop Müller. Against the wishes of Superintendent Ströle and most of the Ravensburg clergy, Müller came to speak in Friedrichshafen, where Steger introduced him as the champion of the Reich Church ideal and claimed that Friedrichshafen German Christians were convinced of the ultimate victory of the Reich Church in Germany.[24]

That same year, Steger widened the scope of his German Christian activity and began to hold meetings in the Bavarian city of Lindau, a few miles east of Friedrichshafen along the shore of the Bodensee. Since Lindau was in the Bavarian Protestant Church, Steger soon ran afoul of both the Württemberg and the Bavarian church authorities. Apparently, Steger had conducted an unauthorized German Christian worship service in the municipal concert hall in Lindau. About 350 people attended the illegal gathering, which was scheduled in direct competition with the local Lutheran church service. Worse yet, Steger had also baptized the child of a German Christian couple from Lindau, even though the parish pastor had expressly denied Steger permission.[25]

Steger tried halfheartedly to justify his action, arguing that he had notified the parish in Lindau two days prior to the service and that he had merely wanted to save the family the expense of traveling to Friedrichshafen for the baptism. The Württemberg Superior Church Council responded with a primer in Bavarian church law, explaining that it demanded express permission from the parish pastor for any non-Bavarian cleric to visit a Bavarian parish. Steger claimed confusion about the service time and blamed the Lindau German Christians for scheduling the event against the local church service.[26] Flouting the authority of his ecclesiastical superiors, Steger continued illegally performing pastoral functions in Lindau for over two years, marrying German Christians, conducting church services, arranging German Christian lectures, speaking at rallies, and even teaching confirmation instruction to Lindau children.[27]

During this period, Steger became increasingly radical in his ideology. In one speech, he compared German Christians to the "old fighters" of the NSDAP, who were once scorned as dreamers but eventually won the day for Hitler's movement. So too, Steger believed, would German Christians from the South march forward in victory for the goal of "one God, one Christ, one German soul." Steger even embraced the neo-pagan German Faith Movement of Tübingen professor Jakob Wilhelm Hauer, declaring that German Christians would work together with Hauer and even the Nazi neo-pagan ideologue Alfred Rosenberg, as long as their goals were similar. Steger affirmed Rosenberg's controversial book *Myth of the 20th Century* as "throughout true," arguing that many Protestant spokesmen had said the same things themselves![28]

During the Hitler era, Steger combined his talents as a speaker and organizer for the German Christians with his role as a writer for the *Friedrichshafen Protestant Parish Newsletter*, which he edited from 1930 until 1941, when it ceased publication because of paper rationing. Time and again, he used the pages of the parish newsletter to praise the Nazi government, urge the church to serve the German nation, and report on German Christian meetings. In April 1933, Steger joyfully greeted Hitler's rise to the chancellorship, describing it as a great moment in German history. The old had collapsed, and the new had taken its place. Looking eagerly into the future,

Steger exhorted his readers to participate fully in the National Socialist renewal of Germany. Two months later, Steger waxed poetic about the many recent changes in Germany: flags fluttered, celebrations erupted, millions had new hope for a better future for their beloved Fatherland, and all because the modest, forthright man of the people, trusted by millions, had become the Führer of the nation. Later that year, Steger celebrated the withdrawal of Germany from the League of Nations and portrayed the upcoming national election as an ideal opportunity for the nation to show its approval for National Socialism.[29]

In virtually every edition of his parish newsletter, Steger praised the many new developments in the Hitler state, including the suppression of the so-called Röhm Putsch in June 1934, the return of the Saar in January 1935, and the rearming of Germany in March 1935. In September 1937, Steger proclaimed that Germany's resurgence was due to the Lord God and the man whom he had sent in Germany's final hour, Adolf Hitler. In January 1938, Steger deflected criticism of the National Socialist regime's religious orientation, asserting that it was an injustice to hold that National Socialism was anti-Christian. Finally, in the edition of May 1940, Steger reiterated his opinion that for Germans and for Christians, Hitler's coming was in no way a matter of chance, but rather the product of God's will and power. In the early years of the Second World War, Steger continued to use the Friedrichshafen parish newsletter to drive home his conviction that God had appointed Hitler as his instrument for the salvation of Germany and his belief that German Protestants should eagerly support the National Socialist movement.[30]

Though Steger was an effective speaker, organizer, and writer on behalf of the German Christian Movement, three factors limited his effectiveness in Friedrichshafen: poor health, local and regional church opposition, and the ravages of the Second World War. The first of these factors, poor health, was one of the constants of Steger's career in Friedrichshafen. As early as 1929, Steger referred to a heart condition that restricted his duties severely in 1931 and forced him to take leaves of absence in late 1934, 1937, and again in 1942, 1943, and 1944.[31] Over time, his inability, or unwillingness, to exert himself on behalf of his parishioners created a truly immense workload for the senior pastor in Friedrichshafen, Eugen Schmid. In May 1942, for instance, while Pastor Duisberg was recovering from a hernia operation and Pastor Immanuel Spellenberg was awaiting his call-up into military service, Pastor Steger (whose heart Schmid described as "four-fifths spent") was about to leave for a cure at a sanatorium in Konstanz.[32] Two years later, in January 1944, the personnel shortage was even worse and Steger's absence even more grating. Schmid complained that Steger had taken his doctor's instructions to "do what gives you pleasure!" to mean that he should perform no work after 4:00 P.M. Apparently, since the spring of 1943, Steger had taught neither the religious instruction classes in the local school, the confirmation classes in the parish, nor the voluntary Christian instruction regularly offered at church. On top of that, he had refused to help with the youth group, the Men's Association, or the Women's Aid, nor had he conducted any Bible studies, gone on any hospital visitation, or officiated at any funerals during the winter of 1943 to 1944. (At one point, on top of all his other duties, Pastor Schmid had officiated at seven funerals in ten days.) Steger had attended only one meeting of the Friedrichshafen parish council since 1940 and, on average, had given only one or two sermons a month in his parish.[33]

In addition to these medical absences and periods of unproductivity, Steger's many positions in the Württemberg Church and the Reich Church often kept him away from Friedrichshafen, diminishing the energy he could give to local church activities. As early as November 1933, Steger asked the Württemberg Church Committee for a vicar for Friedrichshafen to help him, citing his heavy responsibilities in Stuttgart as the grounds for his request.[34] His absence from Friedrichshafen during the turning point of the Württemberg Church Struggle, in October 1934, also necessitated the appointment of a substitute vicar. Steger's frequent absences undermined his ability to propagandize on behalf of the German Christians and National Socialists, not only because he was away but also because the Württemberg Superior Church Council and Superintendent Ströle regularly appointed Confessing Church vicars who worked to undo the influence of his German Christian ideas.[35]

In the vital area of religious instruction, Steger was opposed by three groups: the Württemberg Protestant authorities, the temporary clergy working in his parish, and the Friedrichshafen parish council. For instance, in August 1936, someone in Steger's parish sent Bishop Wurm a typed copy of a new confirmation booklet Steger had compiled, a work that not only deviated from existing confirmation practices but also debased the Württemberg Confession of Faith.[36] When Wurm demanded an explanation, Steger retorted that the booklet was only a draft and that after discussions with parents in the parish, the old booklet and practice remained in place.[37] It is not clear whether this was the truth or merely an expedient way out of trouble—at the very least, it was not the last time Steger would misuse confirmation instruction to further his heterodox brand of Protestantism. Two years later, three young curates substituting for Steger tried to block his return from a medical leave, fearing he would use his role as confirmation instructor to sway young Protestants and their families toward the German Christian Movement and expose the parish to yet another round of division and conflict.[38] Indeed, that was exactly what happened the following year, just after the outbreak of war in 1939. As Steger was reviewing questions and answers from the confirmation booklet one day, a young girl responded that the greatest concern of the present day was for the German nation to emerge victorious from the war that had been forced upon it. Steger agreed with her, noting that although the confirmation booklet had said something else, the girl had given the only right answer for that moment. Then, in the next edition of the parish newsletter, Steger used the exchange in an attempt to arouse the devotion of his parishioners to their "eternally significant" Führer. Invoking biblical language that sanctified marriage, Steger said of Hitler and the Germans: "What God has joined together—our nation and our Führer—man will *not* separate!"[39]

In spite of many absences from Friedrichshafen because of poor health or church-political duties, in spite of the efforts of local clergy and Protestant authorities in Stuttgart, Steger maintained a high profile in Friedrichshafen right through the Nazi era. As Allied military forces advanced toward victory and the end of Nazism was in sight, parishioners in Friedrichshafen began to fear for Steger's position. In February 1945, they circulated a petition calling on Württemberg bishop Wurm to ensure that Steger would remain their pastor and religious instructor. Over three hundred individuals and families signed the petition, some with comments such as "Judge not, lest you be judged," or threats of leaving the church if Steger were "unjustly" dismissed.[40]

As it turned out, the only initiative to remove Steger from his post in 1945 was his own. Late that year, Steger requested a transfer to a small parish close to a suitable doctor, in order to lighten his load (!) and ameliorate his worsening heart condition.[41] Almost a full year dragged on with no response from the Superior Church Council. Then, on December 15, 1946, the Friedrichshafen pastor made a public statement that changed the situation entirely. After a Sunday morning service, Steger attempted to justify his activities during the Church Struggle. Admitting that he had struggled for a unitary Reich Church in 1933 and 1934, Steger claimed that he had expended all his efforts on behalf of the Württemberg Protestant Church ever since 1935. This he supported with a letter from Bishop Wurm thanking him for his loyal service and noting that Steger had intervened successfully with the Württemberg political authorities on behalf of the church. While it was true that Steger had occasionally mediated between Wurm and Steger's radical German Christian colleagues, his own career had been riddled with insubordination and resistance against the Wurm administration.[42]

Not surprisingly, the Friedrichshafen parish council labeled Steger's declaration as both a misrepresentation of past events and a blow to the present unity of the parish. In response, they submitted a formal request for Steger's dismissal, not because of his previous German Christian agitation or his National Socialist sympathies, but because he had publicly lied about his past and was threatening to split the Friedrichshafen parish again.[43] Technically, these were not grounds on which the Superior Church Council could dismiss Steger, so in the end, Stuttgart was forced to construct a case against Steger. Church officials began to delve into Steger's participation in the Church Struggle, quickly finding abundant evidence of Steger's divisiveness and heresy. After a series of official hearings and a fruitless appeal by Steger, the Superior Church Council finally pensioned him off in January 1948.[44]

Even as an outcast in the Ravensburg district, Karl Steger had been a formidable force. Like other German Christians, he believed in the fusion of Nazi ideology and Protestant theology and was convinced that the unification of all the Protestant churches in Germany would unleash a powerful spiritual deepening and strengthening of the National Socialist political revolution. Although he was briefly successful in pursuing that agenda as a leader in the Württemberg church government, ultimately Steger came closer to achieving his goals as pastor in Friedrichshafen than as synod president in Stuttgart. Even in the face of illness, local and regional church opposition, and Germany's defeat in the Second World War, Steger developed and maintained a loyal circle of roughly three hundred Friedrichshafen parishioners who consistently supported him, even after the collapse of Hitler's Germany in 1945.

## Church Politics in Leutkirch

Steger's influence not only dominated the Church Struggle in his Friedrichshafen parish but also helped advance other German Christian groups in the neighboring communities of Leutkirch, Isny, and Bad Waldsee. Pastors in those three parishes remained loyal to Württemberg bishop Wurm and therefore to the Confessing Church. They worked with church officials in Stuttgart to thwart the noisy demands of local German Christians. Leutkirch was an especially important parish for German Christians, who hoped to turn their city into an important center for the movement in the Allgäu region, west of Ravensburg.[45] To that end, prominent German Christian speakers came to Leutkirch in 1935, including Pastor Griesinger of Ulm, who spoke on "Blood, Race, Nation, God," and on "The Book of Nature," a lecture in which he abandoned Scripture and presented a reflection on God out of nature and stories of the Greek and Roman gods. Pastor Karl Steger of Friedrichshafen also lectured in Leutkirch, and both he and Griesinger held German Christian assemblies and holiday celebrations as late as Easter 1937, even though Griesinger had already been forced into retirement in late 1936 on moral and political grounds.[46]

Even though Württemberg Protestant authorities tried to support veteran Leutkirch pastor Theodor Metzger with guest speakers from Stuttgart, Metzger still faced the withering criticism of parishioners like Mrs. Welte, who repeatedly wrote Stuttgart complaining about both her pastor and Bishop Wurm's government. In July 1935, for instance, she described Wurm's "Confessing Front" as "deceitful, treasonous, separatist and reactionary." For a long time, she continued, it had become, "no longer Christian and not Protestant, but Jesuitical and Communistic." When Superintendent Ströle investigated the complaints, however, he found that the agitation against Pastor Metzger was led by "a couple of women." The mayor himself told Ströle that the whole business was "a personal matter of a few individuals." For example, much of the agitation had been caused by the eleven-year-old son of the German Christian leader in Leutkirch, who predicted to his friends that Metzger would soon have to leave the parish. Ströle summarily dismissed the controversy as "an example of what can be spoiled through the rigid, unforgiving attitude of the German Christian people."[47]

Nonetheless, the German Christian campaign in Leutkirch forged ahead. First, after a long string of complaints, the Württemberg Superior Church Council decided to transfer Pastor Metzger away from Leutkirch. Then the Leutkirch German Christians petitioned the Württemberg Protestant authorities to appoint Pastor Griesinger of Ulm, a noted German Christian, as their new pastor. However, rather than accede to this demand, officials in Stuttgart appointed Pastor Hilmar Schieber, an energetic member of the Confessing Church, and planned to support him by sending prominent speakers to combat the German Christians.[48] Still, the German Christians of Leutkirch continued their agitation, launching a lengthy campaign to gain the use of church facilities for their own worship services. It was only thanks to a Ravensburg court ruling overturning the decision of the Leutkirch mayor that Pastor Schieber finally managed to defend the exclusive right of the Württemberg Protestant Church to prohibit German Christians from using its church facilities.[49]

In this matter of access to the local churches, Schieber proved especially resolute in his opposition to his German Christian parishioners. When the German Christians renewed their request to use the Leutkirch Hospital Church—this time for a confirmation ceremony in March 1939—Schieber hurriedly wrote to the Superior Church Council, reminding Württemberg church leaders that they had only just defended their exclusive right to the Leutkirch churches two years earlier. He went on to describe the manner in which Leutkirch German Christians had rejected the authority of the Württemberg Protestant Church in religious instruction, pastoral ministry, church services, and church taxes, and all but demanded that Württemberg church authorities take a firm stand. After a positive reply from Stuttgart, Schieber wrote to the head of the German Christian group in Leutkirch, firmly rejecting the German Christian request for access to the church and laying down the strict conditions required before another request would be considered.[50]

As Schieber's letter illustrated, German Christians in Leutkirch had separated themselves almost completely from the official church during the mid-1930s. For one, they grew more radical, making the shift to the racialist "*Volk* Church" wing of the German Christian Movement sometime in late 1936 or early 1937. About the same time, three German Christians on the parish council resigned their positions, and German Christian parents withdrew their children from Schieber's religious instruction classes and established their own unauthorized confirmation classes. German Christians even quit paying their church taxes. Ultimately, however, the group was unable to gain the upper hand in the parish. Loyal Protestants in Leutkirch grew tired of the polemics of the German Christians, and the group's failure to gain access to Leutkirch church buildings marked the beginning of their decline.[51]

## Controversy in Isny

German Christian agitation also proved problematic for Pastor Siegle and his colleagues in the neighboring parish of Isny im Allgäu. Throughout his ministry in Isny, Siegle was an outspoken supporter of Bishop Wurm and thus a resolute opponent of local German Christians. In April 1934, he collected three hundred signatures for a protest telegram against Reich Bishop Müller's emergency decree and suspension of Wurm, though the Gestapo stopped him before he could send it to Stuttgart. Siegle lodged an official complaint and vowed to try to collect more signatures, but to no avail.[52] Undaunted, Siegle gathered another 210 signatures in early 1935, in protest of Reich Bishop Müller's planned speaking tour of Württemberg. This time Siegle was able to send his petition, which he directed to the Reich Ministry of the Interior in Berlin and the Reich Governor in Stuttgart.[53]

Pastor Siegle was not the only controversial pastor in Isny. Curate Karl Dipper's short career there disintegrated as a result of the ideological opposition of Director Diest of the Überruh convalescent home in Isny, where Dipper was supposed to provide regular pastoral care. Diest became angered at Dipper's outspoken support for Bishop Wurm during Reich Bishop Müller's illegal takeover of the Württemberg church government and prohibited Dipper from ministering in Überruh. The director accused the Isny curate of upsetting the patients and impeding their medical recovery, while Dipper retorted that the director was acting out of church-political motives rather than on medical grounds. In his own defense, Dipper claimed that he had only spoken out in the small circle of his Bible study at the convalescent home, where he defended Bishop Wurm, explained the current state of Württemberg church politics, and upheld the traditional confession of faith that the German Christians had attacked. Most provocatively, Dipper had asserted that the Christian church's ultimate allegiance was to "a lord, who also stands above A. Hitler, namely Jesus Christ." As the rift between Director Diest and Curate Dipper deepened, Dipper vowed that he would only be moved by biblical truth, and not by Diest's institutional authority. He claimed that Diest had accused him of undermining the authority of Hitler, and also that the director had confessed that Hitler was his conscience. For Dipper, this only proved the political nature of Diest's campaign against him. While he may have been right about Diest's motives, Dipper did not win the argument over access to Überruh and was soon transferred from Isny.[54]

Over the next three years, German Christians in Isny employed prominent speakers to attract new followers to their movement, just as the Leutkirch group was doing. The most important of these was none other than Pastor Griesinger of Ulm, who came to Isny soon after his initial forays into Leutkirch. On Sunday, May 5, 1935, Griesinger spoke at a German Christian assembly in Isny, raising false allegations of financial impropriety against Bishop Wurm. From sixty to seventy people were in attendance, about half of them from Isny and half from neighboring communities. Pastor Siegle, who was on holiday at the time, was incensed that Griesinger would dare speak in his parish without permission. He sent the German Christian pastor an angry letter defending his authority as parish pastor in Isny and criticizing Griesinger's church politics. Siegle charged that it was not in the spirit of Christ, the apostles, or the reformers to introduce division into a parish that preached the pure gospel, but that it was sectarian to preach without permission in other pastors' congregations. The fact that Griesinger had possessed the temerity to invite Siegle to the meeting only made the Isny pastor even angrier. In reply, Griesinger claimed he was free to lecture wherever he pleased, justifying his attitude with the argument that the German Christians were preaching the message of National Socialism as a gracious gift of God for the Christian church in Germany. Condescendingly, Griesinger expressed his hope that all pastors in Württemberg would work together to build the church and not "fight over small things."[55]

As in Leutkirch, the Württemberg Protestant authorities responded to the German Christian challenge by sending representatives from Stuttgart to hold special services in Isny. Less than two weeks after Griesinger's lecture, a member of the Württemberg Superior Church Council conducted a Confessing Church service attended by 450 people. This pleased Siegle greatly, not least because between sixty and eighty men had come, a significant number for a Thursday night event.[56]

Apart from the struggle against Griesinger and other German Christians in Isny, Pastor Siegle and his colleague Adolf Wertz also clashed with the local SA leadership in 1935. Siegle was angry because local SA leaders scheduled activities late into Saturday evenings, inhibiting Isny men from attending church services the following morning. In turn, SA leaders were critical of Siegle and Wertz's uncompromising support for Bishop Wurm and the Confessing Church. On June 23, 1935, tensions boiled over at the close of the Sunday morning service, when Pastor Wertz began to read a recent Confessing Church declaration. During Wertz's reading, several young men stood up and walked out, one at a time, grumbling and slamming the church door on their way out. Though Isny parishioners were shocked by the behavior of the young men, Pastor Siegle was unwilling to press charges, since he was unsure whether the action was spontaneous, or whether the local NS Volkszeitung editor had planned it. Siegle also wondered whether the protest stemmed from recent trouble between the pastors and the local SA work camp over the absence of SA men from church.[57]

Church-political conflicts with local party officials and German Christians continued in Isny late into the 1930s. In December 1937 Siegle was stripped of his right to teach religious instruction in the local school over critical remarks he had made. The following year, three parish councilors resigned their offices, based on a misinterpretation of party policy that they took to be an order from Hitler's deputy, Martin Bormann, prohibiting NSDAP leaders from holding leadership positions in any kind of religious association. Around the same time, the Isny German Christian group joined their neighbors in Leutkirch in the radical "*Volk* Church" wing of the German Christian Movement. In spite of these developments, the strength of the German Christians was on the wane in Isny and throughout the Allgäu region. Only forty people came to hear a German Christian guest speaker in February 1937. According to Pastor Siegle, they were mainly women from the local mothers convalescent home, along with Catholics and Red Cross sisters from Biberach. By the time that Siegle retired in early 1938, the Isny German Christians were no longer a problem for the parish.[58]

## Turmoil in Bad Waldsee

In Bad Waldsee, north of Ravensburg, Pastor W. Hartmann endured a turbulent nine years as pastor before being driven from the parish in mid-1937, thanks in part to the efforts of local German Christians. Hartmann's troubles began in 1929, when he clashed with a prominent Waldsee family, the Birkmeyers. Paul Birkmeyer directed the local textile mill and sat on the Waldsee parish council but was brought into disrepute when accusations surfaced that his wife was engaged in an extramarital affair. Controversy was no stranger to Mrs. Birkmeyer, however. The former pastor described her as a "psychopathic personality" and a "person with an unusually bad conscience" who stirred up all manner of trouble if she was not treated with special regard and referred to by her husband's title.[59]

When Pastor Hartmann questioned the Birkmeyers about the affair, they began to make trouble for him. Informal accusations surfaced that Hartmann would not visit certain parishioners and was speaking ill of them. Then a seventeen-name petition was submitted to the Superior Church Council stating that Pastor Hartmann had lost the confidence of many Waldsee parishioners. The parish council defended Hartmann against the charge, gathering 184 signatures on a petition of its own. After several months of accusations and counteraccusations, Hartmann and the Birkmeyers eventually signed an agreement to put aside their conflict and respect one other. While that did not put an end to all the trouble between the Birkmeyers and the parish—there was a subsequent accusation that the Women's Aid was shunning Mrs. Birkmeyer—the agreement did enable Pastor Hartmann to avert the threat of legal charges for slander.[60]

Whether to spite Hartmann or out of inner conviction, sometime after 1933 the Birkmeyers joined the Waldsee German Christian circle, led by Walter Staib, a local schoolteacher, and his wife, who was the church organist. Together the two couples created most of the trouble faced by Hartmann in the middle 1930s. In 1935, Hartmann and Staib clashed when Staib arranged for a Catholic teacher to substitute in his religious instruction classes, and Hartmann, who was chairman of the local Protestant school board, censured him on behalf of outraged parents. When Waldsee parents raised subsequent concerns about Staib's actions as Protestant schoolteacher, Hartmann's relationship with him grew even more strained.[61] Meanwhile, at church Hartmann clashed with Mrs. Staib, accusing her of reporting the content of his sermons to local police. When he summarily dismissed her, she filed a complaint with the Württemberg Superior Church Council, claiming Hartmann had called her a "Judas."[62] Though the council chastised Hartmann for firing Mrs. Staib without proving his accusation, she refused to return to her position, and the matter was dropped.[63]

Relations worsened in 1937, as many Waldsee Protestant parents became alarmed by Staib's German Christian propagandizing and refused to send their children to him for religious instruction. At the same time, Pastor Hartmann, who also gave religious instruction in the school, was coming under fire from other teachers, who mocked the Old Testament as a book of scandals and raised doubts about the Bible as a source of divine revelation.[64] Hartmann was transferred from the Waldsee parish, presumably to give him a new start elsewhere in Württemberg, but the damage had been done. Before the end of the year, the Staibs burned their bridges with the Waldsee parish, withdrawing their church memberships together with the leader of the Hitler Youth and a few other local notables. The Birkmeyers and other members of the German Christian group retained their church memberships but refused to pay their church taxes. Pastor Gottfried Hoffmann, Hartmann's successor, tried in vain to sort out the controversy, until Paul Birkmeyer finally withdrew his church membership in 1941 and the conflict between the German Christians and Waldsee parish subsided.[65]

## Other Parishes in the Ravensburg District

If German Christians in Leutkirch, Isny, and Bad Waldsee stirred up trouble for local pastors during the 1930s, church-political controversy was largely absent from other Ravensburg parishes during the same period. In Ravensburg itself, for instance, one report estimated that there were about two hundred German Christians in Ravensburg and Weingarten, but identified no leadership structure. In Ravensburg itself, there was no evidence of any church-political controversy, apart from the withdrawal of a few local notables from the church in 1937—the local SS leader, two SA leaders, a schoolteacher, and two doctors from Weissenau. In neighboring Weingarten, men in SA or SS uniforms could be seen in church already before 1933; confirmation students attended classes in their Hitler Youth uniforms; and NSDAP members sat on the parish council. Relations between the parish and local political leaders were positive, and there was no German Christian agitation in the parish. Indeed, Weingarteners generally rejected National Socialist neo-pagan ceremonies and adhered to traditional church baptisms, confirmations, weddings, and funerals, and few Nazis felt the need to withdraw from the church. The same holds true for the parish of Wangen im Allgäu, where the parish council reported in 1939 that neither any sect nor the German Christian Movement played any tangible role in the parish.

Despite this absence of open conflict, however, there were still underlying tensions for Protestants involved in Nazi Party politics. Reports indicate that twenty-six parish councilors from nine parishes resigned their positions for ideological or political reasons during the National Socialist era.[66] And while fewer than half of Ravensburg pastors encountered any significant church-political conflict from German Christian groups in their parishes, several clergy did face censure for their church-political actions during and after the Third Reich.

In the Ravensburg parish, two young vicars attracted the attention of the Württemberg Education Ministry for statements they had uttered during religious instruction. In 1935, students reported Vicar Werner Mauch for making a series of slanderous statements during a single religious instruction class. First, Mauch was alleged to have declared that the Führer's program of "common interest before self-interest" was impossible to fulfill because of the sin of human selfishness. This was taken by his students as an attack on Hitler. Next, Mauch's students accused him of denying the power of Aryan people and even calling the notion of Aryan supremacy a clear lie. Though he did not remember speaking that way, Mauch asserted that if he had made such a remark, it would have been for the purpose of exposing the sinfulness of racial pride before God. Mauch was also accused of criticizing the lack of character in Germany, of lamenting the fact that Germans no longer spoke their minds, and of accusing the state of threatening the existence of religious instruction. Allegedly, Mauch had asked his students not to repeat what he had told them, an assertion he denied vigorously.

On another occasion, students reported that Mauch warned that the time was coming when Christians would have to decide who really belonged to their number, and who were not real Christians. In addition, he was said to have declared that the highest calling of humans was the kingdom of God, and that there were stronger ties than blood. Mauch defended himself by citing Matthew 12:46-50, where Jesus declared that the fellowship of those in the kingdom of God was more important than his biological family. Mauch identified himself as both a loyal NSDAP member and a Christian, and argued he had said nothing against the state. Rather, he had been trying to strengthen the foundational forces of the German nation.[67]

Whether this was really his conviction or whether he was only scrambling to escape the consequences of being reported by his students, Mauch seemed unwilling to recognize the far-reaching implications of his comments. His critique touched on the most fundamental incompatibilities between the National Socialist worldview and the Christian faith: the universal condition of sin, the idolization of race, and the ultimate allegiance of the Christian to God. Mauch's forceful critique was all the more significant for coming in 1935, far earlier than many other clergy perceived such fundamental tensions between Nazism and Christianity.

Although there is no record of whether Vicar Mauch faced any legal or professional consequences for his controversial religious instruction, one of his successors in Ravensburg, Vicar Helmut Lamparter, was banned from teaching in religious instruction classes in 1937 on account of slandering the National Socialist state, after he declared that the German nation had gone a long way toward doing away with Jesus. Two years after that, Curate Immanuel Spellenberg of Friedrichshafen-Fischbach escaped investigations by Württemberg Protestant authorities (or perhaps the education ministry) and the NSDAP district court in Friedrichshafen, on account of use of the Old Testament in religious instruction.[68]

Around the same time, on February 12, 1939, four pastors in Ravensburg and Weingarten read Bishop Wurm's banned "Word to the parishes," in spite of a Gestapo warning and the threat of a fine of up to one thousand reichmarks. Superintendent Eugen Kommerell, who read Wurm's message to about 250 parishioners in the Ravensburg church, urged other pastors in his district to do the same, since it addressed current state measures against Protestant religious instruction in Württemberg schools. As he reported to the Ravensburg criminal police, he knew statement had been prohibited, but felt compelled to follow the instructions of Bishop Wurm, knowing he might well be punished. His colleague, Pastor Wolfram Gestrich, admitted to police that he too had read the statement to about fifty parishioners at the early service in Ravensburg. Gestrich shared his superintendent's convictions about the importance of the statement and the need to follow Bishop Wurm's leadership, adding that he was also motivated by his vow of ordination, which bound him to proclaim the gospel by preaching and teaching. Since Wurm's message discussed the threat to Christian religious instruction, Gestrich considered it to be an essential pastoral duty to inform his parishioners. There is no evidence that Kommerell or Gestrich faced any punishment after their initial encounter with police.[69]

In contrast to critics of the Hitler regime, National Socialists like Pastor Martin Kinzler of Tettnang suffered no political consequences for their church activities, at least until the end of the war. After the collapse of the Third Reich, however, Kinzler's Nazi record made him vulnerable to the French military authorities who occupied southwestern Germany. Kinzler was alleged to have stood "wholeheartedly" behind the Nazi state, while his wife, Helene, was a party member and the leader of the National Socialist Women's League in Tettnang. Consequently, French authorities arrested Helene Kinzler. Despite a report that Pastor Kinzler had been a *"fanatical Nazi . . . during the whole war,"* always demanding the Hitler greeting from school children in Tettnang, and that Helene Kinzler had worked "with body and soul" for the National Socialist women's movement, Württemberg bishop Wurm wrote a letter defending Kinzler and asking for the release of his wife from French detention.[70]

In the end, Pastor Martin Kinzler was forced to retire in 1946 and thus received the same treatment as prominent German Christian pastors Griesinger of Ulm and Steger of Friedrichshafen. When their divisive behavior or unsavory ideas became too unbearable, the Württemberg church government simply pensioned them off. If that was the worst that radical German Christians received from the Wurm church administration during and after the war, it was not substantially different from the treatment meted out by the Württemberg educational ministry or Ravensburg Gestapo to Confessing Church pastors in Ravensburg during the Nazi era. A far cry from the arrests, suspensions and fines suffered by clergy in Nauen and Pirna, pastors in Ravensburg were spared from most of the tumult their northern German counterparts experienced in the Church Struggle.

Such was not always the case in Württemberg, however, as the experience of Oberlenningen Pastor Julius von Jan demonstrates. After Pastor von Jan condemned the Kristallnacht Pogrom of November 1938 in a Repentance Day sermon, he was harassed, beaten, tortured, robbed, and arrested by National Socialists. A Nazi Special Court in Stuttgart later sentenced von Jan to a term in prison for an infraction of the 1934 Insidiousness Law, which prohibited any criticism of the government or the NSDAP. In other Württemberg locales, National Socialists ridiculed and beat clergy, fired shots, threw paving stones into a parsonage, and vandalized church property.[71]

In Ravensburg, however, the Church Struggle was far less intense. In part, this was due to the sparse Protestant population. Each of the parishes in the district contained tiny collections of parishioners scattered across the countryside near the towns and small cities in which the pastors lived. These far-flung parishes required pastors to travel more often, teach more classes of religious or confirmation instruction, and conduct more church services. Such a diluted Protestant presence also militated against the development of strong church-political opposition groups, as evidenced by the distances German Christians sometimes traveled to their meetings.

More important, however, was the simple fact that the Church Struggle did not throw the Württemberg Protestant Church into the kind of upheaval that Protestants in Brandenburg (and indeed the entire Old Prussian Union Church) and Saxony experienced. The majority of the clergy, who were patriotic, conservative, and committed to the traditional teachings of the church, were entirely at home in the Württemberg Protestant Church led by Bishop Wurm. Only pastors, curates, and vicars on either extreme of the church-political spectrum encountered any difficulties, whether their support of the Confessing Church led to clashes with local schoolteachers or civic officials, or whether their personal commitment to the fusion of Protestantism and National Socialism led them astray from the traditional biblical and theological teachings of the Württemberg Protestant Church. At no time apart from the brief but contentious period of Reich Bishop Müller's attempted takeover of the Württemberg Church were clergy in Ravensburg ever forced to grapple with heretical confessions of faith, deviant doctrines, or arbitrary administrative decisions from their ecclesiastical superiors. These pastors, curates, and vicars could be thankful that they were spared some of the crises of conscience forced upon their counterparts in Nauen and Pirna.

Indeed, within the basic continuity of church life under Bishop Wurm, parish pastors were quite free to shape their own experiences. The forceful character of Pastor Karl Steger drew sections of the Friedrichshafen parish to the German Christian cause, even if his poor health, frequent absences, and clerical opponents curtailed some of his effectiveness. Most pastors in the district, however, simply tried to minister faithfully under Hitler's regime and to fend off local attempts to turn Protestant religious life into another venue for the propagation of National Socialist values. In this endeavor, they were largely successful, even if they proved unable or unwilling to address the larger questions of the morality of National Socialist movement itself and the nature of its hold over Germany.

# Bibliography

## Archival Sources

*Dekanatsarchiv Ravensburg:*
DA 52–170
Neue Akten A–C
Neue Akten Atzenweiler-Weingarten

*Domstiftsarchiv Brandenburg:*
FL 22–23
Ka 30
Ki 490
Nau 25–56 (Nauen Parish)
NE 46–703 (Nauen District)
Ri 5–7
Schw 19
Sta 18
Tie 11–12

*Ephoralarchiv Pirna:*
EA 013–1168

*Evangelisches Pfarrarchiv Friedrichshafen:*
Abt. 7 Pfarrgeschichte

*Evangelisches Zentralarchiv in Berlin (EZA):*
Altpreußischer Oberkirchenrat 14/10306–10963
Evangelischer Oberkirchenrat 7/11122–13688
Kirchenkampf (Archiv für die Geschichte des Kirchenkampfes) (Bestand 50)

*Landeskirchliches Archiv Stuttgart:*
Allg. Akten-Dekanat Ravensburg
Alt. Reg. Orts. Ravensburg-Besetzung I, II, III
Nachlasse Wurm-Abt. III
PA B/139 Bidlingmaier
PA E/67 Elsenhans
PA H/345 G. Hoffmann
PA K/298 P. Krauss
PA S/446 Siegle

*Staatsarchiv Dresden:*
Amtshauptmannschaft Pirna
Kreishauptmannschaft Dresden
Religionssachen 325–52
Pirna-Gemeindesachen 638–55
Vereine . . . 1094–1179
VI. 113—Kriegsschäden bei Ev.-luth. Kirchenvorstand, Hohnstein
VI. 114—Kriegsschäden bei Ev.-luth. Pfarramt, Sebnitz
IX. Abteilung—Kirchenangelegenheiten

*Stadtarchiv Friedrichshafen:*
Evangelisches Gemeindeblatt Friedrichshafen
Fischbacher Evangelisches Gemeindeblatt

*Stadtarchiv Pirna:*
BIII Kapitalismus II 1907 bis 1945 Band I
BIII-i to BIII-xv
BIII-xv—church matters, church buildings, and cemeteries
BIII Kapitalismus II 1907 bis 1945 Band II
BIII-xvi to BIII-xxxi
BIII-xvi—school grievances
BIII-xx—racial issues

*Stadtarchiv Ravensburg:*
AI 3002–34
Oberschwäbischer Anzeiger

## Published Sources

Babík, Milan. "Nazism as a Secular Religion." *History and Theory* 45, no. 3 (October 2006): 375–96.

Baier, Helmut. *Kirchenkampf in Nürnberg 1933–1945.* Nürnberg: Korn & Berg, 1973.

Bankier, David. *The Germans and the Final Solution: Public Opinion under Nazism.* Oxford: Basil Blackwell, 1992.

Baranowski, Shelley. *The Confessing Church, Conservative Elites, and the Nazi State.* Texts and Studies in Religion 28. New York: Edwin Mellen, 1986.

———. "Consent and Dissent: The Confessing Church and Conservative Opposition to National Socialism." *Journal of Modern History* 59 (March 1987): 53–78.

Barnett, Victoria. *For the Soul of the People: Protestant Protest against Hitler.* New York: Oxford University Press, 1992.

Baumgärtel, Friedrich. *Wider die Kirchenkampf-Legenden.* 2nd ed. Neuendettelsau: Freimund, 1959.

Baynes, Norman H. *Hitler's Speeches,* vol. 1. London: Oxford University Press, 1942.

Beckmann, Joachim. *Artgemässes Christentum oder schriftgemässer Christenglaube.* Essen, 1933.

———, ed. *Kirchliches Jahrbuch für die Evangelische Kirche in Deutschland 1933–1945.* Gütersloh: C. Bertelsmann, 1948.

Bente, F., and W. H. T. Dau, eds. *Triglot Concordia: The Symbolical Books of the Evangelical Lutheran Church.* St. Louis: Concordia, 1921.

Bentley, James. *Martin Niemöller.* London: Oxford University Press, 1984.

Bergen, Doris. "Catholics, Protestants, and Antisemitism in Nazi Germany." *Central European History* 27, no. 3 (1994): 329–48.

———. *Twisted Cross: The German Christian Movement in the Third Reich.* Chapel Hill: University of North Carolina Press, 1996.

Besier, Gerhard. "Ansätze zum politischen Widerstand in der Bekennenden Kirche: Zur gegenwärtigen Forschungslage." In *Die Evangelische Kirche in den Umbrüchen des 20. Jahrhunderts.* Historisch-Theologische Studien zum 19. und 20. Jahrhundert 5/1. Neukirchen-Vluyn: Neukirchner, 1994.

———. *Der SED-Staat und die Kirche 1969–1990: Die Vision vom "Dritten Weg."* Berlin: Propyläen, 1995.

———. *Der SED-Staat und die Kirche 1983–1991: Höhenflug und Absturz.* Frankfurt am Main: Propyläen, 1995.

———. "Widerstand im Dritten Reich—Ein kompatibler Forschungsgegenstand—Verständigung heute." In *Die Evangelische Kirche in den Umbrüchen des 20. Jahrhunderts.* Historisch-Theologische Studien zum 19. und 20. Jahrhundert 5/1. Neukirchen-Vluyn: Neukirchner, 1994.

Besier, Gerhard, and Gerhard Ringshausen, eds. *Bekenntnis, Widerstand, Martyrium: Von Barmen 1934 bis Plötzensee 1944*. Göttingen: Vandenhoeck & Ruprecht, 1986.

Besier, Gerhard, and Stephen Wolf, eds. *"Pfarrer, Christen und Katholiken": Das Ministerium für Staatssicherheit der ehemaligen DDR und die Kirchen*. 2 vols. Neukirchen-Vluyn: Neukirchener, 1991.

Bethge, Eberhard, "Troubled Self-Interpretation and Uncertain Reception in the Church Struggle." In *The German Church Struggle and the Holocaust*, edited by Franklin Littell and Hubert Locke, 167–84. Detroit: Wayne State University Press, 1974.

————. "Zwischen Bekenntnis und Widerstand: Erfahrungen in der Altpreußischen Union." In *Der Widerstand gegen den Nationalsozialismus: Die deutsche Gesellschaft und der Widerstand gegen Hitler*, edited by Jürgen Schmädeke and Peter Steinbach, 281–94. Munich: Piper, 1985.

Bethge, Eberhard, and Victoria Barnett. *Dietrich Bonhoeffer: A Biography*. Rev. ed. Minneapolis: Fortress Press, 2000.

Boberach, Heinz, ed. *Meldungen aus dem Reich: Die geheimen Lageberichte des Sicherheitsdienstes der SS, 1938–1945*. 17 vols. Herrsching: Pawlack, 1984.

Böhm, Boris, and Thomas Schilter. "Pirna-Sonnenstein: Von der Reformpsychiatrie zur Tötung psychisch Kranker." In *Nationalsozialistische Euthanasie-Verbrechen in Sachsen: Beiträge zu ihrer Aufarbeitung*, edited by Kuratorium Gedenkstätte Sonnenstein e.V. und Sächsische Landeszentrale für politische Bildung, 11–51. Dresden/Pirna: Kuratorium Gedenkstätte Sonnenstein e.V. und Sächsische Landeszentrale für politische Bildung, 1993.

Borg, Daniel. *The Old-Prussian Church and the Weimar Republic: A Study in Political Adjustment, 1917–1927*. Hanover, N.H.: University Press of New England, 1984.

Bracher, Karl Dietrich. *The German Dictatorship: The Origins, Structure, and Effects of National Socialism*. New York: Praeger, 1970.

Breitman, Richard. *The Architect of Genocide: Himmler and the Final Solution*. New York: Knopf, 1991.

Broszat, Martin. "Resistenz und Widerstand: Eine Zwischenbilanz des Forschungsprojekts." In *Bayern in der NS-Zeit: Herrschaft und Gesellschaft im Konflikt*, edited by Martin Broszat et al., vol. 4. Munich: Oldenbourg, 1981.

Buchheim, Hans. *Glaubenskrise im Dritten Reich: Drei Kapitel nationalsozialistischer Religionspolitik*. Veröffentlichungen des Instituts für Zeitgeschichte. Stuttgart: Deutsche Verlags-Anstalt, 1953.

Burleigh, Michael. "Political Religion and Social Evil." *Totalitarian Movements and Political Religions* 3, no. 2 (Autumn 2002): 1–60.

Chadwick, Owen. "The Present Stage of the 'Kirchenkampf' Enquiry." *Journal of Ecclesiastical History* 24, no. 1 (January 1973): 33–50.

Childers, Thomas, and Jane Caplan, eds. *Reevaluating the Third Reich*. Europe Past and Present. New York: Holmes & Meier, 1993.

Cochrane, Arthur C. *The Church's Confession under Hitler*. Philadelphia: Westminster, 1962.

Conrad, Walter. *Der Kampf um die Kanzeln: Erinnerungen und Dokumente aus der Hitlerzeit*. Berlin: A. Töpelmann, 1957.

Conway, John S. "The German Church Struggle: Its Making and Meaning." In *The Church Confronts the Nazis: Barmen Then and Now*, edited by Hubert G. Locke, 94–96. Toronto Studies in Theology 16. Toronto: Edwin Mellen, 1984.

————. "National Socialism and the Christian Churches during the Weimar Republic." In *The Nazi Machtergreifung*, edited by Peter D. Stachura, 124–45. London: Allen & Unwin, 1983.

————. *The Nazi Persecution of the Churches 1933–1945*. New York: Basic Books, 1968.

Dehn, Günther. *Die alte Zeit, die vorigen Jahre: Lebenserinnerungen*. Munich: Christian Kaiser, 1962.

Demps, Laurenz. "Die Provinz Brandenburg in der NS-Zeit (1933 bis 1945)." In *Brandenburgische Geschichte*, edited by Ingo Materna and Wolfgang Ribbe, 619–76. Berlin: Akademie, 1995.

Dibelius, Otto. *Das Jahrhundert der Kirche: Geschichte, Betrachtung, Umschau und Ziel*. Berlin: Furchte, 1927.

Diehn, Otto. *Bibliographie zur Geschichte des Kirchenkampfes 1933–1945*. Arbeiten zur Geschichte des Kirchenkampfes 1. Göttingen: Vandenhoeck & Ruprecht, 1958.

Diephouse, David J. *Pastors and Pluralism in Württemberg, 1918–1933*. Princeton: Princeton University Press, 1987.

————. "Theophil Wurm (1868–1953)." In *Wir konnten uns nicht entziehen: 30 Porträts zu Kirche und Nationalsozialismus in Württemberg*, edited by Rainer Lächele and Jörg Thierfelder, 13–33. Stuttgart: Quell, 1998.

Dierker, Wolfgang. *Hitlers Glaubenskrieger*. Paderborn: Schöningh, 2003.

Dipper, Theodor. *Die evangelische Bekenntnisgemeinschaft in Württemberg 1933–1945*. Arbeiten zur Geschichte des Kirchenkampfes 17. Göttingen: Vandenhoeck & Ruprecht, 1966.

Ehrenforth, Gerhard. *Die schlesische Kirche im Kirchenkampf 1932–1945*. Arbeiten zur Geschichte des Kirchenkampfes 4. Göttingen: Vandenhoeck & Ruprecht, 1968.

Ericksen, Robert P. "The Barmen Synod and Its Declaration: A Historical Synopsis." In *The Church Confronts the Nazis: Barmen Then and Now*, edited by Hubert G. Locke, 27–93. Toronto Studies in Theology 16. Toronto: Edwin Mellen, 1984.

————. *Theologians under Hitler: Gerhard Kittel, Paul Althaus, and Emanuel Hirsch*. New Haven: Yale University Press, 1985.

Ericksen, Robert P., and Susannah Heschel, eds. *Betrayal: German Churches and the Holocaust*. Minneapolis: Fortress Press, 1999.

Evans, Richard J. "Nazism, Christianity and Political Religion: A Debate," *Journal of Contemporary History* 42, no. 1 (January 2007): 5-7.

Evans, Richard J. *Rethinking German History: Nineteenth-Century Germany and the Origins of the Third Reich.* London: Allen & Unwin, 1987.

Falter, Jürgen. *Hitlers Wähler.* Munich: Beck, 1991.

Fest, Joachim. *Hitler.* New York: Harcourt Brace Jovanovich, 1974.

Feurich, Walter. "Die Ev.-Luth. Landeskirche Sachsens an der Wende der Jahre 1933/34." *Evangelische Theologie* 21 (1961): 368–81.

Fiege, Franz G. M. *The Varieties of Protestantism in Nazi Germany. Five Theological Positions.* Toronto Studies in Theology 50. Lewiston, N.Y.: Edwin Mellen, 1990.

Fischer, Joachim. *Die sächsische Landeskirche im Kirchenkampf 1933–1937.* Arbeiten zur Geschichte des Kirchenkampfes, Supplementary Series 8. Göttingen: Vandenhoeck & Ruprecht, 1972.

Flade, Lissa. "Erinnerung an meine Mutter—ein Opfer der Tötungsanstalt Sonnenstein." In *Nationalsozialistische Euthanasie-Verbrechen in Sachsen: Beiträge zu ihrer Aufarbeitung*, edited by Kuratorium Gedenkstätte Sonnenstein e.V. und Sächsische Landeszentrale für politische Bildung, 101–3. Dresden/Pirna: Kuratorium Gedenkstätte Sonnenstein e.V. und Sächsische Landeszentrale für politische Bildung, 1993.

Forner, Willy. *Das Verbrechen von La Mornasse: Berichte über faschistische Gewalttaten.* N.p.: Militärverlag der Deutschen Demokratischen Republik, 1981.

Geck, Helmut. *Der Kirchenkampf in Recklinghausen: Die Auseinandersetzungen zwischen der Bekennenden Kirche und den Deutschen Christen in der evangelischen Kirchengemeinde Recklingshausen-Altstadt von 1933 bis 1939.* Vestischen Zeitschrift 81. Recklinghausen: Druck und Verlagshaus W. Bitter, 1982.

Gellately, Robert. *The Gestapo and German Society: Enforcing Racial Policy, 1933–1945.* Oxford: Oxford University Press, 1990.

Gerlach, Wolfgang. *And the Witnesses Were Silent: The Confessing Church and the Persecution of the Jews.* Translated and edited by Victoria Barnett. Lincoln: University of Nebraska Press, 2000.

———. "The Attitude of the Confessing Church Toward German Jews in the Third Reich, and the Way After." In *The Barmen Confession: Papers from the Seattle Assembly*, edited by Hubert G. Locke. Toronto Studies in Theology 26. Lewiston, N.Y.: Edwin Mellen, 1986, 91-118.

Gordon, Sarah. *Hitler, Germans, and the "Jewish Question."* Princeton: Princeton University Press, 1984.

Gregor, Neil. "Politics, Culture, Political Culture: Recent Work on the Third Reich and Its Aftermath." *Journal of Modern History* 78, no. 3 (September 2006): 643–83.

Griffin, Roger. "Introduction: God's Counterfeiters? Investigating the Triad of Fascism, Totalitarianism, and (Political) Religion." *Totalitarian Movements and Political Religions* 5, no. 3 (December 2004): 291–325.

Grünberg, Reinhold, ed. *Sächsisches Pfarrerbuch: Die Parochien und Pfarrer der Ev.-luth. Landeskirche Sachsens (1539–1939).* Freiburg i. Sa.: E. Mauckisch, 1939–1940.

Hamilton, Richard F. *Who Voted for Hitler?* Princeton: Princeton University Press, 1982.

Hamm, Berndt. "Werner Elert als Kriegstheologe: Zugleich ein Beitrag zur Diskussion 'Luthertum und Nationalsozialismus.'" *Kirchliche Zeitgeschichte* 11, no. 2 (1998): 206–54.

Harder, Günther. "Rechenschaftsbericht." In *Bekenntnissynode der Mark Brandenburg vom 22. bis 24. Oktober 1945 in Berlin-Spandau Evangelisches Johannesstift.* Berlin: R. Schröter, n.d.

Harder, Günther, and Wilhelm Niemöller, eds. *Die Stunde der Versuchung: Gemeinden im Kirchenkampf 1933–1945. Selbstzeugnisse.* Munich: Christian Kaiser, 1963.

Hase, Hans Christoph von, ed. *Evangelische Dokumente zur Ermordung der "unheilbar Kranken" unter der nationalsozialistischen Herrschaft in den Jahren 1939–1945* Stuttgart: Evangelisches Verlagswerkes, 1964.

Heine, Ludwig. *Geschichte des Kirchenkampfes in der Grenzmark—Posen—Westpreußen 1930–1940.* Arbeiten zur Geschichte des Kirchenkampfes 9. Göttingen: Vandenhoeck & Ruprecht, 1961.

Heinonen, Reijo E. *Anpassung und Identität: Theologie und Kirchenpolitik der Bremer Deutschen Christen, 1933–1945.* Arbeiten zur kirchlichen Zeitgeschichte, Reihe B, Darstellungen 5. Göttingen: Vandenhoeck & Ruprecht, 1978.

Helmreich, Ernst Christian. *The German Churches under Hitler: Background, Struggle, and Epilogue.* Detroit: Wayne State University Press, 1979.

———. "The Nature and Structure of the Confessing Church in Germany under Hitler." *Journal of Church and State* 12 (Autumn 1970): 405–20.

Hermelink, Heinrich, ed., *Kirche in Kampf: Dokumente des Widerstands und des Aufbaus in der evangelischen Kirche Deutschlands von 1933 bis 1945.* Tübingen: R. Wunderlich, 1950.

Heschel, Susannah. "Nazifying Christian Theology: Walter Grundmann and the Institute for the Study and Eradication of Jewish Influence on German Church Life." *Church History* 63 (1994): 587–605.

Hey, Bernd. *Die Kirchenprovinz Westfalen 1933–1945.* Beiträge zur westfälischen Kirchengeschichte 2. Bielefeld: Luther-Verlag, 1974.

Hilberg, Raul. *The Destruction of the European Jews 1933–1945.* 3 vols. New York: Holmes & Meier, 1985.

Hornig, Ernst. *Die Bekennende Kirche in Schlesien 1933–1945: Geschichte und Dokumente.* Arbeiten zur Geschichte des Kirchenkampfes 10. Göttingen: Vandenhoeck & Ruprecht, 1977.

Huber, Ernst Rudolf, and Wolfgang Huber, eds. *Staat und Kirche im 19. und 20. Jahrhundert: Dokumente zur Geschichte des deutschen Staatskirchenrechts.* Vol. 4, *Staat und Kirche in der Zeit der Weimarer Republik.* Berlin: Duncker & Humblot, 1987.

Jäckel, Eberhard. *Hitler in History*. Hanover, N.H.: University Press of New England, 1989.

Jacobs, Manfred. "Kirche, Weltanschauung, Politik: Die evangelischen Kirchen und die Option zwischen dem zweiten und dritten Reich." *Vierteljahrshefte für Zeitgeschichte* 31, no. 1 (1983): 108–35.

Kandler, Hans-Joachim. "Kirche und Juden während des deutsch-christlichen Kirchenregiments in Sachsen 1933–1945." *Theologische Versuche* 14 (1985): 93–103.

Kaul, F. K. *Nazimordaktion T4: Ein Bericht über die erste industriemäßig durchgeführte Mordaktion des Naziregimes.* Berlin: VEB Verlag Volk und Gesundheit, 1973.

Kershaw, Ian. *The Nazi Dictatorship: Problems and Perspectives of Interpretation.* 3rd ed. London: Edward Arnold, 1993.

Kersting, Andreas. *Kirchenordnung und Widerstand: Der Kampf um den Aufbau der Bekennenden Kirche der altpreußischen Union aufgrund des Dahlemer Notrechts von 1934 bis 1937.* Heidelberger Untersuchungen zu Widerstand, Judenverfolgung und Kirchenkampf im Dritten Reich 4. Gütersloh: Christian Kaiser, 1994.

Klee, Ernst. *Dokumente zur "Euthanasie."* Frankfurt: Taschenbuch, 1985.

Klemm, Hermann. *Ich konnte nicht Zuschauer bleiben: Karl Fischers theologische Arbeit für die Bekennende Kirche Sachsens.* Berlin: Evangelische Verlagsanstalt, 1985.

Klemperer, Klemens von. "Glaube, Religion, Kirche und der deutsche Widerstand gegen den Nationalsozialismus." *Vierteljahrshefte für Zeitgeschichte* 28, no. 3 (1980): 293–309.

Köhle-Hezinger, Christel. "Schwester Maria Benedikta Ströle (Getrud Ströle, geboren 1918)" In *Wir konnten uns nicht entziehen: 30 Porträts zu Kirche und Nationalsozialismus in Württemberg,* edited by Rainer Lächele and Jörg Thierfelder, 505–22. Stuttgart: Quell, 1998.

[Krause, Reinhold]. *Rede des Gauobmannes der Glaubensbewegung "Deutsche Christen" i. Groß-Berlin Dr Krause gehalten im Sportpalast am 13. November 1933.* Berlin: n.p. 1933.

Krumpolt, Holm. "Die Landesheilanstalt Großschweidnitz als 'T4'-Zwischenanstalt und Tötungsanstalt (1939–1945)" In *Nationalsozialistische Euthanasie-Verbrechen in Sachsen: Beiträge zu ihrer Aufarbeitung,* edited by Kuratorium Gedenkstätte Sonnenstein e.V. und Sächsische Landeszentrale für politische Bildung, 91–100. Dresden/Pirna: Kuratorium Gedenkstätte Sonnenstein e.V. und Sächsische Landeszentral für politische Bildung, 1993.

Lächele, Rainer. *Ein Volk, ein Reich, ein Glaube: Die 'Deutsche Christen' in Württemberg 1925–1960.* Quellen und Forschungen zur württembergischen Kirchengeschichte 12. Stuttgart: Calwer, 1994.

Lächele, Rainer, and Jörg Thierfelder, eds. *Wir konnten uns nicht entziehen: 30 Porträts zu Kirche und Nationalsozialismus in Württemberg.* Stuttgart: Quell, 1998.

Lehman, Hartmut. "Martin Luther als deutscher Nationalheld im 19. Jahrhundert." *Luther: Zeitschrift der Luthergesellschaft* 55, no. 2 (1984): 53–65.

Lessing, Eckard. *Zwischen Bekenntnis und Volkskirche: Der theologische Weg der Evangelischen Kirche der altpreußischen Union (1922–1953) unter besonderer Berücksichtigung ihrer Synoden, ihrer Gruppen und der theologischen Begründungen.* Unio und Confessio 17. Bielefeld: Luther-Verlag, 1992.

Linck, Hugo. *Der Kirchenkampf in Ostpreußen 1933–1945: Geschichte und Dokumentation.* Munich: Gräfe und Unzer, 1968.

Littell, Franklin, and Hubert Locke, eds. *The German Church Struggle and the Holocaust.* Detroit: Wayne State University Press, 1974.

Locke, Hubert G., ed. *The Barmen Confession. Papers from the Seattle Assembly.* Toronto Studies in Theology. Lewiston, N.Y.: Edwin Mellen, 1986.

———. *The Church Confronts the Nazis: Barmen Then and Now.* Toronto Studies in Theology. Toronto: Edwin Mellen, 1984.

Ludwig, Hartmut. "Die Entstehung der Bekennenden Kirche in Berlin." In *Beiträge zur Berliner Kirchengeschichte*, edited by Günther Wirth, 264ff. East Berlin: Union, 1987.

———. "Die 'Illegalen' im Kirchenkampf." In *Predigtamt ohne Pfarramt? Die "Illegalen" im Kirchenkampf*, edited by Karl-Adolf Bauer, 23–70. Neukirchen-Vluyn: Neukirchener, 1993.

Maser, Peter, ed. *Der Kirchenkampf im deutschen Osten und in den deutschsprächigen Kirchen Osteuropas.* Kirche im Osten 22. Göttingen: Vandenhoeck & Ruprecht, 1992.

Matheson, Peter, ed. *The Third Reich and the Christian Churches.* Grand Rapids: Eerdmans, 1981.

Mayer, Eberhard. *Die evangelische Kirche in Ulm 1918–1945.* Forschungen zur Geschichte der Stadt Ulm 26. Stuttgart: Kohlhammer, 1998.

McLeod, Hugh. "Protestantism and the Working Class in Imperial Germany." *European Studies Review*, 12 no. 3 (1982): 323-344.

Meier, Kurt. *Die Deutschen Christen: Das Bild einer Bewegung im Kirchenkampf des Dritten Reiches.* Göttingen: Vandenhoeck & Ruprecht, 1964.

———. *Der evangelische Kirchenkampf.* 3 vols. Göttingen: Vandenhoeck & Ruprecht, 1976–1984.

———. *Kreuz und Hakenkreuz. Die evangelische Kirche im Dritten Reich.* Munich: Deutscher Taschenbuch, 1992.

Michael, Robert. "Theological Myth, German Antisemitism and the Holocaust: The Case of Martin Niemoeller." *Holocaust and Genocide Studies* 2, no. 1 (1987): 105–22.

Müller, Manfred. *Jugend in Zerreißprobe: Persönliche Erinnerungen und Dokumente eines Jugendpfarrers im Dritten Reich.* Stuttgart: Quell, 1982.

Närger, Nikolaus. *Das Synodwahlsystem in den deutschen evangelischen Landeskirchen im 19. und 20. Jahrhundert.* Tübingen: J. C. B. Mohr (Paul Siebeck), 1988.

Nicolaisen, Carsten, and Georg Kretschmar, eds. *Dokumente zur Kirchenpolitik des Dritten Reiches.* Vol. 1, *Das Jahr 1933.* Munich: Christian Kaiser, 1971.

Niemöller, Wilhelm. *Die evangelische Kirche im Dritten Reich: Handbuch des Kirchenkampfes.* Bielefeld: Ludwig Bechauf, 1956.

————. *Kampf und Zeugnis der Bekennenden Kirche.* Bielefeld: Ludwig Bechauf, 1948.

————. *Kirchenkampf in Dritten Reich.* Bielefeld: Ludwig Bechauf, 1946.

————. *Kirchenkampf in Westfalen.* Bielefeld: Ludwig Bechauf, 1952.

————. *Macht geht vor Recht: Der Prozess Martin Niemöllers.* Munich: Christian Kaiser Verlag, 1952.

Niesel, Wilhelm. *Kirche unter dem Wort: Der Kampf der Bekennenden Kirche der altpreußischen Union 1933–1945.* Arbeiten zur Geschichte des Kirchenkampfes 11. Göttingen: Vandenhoeck & Ruprecht, 1978.

Noakes, Jeremy. *Nazism 1919–1945.* Vol. 4, *The German Home Front in World War II: A Documentary Reader.* Exeter: University of Exeter Press, 1998.

Norden, Günther van. "Der Kirchenkampf im Rheinland 1933 bis 1934." In *Kirchenkampf im Rheinland: Die Entstehung der Bekennenden Kirche und die Theologische Erklärung von Barmen 1934.* Cologne: Rheinland, 1984.

————. "Zwischen Kooperation und Teilwiderstand: Die Rolle der Kirchen und Konfessionen—Ein Überblick über Forschungspositionen." In *Der Widerstand gegen den Nationalsozialismus: Die deutsche Gesellschaft und der Widerstand gegen Hitler,* edited by Jürgen Schmädeke and Peter Steinbach, 227–39. Munich: Piper, 1985.

Nowak, Kurt. "Evangelische Kirche und Widerstand im Dritten Reich: Kirchenhistorische und gesellschaftsgeschichtliche Perspektiven." *Geschichtswissenschaft und Unterricht* 6 (1987): 352–64.

Peukert, Detlev. *Inside Nazi Germany: Conformity, Opposition, and Racism in Everyday Life.* New Haven: Yale University Press, 1987.

Pierard, Richard V. "Why Did Protestants Welcome Hitler?" *Fides et Historia* 10 (Spring 1978): 8–29.

Poewe, Karla. *New Religions and the Nazis.* New York: Routledge, 2006.

Poewe, Karla, and Irving Hexham. "Jakob Wilhelm Hauer's New Religion and National Socialism." *Journal of Contemporary Religion* 20, no. 2 (2005): 195–215.

Prolingheuer, Hans. "Der ungekämpfte Kirchenkampf 1933–1945—das politische Versagen der Bekennenden Kirche." *Neue Stimme* Sonderheft 6 (1983): 3–34.

Rehmann, Jan. *Die Kirchen im NS-Staat: Untersuchung zur Interaktion ideologischer Mächte.* Ideologische Mächte im deutschen Faschismus 2. Berlin: Argument, 1986.

Rexer, Martin, and Bodo Rüdenburg. "Zweifalten as 'Halfway House' on the Road to Grafeneck." In *Administered Killings at the Time of National Socialism: Involvement—Suppression—Responsibility of Psychiatry and Judicial System*, edited by Ulrich Jockusch and Lothar Scholz, 110–46. Regensburg: Roderer, 1992.

Rothfels, Hans. *The German Opposition to Hitler: An Assessment*. London: Oswald Wolff, 1970.

Ruff, Mark. "The Nazis' Religionspolitik: An Assessment of Recent Literature." *Catholic Historical Review* 92, no. 3 (September 2006): 252–67.

Sauer, Paul, ed. *Dokumente über die Verfolgung der jüdischen Bürger in Baden-Württemberg durch das nationalsozialistische Regime 1933–1945*, vol. 1. Veröffentlichungen der Staatlichen Archivverwaltung Baden-Württemberg 16. Stuttgart: Kohlhammer, 1966.

Sax, Benjamin, and Dieter Kuntz, eds. *Inside Hitler's Germany: A Documentary History of Life in the Third Reich*. Toronto: D. C. Heath, 1992.

Schäfer, Gerhard, ed. *Die Evangelische Landeskirche in Württemberg unter Nationalsozialismus: Eine Dokumentation zum Kirchenkampf*. 6 vols. Stuttgart: Calwer, 1971–1986.

———. *Landesbischof D. Wurm und der nationalsozialistische Staat, 1940–1945: Eine Dokumentation*. Stuttgart: Calwer, 1968.

Schäfer, Hans-Dieter, ed., *Evangelische Kirchengemeinde Wälde-Winterbach*. Ravensburg, 1991.

Scholder, Klaus. *The Churches and the Third Reich*. 2 vols. Translated by John Bowden. Philadelphia: Fortress Press, 1988.

———. "Politische Widerstand oder Selbstbehauptung als Problem der Kirchenleitungen." In *Der Widerstand gegen den Nationalsozialismus: Die deutsche Gesellschaft und der Widerstand gegen Hitler*, edited by Jürgen Schmädeke and Peter Steinbach, 254–64. Munich: Piper, 1985.

———. *A Requiem for Hitler, and Other New Perspectives on the German Church Struggle*. London: SCM, 1989.

Schröter, Sonja. "Waldheim als 'Euthanasie'-Zwischenanstalt von Kranken-Sammel-Transporten an die Tötungsanstalt Sonnenstein im Rahmen der sog. 'Aktion T4' in den Jahren 1940 und 1941." In *Nationalsozialistische Euthanasie-Verbrechen in Sachsen: Beiträge zu ihrer Aufarbeitung*, edited by Kuratorium Gedenkstätte Sonnenstein e.V. und Sächsische Landeszentrale für politische Bildung, 77–89. Dresden/Pirna: Kuratorium Gedenkstätte Sonnenstein e.V. und Sächsische Landeszentrale für politische Bildung, 1993.

Schumann, Dora. "Erinnerungen an die Tötungsanstalt Pirna-Sonnenstein." In *Nationalsozialistische Euthanasie-Verbrechen in Sachsen: Beiträge zu ihrer Aufarbeitung*, edited by Kuratorium Gedenkstätte Sonnenstein e.V. und Sächsische Landeszentrale für politische Bildung, 53–55. Dresden/Pirna: Kuratorium

Gedenkstätte Sonnenstein e.V. und Sächsische Landeszentrale für politische Bildung, 1993.

See, Wolfgang, and Rudolf Weckerling. *Frauen im Kirchenkampf: Beispiele aus der Bekennenden Kirche Berlin-Brandenburg*. Berlin: Wichern, 1984.

Smith, Helmut Walser. *German Nationalism and Religious Conflict: Culture, Ideology, Politics, 1870–1914*. Princeton: Princeton University Press, 1995.

Spicer, Kevin P. *Resisting the Third Reich: The Catholic Clergy in Hitler's Berlin*. DeKalb: Northern Illinois University Press, 2004.

Spicer, Kevin P., ed. *Antisemitism, Christian Ambivalence, and the Holocaust*. Bloomington: Indiana University Press, 2007.

Spotts, Frederic. *The Churches and Politics in Germany*. Middletown, Conn.: Wesleyan University Press, 1973.

Stegmann, Eric. *Der Kirchenkampf in der Thüringer Evangelischen Kirche, 1933–1945*. Berlin: Evangelischer Verlagsanstalt, 1984.

Steigmann-Gall, Richard. *The Holy Reich: Nazi Conceptions of Christianity, 1919–1945*. Cambridge: Cambridge University Press, 2003.

————. "Nazism and the Revival of Political Religion Theory." *Totalitarian Movements and Political Religions* 5, no. 3 (December 2004): 376–96.

Steinert, Tilman. "Reactions in Psychiatric Institutions to the Murder of Their Patients in Grafeneck." In *Administered Killings at the Time of National Socialism: Involvement–Suppression–Responsibility of Psychiatry and Judicial System*, edited by Ulrich Jockusch and Lothar Scholz, 105–9. Regensburg: Roderer, 1992.

Stoevesandt, Karl. *Bekennende Gemeinden und deutschgläubige Bischofsdiktatur in Bremen 1933–1945*. Arbeiten zur Geschichte des Kirchenkampfes 10. Göttingen: Vandenhoeck & Ruprecht, 1961.

Thielicke, Helmut. *Notes from a Wayfarer: The Autobiography of Helmut Thielicke*. Translated by David R. Law. New York: Paragon House, 1995.

Tiefel, Hans. "The German Lutheran Church and the Rise of National Socialism." *Church History* 41 (1972): 326–36.

*Triglot Concordia: The Symbolical Books of the Evangelical Lutheran Church*. Translated by F. Bente and W. H. T. Dau. St. Louis: Concordia, 1921.

U.S. Chief of Counsel for the Prosecution of Axis Criminality. *Nazi Conspiracy and Aggression*. 8 vols. Washington: U.S. Government Printing Office, 1946–1948.

Usdorf, Werner. "Confronting Political Religion with Divine Religion: Christian Strategies of Re-Evangelization in the 1930s." *Political Theology* 3, no. 1 (November 2001): 22–31.

Vondung, Klaus. "National Socialism as a Political Religion: Potentials and Limits of an Analytical Concept." *Totalitarian Movements and Political Religions* 6, no. 1 (June 2005): 87–95.

Wall, Donald. "The Confessing Church and the Second World War." *Journal of Church and State* 23, no. 1 (Winter 1981): 15–34.

————. "Karl Barth and National Socialism, 1921–1946." *Fides et Historia* 15 (Spring–Summer 1983): 80–95.

Weiling, Christoph. *Die "Christliche-deutsche Bewegung": Eine Studie zum konservativen Protestantismus in der Weimarer Republik.* Arbeiten zur kirchlichen Zeitgeschichte, Reihe B, Darstellungen 28. Göttingen: Vandenhoeck & Ruprecht, 1998.

[Weingarten Protestant Parish]. *Evangelisches Stadtkirche Weingarten 1883–1983.* Weingarten: Franz Harder, 1983.

Wilhelmi, Heinrich. *Die Hamburger Kirche in der nationalsozialistischen Zeit, 1933–1945.* Arbeiten zur Geschichte des Kirchenkampfes 5. Göttingen: Vandenhoeck & Ruprecht, 1968.

Witetschek, Helmut. *Die kirchliche Lage in Bayern nach den Regierungspräsidenten-berichten 1933–1943.* Vol. 1, *Regierungsbezirk Oberbayern.* Katholische Akademie in Bayern, Kommission für Zeitgeschichte, Ver öffentlichungen, Reihe A, Quellen 3. Mainz: Matthias Grünewald. 1996.

Wolf, Ernst. *Barmen : Kirche zwischen Versuchung und Gnade.* Munich: Christian Kaiser, 1957.

————. *Kirche im Widerstand? Protestantische Opposition in der Klammer der Zweireichlehre.* Munich: Christian Kaiser, 1965.

Wright, Jonathan R.C. *"Above Parties": The Political Attitudes of the German Protestant Church Leadership, 1918–1933.* Oxford Historical Monographs. London: Oxford University Press, 1974.

————. "The German Protestant Church and the NSDAP in the Period of the Seizure of Power 1932–33." In *Renaissance and Renewal in Christian History,* edited by Derek Baker, 393–418. Oxford: Oxford University Press, 1977.

Zabel, James. *Nazism and the Pastors: A Study of the Ideas of Three "Deutsche Christen" Groups.* American Academy of Religion Dissertation Series 14. Missoula, Mont.: Scholars Press for the American Academy of Religion, 1976.

# Appendix: Church Seals

**Preface:** This is the seal of the Brandenburg Provincial Council of the Confessing Church. Its motto "Christ alone the Lord" surrounds a Christian cross and signifies the Confessing Church's commitment to remain faithful to the lordship of Christ as understood from the Bible and Reformation confessions of faith.

**Introduction:** This is the seal of the Reich Ministry of Church Affairs, an office created in July 1935 and headed by Hans Kerrl. Although the eagle and swastika on the symbol emphasize the National Socialist intervention in German church life, Kerrl's mandate was actually to mediate between the Nazi Party and the Protestant and Catholic churches.

**Chapter 1:** This is the seal of the local chapter of the German Christian (National Church) group in Leutkirch, Württemberg. Its combination of Christian cross and Nazi swastika illustrates the German Christians' attempt to fuse key elements of National Socialist ideology and traditional German Protestantism. More broadly, this seal evokes the power of religious nationalism in the Third Reich.

**Chapter 2:** This is the seal for the parish of Groß and Klein Behnitz. The image of the church building in the middle of the seal calls to mind the importance of the traditional village church. In Groß and Klein Behnitz, the rise of the National Socialist Party injected great excitement into the parish during the first months of Hitler's rule in 1933, and restored the local church and pastor to a place of importance not enjoyed for several decades.

**Chapter 3:** This is the seal from the city of Nauen, a district capital in the Havelland, a region named after the Havel River and noted for its many lakes and canals. The seal serves as a reminder that local political authorities were often important voices in parish debates. In Nauen, the mayor was the parish patron, responsible for nominating candidates for pastoral positions. As a result, he was frequently caught up in conflict between local German Christians and members of the Confessing Church.

**Chapter 4:** This is the seal from the Nauen church district superintendent's office. In Nauen, responses to Nazi racial ideology were mixed, ranging from Friedrich Siems' strident anti-Semitism to Günther Harder and Herbert Posth's criticism of the idolization of the German race.

**Chapter 5:** This is the parish seal for Beetz and Sommerfeld, in the Nauen church district. Its eagle is a symbol of the majesty of the Word of God, but also recalls German political power. Pastor Ulrich Bettac of Beetz became one of the most important figures in Nauen during the time of the German Church Struggle. As interim superintendent for much of the 1930s and early 1940s, he supported the Confessing Church in the district and tried to keep the peace as best he could.

**Chapter 6:** This is the seal of the Lutheran district superintendent in Pirna. A simple seal consisting of a Christian cross, it is a reminder of the importance of the district superintendent as overseer of the spiritual and ecclesiastical life of a church district. In Pirna, Superintendent Max Zweynert worked hard to mediate between German Christians and members of the Confessing Church. His successor, Heinrich Leichte, persecuted Confessing Church pastors and supported the work of local German Christians and National Socialists.

**Chapter 7:** This is the seal of the senior parish pastor in Ravensburg, Württemberg. Its simple design was based on the Württemberg Protestant Church symbol of a Christian cross attached to the letter *W*, a reminder of the strong leadership of Württemberg Bishop Theophil Wurm, who kept the Württemberg church *intact*, free from the control of the German Christians who siezed power in most of the other regional churches in Germany.

# Notes

## Introduction

1. Arthur C. Cochrane, *The Church's Confession under Hitler* (Philadelphia: Westminster, 1962), 275.

2. Wolfgang Gerlach, *And the Witnesses Were Silent: The Confessing Church and the Persecution of the Jews*, trans. and ed. Victoria J. Barnett (Lincoln: University of Nebraska Press, 2000); Andreas Kersting, *Kirchenordnung und Widerstand: Der Kampf um den Aufbau der Bekennenden Kirche der altpreußischen Union aufgrund des Dahlemer Notrechts von 1934 bis 1937*, Heidelberger Untersuchungen zu Widerstand, Judenverfolgung und Kirchenkampf im Dritten Reich 4 (Gütersloh: Christian Kaiser, 1994); Victoria Barnett, *For the Soul of the People: Protestant Protest against Hitler* (New York: Oxford University Press, 1992, title notwithstanding); Shelley Baranowski, "Consent and Dissent: The Confessing Church and Conservative Opposition to National Socialism," *Journal of Modern History* 59 (March 1987): 53–78; Shelley Baranowski, *The Confessing Church, Conservative Elites, and the Nazi State*, Texts and Studies in Religion 28 (New York: Edwin Mellen, 1986); Hans Prolingheuer, "Der ungekämpfte Kirchenkampf 1933–1945—das politische Versagen der Bekennenden Kirche," *Neue Stimme* Sonderheft 6 (1983): 3–34.

3. Klaus Scholder, "Modern German History and Protestant Theology," in *A Requiem for Hitler, and Other New Perspectives on the German Church Struggle* (London: SCM, 1989), 35–60, here 51–52.

4. Hans Rothfels, *The German Opposition to Hitler: An Assessment* (London: Oswald Wolff, 1970), 42.

5. Kersting, *Kirchenordnung und Widerstand*, 7–14; Hartmut Ludwig, "Die 'Illegalen' im Kirchenkampf," in *Predigtamt ohne Pfarramt? Die "Illegalen" im Kirchenkampf*, ed. Karl-Adolf Bauer (Neukirchen-Vluyn: Neukirchener, 1993), 23–70.

6. Ludwig, "Die 'Illegalen' im Kirchenkampf," 30–31.

7. Richard Steigmann-Gall, *The Holy Reich: Nazi Conceptions of Christianity, 1919–1945* (Cambridge: Cambridge University Press, 2003). On Steigmann-Gall, see articles by Richard Evans, Stanley Stowers, Doris Bergen, Manfred Gailus, Ernst Piper, and Irving Hexham, all published in the *Journal of Contemporary History* 42, no. 1 (January 2007). See also Milan Babík, "Nazism as a Secular Religion," *History and Theory* 45, no. 3 (October 2006): 375–96; Neil Gregor, "Politics, Culture, Political Culture: Recent Work on the Third Reich and Its Aftermath," *Journal of Modern History* 78, no. 3 (September 2006): 643–83; Mark Ruff, "The Nazis' Religionspolitik: An Assessment of Recent Literature," *Catholic Historical Review* 92, no. 3 (September 2006): 252–67; Karla Poewe, *New Religions and the Nazis* (New York: Routledge, 2006); Karla Poewe and Irving Hexham, "Jakob Wilhelm Hauer's New Religion and National Socialism," *Journal of Contemporary Religion* 20, no. 2 (2005): 195–215; Klaus Vondung, "National Socialism as a Political Religion: Potentials and Limits of an Analytical Concept," *Totalitarian Movements and Political Religions* 6, no. 1 (June 2005): 87–95; Roger Griffin, "Introduction: God's Counterfeiters? Investigating the Triad of Fascism, Totalitarianism, and (Political) Religion," *Totalitarian Movements and Political Religions* 5, no. 3 (December 2004): 291–325; Richard Steigmann-Gall, "Nazism and the Revival of Political Religion Theory," *Totalitarian Movements and Political Religions* 5, no. 3 (December 2004): 376–96; Wolfgang Dierker, *Himmlers Glaubenskrieger: Der Sicherheitsdienst der SS und seine Religionspolitik, 1933–1941*, Veröffentlichung der Kommission für Zeitgeschichte: Reihe B, Forschungen 92 (Paderborn: Schöningh, 2002); Michael Burleigh, "Political Religion and Social Evil," *Totalitarian Movements and Political Religions* 3, no. 2 (Autumn 2002): 1–60; Werner Usdorf, "Confronting Political Religion with Divine Religion: Christian Strategies of Re-Evangelization in the 1930s," *Political Theology* 3, no. 1 (November 2001): 22–31.

8. Klaus Scholder, *The Churches and the Third Reich*, vol. 1, *Preliminary History and the Time of Illusions 1918–1934*, trans. John Bowden (Philadelphia: Fortress Press, 1988), 32.

## Chapter 1: Faith and Fatherland through the Eyes of Clergy

1. "Festgottesdienst in der evangelische Stadtkirche Ravensburg," *Oberschwäbischer Anzeiger*, November 20, 1933, Stadtarchiv Ravensburg.

2. "Kreiskirchentag in Nauen" (newspaper clipping), n.d., Domstiftsarchiv Brandenburg NE 300/590. "So if anyone is in Christ, there is a new creation: everything old has passed away; see, everything has become new!" (2 Corinthians 5:17).

3. Ibid.

4. "Ephoralkonferenz des Kirchenbezirks Pirna" (newspaper clipping), n.d., Ephoralarchiv Pirna 814.

5. "Bericht des Dekans," Kirchenbezirkstag, December 14, 1933, Dekanatsarchiv Ravensburg 88e.

6. Klaus Scholder, *The Churches and the Third Reich*, vol. 1, *Preliminary History and the Time of Illusions 1918–1934*, trans. John Bowden (Philadelphia: Fortress Press, 1988), 232, 236.

7. Walter Feurich, "Die Ev.-Luth. Landeskirche Sachsens an der Wende der Jahre 1933/34," *Evangelische Theologie* 21 (1961): 368–81, here 370.

8. To be fair, Wurm's adoption of the title of bishop may well have been a clever adaptation of Nazi-style authority for the defense of traditional church institutions. Gerhard Schäfer, ed., *Die evangelische Landeskirche in Württemberg unter Nationalsozialismus: Eine Dokumentation zum Kirchenkampf*, vol. 1, *Um das politische Engagement der Kirche 1932–1933* (Stuttgart: Calwer, 1971), 234; Jan Rehmann, *Die Kirchen im NS-Staat: Untersuchung zur Interaktion ideologischer Mächte*, Ideologische Mächte im deutschen Faschismus 2 (Berlin: Argument, 1986), 52; Scholder, *Churches and the Third Reich*, 1:220, 228; Wilhelm Niemöller, *Die evangelische Kirche im Dritten Reich: Handbuch des Kirchenkampfes* (Bielefeld: Ludwig Bechauf, 1956), 81, quoted in Friedrich Baumgärtel, *Wider die Kirchenkampf-Legenden,* 2nd ed. (Neuendettelsau: Freimund, 1959), 11; David J. Diephouse, *Pastors and Pluralism in Württemberg, 1918–1933* (Princeton: Princeton University Press, 1987), 356–57; idem, "Theophil Wurm (1868–1953)," in *Wir konnten uns nicht entziehen: 30 Porträts zu Kirche und Nationalsozialismus in Württemberg,* ed. Rainer Lächele and Jörg Thierfelder (Stuttgart: Quell, 1998), 13–33, here 15–21.

9. Superintendent Graßhoff in Nauen to the Brandenburg Consistory, May 3, 1934; Pastor Kahle in Linum to the District Superintendent's Office, Nauen, "Bericht über das kirchliche Leben der Kirchengemeinde," April 26, 1934, Domstiftsarchiv Brandenburg NE 48/658; Pastor Lux in Groß Behnitz to District Superintendent's Office, Nauen, May 8, 1933, Domstiftsarchiv Brandenburg NE 101/647.

10. Superintendent's Office in Pirna to the pastors of the district, September 18, 1933, Ephoralarchiv 80.

11. Scholder, *Churches and the Third Reich*, 1:545.

12. "Festgottesdienst in der evangelischen Stadtkirche Ravensburg," *Oberschwäbischer Anzeiger*, November 20, 1933; "Evangelischer Gemeindeabend zum Luthertag," *Oberschwäbischer Anzeiger*, November 21, 1933, Stadtarchiv Ravensburg.

13. "Kundgebung der Deutschen Evang. Kirche zur Abstimmung des 19. August 1934," Dekanatsarchiv Ravensburg 85b.

14. "Sehr geehrter Herr Dekan!" February 27, 1935, Dekanatsarchiv Ravensburg 73l. For a comparison with German Christian ideology, see James Zabel, *Nazism and the Pastors: A Study of the Ideas of Three "Deutsche Christen" Groups,* American Academy of Religion Dissertation Series 14 (Missoula, Mont.: Scholars Press for the American Academy of Religion, 1976), 21–43, 199–218.

15. *Völkischer Beobachter*, February 2, 1933, quoted in Benjamin Sax and Dieter Kuntz, eds., *Inside Hitler's Germany: A Documentary History of Life in the Third Reich* (Toronto: D.C. Heath, 1992), 132.

16. Carsten Nicolaisen and Georg Kretschmar, eds., *Dokumente zur Kirchenpolitik des Dritten Reiches*, vol. 1, *Das Jahr 1933* (Munich: Christian Kaiser, 1971), 8–9, quoted in Ernst Christian Helmreich, *The German Churches under Hitler: Background, Struggle, and Epilogue* (Detroit: Wayne State University Press, 1979), 129.

17. Norman H. Baynes, *Hitler's Speeches*, vol. 1 (London: Oxford University Press, 1942), 370–71, quoted in Helmreich, *German Churches under Hitler*, 131.

18. Pastor Kahle in Linum to the District Superintendent's Office, Nauen, "Bericht über das kirchliche Leben der Kirchengemeinde," April 26, 1934, Domstiftsarchiv Brandenburg NE 48/658; "Kreiskirchentag in Nauen" (newspaper clipping), n.d., Domstiftsarchiv Brandenburg NE 300/590.

19. "Mit aufrichtiger Freude . . . ," April 18, 1933, Ephoralarchiv Pirna 814; "Timely Preaching," Struppen, March 1934, Ephoralarchiv Pirna 290.

20. Superintendent Max Zweynert to the pastors in the district of Pirna, August 17, 1934, Ephoralarchiv Pirna 80.

21. Report from the Müglitztaler Conference of February 5, 1934, Ephoralarchiv Pirna 290.

22. Zeitgemässe Verkundigung, March 1934, Ephoralarchiv Pirna, 290.

23. Superintendent Max Zweynert to all clergy in the Pirna district, January 7 and 11, 1935, Ephoralarchiv Pirna 80.

24. Superintendent's Instructions 120, November 19, 1937; Superintendent's Instructions 123, March 25, 1938, Ephoralarchiv Pirna 80; Pastor Ploedterll of Königstein to Superintendent Leichte of Pirna, March 30, 1938, Ephoralarchiv Pirna 119.

25. Evangelisches Gemeindeblatt Friedrichshafen, November 1936, Stadtarchiv Friedrichschafen.

26. "Bericht des Dekans," Kirchenbezirkstag, December 14, 1933, 3, Dekanatsarchiv Ravensburg 88e; Gemeindeblatt Wälde-Winterbach/Bavendorf, Nr. 1, 1934, in Hans-Dieter Schäfer, ed., Evangelische KirchengemeindeWälde-Winterbach (Ravensburg, 1991), 26; "Oberschwäb. evang. Diaspora-Versammlung," Oberschwäbischer Anzeiger, December 11, 1933; Evangelisches Gemeindeblatt Friedrichshafen, May 1933, Stadtarchiv Friedrichshafen; Evangelisches Gemeindeblatt Friedrichshafen, November 1936, Stadtarchiv Friedrichshafen; Brandenburg Consistory circular, April 13, 1937, Domstiftsarchiv Brandenburg NE 71/737.

27. Oberschwäbischer Anzeiger, January 14 and 16, 1932, Stadtarchiv Ravensburg; "Kreiskirchentag in Nauen" (newspaper clipping), n.d., Domstiftsarchiv Brandenburg NE 300/590; "Wesen und Grund der christlichen Hoffnung," by Pastor Schmidt of Weingarten, October 1933, 1–2, Dekanatsarchiv Ravensburg 83b; "Evangelischer Männerverein," Oberschwäbischer Anzeiger, August 29, 1933, Stadtarchiv Ravensburg; "Kreiskirchentag in Pirna" (newspaper clipping), n.d., Ephoralarchiv Pirna 92; Evangelisches Gemeindeblatt Friedrichshafen, July 1935, Dekanatsarchiv Ravensburg 54d.

28. Anna von Hofsten, "Det Andliga Livet I Tyskland," Östgöta Correspondenten, February 8, 1939, translated into German by von Hofsten, Domstiftsarchiv Brandenburg Nau 26/21. Von Hofsten had become acquainted with Pastor Friedrich Siems during a visit to Nauen and had written an article describing his ministry, which she then translated from Swedish to German for him.

29. Hans Tiefel, "The German Lutheran Church and the Rise of National Socialism," Church History 41 (1972): 326–36; Scholder, Churches and the Third Reich, 1:99–119; Berndt Hamm, "Werner Elert als Kriegstheologe: Zugleich ein Beitrag zur Diskussion 'Luthertum und Nationalsozialismus,'" Kirchliche Zeitgeschichte 11, no. 2 (1998): 206–54; and particularly Robert Ericksen, Theologians under Hitler: Gerhard Kittel, Paul Althaus, and Emanuel Hirsch (New Haven: Yale University Press, 1985).

30. Tiefel, "German Lutheran Church and the Rise of National Socialism," 331–32.

31. Victoria Barnett, For the Soul of the People: Protestant Protest against Hitler (New York: Oxford University Press, 1992), 9–17; Hans Rothfels, The German Opposition to Hitler: An Assessment (London: Oswald Wolff, 1970), 39.

32. "Bericht über die Sitzung der Stolpener Konferenz am 22. Januar 1934," Ephoralarchiv Pirna 290.

33. Von Hofsten, "Det Andliga Livet I Tyskland," Östgöta Correspondenten, February 8, 1939, Domstiftsarchiv Brandenburg Nau 26/21.

34. Pastor Siems in Nauen to Frau von Hofsten, Upsala, Sweden, Domstiftsarchiv Brandenburg Nau 26/21.

35. Pastor Wertz of Isny, "Staat und Kirche," November 1936, 2, Dekanatsarchiv Ravensburg 83b.

36. Both the ennobling of the soil and the need for authority were based on Genesis 1:28 and 3:19.

37. Joachim Beckmann, Artgemässes Christentum oder schriftgemässer Christenglaube (Essen, 1933), 11, quoted in John S. Conway, The Nazi Persecution of the Churches 1933–1945 (New York: Basic Books, 1968), 46.

38. Pastor Klemm of Burkhardswalde to the Saxon Church Office, July 12, 1945, Ephoralarchiv Pirna 180.

39. The church-political orientation of Nauen clergy was determined based on lists compiled by the Confessing Church (Domstiftsarchiv Brandenburg NE 142/94), supplemented by marginal notations from the list of delegates to the 1934 district synod (Domstiftsarchiv Brandenburg NE 48/658), correspondence between the pastors, superintendents and the Brandenburg Consistory (Domstiftsarchiv Brandenburg NE 122/742), official private correspondence between pastors and superintendents (Domstiftsarchiv Brandenburg NE 140/814 and 141/835), correspondence concerning the monthly pastoral convents (Domstiftsarchiv Brandenburg NE 200/734) and the "Brotherly Get-Togethers" that replaced them (Domstiftsarchiv Brandenburg NE 202/860), as well as material relating to pastoral appointments and the Church Struggle in Nauen (Domstiftsarchiv Brandenburg NE 703/770).

40. Superintendent Zweynert of Pirna to Saxon Bishop Coch, February 6, 1934, Ephoralarchiv Pirna 814.

41. Superintendent Meinel of Pirna to the Saxon Church Committee, July 30, 1937; Superintendent Leichte, Handwritten Lists, 1938; Superintendent Leichte of Pirna to the Saxon Church Office, October 18, 1938, Ephoralarchiv Pirna 403.

42. Unidentified correspondent from Nauen to Lic. Kummel in Stahnsdorf, Westhavelland, July 27, 1933, Domstiftsarchiv Brandenburg NE 120/596.

43. "Bericht über die Pastoralkonferenz in Bad Schandau am 19.3.1934," Ephoralarchiv Pirna 290.

44. Pastor Isleib in Hakenberg to Interim Superintendent Bettac in Beetz, January 7, 1939, Domstiftsarchiv Brandenburg NE 140/814; Pastor Gartenschläger in Bötzow, "Die Deutschen Christen rufen zur Volksmission," n.d., Domstiftsarchiv Brandenburg Nau 56/85.

45. *Ev. Gemeindeblatt für die Leutkirchner Diaspora*, July/August 1933, Dekanatsarchiv Ravensburg 66f.

46. "75 Jahre evangelische Kirchengemeinde Tettnang" (newspaper clipping), March 17, 1936, Dekanatsarchiv Ravensburg 67h.

47. *Evang. Gemeindeblatt Friedrichshafen*, November 1936, and "Evangelischer Männerverein Friedrichshafen, Bericht, Juni 1937," Dekanatsarchiv Ravensburg 54d.

48. "Kreiskirchentag in Nauen" (newspaper clipping), n.d., Domstiftsarchiv Brandenburg NE 300/590.

49. *Evang. Sonntagsblatt für den Kirchenkreis Nauen*, March 3, 1940, Domstiftsarchiv Brandenburg Ki 490.

50. Pastor Heinrich Zweynert of Neustadt, "Bericht über die Sitzungen der Stolpener Konferenz am 1. und 22. Juli 35," Ephoralarchiv Pirna 291.

51. Pastor Martin Rasch in Reinhardtsdorf to Superintendent Zweynert in Pirna, May 19, 1933, Ephoralarchiv Pirna 814.

52. Interim Superintendent Bettac in Beetz to Pastor Knuth in Berlin, July 18, 1938, Domstiftsarchiv Brandenburg NE 140/814.

53. Interim Superintendent Bettac in Beetz to Pastor Isleib in Hakenberg, January 10, 1939, Domstiftsarchiv Brandenburg NE 140/814.

54. *Evang. Sonntagsblatt für den Kirchenkreis Nauen*, March 3, 1935, Domstiftsarchiv Brandenburg Ki 490; Pastor Posth in Berge to the Brandenburg Consistory, October 20, 1938, Domstiftsarchiv Brandenburg Ri 6/26.

55. Pastor Posth in Berge to the Prussian Superior Church Council, Berlin, December 1, 1943, Evangelisches Zentralarchiv Berlin 7/11934.

56. Fifty-Five Groß Behnitz parishioners to the Brandenburg Consistory, March 7, 1938, Evangelisches Zentralarchiv Berlin 7/12233.

57. Helmut Thielicke, *Notes from a Wayfarer: The Autobiography of Helmut Thielicke*, trans. David R. Law (New York: Paragon House, 1995), 140.

58. "Abschied von Stadtpfarrer Sigle [*sic*], Isny, am 21.2.1938. aus dem Diözesanverein in Ravensburg," Landeskirchliches Archiv Stuttgart PA S/446.

# Chapter 2: National Socialism as a Catalyst for German Protestant Renewal?

1. Klaus Scholder, *The Churches and the Third Reich*, vol. 1, *Preliminary History and the Time of Illusions 1918–1934*, trans. John Bowden (Philadelphia: Fortress Press, 1988), 231.

2. The account of the 1933 district church assembly is based on "Kreiskirchentag in Nauen" (newspaper article), n.d, Domstiftsarchiv Brandenburg NE 300/590.

3. Pastor Gartenschläger in Bötzow to Superintendent Graßhoff in Nauen, STN 1427 1933, Domstiftsarchiv Brandenburg NE 101/647.

4. Pastor Günther Harder in Fehrbellin to Superintendent Graßhoff in Nauen, STN 1577 1933, Domstiftsarchiv Brandenburg NE 101/647.

5. Pastor Lux in Groß Behnitz to Superintendent Graßhoff in Nauen, May 8, 1933, Domstiftsarchiv Brandenburg NE 101/647.

6. Pastor Schmidt in Flatow to Superintendent Graßhoff in Nauen, STN 1348 1933, Domstiftsarchiv Brandenburg NE 101/647.

7. Pastor Cramer in Kremmen to Superintendent Graßhoff in Nauen, STN 1335 1933; Pastor Feder in Vehlefanz to Graßhoff, STN 1435 1933, Domstiftsarchiv Brandenburg NE 101/647.

8. Superintendent Graßhoff in Nauen to the Brandenburg Consistory, August 15, 1933, Domstiftsarchiv Brandenburg NE 50/825; "Personalbestand" lists of synodal representatives, NE 48/658.

9. All statistics are compiled from tables in Domstiftsarchiv Brandenburg NE 96/754 "Statistische Übersichten über Äußerungen des kirchlichen Lebens im Kirchenkreis, 1929–1944."

10. All statistics are compiled from tables in Ephoralarchiv Pirna 13, "Wiedereintrittsbewegung 1933" Ephoralarchiv Pirna 14, "Kirchenein- und Austrittsbewegung (Statistik) 1938–9"; Ephoralarchiv Pirna 15, "Kirchenein- und Austrittsbewegung (Statistik) betr. 1939–1940"; Ephoralarchiv Pirna 834, "Übersicht über Gottesdienst Besucher 1943–1945"; Ephoralarchiv Pirna 847, "Statistik kirchlicher Einrichtungen . . . 1928–1939"; Ephoralarchiv Pirna 915, "Statistik . . ."; and Ephoralarchiv Pirna 925, "Statistik. . . ."

11. Superintendent's Office in Pirna to pastors in the district, July 25, 1933, Ephoralarchiv Pirna 80.

12. This number does not include clergy who had been German Christians, but who abandoned the movement after the scandalous Berlin Sport Palace assembly of November 13, 1933.

13. "Bericht über die Pastoralkonferenz in Bad Schandau am 19.3.1934," Ephoralarchiv Pirna 290.

14. "Timely Preaching," Struppen, March 1934, Ephoralarchiv Pirna 290.

15. "Kreiskirchentag in Pirna" (newspaper clipping), n.d., Ephoralarchiv Pirna 92.

16. Various pastoral correspondence, Ephoralarchiv Pirna 184.

17. Stolpen Pastoral Conference to the Regional Church Office in Dresden, May 20, 1935, Ephoralarchiv Pirna 290.

18. "Es sei noch einmal betont . . ." (newspaper clipping), 1932, Ephoralarchiv Pirna 216; Pastor Klemm in Burkhardswalde to the Superintendent's Office in Pirna, July 1, 1933, Ephoralarchiv Pirna 210.

19. Pastor Heinrich Zweynert of Neustadt, "Bericht über die Sitzung der Stolpener Konferenz am 9. März 1936," Ephoralarchiv Pirna 291.

20. "Nazi Flag in the Church!" (newspaper clipping), January 13, 1933, Ephoralarchiv Pirna 216.

21. The following account is based on correspondence sent from Superintendent Max Zweynert of Pirna to Saxon Church Office, March 10, 1933; Pastor Peter of Pirna to Mr. Killinger, Reich Plenipotentiary for Saxony, March 10, 1933; Peter to the Saxon Consistory, May 7, 1933, Ephoralarchiv Pirna 814.

22. Pastor Rudolf Peter of Pirna to Superintendent Max Zweynert of Pirna, May 8, 1933, and Pastor Adolf Müller of the Consistory to Superintendent Zweynert in Pirna, July 18, 1933, Ephoralarchiv Pirna 814.

23. Superintendent Max Zweynert to the city councils and municipal authorities in the church district of Pirna, May 31, 1933, Ephoralarchiv Pirna 184.

24. Superintendent's Office to the pastors in the district, April 26, 1934; Superintendent Max Zweynert to all clergy in the Pirna district, March 19, 1937; and Superintendent's Instructions 112, March 23, 1937, Ephoralarchiv Pirna 80.

25. Superintendent's Instructions 127, May 19, 1938, Ephoralarchiv Pirna 80.

26. Pastor Heinrich Zweynert of Neustadt, "Bericht über die Sitzung der Stolpener Konferenz am 28.5.1934," Ephoralarchiv Pirna 290.

27. Pastor Scherffig of Heidenau-Christus to Superintendent Max Zweynert of Pirna, August 17, 1934, Ephoralarchiv Pirna 403.

28. Pastor Ebert of Pirna to Superintendent Max Zweynert in Pirna, December 17, 1935, Ephoralarchiv Pirna 403.

29. Superintendent Max Zweynert of Pirna to the Regional Church Committee, November 23, 1936, Ephoralarchiv Pirna 403.

30. Pastor Börner of Ottendorf to Superintendent Leichte in Pirna, February 21, 1939, Ephoralarchiv Pirna 184.

31. Pastor Ebert of Pirna to Superintendent Leichte in Pirna, February 23, 1939, Ephoralarchiv Pirna 184.

32. Pastor Werner of Dohna to Superintendent Leichte, February 13, 1941, Ephoralarchiv Pirna 915.

33. "Bericht des Dekans," Kirchenbezirkstag, December 14, 1933, Dekanatsarchiv Ravensburg 88e.

34. "Evangelischer Männerverein," *Oberschwäbischer Anzeiger*, August 29, 1933, Stadtarchiv Ravensburg.

35. Unidentified newspaper clipping, February 6, 1935, Dekanatsarchiv Ravensburg 54d.

36. On the land transactions, see correspondence in Dekanatsarchiv Ravensburg 54a, 54c, and 60a, among others. On the rental of facilities, see correspondence and contracts in Dekanatsarchiv Ravensburg 55c, 56h, 58c, 60a, 69c, and 168g.

37. For correspondence, plans, and contracts, see Dekanatsarchiv Ravensburg 54a, 54c, 55c, 55e, 56h, 57a, 58a, 58c, 60a, 61a, 64c, 66d, 67a, 67g, 80c, 168g, and Neue Akten/Langenargen.

38. For correspondence and contracts, see Dekanatsarchiv Ravensburg 52b, 53e, 55e, 56e, 58a, 61a, 62l, 64e, 66d, 67a, 69c, 69d, 69e, 72c, 74e, 76d, Neue Akten/Langenargen, and Neue Akten/Wangen.

39. Correspondence in Dekanatsarchiv Ravensburg 61a, 63a, 64e and 64g; Willi Eberle, *400 Jahre Evangelische Gemeinde in Leutkirch (1546–1946)*, Sondernummer Trinitatis 1946, *Evangelisches Gemeindeblatt für Leutkirch und seine Diaspora*, 32, Dekanatsarchiv Ravensburg Neue Akten/Leutkirch A II 1.

40. Various pastoral correspondence, Dekanatsarchiv Ravensburg 53c and 62a.

41. Pastor Ludwig Schmidt of Friedrichshafen to the Württemberg Superior Church Council, May 1, 1944; Württemberg Superior Church Council to the Ravensburg Superintendent, May 4, 1944, and May 17, 1944, Dekanatsarchiv Ravensburg 54d.

42. Pastor Ludwig Schmidt of Friedrichshafen to the Württemberg Superior Church Council, July 20, 1944, Dekanatsarchiv Ravensburg 54d; Pastor Waldbaur of Langenargen, "Report over the events in the parish hall during the last air raid on our city, July 18 and 20, 1944," July 23, 1944, Dekanatsarchiv Ravensburg 56h.

43. All statistics are compiled from tables in Dekanatsarchiv Ravensburg 89.

44. Günther Dehn, *Die alte Zeit, die vorigen Jahre: Lebenserinnerungen* (Munich: Christian Kaiser, 1962), 346–48; Frederic Spotts, *The Churches and Politics in Germany* (Middletown, Conn.: Wesleyan University Press, 1973), 48–49; Laurenz Demps, "Die Provinz Brandenburg in der NS-Zeit (1933 bis 1945)," in *Brandenburgische Geschichte,* ed. Ingo Matema and Wolfgang Ribbe (Berlin: Akademie, 1995), 625.

45. Dehn, *Die alte Zeit,* 343-344; *Oberschwäbischer Anzeiger*, August 1, 1932, November 7, 1932, and March 6, 1933, Stadtarchiv Ravensburg. On German voting patterns in the Nazi era, see Richard F. Hamilton, *Who Voted for Hitler?* (Princeton: Princeton University Press, 1982); and Jürgen Falter, *Hitlers Wähler* (Munich: Beck, 1991).

# Chapter 3: Pastoral Appointments and the Local Church Struggle

1. "Bericht über unsere Reise am Ostersamstag bis einschl. Ostermontag 1929 nach Massenbach O/A. Brackenheim zu Herrn Pfarrer Dr. Steger, Massenbach, Herrn Dekan Metzger in Brackenheim, Herrn Prälat Wurm in Heilbronn und Herrn Stadtpfarrer Eifert in Heilbronn," April 5, 1929, Dekanatsarchiv Ravensburg 53b.

2. Gottfried Hoffmann, "Aufstellung der persönlichen Verhältnisse," Landeskirchliches Archiv Stuttgart PA H/345.

3. Correspondence concerning Hoffmann's conflict with a prominent manufacturing family and the principal Protestant schoolteacher in Waldsee is in Dekanatsarchiv Ravensburg 71a, 71b ("Fall Birkmeyer"), 72c, 72d, and 72f.

4. Württemberg Superior Church Council to the District Superintendent's Office, Ravensburg, October 20, 1939, Dekanatsarchiv Ravensburg 53a.

5. Friedrichshafen had doubled in size over the previous five years thanks to its important military industries—it was the home of the Zeppelin—and an influx of Protestant factory workers from across Germany had turned it into a heterogeneous parish of close to seven thousand souls. "Protokollauszug of the Kirchengemeinderat Friedrichshafen," August 27, 1939, Dekanatsarchiv Ravensburg 53a.

6. Helmut Thielicke, *Notes from a Wayfarer: The Autobiography of Helmut Thielicke*, trans. David R. Law (New York: Paragon House, 1995), 110–25, 147; Württemberg Superior Church Council to the District Superintendent's Office, Ravensburg, January 20, 1941, Dekanatsarchiv Ravensburg 151e; Pastor Daur in Ravensburg to the Württemberg Superior Church Council, January 16, 1942, Landeskirchliches Archiv Stuttgart Alt. Reg. Ravensburg Besetzung III; Minutes of the Ravensburg parish council meeting of September 24, 1942, *Verhandlungsbuch*, Band VI, 362, Dekanatsarchiv Ravensburg 125.

7. Württemberg Superior Church Council to the District Superintendent's Office, Ravensburg, November 21, 1942, Dekanatsarchiv Ravensburg 151e; Minutes of the Ravensburg parish council meeting of December 14, 1942, *Verhandlungsbuch*, Band VI, 367, Dekanatsarchiv Ravensburg 125.

8. On the Dehn Case, see Günther Dehn, *Die alte Zeit, die vorigen Jahre: Lebenserinnerungen* (Munich: Christian Kaiser, 1962), 247–85; Klaus Scholder, *The Churches and the Third Reich*, vol. 1, *Preliminary History and the Time of Illusions 1918–1934*, trans. John Bowden (Philadelphia: Fortress Press, 1988), 172–77; Ernst Rudolf Huber and Wolfgang Huber, eds., *Staat und Kirche im 19. und 20. Jahrhundert: Dokumente zur Geschichte des deutschen Staatskirchenrechts*, vol. 4, *Staat und Kirche in der Zeit der Weimarer Republik* (Berlin: Duncker & Humblot, 1987), 785–803.

9. Dehn, *Die alte Zeit,* 346; Thielicke, *Notes from a Wayfarer*, 184; Prelate Buder in Ulm to the Württemberg Superior Church Council, October 16, 1945 (and reply of November 3, 1945), Prelate Buder to the Württemberg Superior Church Council, December 14, 1945, Landeskirchliches Archiv Stuttgart Alt. Reg. Ravensburg Besetzung I.

10. "Herr, auf dein Wort! Abschiedspredigt von Oberkirchenrat Dr. Zweynert in der Marienkirche zu Pirna am 27. Juni 1937," Ephoralarchiv Pirna 422.

11. Superintendent Max Zweynert to all pastors in the Pirna district, June 7, 1933; Various replies from pastors, June and July 1933, Ephoralarchiv Pirna 814.

12. Superintendent's Instructions 113, April 5, 1937; Superintendent's Instructions 115, June 25, 1937; Pirna Superintendent to district clergy, January 19, 1934, Ephoralarchiv Pirna 80.

13. Klotsche and Kretzschmar, Saxon Church Office, to Pastor Meinel in Bad Schandau, November 11, 1937, Ephoralarchiv Pirna 422.

14. Letter to the Pirna political police, November 18, 1937, Ephoralarchiv Pirna 422; Superintendent's Instructions 120, November 19, 1937, Ephoralarchiv Pirna 80. This was not the first time that Meinel had run afoul of the Saxon church authorities. Early in the Third Reich, he joined the Pastors' Emergency League. Though he withdrew from the League in mid-1934, Meinel remained an opponent of the Saxon German Christians, who dominated the regional church government. In 1937, he joined the *Middle* church group and worked actively against the German

Christians in the Pirna district. Saxon Church Office to Superintendent Zweynert in Pirna, July 25, 1934; Pastor Meinel in Bad Schandau to the Saxon Church Office, November 8, 1934, Ephoralarchiv Pirna 815; Meinel to Zweynert, March 23, 1937, Ephoralarchiv Pirna 819.

15. List of district clergy who acknowledge the authority of the Saxon Lutheran Church government, 1934, Ephoralarchiv Pirna 815; "Wiederbesetzung der ersten Pfarrstelle in Pirna" (newspaper clipping), May 30, 1938; Heinrich Leichte, "Lebenslauf," Ephoralarchiv Pirna 422.

16. Pastor Heinrich Leichte to the District Superintendent's Office, Pirna, June 13, 1938, June 15, 1938, and June 21, 1938, Ephoralarchiv Pirna 422.

17. Maximilian Zweynert to Superintendent Heinrich Leichte, April 24, 1939, Ephoralarchiv Pirna 422.

18. The relevant material includes many circular letters from Pirna superintendents in Ephoralarchiv Pirna 80 and 81, as well as the large file containing the cases of fourteen Pirna pastors, Ephoralarchiv Pirna 816.

19. Herr von Ribbeck to the Brandenburg Consistory, October 5 and 16, 1933; Pastor Posth of Berge to the Brandenburg Consistory, February 10, 1934, Evangelisches Zentralarchiv Berlin 14/10649.

20. Filial churches were village congregations that were part of larger parishes in neighboring towns.

21. Prussian Superior Church Council EO II 3050, September 27, 1935; report on Groß Behnitz, July 1, 1935, Evangelisches Zentralarchiv Berlin 7/12233.

22. Interim Superintendent Schmidt in Flatow to the Brandenburg Consistory, August 8, 1936, Evangelisches Zentralarchiv Berlin 14/10317.

23. Interim Superintendent Bettac in Beetz to the Brandenburg Consistory, Finance Department, December 23, 1936, Evangelisches Zentralarchiv Berlin 14/10317.

24. Pastor Posth of Berge to the Brandenburg Consistory, December 8, 1936, Evangelisches Zentralarchiv Berlin 14/10317.

25. Pastor Posth of Berge to the Brandenburg Consistory, December 15, 1936, Evangelisches Zentralarchiv Berlin 14/10317; Interim Superintendent Bettac in Beetz to the Nauen district synod executive, February 18, 1937, Domstiftsarchiv Brandenburg NE 59/646.

26. Prussian Superior Church Council EO II 398/37, February 12, 1937, Evangelisches Zentralarchiv Berlin 7/12233; Brandenburg Consistory to the Prussian Superior Church Council, March 13, 1937, Evangelisches Zentralarchiv Berlin 7/11934 and 7/12765; Interim Superintendent Bettac in Beetz to the Brandenburg Consistory, March 22, 1937, Evangelisches Zentralarchiv Berlin 14/10753.

27. Prussian Superior Church Council EO II 56/38, January 28, 1938, Evangelisches Zentralarchiv Berlin 7/12233.

28. Pastor Höft of Zeestow to the Brandenburg Consistory, December 5, 1936, and January 2, 1937; Interim Superintendent Schmidt in Flatow to the Brandenburg Consistory, April 8, 1936; Höft to the District Superintendent's Office, Nauen, October 8, 1936; Höft to the Brandenburg Consistory, November 16, 1936; December 5, 1936; January 2, 1937; and March 6, 1937; Brandenburg Consistory, Finance Department, to Curate Dreves, the Markau Parish Council and the District Superintendent's Office, Nauen, March 19 and July 13, 1937; Höft to the Brandenburg Consistory, December 5, 1936; Schmidt to the Brandenburg Consistory, October 20, 1936, Evangelisches Zentralarchiv Berlin 14/10800.

29. Prussian Superior Church Council EO II 3050, September 27, 1935, Evangelisches Zentralarchiv Berlin 7/12233; Interim Superintendent Schmidt in Flatow to the Brandenburg Consistory, January 31 and March 18, 1936; Patron Schoch in Markau to the Brandenburg Consistory, March 18, 1936, Evangelisches Zentralarchiv Berlin 14/10317.

30. Brandenburg Consistory to the Prussian Superior Church Council, March 13, 1937, Evangelisches Zentralarchiv Berlin 7/11934.

31. Pastor Scharf of the Brandenburg Confessing Church Council to Interim Superintendent Bettac in Beetz, January 30, 1938; Bettac to Consistorial Councilor Kegel, February 2, 1938; Bettac to Scharf, February 2, 1938; Kegel to Bettac, February 3, 1938; Bettac to Güterdirektor Schoch of

the Lynarschen Güterverwaltung, Patron of Markau, February 28, 1938; Schoch to Curate Krafft in Markau, March 4, 1938; Schoch to Bettac, March 4, 1938, Domstiftsarchiv Brandenburg NE 140/814.

32. Fürstlich Lynar-Gräflich Redern'sche Generalverwaltung (Schoch) to the Brandenburg Consistory, April 5, 1939; Brandenburg Consistory to Schoch, April 24, 1939, Evangelisches Zentralarchiv Berlin 14/10800; Interim Superintendent Bettac in Beetz to Prelate Bormann in Angermünde, November 23, 1939, Domstiftsarchiv Brandenburg NE 141/835.

33. Pastor Posth of Berge to Interim Superintendent Bettac in Beetz, October 21, 1940; Bettac to Posth, October 24, 1940; Interim Superintendent Bettac in Beetz to Pastor Born of Leegebruch, December 2, 1940, Domstiftsarchiv Brandenburg NE 141/835. Bettac's divorce is documented in Evangelisches Zentralarchiv Berlin 14/10879.

34. Fürstlich Lynar-Gräflich Redern'sche Generalverwaltung to the Brandenburg Consistory, May 15, 1942; Markau Parish Council to the Brandenburg Consistory, May 27, 1942, Evangelisches Zentralarchiv Berlin 14/10800.

35. Interim Superintendent Bettac in Beetz to Pastor Isleib of Hakenberg, February 19, 1940, Domstiftsarchiv Brandenburg NE 141/835.

36. Interim Superintendent Bettac in Beetz to Mrs. Eichler of Leegebruch, October 27, 1939, Domstiftsarchiv Brandenburg 141/835; Bettac to the Brandenburg Consistory, October 31, 1939, Domstiftsarchiv Brandenburg NE 127/751.

37. Information about the tenure of interim superintendents is based on the flow of correspondence between the district superintendent's office and the pastors, found in Domstiftsarchiv Brandenburg NE 70/736, NE 71/737 and NE 72/738, and between the superintendency and the Brandenburg Consistory from 1932 to 1946, in Domstiftsarchiv Brandenburg NE 122/742, NE 124/743, NE 125/744, NE 127/751, NE 128/752, NE 129/900, NE 130/840, NE 131/803, NE 132/759 and NE 133/830.

38. *Berufsurkunde*, October 28, 1937; Groß Behnitz Parish Councilor Rudolf Günther to the Brandenburg Consistory, January 16, 1938; Groß Behnitz School Principal and Church Organist Th. Lehmann to the Brandenburg Consistory, January 16 and 17, 1938; Groß Behnitz Mayor and Parish Councilor Stackebrandt to the Brandenburg Consistory, January 16, 1938, Evangelisches Zentralarchiv Berlin 14/10318.

39. R. Günther, Mayor Stackebrandt et al. to the Brandenburg Consistory, March 7, 1938, Evangelisches Zentralarchiv Berlin 7/12233 and 14/10318. Copies were also sent directly to Reich Minister for Ecclesiastical Affairs Kerrl, the Ecclesiastical Chancellery of the German Evangelical Church and the president of the Old Prussian Union Church.

40. Petitions from the parish council in Groß and Klein Behnitz, March 9, 1938, Evangelisches Zentralarchiv Berlin 14/10318.

41. Dr. Ernst von Borsig to the Brandenburg Consistory, March 14, 1938; Brandenburg Confessing Church Council, "Notice for Sunday, the February 27, 1938 in the morning and evening church services"; Dr. Ernst von Borsig to the Brandenburg Consistory, March 14, 1938, Evangelisches Zentralarchiv Berlin 14/10318.

42. "Beglaubigte Abschrift aus dem Protokollbuch Gr. Behnitz," April 21, 1938, Evangelisches Zentralarchiv Berlin 14/10318; Brandenburg Consistory to the Prussian Superior Church Council, May 5, 1938; "Beglaubigte Auszug aus dem Verhandlungsbuche der evangelischen Kirchengemeinde Großbehnitz. Sitzung . . . den 28. Mai 1937"; Brandenburg Consistory to the Groß Behnitz Parish Council and Nauen District Church Office, July 30, 1938, Evangelisches Zentralarchiv Berlin 7/12233.

43. Interim Superintendent Bettac in Beetz to the Brandenburg Confessing Church Council, August 23, 1938; Bettac to Pastor Pachali of Retzow, December 16, 1938, Domstiftsarchiv Brandenburg NE 140/814; Bettac to Pastor Harder of Fehrbellin, January 10, 1939, Domstiftsarchiv Brandenburg NE 142/944; Pessin Parish Council to the Brandenburg Consistory, December 5, 1938; Confirmation of Pastor Bedorf's appointment, January 29, 1939, Evangelisches Zentralarchiv Berlin 14/10770; List of neutral pastors in the Nauen church district, n.d., Domstiftsarchiv Brandenburg NE 142/944.

44. Interim Superintendent Bettac in Beetz to Consistorial Councilor Kegel, March 12, 1940; Pastor Isleib in Hakenberg to Bettac, February 13, 1940, Domstiftsarchiv Brandenburg NE 141/835.

45. Interim Superintendent Bettac in Beetz to Pastor Harder of Fehrbellin, April 16, 1940; Herr Quehl to Interim Superintendent Bettac in Beetz, August 8, 1940; Interim Superintendent Bettac in Beetz to Curate Born, August 21, 1940; Bettac to Patron Oberamtmann Demuth, Linum, August 21, 1940, Domstiftsarchiv Brandenburg NE 141/835 and 143/948; Bettac to the Brandenburg Consistory, April 26, 1940; Letter of the Brandenburg Consistory, January 19, 1941, Evangelisches Zentralarchiv Berlin 14/10669.

46. Already in August 1933, Posth complained that his duties were too burdensome. Preaching in Berge, Lietzow, and a hemp factory three miles away (a total of 1,558 parishioners), along with regular youth and women's meetings in Berge made Ribbeck too great a challenge for Posth, who suffered from chronic lung problems. Posth suggested giving the work to Pastor Koch of Retzow, who had only two towns less that two miles apart, and only 1,020 parishioners. Koch refused, and Posth took on the task. Pastor Posth of Berge to the Brandenburg Consistory, August 15, 1933; Nauen district synod executive to the Brandenburg Consistory, October 11, 1933; Herr von Ribbeck to the Brandenburg Consistory, October 5, 1933; Herr von Ribbeck to the Brandenburg Consistory, October 16, 1933; Pastor Posth in Berge to the Brandenburg Consistory, February 10, 1934, Evangelisches Zentralarchiv Berlin 14/10649.

47. Ribbeck Parish Council to Pastor Pachali in Retzow, October 6, 1937; Pastor Pachali of Retzow to the Ribbeck Parish Council, October 15, 1937; Ribbeck Parish Council to the Brandenburg Consistory, October 21, 1937, Evangelisches Zentralarchiv Berlin 14/10649; lists of Confessing Church membership are in Domstiftsarchiv Brandenburg NE 142/944.

48. Pastor Posth of Berge to Interim Superintendent Bettac in Beetz, November 8, 1937, Domstiftsarchiv Brandenburg NE 69/741.

49. Interim Superintendent Bettac in Beetz to the Brandenburg Consistory, June 24, 1938, Evangelisches Zentralarchiv Berlin 14/10649; Pastor Posth of Berge to the Prussian Superior Church Council, Berlin, April 11, 1939, Domstiftsarchiv Brandenburg NE 143/948.

50. Ribbeck Parish Council to the Brandenburg Consistory, October 21, 1937; Report on a meeting between Consistorial Councilor Hermann, Interim Superintendent Bettac of Beetz, and Pastors Posth of Berge and Pachali of Retzow, February 22, 1938; Pastor Pachali in Retzow to the Brandenburg Consistory, June 22, 1938; Pastor Posth in Berge to the Brandenburg Consistory, July 12, 1938, and October 20, 1938; Interim Superintendent Bettac in Beetz to the Brandenburg Consistory, December 9, 1938; "Beglaubigter Auszug aus dem Verhandlungsbuch der Kirchengemeinde Ribbeck," January 19, 1941, Evangelisches Zentralarchiv Berlin 14/10649; Interim Superintendent Bettac in Beetz to the Brandenburg Consistory (annual reports on the administration of vacant parishes), May 11, 1939, Domstiftsarchiv Brandenburg NE 130/840; July 22, 1940, Domstiftsarchiv Brandenburg NE 127/751; March 5, 1941, Domstiftsarchiv Brandenburg NE 128/752.

51. Interim Superintendent Bettac in Beetz to Pastor Posth of Berge, April 19, 1940, Domstiftsarchiv Brandenburg NE 141/835.

52. Interim Superintendent Pastor Bettac in Beetz to the Brandenburg Consistory, re: "Pfarrstellenbesetzungen bei Stadtpatronen," February 12, 1937, Domstiftsarchiv Brandenburg NE 126/750.

53. "Einspruch gegen die Wahl des Herrn Pfarrer Andrich . . . ," n.d., Domstiftsarchiv Brandenburg NE 703/770.

54. Ibid. There is also a similar grievance from three Nauen women, June 11, 1939, Domstiftsarchiv Brandenburg NE 703/770 (also in Domstiftsarchiv Brandenburg NE 143/948, attributed there to Confessing Church Curate Ossenkop in Fehrbellin).

55. Ibid. There is also a similar grievance from three Nauen women, June 11, 1939, Domstiftsarchiv Brandenburg NE 703/770 (also in Domstiftsarchiv Brandenburg NE 143/948, attributed there to Confessing Church Curate Ossenkop in Fehrbellin).

56. Interim Superintendent Bettac in Beetz to Mrs. Krüger of Nauen, April 5, 1939; Mrs. Krüger to Mayor Urban of Nauen, April 18, 1939, Domstiftsarchiv Brandenburg NE 703/770.

57. "Predigt gehalten bei der Probeaufstellung am 21. Jan. 1940 in Nauen durch P. Gille," Evangelisches Zentralarchiv Berlin 14/10559; "Wir Endesunterzeichneten erheben hiermit Enspruch gegen Lehre, Gaben und Wandel des Herrn Hilfspredigers Gille," February 19, 1940; Minutes of the Nauen district synod executive, August 23, 1940, Evangelisches Zentralarchiv Berlin 14/10559 and Domstiftsarchiv Brandenburg 59/646.

58. The representative of those in the parish protesting against the election of Pastor Gille in Nauen to the Prussian Superior Church Council, May 31, 1940, Domstiftsarchiv Brandenburg NE 141/835; "Ich erhebe Einspruch gegen die Lehre von Herrn Pfarrer Gille aus Raguhn aus folgenden Gründen . . . ," n.d., Evangelisches Zentralarchiv Berlin 14/10559. Edith Troost of the Women's Aid and three women, two of them children's church helpers, signed the grievance. It was then forwarded with a letter to President Heinrich of the Prussian Superior Church Council, signed by the widow Emma Preuss and two other Nauen women (also in Evangelisches Zentralarchiv Berlin 14/10559). Other grievances and related correspondence, including evidence of Gille's leadership in the German Christian National Church Movement and his dedication to German anti-Jewish, völkisch piety are in Domstiftsarchiv Brandenburg NE 141/835 and Evangelisches Zentralarchiv Berlin 14/10559.

59. Brandenburg Consistory to the Prussian Superior Church Council, March 16, 1940; Brandenburg Consistory to the protesting parishioners in Nauen, May 18, 1940, Evangelisches Zentralarchiv Berlin 14/10559; Letter from Nauen parishioners, July 17, 1940, Domstiftsarchiv Brandenburg NE 143/948.

60. Brandenburg Consistory to the Prussian Superior Church Council, October 8, 1940, Evangelisches Zentralarchiv Berlin 14/10559.

61. Sitting of the Nauen district synod executive, August 23, 1940, Domstiftsarchiv Brandenburg NE 59/646 and Evangelisches Zentralarchiv Berlin 14/10559.

62. Nauen district synod executive to the Brandenburg Consistory, August 29, 1940; Pastor Gustav Gille in Raguhn/Anhalt, at present in the army, to the Brandenburg Consistory, October 19, 1940; Pastor Siems of Nauen to the Brandenburg Consistory, October 11, 1940, Evangelisches Zentralarchiv Berlin 14/10559.

63. Mayor Urban of Nauen to the Brandenburg Consistory, January 20, 1941, Evangelisches Zentralarchiv Berlin 14/10559.

64. Mayor Urban of Nauen to the Brandenburg Consistory, June 23, 1941, Evangelisches Zentralarchiv Berlin 14/10559; Mayor Urban of Nauen to the Brandenburg Consistory, April 27, 1942; Military Chaplain Schröder to Interim Superintendent Simon in Oranienburg, August 10, 1942, and January 12, 1943; Schröder's nomination and signature of acceptance are in Evangelisches Zentralarchiv Berlin 14/10556.

# Chapter 4: Clerical Responses to Euthanasia and Anti-Semitism

1. It is both unfortunate and unavoidable that anyone who wishes to discuss modern anti-Semitism and Hitler's racial policy must engage with the Nazi mental world, including its categories and language. The use of Hitler's propagandistic vocabulary is a necessary evil and is not meant to obscure the artificiality of the Nazi construct of race.

2. Heinrich Himmler to SS Leaders, September 13, 1936, and October 28, 1939, U.S. Chief of Counsel for the Prosecution of Axis Criminality, *Nazi Conspiracy and Aggression* (Washington: U.S. Government Printing Office, 1946), 2:190–91.

3. Two examples of such "wild euthanasia" were institutions previously used as collection centers for further transport, Zweifalten in Württemberg and Großschweidnitz in Saxony. Martin Rexer and Bodo Rüdenburg, "Zweifalten as 'Halfway House' on the Road to Grafeneck," in *Administered Killings at the Time of National Socialism: Involvement–Suppression–Responsibility of Psychiatry and Judicial System,* ed. Ulrich Jockusch and Lothar Scholz (Regensburg: Roderer, 1992), 110–46; Holm Krumpolt, "Die Landesheilanstalt Großschweidnitz als 'T4'-Zwischenanstalt und Tötungsanstalt (1939–1945)," in *Nationalsozialistische Euthanasie-Verbrechen in Sachsen: Beiträge zu ihrer Aufarbeitung* (Dresden/Pirna:

Kuratorium Gedenkstätte Sonnenstein e.v. und Sächsische Landeszentral für politische Bildung, 1993), 91–100.

4. Wolfgang Gerlach, *And the Witnesses Were Silent: The Confessing Church and the Persecution of the Jews*, trans. and ed. Victoria Barnett (Lincoln: University of Nebraska Press, 2000), 230–36.

5. Otto L. Elias, "Die Evangelische Kirchenkampf und die Judenfrage," *Informations-blatt für die Gemeinden in den niederdeutschen lutherischen Landeskirchen* 10 (1961): 217, quoted in Gerlach, *And the Witnesses Were Silent*, 232–33.

6. *Oberschwäbischer Anzeiger*, January 20, 1932, Stadtarchiv Ravensburg.

7. *Oberschwäbischer Anzeiger*, September 12, 1933, Stadtarchiv Ravensburg.

8. "Evangelischer Gemeindeabend zum Luthertag," *Oberschwäbischer Anzeiger*, November 21, 1933, Stadtarchiv Ravensburg.

9. Pastor Heinrich Zweynert of Neustadt, "Bericht über die Sitzung der Stolpener Pfarrkonferenz am 26.11.1934." Ephoralarchiv Pirna 291.

10. Pastor Wertz of Isny, "Staat und Kirche," [November 1936], 2, Dekanatsarchiv Ravensburg 83b.

11. Michael Jag, *Karl Steger: ein Pfarrer in Friedrichshafen als Deutscher Christ*, Prüfungsarbeit zur II. theologischen Dienstprüfung (1988/1989), June 1988, 13–14, Stadtarchiv Friedrichshafen.

12. Schoolteacher Voigt in Lietzow and NSDAP Local Group Leader Städicke to the Governing President in Potsdam and the Brandenburg Consistory, January 12–13, 1936; Curate Priester to Pastor Posth of Berge, September 10, 1936; "Erklärung des Vikars Priester [...] am 4. February 1936," Evangelisches Zentralarchiv Berlin 14/10859.

13. "Vikariatsbericht über Spellenberg, Immanuel," February 1, 1939; Immanuel Spellenberg, "Erklärung zu meiner Unterschrift am 13.I.39." Dekanatsarchiv Ravensburg 56h.

14. Pastor Siems of Nauen to Anna von Hofsten of Uppsala, Sweden, July 12, 1939, Domstiftsarchiv Brandenburg Nau 26/21. Susannah Heschel and Doris Bergen have both pointed out that the questioning of Jesus' racial identity was a German Christian strategy for dismissing the Jewish roots of the Christian faith. Susannah Heschel, "Nazifying Christian Theology: Walter Grundmann and the Institute for the Study and Eradication of Jewish Influence on German Church Life," *Church History* 63 (1994): 587–605; Doris Bergen, *Twisted Cross: The German Christian Movement in the Third Reich* (Chapel Hill: University of North Carolina Press, 1996), 195.

15. "Bericht betr. die Adventistenbewegung und die von den Adventisten verbreiteten Schriften," n.d., Ephoralarchiv Pirna 196.

16. "Kreiskirchentag zu Pirna" (newspaper clipping), October 9, 1935, Ephoralarchiv Pirna 92; "Kreiskirchentag in Pirna" (handwritten notes), October 9, 1935, Ephoralarchiv Pirna 100.

17. *Evangelisches Gemeindeblatt Friedrichshafen*, May 1936, Stadtarchiv Friedrichshafen.

18. Schoolteacher Lehmann of Groß Behnitz to the Brandenburg Consistory, November 14, 1938; "Folgendes Protokoll ist durch freiwillige Aussagen der Schulkinder entstanden, die am 11.11.38 am Konfirmandenunterricht des Herrn Pfarrer Fritzsche teilnahmen." Groß Behnitz, November 15, 1938, Evangelisches Zentralarchiv Berlin 7/12233. The last statement is a reference to the Jewish youth Herschel Grynszpan, who murdered a German embassy official in Paris and provided the pretext for the anti-Semitic pogrom.

19. Schoolteacher Lehmann of Groß Behnitz to Pastor Fritzsche of Groß Behnitz, November 13, 1938; Fritzsche to the Brandenburg Consistory, May 11, 1939; EO.II 3278 II/39 Prussian Superior Church Council to the Brandenburg Consistory, September 1939, Evangelisches Zentralarchiv Berlin 7/12233.

20. Letter from Reich Minister Kerrl, November 14, 1936, Evangelisches Zentralarchiv Berlin, Archives of the EKD-Kanzlei, Akte C 3/171, as quoted in Gerlach, *And the Witnesses Were Silent*, 116–17; Brandenburg Consistory to the Prussian Superior Church Council, February 10, 1937, Evangelisches Zentralarchiv Berlin 7/12233; Reich Church Committee to the Prussian Church Committee, December 4, 1936, Evangelisches Zentralarchiv Berlin 7/12127.

21. "Aufstellung über Massnahmen gegen BK-Brüder Kirchenkreis Nauen," September 11, 1939, Domstiftsarchiv Brandenburg NE 142/944; Pastor Posth of Berge to Pastor Harder of Fehrbellin, March 2, 1939, Domstiftsarchiv Brandenburg NE 143/948.

22. Pastor Posth of Berge to Mr. Hoppe, Financial Plenipotentiary for the Ribbeck parish, June 13, 1939, Domstiftsarchiv Brandenburg Ri 5/11; Wolfgang See and Rudolf Weckerling, *Frauen im Kirchenkampf: Beispiele aus der Bekennenden Kirche Berlin-Brandenburg* (Berlin: Wichern, 1984), 127.

23. Superintendent's Instructions 7 and 8, October 1, 1941, and November 11, 1941, Ephoralarchiv Pirna 81.

24. Saxon Church Office to Superintendent Max Zweynert, March 7, 1935; Zweynert to the Saxon Church Office, May 8, 1935, Ephoralarchiv Pirna 403; Zweynert to all clergy in the Pirna district, August 28, 1935; Superintendent's Instructions 15, June 8, 1939; Superintendent's Instructions 17, October 13, 1939, Ephoralarchiv Pirna 80.

25. Superintendent's Instructions 20, July 9, 1940, Ephoralarchiv Pirna 81.

26. Superintendent's Instructions 1, January 11, 1941, Ephoralarchiv Pirna 81.

27. Boris Böhm and Thomas Schilter, "Pirna-Sonnenstein: Von der Reformpsychiatrie zur Tötung psychisch Kranker," in *Nationalsozialistische Euthanasie-Verbrechen in Sachsen: Beiträge zu ihrer Aufarbeitung* (Dresden/Pirna: Kuratorium Gedenkstätte Sonnenstein e.V. und Sächsische Landeszentrale für politische Bildung, 1993), 12–16.

28. Ernst Klee, *Dokumente zur 'Euthanasie'* (Frankfurt: Taschenbuch, 1985), 232–33; Willy Forner, *Das Verbrechen von La Mornasse: Berichte über faschistische Gewalttaten* (n.p.: Militärverlag der Deutschen Demokratischen Republik, 1981), 45–50; F. K. Kaul, *Nazimordaktion T4: Ein Bericht über die erste industriemäßig durchgeführte Mordaktion des Naziregimes* (Berlin: VEB Verlag Volk und Gesundheit, 1973), passim; Böhm and Schilter, "Pirna-Sonnenstein," 28.

29. The normal death rate at the Waldheim institution was between three and seven deaths annually. Krumpolt, "Die Landesheilanstalt Großschweidnitz als 'T4'-Zwischenanstalt und Tötungsanstalt (1939-1945)," 98; Sonja Schröter, "Waldheim als 'Euthanasie'-Zwischenanstalt von Kranken-Sammel-Transporten an die Tötungsanstalt Sonnenstein im Rahmen der sog. 'Aktion T4' in den Jahren 1940 und 1941," in *Nationalsozialistische Euthanasie-Verbrechen in Sachsen: Beiträge zu ihrer Aufarbeitung* (Dresden/Pirna: Kuratorium Gedenkstätte Sonnenstein e.V. und Sächsische Landeszentrale für politische Bildung, 1993), 85.

30. Klee, *Dokumente zur 'Euthanasie,'* 66.

31. Böhm and Schilter, "Pirna-Sonnenstein," 35.

32. Dora Schumann, "Erinnerungen an die Tötungsanstalt Pirna-Sonnenstein," in *Nationalsozialistische Euthanasie-Verbrechen in Sachsen: Beiträge zu ihrer Aufarbeitung* (Dresden/Pirna: Kuratorium Gedenkstätte Sonnenstein e.V. und Sächsische Landeszentrale für politische Bildung, 1993), 54–55.

33. Lissa Flade, "Erinnerung an meine Mutter—ein Opfer der Tötungsanstalt Sonnenstein," in *Nationalsozialistische Euthanasie-Verbrechen in Sachsen: Beiträge zu ihrer Aufarbeitung* (Dresden/Pirna: Kuratorium Gedenkstätte Sonnenstein e.V. und Sächsische Landeszentrale für politische Bildung, 1993), 101–3.

34. Tilman Steinert, "Reactions in Psychiatric Institutions to the Murder of Their Patients in Grafeneck," in *Administered Killings at the Time of National Socialism: Involvement–Suppression–Responsibility of Psychiatry and Judicial System,* ed. Ulrich Jockusch and Lothar Scholz (Regensburg: Roderer, 1992), 105–9.

35. Hans Christoph von Hase, ed., *Evangelische Dokumente zur Ermordung der "unheilbar Kranken" unter der nationalsozialistischen Herrschaft in den Jahren 1939–1945* (Stuttgart: Evangelisches Verlagswerkes, 1964), 69–70; Gerhard Schäfer, ed., *Landesbischof D. Wurm und der nationalsozialistische Staat, 1940–1945: Eine Dokumentation* (Stuttgart: Calwer, 1968) 115, 140.

36. Hase, *Evangelische Dokumente,* 69–70, 91, 92; Schäfer, *Landesbischof D. Wurm,* 116.

37. Württemberg Superior Church Council to all district superintendents, July 27, 1940, Dekanatsarchiv Ravensburg 88b.

38. Gerlach, *And the Witnesses Were Silent,* 192–94, 281 n. 62.

39. Conference of Regional Councils of Brethren to the German Protestant Church Chancellery, February 5, 1942, in Joachim Beckmann, *Kirchliches Jahrbuch für die Evangelische Kirche in Deutschland 1933–1945* (Gütersloh: C. Bertelsmann, 1948), 484–85, as cited in Gerlach, *And the Witnesses Were Silent,* 196.

40. Günther Harder, "Rechenschaftsbericht," in *Bekenntnissynode der Mark Brandenburg vom 22. bis 24. Oktober 1945 in Berlin-Spandau Evangelisches Johannesstift* (Berlin: R. Schröter, n.d.), 22–23; Wilhelm Niesel, *Kirche unter dem Wort: Der Kampf der Bekennenden Kirche der altpreußischen Union 1933–1945* (Göttingen: Vandenhoeck & Ruprecht, 1978), 259, 275–77; Ernst Christian Helmreich, *The German Churches under Hitler: Background, Struggle, and Epilogue* (Detroit: Wayne State University Press, 1979), 336.

# Chapter 5: The Church Struggle in Nauen, Brandenburg

1. Superintendent Graßhoff in Nauen to the pastors of the Nauen district, March 23, 1935, Domstiftsarchiv Brandenburg NE 70/736.

2. The calculation of the terms of service of the interim superintendents is based on the flow of correspondence between the Superintendent's Office and the pastors in Domstiftsarchiv Brandenburg NE 70/736, NE 71/737 and NE 72/738, and between the Superintendent's Office and the Brandenburg Consistory from 1932 to 1946, in Domstiftsarchiv Brandenburg NE 122/742, NE 124/743, NE 125/744, NE 127/751, NE 128/752, NE 129/900, NE 130/840, NE 131/803, NE 132/759 and NE 133/830.

3. The church-political orientation of Nauen clergy was determined based on lists compiled by the Confessing Church (Domstiftsarchiv Brandenburg NE 142/94), supplemented by marginal notations from the list of delegates to the 1934 district synod (Domstiftsarchiv Brandenburg NE 48/658), correspondence between the pastors, superintendents, and the Brandenburg Consistory (Domstiftsarchiv Brandenburg NE 122/742), official private correspondence between pastors and superintendents (Domstiftsarchiv Brandenburg NE 140/814 and 141/835), correspondence concerning the monthly pastoral convents (Domstiftsarchiv Brandenburg NE 200/734 and NE 202/860), as well as material relating to pastoral appointments and the Church Struggle in Nauen (Domstiftsarchiv Brandenburg NE 703/770).

4. Günther Harder, "Rechenschaftsbericht," in *Bekenntnissynode der Mark Brandenburg vom 22. bis 24. Oktober 1945 in Berlin-Spandau Evangelisches Johannesstift* (Berlin: R. Schröter, n.d.), 22–23; Wilhelm Niesel, *Kirche unter dem Wort: Der Kampf der Bekennenden Kirche der altpreußischen Union 1933–1945* (Göttingen: Vandenhoeck & Ruprecht, 1978) , 118, 134, 224, 259–60, 275–77.

5. Wolfgang See and Rudolf Weckerling, *Frauen im Kirchenkampf: Beispiele aus der Bekennenden Kirche Berlin-Brandenburg* (Berlin: Wichern, 1984), 125.

6. List of Confessing Church clergy, Domstiftsarchiv Brandenburg NE 142/944; Pastor Bettac of Beetz to Interim Superintendent Simon of Oranienburg, March 4, 1941, Domstiftsarchiv Brandenburg NE 202/860.

7. Günther Harder, "Fehrbellin," in *Die Stunde der Versuchung: Gemeinden im Kirchenkampf 1933–1945; Selbstzeugnisse,* ed. Günther Harder and Wilhelm Niemöller (Munich: Christian Kaiser, 1963), 131, 143. A draft of the chapter is in Evangelisches Zentralarchiv Berlin 50/D1.

8. Harder, "Fehrbellin," 132–33.

9. Joachim Beckmann, ed., *Kirchliches Jahrbuch für die evangelische Kirche in Deutschland, 1933–1945* (Gütersloh: C. Bertelsmann, 1948), 84–86; Ernst Christian Helmreich, *The German Churches under Hitler: Background, Struggle, and Epilogue* (Detroit: Wayne State University Press, 1979), 178–79; Harder, "Fehrbellin," 139.

10. "Aufstellung über Massnahmen gegen BK-Brüder, Kirchenkreis Nauen," September 11, 1939, Domstiftsarchiv Brandenburg NE 142/944; Helmreich, *German Churches under Hitler,* 179.

11. Harder, "Fehrbellin," 143.

12. "Aufstellung über Massnahmen gegen BK-Brüder, Kirchenkreis Nauen," September 11, 1939, Domstiftsarchiv Brandenburg NE 142/944; Harder, "Fehrbellin," 143–44; See and Weckerling, *Frauen im Kirchenkampf,* 126; Shelley Baranowski, "Consent and Dissent: The Confessing Church and Conservative Opposition to National Socialism," *Journal of Modern History* 59 no. 1 (March 1987): 72; Interim Superintendent Bettac in Beetz to the Brandenburg Consistory, October 31, 1939, Domstiftsarchiv Brandenburg NE 127/751.

13. Harder, "Fehrbellin," 143; Niesel, *Kirche unter dem Wort*, 310–11.

14. "Aufstellung über Massnahmen gegen BK-Brüder, Kirchenkreis Nauen," September 11, 1939, Domstiftarchiv Brandenburg NE 142/944; "Landeskirchenausschuß warnt vor Verlesung der Kanzelabkündigung der Bekenntniskirche," n.d.; Interim Superintendent Schmidt in Flatow to the Brandenburg Consistory, August 25, 1936, Domstiftsarchiv Brandenburg NE 138/745.

15. "Entwurf eines Beschlusses über den Anschluß an die Bekennende Kirche (BK)," May 25, 1937, Domstiftsarchiv Brandenburg Ri 6/26.

16. Herbert Posth, "Betr. Abgabe der Pfarrstelle Ribbeck," October 20, 1938, Domstiftsarchiv Brandenburg Ri 6/26; Brandenburg Consistory to Posth of Berge, October 14, 1938, Domstiftsarchiv Brandenburg NE 69/741.

17. Herbert Posth, "Betr. Abgabe der Pfarrstelle Ribbeck," October 20, 1938, Domstiftsarchiv Brandenburg Ri 6/26; Philip Melanchthon, "The Confession of Faith: Which Was Submitted to His Imperial Majesty Charles V at the Diet of Augsburg in the Year 1530," trans. F. Bente and W. H. T. Dau, in *Triglot Concordia: The Symbolical Books of the Evangelical Lutheran Church* (St. Louis: Concordia, 1921), 37–95; Martin Luther, "Smalcald Articles," trans. F. Bente and W. H. T. Dau, in *Triglot Concordia,* 453–529.

18. Pastor Posth of Berge to Interim Superintendent Bettac in Beetz, October 11, 1938, Domstiftsarchiv Brandenburg NE 69/741.

19. Financial Plenipotentiary Hoppe to Ribbeck Parish Treasurer Behrendt, May 30, 1939, Domstiftsarchiv Brandenburg Ri 5/11.

20. Financial Plenipotentiary Hoppe in Ribbeck to Interim Superintendent Bettac in Beetz, May 28, 1939; Hoppe to Pastor Posth of Berge, June 19, June 20, and July 10, 1939; Hoppe in Ribbeck to Parish Treasurer Behrendt in Ribbeck, May 30, 1939; Finance Department of the Brandenburg Consistory to the Governing President in Potsdam, June 1, 1939, Domstiftsarchiv Brandenburg Ri 5/11.

21. Pastor Posth of Berge to Financial Plenipotentiary Hoppe, July 8, 1939, Domstiftsarchiv Brandenburg Ri 5/11.

22. Pastor Posth of Berge to Financial Plenipotentiary Hoppe, November 5, 1939, Domstiftsarchiv Brandenburg Ri 5/11.

23. Financial Plenipotentiary Hoppe to the Finance Department of the Brandenburg Consistory, April 22, 1940, Domstiftsarchiv Brandenburg Ri 5/11.

24. Brandenburg Confessing Church Council to Pastor Posth of Berge, August 7, 1940, Domstiftsarchiv Brandenburg Ri 7/35.

25. "Aufstellung über Massnahmen gegen BK-Brüder Kirchenkreis Nauen," September 11, 1939, Domstiftsarchiv Brandenburg NE 142/944; Interim Superintendent Bettac in Beetz to retired Superintendent Graßhoff in Ketchendorf, July 25, 1938; Bettac to Pastor Knuth of Berlin, July 18, 1938, Domstiftsarchiv Brandenburg NE 140/814.

26. Interim Superintendent Bettac in Beetz to Vicar Böck of Staffelde, December 7, 1938, Domstiftsarchiv Brandenburg NE 140/814.

27. Interim Superintendent Bettac in Beetz to Pastor Knuth in Berlin, July 18, 1938; Interim Superintendent Bettac in Beetz to Pastor Posth of Berge, December 6, 1938, Domstiftsarchiv Brandenburg NE 140/814.

28. Interim Superintendent Bettac in Beetz to the Brandenburg Consistory, January 12, 1939, and December 2, 1940, Domstiftsarchiv Brandenburg NE 128/752.

29. Pastor Gartenschläger of Potsdam to Interim Superintendent Bettac in Beetz, February 28, 1938, Domstiftsarchiv Brandenburg NE 59/646.

30. Pastor Isleib of Hakenberg to Interim Superintendent Bettac in Beetz, January 7, 1939, Domstiftsarchiv Brandenburg NE 140/814.

31. Interim Superintendent Bettac in Beetz to Pastor Isleib of Hakenberg, January 10, 1939, Domstiftsarchiv Brandenburg NE 140/814.

32. Interim Superintendent Bettac of Nauen to the Brandenburg Consistory, October 20, 1937, Domstiftsarchiv Brandenburg NE 140/814.

33. Pastor Siems of Nauen to Interim Superintendent Bettac, April 18, 1939, and June 12, 1939; Bettac to Siems, April 21, 1939, and May 11, 1939; Bettac to the Brandenburg Consistory, June 12, 1939 (two letters); Siems to the Brandenburg Consistory, June 18, 1939 (two letters), Evangelisches

Zentralarchiv Berlin 14/10884; Bettac to Mrs. Krüger of Nauen, April 28, 1939, Domstiftsarchiv Brandenburg NE 703/770.

34. Pastor Siems of Nauen to Interim Superintendent Bettac, January 2, 1940, Domstiftsarchiv Brandenburg NE 141/835.

35. Carl Quehl of Nauen to Pastor Siems of Nauen, January 27, 1940, Domstiftsarchiv Brandenburg NE 141/835.

36. Pastor Rehfeldt of Kremmen to Interim Superintendent Bettac in Beetz, July 25, 1940, Domstiftsarchiv Brandenburg NE 141/835; Brandenburg Consistory to the Prussian Superior Church Council, November 7, 1940, Evangelisches Zentralarchiv Berlin 7/12410.

37. Copy of "St. Halifax und die Pimpfe," *Das Schwarze Korps*, Folge 37, September 12, 1940, Evangelisches Zentralarchiv Berlin 7/12410.

38. Brandenburg Consistory to the Prussian Superior Church Council, November 7, 1940, Evangelisches Zentralarchiv Berlin 7/12410

39. Copy of the judgment against Rumpf, "IM NAMEN DES DEUTSCHEN VOLKES! . . . ," December 12, 1944; Brandenburg Consistory to the Prussian Superior Church Council, September 23, 1944, October 15, 1944, and December 12, 1944, Evangelisches Zentralarchiv Berlin 7/12837.

40. *"Entscheidung* in dem Verfahren betreffend die Beschwerde des . . . Otto Bellin. . . ," February 3, 1938, Evangelisches Zentralarchiv Berlin 14/10393.

41. Hilde Lehmann to the Finance Department of the Brandenburg Consistory, September 14, 1941; Interim Superintendent Simon of Oranienburg to the Brandenburg Consistory, September 16, 1941, Evangelisches Zentralarchiv Berlin 14/10393.

# Chapter 6: The Church Struggle in Pirna, Saxony

1. *Pirnaer Anzeiger*, "Ephoralkonferenz des Kirchenbezirks Pirna," May 1933, Ephoralarchiv Pirna 814.

2. Bund für Luthers Kirche in Sachsen und im Reich, Information Letter, April 22, 1933; "Gleichschaltung in der Kirche," *Freiheitskampf*, May 26, 1933, Ephoralarchiv Pirna 814; Joachim Fischer, *Die sächsische Landeskirche im Kirchenkampf 1933–1937*, Arbeiten zur Geschichte des Kirchenkampfes, Supplementary Series 8 (Göttingen: Vandenhoeck & Ruprecht, 1972), 13–18; Hermann Klemm, *Ich konnte nicht Zuschauer bleiben: Karl Fischers theologische Arbeit für die Bekennende Kirche Sachsens* (Berlin: Evangelische Verlagsanstalt, 1985), 14–17.

3. Pastor Martin Rasch of Reinhardtsdorf to Superintendent Zweynert, May 19, 1933, Ephoralarchiv Pirna 814.

4. Pastor Peter of Pirna to Superintendent Zweynert, June 30 and July 1, 1933, Ephoralarchiv Pirna 814; Klemm, *Ich konnte nicht Zuschauer bleiben*, 15.

5. Superintendent Zweynert to all clergy from the district of Pirna, June 7, 1933; Pastor Ranft of Helmsdorf to Zweynert, n.d.; Pastor Leonard of Stolpen to Zweynert, July 1, 1933, Ephoralarchiv Pirna 814.

6. Various articles from the *Dresdner Anzeiger* of July 1 and 2, 1933, along with other newspaper clippings, circular letters, and legal notices describing the new state of the Saxon Lutheran Church in Ephoralarchiv Pirna 814.

7. Fischer, *Die sächsische Landeskirche im Kirchenkampf*, 22–41; Klemm, *Ich konnte nicht Zuschauer bleiben*, 16-22; "Schreiben von 47 Leipziger Pfarrern der Mittelgruppe an Landesbischof Coch," November 17, 1934, in Fischer, *Die sächsische Landeskirche im Kirchenkampf*, 194–195.

8. Pastor Schumann of Hohnstein to Superintendent Zweynert, November 24, 1933; Pastor Carl of Cotta to Zweynert, November 24, 1933, Ephoralarchiv Pirna 814.

9. Superintendent Zweynert of Pirna to Pastors Schumann of Hohnstein and Carl of Cotta, November 27, 1933, Ephoralarchiv Pirna 814.

10. Saxon Bishop Coch, "Zur kirchlichen Lage," *Schulungsbriefe der volksmissionarischen Bewegung Deutsche Christen in Sachsen*, December 12, 1933, ed. M. Heinz Poppe, Ephoralarchiv Pirna 814.

11. "Die 28 Thesen der sächsischen Volkskirche zum inneren Aufbau der Deutschen Evangelischen Kirche," *Schulungsbriefe der volksmissionarischen Bewegung Deutsche Christen in Sachsen*, December 12, 1933, ed. M. Heinz Poppe, Ephoralarchiv Pirna 814.

12. Superintendent Zweynert to the Working Group of National Socialist Pastors, December 20, 1933; Zweynert to "Herr Oberstudiendirektor," January 16, 1934, Ephoralarchiv Pirna 814.

13. Superintendent Zweynert to Saxon Bishop Coch, December 29, 1933, Ephoralarchiv Pirna 814; Zweynert to Superintendent Spranger, August 28, 1934, Ephoralarchiv Pirna 815.

14. Pastor Meinel of Bad Schandau to Superintendent Zweynert, New Year 1934; Pastor Müller of Heidenau (Luther) to Zweynert, December 31, 1933, Ephoralarchiv Pirna 814.

15. Superintendent Zweynert to the pastors in the district, December 28, 1933, Ephoralarchiv Pirna 80; Pastor Meier of Sebnitz to Zweynert, December 31, 1933, Ephoralarchiv Pirna 814.

16. Pastor Meinel of Bad Schandau to Superintendent Zweynert, March 28, 1935, and March 20, 1934 [*sic*], Ephoralarchiv Pirna 290.

17. Declaration of 15 Superintendents to Saxon Bishop Coch, January 6, 1934; Superintendents Arnold, Böhme, et al., "Um unserer Landeskirche willen. . . ," January 9, 1934; Pastor Bruhns of Leipzig to Superintendent Zweynert, January 8, 1934, Ephoralarchiv Pirna 814.

18. Superintendent Zweynert to the pastors in the district, April 13, 1934, Ephoralarchiv Pirna 80; Pastor Schmeißer of Struppin to Zweynert, January 10, 1934; Pastor Schumann of Hohnstein to Zweynert, January 16, 1934, Ephoralarchiv Pirna 814; Zweynert to the Saxon Church Office, April 18, 1934, Ephoralarchiv Pirna 815; Pastor Meier of Sebnitz to Zweynert, February 20, 1934, Ephoralarchiv Pirna 815.

19. Amtshauptmannschaft Pirna to Pastor Carl of Cotta (copy to Superintendent Zweynert), January 24, 1934, Ephoralarchiv Pirna 814. On the back of his copy, Zweynert scratched the draft of a letter urging Carl to comply with the order.

20. Pastor Plotz of Pirna (Hospital) to the Saxon Church Office in Dresden, January 26, 1934, Ephoralarchiv Pirna 814.

21. Pastor Müller of Heidenau (Luther) to Superintendent Zweynert, April 16, 1934; Pastor Ploedterll of Königstein to Zweynert, April 17, 1934; Pastor Klemm of Burkhardswalde to Zweynert, April 14, 1934, Ephoralarchiv Pirna 815.

22. Pastors Otto Scriba of Wehlen Stadt, Schumann of Hohnstein et al. to Superintendent Zweynert, April 17, 1934, Ephoralarchiv Pirna 814; Klaus Scholder, *The Churches and the Third Reich*, vol. 2, *The Year of Disillusionment: 1934 Barmen and Rome*, trans. John Bowden (Philadelphia: Fortress Press, 1988), 20, 81–82.

23. Superintendent Zweynert to Pastors Martin Meinel of Bad Schandau, Martin Rasch of Reinhardtsdorf, and Gerhard Zweynert of Papstdorf, April 23, 1934, Ephoralarchiv Pirna 814.

24. Robert Ericksen, "The Barmen Synod and Its Declaration: A Historical Synopsis," in *The Church Confronts the Nazis: Barmen Then and Now*, ed. Hubert Locke, Toronto Studies in Theology 16 (Toronto: Edwin Mellen, 1984), 27–93, here 55.

25. Confessing Community of the Saxon Lutheran Church, "To the 16th Saxon Lutheran Synod," May 3, 1934, Ephoralarchiv Pirna 814; Superintendent Zweynert to the pastors in the district, April 26, 1934, Ephoralarchiv Pirna 80; Cathedral Preacher Arndt von Kirchbach, in the name of 110 Emergency League pastors, to Saxon Bishop Coch, May 17, 1934, Ephoralarchiv Pirna 814.

26. Pastor Martin Meinel of Bad Schandau, "Eine Bitte am Pfingstfest 1934 an alle ev.-luth. Geistlichen in Sachsen." Ephoralarchiv Pirna 814.

27. Pastor Meinel of Bad Schandau to Superintendent Zweynert, July 10, 1934; Pastor Rasch of Reinhardtsdorf to Zweynert, July 10, 1934; Pastor Rasch of Reinhardtsdorf to Superintendent Hugo Hahn of Dresden, July 10, 1934, Ephoralarchiv Pirna 815. The biblical text is my translation of Meinel's text.

28. Superintendent Zweynert to the Saxon Church Office, October 26, 1934; "Botschaft der Bekenntnissynode der Deutschen Evangelischen Kirche," Berlin-Dahlem, October 20, 1934, Ephoralarchiv Pirna 815.

29. Superintendent Zweynert to clergy in the district, November 5, 1934, Ephoralarchiv Pirna 80 and 815; Saxon Church Office to Zweynert, November 2, 1934, Ephoralarchiv Pirna 815.

30. Pastor Peter of Pirna to Superintendent Zweynert, November 6, 1934; Peter to the Saxon Pastors' Emergency League Council of Brethren, November 6, 1934, Ephoralarchiv Pirna 815; Peter to Pastor Klemm of Burkhardswalde, December 7, 1934, Ephoralarchiv Pirna 818.

31. Pastor Hellner of Dohna to Superintendent Zweynert, November 6, 1934; Pastor Ploedterll of Königstein to Zweynert, November 7, 1934; Pastor Herbert Dittmann of Ehrenberg to Zweynert, November 6, 1934, Ephoralarchiv Pirna 815.

32. Pastor Herz of Berggießhübel to Superintendent Zweynert, November 13, 1934, Ephoralarchiv Pirna 815.

33. Saxon Church Office to Saxon parish councilors, November 5, 1934; Saxon Church Office to all clergy, November 7, 1934; Pastor Rasch of Reinhardtsdorf to "Colleagues," November 19, 1934, Ephoralarchiv Pirna 815.

34. Response of the Dresden Clergy to the Message of Saxon Bishop Coch, November 19, 1934; Superintendent Zweynert to clergy in the district, November 20, 1934; Zweynert to Saxon Bishop Coch (open letter), November 26, 1934, Ephoralarchiv Pirna 815.

35. Pastor Partecke of Sebnitz to Superintendent Zweynert, December 20, 1934; Pastor Meinel of Bad Schandau to Zweynert, November 29, 1934, Ephoralarchiv Pirna 815.

36. Saxon Church Office to Superintendent Zweynert, December 10 and 31, 1934; Zweynert to the clergy in the district, December 17, 1934, Ephoralarchiv Pirna 815; Zweynert to the Saxon Church Office, April 15, 1935, and June 1935, Ephoralarchiv Pirna 818.

37. NSDAP District leadership in Pirna to the Saxon Church Office, December 19, 1933; Copy of a declaration of Pastor Schumann of Hohnstein, signed by Superintendent Zweynert and Schumann in Pirna, January 8, 1934, Ephoralarchiv Pirna 816.

38. Pastors' Emergency League, "Pulpit Declaration," January 1934, Ephoralarchiv Pirna 814; Saxon Church Office, "*Beschluß*" [against Pastor Walter Schumann], February 6, 1934, Ephoralarchiv Pirna 816.

39. Superintendent Zweynert of Pirna to Saxon Bishop Coch, February 6, 1934, Ephoralarchiv Pirna 814.

40. Consistorial Councilor Adolf Müller to Superintendent Zweynert of Pirna, February 9, 1934, Ephoralarchiv Pirna 814.

41. The Protestant Youth of the Parish Hohnstein-Rathewalde to the Saxon Bishop, February 8, 1934; Rathewalde parishioners to the Saxon Church Office, February 9, 1934; Parish Councilor von Zeschnig to the Saxon Bishop, February 11, 1934, Ephoralarchiv Pirna 816.

42. Pastor Dittmann of Ehrenberg to Superintendent Zweynert, March 23, 1934, March 27, 1934, and April 29, 1934, Ephoralarchiv Pirna 816.

43. Saxon Church Office to Superintendent Zweynert, April 9, 1934, Ephoralarchiv Pirna 816.

44. Saxon Church Office to Superintendent Zweynert, March 10, 1934; Amtshauptmannschaft Pirna to Zweynert and Pastor Schumann, June 25, 1934; Saxon Bishop Coch to Schumann, April 21, 1934; Coch to the Marienberg Superintendent, April 28, 1934; and Saxon Church Office to Zweynert, May 26, 1934; Schumann to the Saxon Church Office, May 5, 1934; Saxon Church Office to Schumann, June 7, 1934, Ephoralarchiv Pirna 816.

45. Superintendent Zweynert to the Saxon Church Office, July 31, 1934; Pastor Schumann to Zweynert, August 10, 1934, Ephoralarchiv Pirna 816.

46. Pastor Schumann, "Why Can I Not Abandon My Parish Hohnstein?" Summer 1934, Ephoralarchiv Pirna 816.

47. Saxon Bishop Coch to Pastor Schumann, September 7, 1934; Coch to Superintendent Zweynert, September 8, 1934; Schumann to Zweynert, March 2, 1935, Ephoralarchiv Pirna 816.

48. Saxon Church Office to Superintendent Zweynert, January 31, 1935, and August 4, 1935, Ephoralarchiv Pirna 816.

49. Saxon Church Committee to Pastor Schumann of Hohnstein, December 16 and 17, 1935, Ephoralarchiv Pirna 816.

50. Mayor of Hohnstein to Superintendent Zweynert, February 16, 1935; Pastor Schumann of Hohnstein to the Saxon Ministry of the Interior, June 24, 1935; Saxon Church Office to Zweynert, August 24, 1935, Ephoralarchiv Pirna 816.

51. Pastor Schumann of Hohnstein to Superintendent Zweynert, March 2, 1935, Ephoralarchiv Pirna 816.

52. Pastor Rosenthal of Lohmen to Superintendent Zweynert, May 29, 1936, Ephoralarchiv Pirna 816.

53. Superintendent's Instructions 101a, June 4, 1936, Ephoralarchiv Pirna 80; Superintendent Zweynert to Pastor Rosenthal of Lohmen, June 22, 1936, Ephoralarchiv Pirna 816; Superintendent's Instructions 106a, October 13, 1936, Ephoralarchiv Pirna 80.

54. Walter Eichenberg to Superintendent Zweynert, November 26, 1933, Ephoralarchiv Pirna 816. The quotations are references to Matthew 5:44; 22:21; and Romans 13:1.

55. Patroness Dora von Eschwege to Superintendent Zweynert, December 27, 1933, Ephoralarchiv Pirna 816.

56. Patroness Dora von Eschwege to Superintendent Zweynert, January 7, 1934; Zweynert to von Eschwege, January 9, 1934, Ephoralarchiv Pirna 816.

57. Patroness Dora von Eschwege to Superintendent Zweynert, February 11, 1934, Ephoralarchiv Pirna 816.

58. Patroness Dora von Eschwege to Superintendent Zweynert, February 21, 1934; Pastor Carl of Cotta to Zweynert, February 23, 1934; Zweynert to von Eschwege, March 6, 1934; von Eschwege to Zweynert, March 8, 1934, Ephoralarchiv Pirna 816.

59. Amtshauptmannschaft Pirna to Pastor Carl of Cotta, May 29, 1934; Saxon Bishop Coch to Superintendent Zweynert, August 20, 1934; Saxon Church Office to Zweynert, August 23, 1934, Ephoralarchiv Pirna 816.

60. Superintendent Zweynert to the Saxon Church Office, August 24, 1935, Ephoralarchiv Pirna 816.

61. Superintendent Zweynert to the Saxon Church Office, February 8, 1935; Saxon Church Office to Zweynert, February 12, 1935, Ephoralarchiv Pirna 816.

62. Pastor Carl of Cotta to Martin Mühlbach et al., May 20, 1935; Consistorial Councilor Adolf Müller, "Besprechung mit Vorsitzenden des Kirchenvorstands zu Cotta, Herrn Mühlbach," May 22, 1935, Ephoralarchiv Pirna 816.

63. Saxon Church Office to Superintendent Zweynert, January 31, 1935, July 23, 1935, and August 4, 1935; Saxon Church Committee to Zweynert, December 17, 1935; Saxon Church Office to Pastor Carl of Cotta, December 16, 1935; Zweynert to the Saxon Church Office, September 3, 1935, Ephoralarchiv Pirna 816.

64. Superintendent Zweynert to the Saxon Church Office, June 5, 1935; Martin Mühlbach to Zweynert, June 16, 1935; Saxon Church Office to Zweynert, June 24, 1935; Zweynert to the Saxon Church Office, September 3, 1935, Ephoralarchiv Pirna 816.

65. Saxon Church Office to Superintendent Zweynert, December 11, 12, and 17, 1935; Saxon Church Office to Pastor Carl of Cotta, December 16, 1935, Ephoralarchiv Pirna 816.

66. Copy of Pastor Carl of Cotta to Mrs. Mühlbach, January 6, 1936; Copy of Carl to Martin Mühlbach, January 7, 1936, Ephoralarchiv Pirna 816.

67. Patroness Dora von Eschwege to Superintendent Zweynert, January 9, 1936, Ephoralarchiv Pirna 816.

68. Superintendent Zweynert to the Saxon Church Committee, January 13, 1936, Ephoralarchiv Pirna 816.

69. Superintendent Zweynert to the Saxon Church Committee, February 6, 1936; Pastor Carl to Zweynert, April 1, 1936; Saxon Church Committee to Zweynert, May 18, 1936; Zweynert to Carl, April 15, 1936; Carl to Zweynert, April 21 and May 18, 1936; Saxon Church Committee to Zweynert, April 15, 1936; "Vorgelesen, genehmigt und unterschrieben: Saxon Church Office Councilor Dr. Ziemann und Pfarrer Carl . . . ," March 6, 1936; Saxon Church Committee to the Amtshauptmann zu Pirna, April 14, 1936, Ephoralarchiv Pirna 816; Superintendent's Instructions 8, November 10, 1941, Ephoralarchiv Pirna 81.

70. Superintendent Zweynert to the Saxon Church Office, April 18, 1934; Zweynert to all clergy in the Pirna district, November 5, 1934; Pastor Meier of Sebnitz to Zweynert, January 23, 1935, Ephoralarchiv Pirna 815.

71. Saxon Church Office to Superintendent Zweynert, January 31, 1935; Amtshauptmannschaft Pirna to Zweynert, April 19, 1935; Zweynert to the Saxon Church Office, April 23, 1935; Zweynert to Pastor Voigtländer of Maxen, April 20, 1935; Voigtländer to Zweynert, May 6, 1935; Zweynert to the Saxon Church Office, April 26, 1935; Zweynert to Pastor Werner of Dohna, May 8, 1935, Ephoralarchiv Pirna 816.

72. Superintendent Zweynert to the Saxon Church Office, May 8, 1935, Ephoralarchiv Pirna 816.

73. Pastor Werner of Dohna to Superintendent Zweynert, May 11, 1935, Ephoralarchiv Pirna 816.

74. Pastor Werner of Dohna to Superintendent Zweynert, May 15, 1935, Ephoralarchiv Pirna 816.

75. Superintendent Zweynert to Pastor Klemm, June 5, 1935, Ephoralarchiv Pirna 816.

76. Saxon Confessing Church council to Superintendent Zweynert, June 7, 1935, Ephoralarchiv Pirna 816.

77. Pastor Teichgräber of Pirna to Superintendent Zweynert, June 9, 1935, Ephoralarchiv Pirna 816.

78. Pastor Teichgräber of Pirna to Superintendent Zweynert, June 9, 1935; Zweynert to the Saxon Church Office, June 11, 1935, Ephoralarchiv Pirna 816.

79. Pastor Werner of Dohna to Superintendent Zweynert, June 12, 1935, Ephoralarchiv Pirna 816.

80. Pastor Werner of Dohna to Superintendent Zweynert, June 18, 1935; Pastor Werner to Confirmation Parents, June 14, 1935; Pastor Lieschke to Confirmation Parents, June 17, 1935, Ephoralarchiv Pirna 816.

81. Pastor Börner of Ottendorf to Pastor Werner of Dohna, June 17, 1935, Ephoralarchiv Pirna 816.

82. Pastor Werner to Superintendent Zweynert, June 23, 1935; Werner to the Amtshauptmannschaft Pirna, June 23, 1935, Ephoralarchiv Pirna 816.

83. Pastor Werner of Dohna to Superintendent Zweynert, July 1, 1935, Ephoralarchiv Pirna 816.

84. Pastor Werner of Dohna to Pastor Klemm of Burkhardswalde, July 5, 1935; Werner to Superintendent Zweynert, July 5, 1935, Ephoralarchiv Pirna 816.

85. Mayor Schmidt of Weesenstein to Superintendent Zweynert, July 10, 1935, Ephoralarchiv Pirna 816.

86. Saxon Church Office, "Beschluß" [against Pastor Klemm], July 30, 1935; Saxon Church Office to Superintendent Zweynert July 30, 1935; Zweynert to Pastor Werner of Dohna, August 30, 1935; Zweynert to the Saxon Church Office, September 3, 1935; Mayor Schmidt of Weesenstein to Zweynert, September 11, 1935; Weesenstein Parish Council to the Saxon Church Office, August 31, 1935, Ephoralarchiv Pirna 816.

87. Saxon Bishop Coch to Pastor Klemm of Burkhardswalde, October 23, 1935; Superintendent Zweynert to Cantor Aehnelt, November 7, 1935; Saxon Church Committee to Klemm, December 16, 1935 (twice), Ephoralarchiv Pirna 816.

88. Bezirksschulrat zu Pirna (personally) to Superintendent Zweynert, November 18, 1935, Ephoralarchiv Pirna 816. The reference to time in jail was the district school councilor's way of describing Klemm's Gestapo detention.

89. Saxon Church Committee to Superintendent Zweynert, January 18, 1936; Zweynert, handwritten notes from Pastor Klemm's hearing with the Saxon Church Committee, n.d., Ephoralarchiv Pirna 816.

90. Saxon Church Committee to Superintendent Zweynert, April 23 and 24, 1936; Burkhardswalde NSDAP leader Heine to Zweynert, April 25, 1936; Zweynert to Heine, April 29, 1936, Ephoralarchiv Pirna 816.

91. Superintendent Zweynert to the Saxon Church Office, September 3, 1935; Mayor Erich Schmidt of Weesenstein to Zweynert, September 11, 1935, Ephoralarchiv Pirna 816.

92. Correspondence concerning the actions of Pastors Hagar, Meier, Scriba, Sherffig, Herz, von Schmidt, Müller, Vorwerk, Hellner, and Friedrich from 1934 to 1936 in Ephoralarchiv Pirna 816, 1–59, 139–58, and 344–454.

93. Pastor Meinel of Bad Schandau to Zweynert, February 6, 1937; Zweynert to the Saxon Church Committee, June 24, 1936; Reich governor for Saxony to the Saxon government . . . , January 26, 1937; Meinel, "Bericht über das Eindringen der Nationalkirchlichen Bewegung Deutsche Christen in Bad Schandau," February 6, 1937, Ephoralarchiv Pirna 818.

94. Saxon Church Office to Pastors von Schmidt, Friedrich, and Grießdorf, July 27, 1938; Saxon Church Office to Pastors von Schmidt and Klemm, May 10, 1938, Ephoralarchiv Pirna 817.

95. Pastor Bahrmann of Sebnitz to Superintendent Leichte, October 17, 1938; "Erklärung!" n.d.; Herr Heinecke to the Dohna and Heidenau parish councils, November 14, 1938, Ephoralarchiv Pirna 819.

96. Pastor Vorwerk of Liebstadt to the Reich Church Minister, July 30, 1938; Superintendent Leichte to the Saxon Church Office, September 30, 1938, Ephoralarchiv Pirna 819.

97. Superintendent's Instructions 23, November 2, 1940, Ephoralarchiv Pirna 81.

98. Pastor Dr. Brunner of Heidenau (Christus) to Superintendent Leichte, February 26, 1941, Ephoralarchiv Pirna 915.

99. Vicar Philipp of Neustadt to Superintendent Leichte, February 20, 1941; Pastor Werner of Dohna to Leichte, February 13, 1941, Ephoralarchiv Pirna 915.

100. Superintendent's Instructions 18, December 30, 1939, Ephoralarchiv Pirna 80; Superintendent's Instructions 25, December 28, 1940, Ephoralarchiv Pirna 81.

101. Leichte made his announcement one and a half years after Goebbels had announced the implementation of "total war" on February 18, 1943, but Leichte was surely responding to new measures from August 11, 1944, which included the imposition of a total ban on vacations, the closure of theaters, coffee shops, and schools, the mobilization of children for farm labor and anti-aircraft support and the establishment of the *Volkssturm*, a defense force consisting of underage boys and overage men. Jeremy Noakes, *Nazism 1919–1945*, vol. 4, *The German Home Front in World War II: A Documentary Reader* (Exeter: University of Exeter Press, 1998), 247–49, 487–94.

102. Superintendent's Instructions 4/44, September 30, 1944, and 1/1945, January 6, 1945, Ephoralarchiv Pirna 81.

103. Superintendent's Instructions 2/1945, February 28, 1945, Ephoralarchiv Pirna 81.

104. Superintendent's Instructions 6/1945, July 12, 1945, Ephoralarchiv Pirna 81.

105. "An die Führer der kirchlichen Männerkreise im Kreis Pirna!" July 9, 1945, Ephoralarchiv Pirna 120; Interim Superintendent Meinel to a colleague, August 23, 1945, Ephoralarchiv Pirna 292.

106. Superintendent's Instructions 19/1945, November 23, 1945, Ephoralarchiv Pirna 81; Klemm to the Saxon Church Office, July 12, 1945, Ephoralarchiv Pirna 180.

107. Superintendent's Instructions 1, March 4, 1942, Ephoralarchiv Pirna 81.

# Chapter 7: The Church Struggle in Ravensburg, Württemberg

1. Karl Steger, *Die politicke Gedanken Moritz Mohls*, Dissertation, Tübingen 1923, cited in Michael Jag, *Karl Steger: Ein Pfarrer in Friedrichshafen als Deutscher Christ*, Prüfungsarbeit zur II. theologischen Dienstprüfung (1988/1989), June 1988, 1, Stadtarchiv Friedrichshafen.

2. David J. Diephouse, *Pastors and Pluralism in Württemberg, 1918–1933* (Princeton: Princeton University Press, 1987), 280.

3. *Aktennotiz*, 10, Dekanatsarchiv Ravensburg Neue Akten/Friedrichshafen, Steger; Jag, *Karl Steger*, 2, Stadtarchiv Friedrichshafen; *Bericht über unsere Reise am Ostersamstag bis einschl. Ostermontag 1929 nach Massenbach O/A. Brackenheim zu Herrn Pfarrer Dr. Steger, Massenbach, Herrn Dekan Metzger in Brackenheim, Herrn Prälat Wurm in Heilbronn und Herrn Stadtpfarrer Eifert in Heilbronn*, April 5, 1929, Dekanatsarchiv Ravensburg 53b.

4. *Bericht über unsere Reise am Ostersamstag*; Letter of Prälat Wurm, April 1, 1929, Dekanatsarchiv Ravensburg 53b; Kurt Meier, *Die Deutschen Christen: Das Bild einer Bewegung im Kirchenkampf des Dritten Reiches* (Göttingen: Vandenhoeck & Ruprecht, 1964), 328; Gerhard Schäfer, ed., *Die evangelische Landeskirche in Württemberg: Eine Dokumentation zum Kirchenkampf*, vol. 2, *Um eine deutsche Reichskirche* (Stuttgart: Calwer, 1972), 304–6, 376–77, 454, 527, 572; *Zusammenstellung der Wahlbewerber für die Wahl zum Landeskirchentag am 23. Juli 1933, vorgeschlagen von der Glaubensbewegung Deutsche Christen, Gruppe I und Gruppe II*, July 18, 1933, Dekanatsarchiv Ravensburg 84a.

5. Gerhard Schäfer, ed., *Die evangelische Landeskirche in Württemberg*, vol. 3, *Der Einbruch des Reichsbischofs in die Württembergische Landeskirche 1934* (Stuttgart: Calwer, 1974), 442; Württemberg Superior Church Council to the District Superintendent's Office, Ravensburg, March 3, 1934, Dekanatsarchiv Ravensburg 53b.

6. Schäfer, ed., *Die evangelische Landeskirche in Württemberg*, 2:591–99; *Aktennotiz*, 1, Dekanatsarchiv Ravensburg Neue Akten/Friedrichshafen, Steger.

7. [Reinhold Krause], *Rede des Gauobmannes der Glaubensbewegung "Deutsche Christen" i. Groß-Berlin Dr Krause gehalten im Sportpalast am 13. November 1933*, 6–8; Schäfer, ed., *Die evangelische Landeskirche in Württemberg*, 2:828–50; Arthur C. Cochrane, *The Church's Confession under Hitler* (Philadelphia: Westminster, 1962), 111–13; Klaus Scholder, *The Churches and the Third Reich*, vol. 1, *Preliminary History and the Time of Illusions 1918–1934*, trans. John Bowden (Philadelphia: Fortress Press, 1988), 551–53.

8. Pastor Lachemann in Stuttgart to Pastor Martin Niemöller of Berlin, Schäfer, ed., *Die evangelische Landeskirche in Württemberg*, 2:995–96.

9. Schäfer, ed., *Die evangelische Landeskirche in Württemberg*, 2:1065–67, and 3:15, 37–42; see also Rainer Lächele, *Ein Volk, ein Reich, ein Glaube: Die "Deutsche Christen" in Württemberg 1925–1960*, Quellen und Forschungen zur württembergischen Kirchengeschichte 12 (Stuttgart: Calwer, 1994), 58.

10. Schäfer, ed., *Die evangelische Landeskirche in Württemberg*, 3:112–15; Jag, *Karl Steger*, 6–7, Stadtarchiv Friedrichshafen; Lächele, *Ein Reich, ein Volk, ein Glaube*, 33–35.

11. Schäfer, ed., *Die evangelische Landeskirche in Württemberg*, 3:117–21, 127–28, 145–57; *Aktennotiz*, 1–2, Dekanatsarchiv Ravensburg Neue Akten/Friedrichshafen, Steger.

12. *Auszug aus der Chronik der Kirchenwirren von Dr. Joachim Gauger (Gotthard-Briefe)*, 1, and *Aktennotiz*, 2, Dekanatsarchiv Ravensburg Neue Akten/Friedrichshafen, Steger; OKR A. 7983 (letter), September 7, 1934, Dekanatsarchiv Ravensburg 84c; Schäfer, ed., *Die evangelische Landeskirche in Württemberg*, 3:176–77, 199–200, 203–8, and 216–21; Württemberg Superior Church Council A. 3651, April 23, 1934, Dekanatsarchiv Ravensburg 84a.

13. Copy of *Gesetzblatt der Deutschen Evangelischen Kirche*, Teil II, Nr. 56, September 17, 1934, 167, in Dekanatsarchiv Ravensburg 84c; Schäfer, ed., *Die evangelische Landeskirche in Württemberg*, 3:232, 257, 272f., 285–86 n. 23, 309–10 n. 67, 406 n. 187, 454, 493, 494.

14. Pf. Reg. III C 27, September 15, 1934, and Württemberg Superior Church Council A. 8818, October 5, 1934, Dekanatsarchiv Ravensburg 84c. *Aktennotiz*, 2-3, and *Auszug aus der Chronik der Kirchenwirren von Dr. Joachim Gauger (Gotthard-Briefe)*, 1-3, Dekanatsarchiv Ravensburg Neue Akten/Friedrichshafen, Steger; Schäfer, ed., *Die evangelische Landeskirche in Württemberg*, 3:597 n. 102, 4:125, 130.

15. Schäfer, ed., *Die evangelische Landeskirche in Württemberg*, 3:524–672; Lächele, *Ein Volk, ein Reich, ein Glaube*, 62–64; *Aktennotiz*, 3–4, and *Auszug aus der Chronik der Kirchenwirren von Dr. Joachim Gauger (Gotthard-Briefe)*, 4, Dekanatsarchiv Ravensburg Neue Akten/Friedrichshafen, Steger.

16. Superintendent Ströle in Ravensburg and Pastor Schmidt in Weingarten to Pastor Krauss of Ebingen, September 20, 1934; "Auf dem Erlaß des kommissar. Oberkirchenrats vom 24.9 . . ."; "Zur Verwendung im Gottesdienst am 16.9.," Dekanatsarchiv Ravensburg 84c.

17. Jag, *Karl Steger*, 13–14, Stadtarchiv Friedrichshafen.

18. Gerhard Schäfer, ed., *Die evangelische Landeskirche in Württemberg und der Nationalsozialismus: Eine Dokumentation zum Kirchenkampf*, vol. 4, *Die Intakte Landeskirche 1935–1936* (Stuttgart: Calwer, 1977), 119–20.

19. Pastor Karl Steger in Friedrichshafen to Dekan Schnaufer, November 4, 1946, Dekanatsarchiv Ravensburg Neue Akten/Friedrichshafen, Steger; Schmid to the Württemberg Superior Church Council, January 10, 1944, Dekanatsarchiv Ravensburg 53b.

20. *Evangelisches Gemeindeblatt Friedrichshafen*, July 1935, Protestant Men's Association of Friedrichshafen circular letter, October 1935, and Annual Report of the Friedrichshafen Protestant Men's Association, 1935 and 1938, Dekanatsarchiv Ravensburg 54d; *Evangelische Kirchengemeinde Friedrichshafen*, 1957, 17–18, Dekanatsarchiv Ravensburg Neue Akten/Friedrichshafen AII2.

21. *Evangelisches Gemeindeblatt Friedrichshafen*, July 1935, Dekanatsarchiv Ravensburg 54d.

22. Württemberg Superior Church Council A.13415 to the Württemberg Land Church Court of Complaint, October 31, 1947, 11, Dekanatsarchiv Ravensburg Neue Akten/Friedrichshafen, Steger.

23. Württemberg Superior Church Council A.13415 to the Württemberg Land Church Court of Complaint, October 31, 1947, 14, *Aktennotiz*, 7, Dekanatsarchiv Ravensburg Neue Akten/Friedrichshafen, Steger.

24. *Aktennotiz*, 5, 9, Dekanatsarchiv Ravensburg Neue Akten/Friedrichshafen, Steger.

25. Württemberg Superior Church Council A.6046 to the District Superintendent's Office, Ravensburg, June 18, 1935, Dekanatsarchiv Ravensburg 53b; *Aktennotiz*, 4, Dekanatsarchiv Ravensburg Neue Akten/Friedrichshafen, Steger.

26. Württemberg Superior Church Council A.6046 to the District Superintendent's Office, Ravensburg, June 18, 1935, Württemberg Superior Church Council A.7385 to the District Superintendent's Office, Ravensburg, July 23, 1935, Dekanatsarchiv Ravensburg 53b.

27. Württemberg Superior Church Council A.8473 and A.11644 to the District Superintendent's Office, Ravensburg, August 23 and November 22, 1935, Dekanatsarchiv Ravensburg 53b; *Aktennotiz*, 4, Dekanatsarchiv Ravensburg Neue Akten/Friedrichshafen, Steger.

28. Helmut Witetschek, *Die kirchliche Lage in Bayern nach den Regierungspräsidentenberichten 1933–1943*, vol. 1, *Regierungsbezirk Oberbayern* (Mainz: Matthias Grünewald, 1966), 114–15.

29. *Evangelisches Gemeindeblatt Friedrichshafen*, April, June, and November 1933, Stadtarchiv Friedrichshafen.

30. *Evangelisches Gemeindeblatt Friedrichshafen*, July 1934, February 1935, and April 1935, Stadtarchiv Friedrichshafen; Jag, *Karl Steger*, 36, Stadtarchiv Friedrichshafen; Württemberg Superior Church Council A.13415 to the Württemberg Land Church Court of Complaint, October 31, 1947, 12–13; *Aktennotiz*, 10, Dekanatsarchiv Ravensburg Neue Akten/Friedrichshafen, Steger.

31. Württemberg Superior Church Council to the Ravensburg Superintendent, November 17, 1934, June 3, 1937, and March 22, 1943; Pastor Schmid of Friedrichshafen to the Württemberg Superior Church Council, January 10, 1944; Württemberg Superior Church Council to the Ravensburg Superintendent, April 14, 1944, Dekanatsarchiv Ravensburg 53b.

32. Pastor Schmid of Friedrichshafen to the Ravensburg Superintendent, May 15, 1942, Dekanatsarchiv Ravensburg 53a.

33. Pastor Eugen Schmid in Friedrichshafen to Württemberg Superior Church Council, January 10, 1944, Dekanatsarchiv Ravensburg 53b.

34. Württemberg Superior Church Council O. 12061 to the District Superintendent's Office, Ravensburg, November 30, 1933; Superintendent Ströle in Ravensburg to the Württemberg Superior Church Council and Regional Superintendent's Office, Ulm, December 12, 1933, Dekanatsarchiv Ravensburg 53c.

35. Superior Church Councilor Walzer to Pastor Karl Steger in Friedrichshafen, September 10, 1934; Steger to the District Superintendent's Office, Ravensburg, September 11, 1934; Württemberg Superior Church Council A. 9462 to the District Superintendent's Office, Ravensburg, October 29, 1934, Dekanatsarchiv Ravensburg 84c.

36. Württemberg Superior Church Council A.8866 to the District Superintendent's Office, Ravensburg, August 19, 1936, Dekanatsarchiv Ravensburg 53b.

37. Pastor Steger in Friedrichshafen to the Württemberg Superior Church Council, August 21, 1936, Dekanatsarchiv Ravensburg 53b.

38. Curate Hauff to an unidentified Superior Church Councilor, on behalf of Curates Fleck and Fritz, May 16, 1938, Dekanatsarchiv Ravensburg 53b.

39. Württemberg Superior Church Council A.13415 to the Württemberg Land Church Court of Complaint, October 31, 1947, 13, Dekanatsarchiv Ravensburg Neue Akten/Friedrichshafen, Steger.

40. "Die Unterzeichneten bitten den Herrn Landesbischof . . . ," February 1945, Dekanatsarchiv Ravensburg Neue Akten/Friedrichshafen, Steger.

41. First Pastor's Office in Friedrichshafen to the Württemberg Superior Church Council, December 4, 1945. Dekanatsarchiv Ravensburg Neue Akten/Friedrichshafen, Steger.

42. Friedrichshafen Parish Council to the Württemberg Superior Church Council, December 27, 1946, Dekanatsarchiv Ravensburg Neue Akten/Friedrichshafen, Steger; Schäfer, ed., *Die evangelische Landeskirche in Württemberg*, 4:143, 147–48, 160–61, 165, 366, 459.

43. Friedrichshafen Parish Council to the Württemberg Superior Church Council, December 27, 1946, Dekanatsarchiv Ravensburg Neue Akten/Friedrichshafen, Steger.

44. Various correspondence, including Württemberg Superior Church Council A.1570, A.2161, and A.12078 to the District Superintendent's Office, Ravensburg, February 4, February 18, and October 2, 1947, Dekanatsarchiv Ravensburg Neue Akten/Friedrichshafen, Steger.

45. Willi Eberle, *400 Jahre Evangelische Gemeinde in Leutkirch (1546–1946)*, Sondernummer Trinitatis 1946, *Evangelisches Gemeindeblatt für Leutkirch und seine Diaspora*, 30, Dekanatsarchiv Ravensburg Neue Akten/Leutkirch A II 1.

46. German Christian Group in Leutkirch to the pastor in Leutkirch, February 18, 1935, Dekanatsarchiv Ravensburg 64e; Pastor Griesinger of Ulm to Pastor Siegle of Isny, May 15, 1935, Dekanatsarchiv Ravensburg 61a; German Christian postcard notice, October 1935; Wolfgang Cramer to the Ravensburg Superintendent, October 14, 1935; Reich Movement of the German Christians in Leutkirch to the Württemberg Superior Church Council, June 4, 1936; Invitation from the Leutkirch National Church German Christian Group, March 1937; Württemberg Superior Church Council to the Reich and Prussian Minister for Church Affairs, February 22, 1936, and Württemberg Protestant Church Disciplinary Court, "Decision of 9 December 1936 . . . ," Dekanatsarchiv Ravensburg 64e; Manfred Müller, *Jugend in Zerreißprobe: Persönliche Erinnerungen und Dokumente eines Jugendpfarrers im Dritten Reich* (Stuttgart: Quell, 1982), 19–21.

47. Mrs. Welte to Superintendent Ströle of Ravensburg, July 4, 1935; Superintendent Ströle of Ravensburg to the Württemberg Superior Church Council, March 10 and April 12, 1936; Württemberg Superior Church Council to the Ravensburg Superintendent, November 12, 1935; Superintendent Ströle of Ravensburg to the Württemberg Superior Church Council, March 10, 1936, Dekanatsarchiv Ravensburg 63a.

48. Regional Superintendent Mayer-List to Pastor Metzger of Leutkirch, September 3, 1936; Württemberg Superior Church Council to the Ravensburg Superintendent, October 19, 1936; Württemberg Superior Church Council to the Ravensburg Superintendent, July 5, 1937; Superior Church Councilor Eichler to Superintendent Ströle of Ravensburg, January 19, 1938, Dekanatsarchiv Ravensburg 63a.

49. Willi Eberle, *400 Jahre Evangelische Gemeinde in Leutkirch (1546–1946)*, Sondernummer Trinitatis 1946, *Evangelisches Gemeindeblatt für Leutkirch und seine Diaspora*, 30, Dekanatsarchiv Ravensburg Neue Akten/Leutkirch A II 1; various correspondence between Leutkirch German Christians, the Superior Church Council, Superintendent Ströle and Pastors Metzger and Schieber of Leutkirch, December 24, 1935, to March 2, 1939, Dekanatsarchiv Ravensburg 64e.

50. Pastor Schieber of Leutkirch to the Württemberg Superior Church Council, March 2, 1939; Schieber to the leader of the German Christian Group in Leutkirch, March 9, 1939, Dekanatsarchiv Ravensburg 64e.

51. Georg Sailor to the Leutkirch Pastor, March 25, 1937, Dekanatsarchiv Ravensburg 64e; E. Frauer and Georg Hayn to the Leutkirch Pastor, September 25 and 27, 1936; Württemberg Superior Church Council to the Ravensburg Superintendent, September 23, 1936, Dekanatsarchiv Ravensburg 64f; Württemberg Superior Church Council to the Ravensburg Superintendent, May 14, 1937, Dekanatsarchiv Ravensburg 64e; Leutkirch Protestant Parish, "Excerpt from the Book of Minutes of the Parish Council, Volume 7, Page 224 . . . ," May 18, 1937, Dekanatsarchiv Ravensburg 63a; Württemberg Superior Church Council to the Ravensburg Superintendent, September 12, 1935, September 6, 1938, May 3, 1939, and June 14, 1941, Dekanatsarchiv Ravensburg 65b; Willi Eberle, *400 Jahre Evangelische Gemeinde in Leutkirch (1546–1946)*, Sondernummer Trinitatis 1946, *Evangelisches Gemeindeblatt für Leutkirch und seine Diaspora*, 30, Dekanatsarchiv Ravensburg Neue Akten/Leutkirch A II 1.

52. Pastor Siegle of Isny to Superintendent Ströle of Ravensburg, April 26, 1934, Dekanatsarchiv Ravensburg 57b.

53. Pastor Siegle of Isny to Superintendent Ströle of Ravensburg, May 20, 1935, Dekanatsarchiv Ravensburg 61a.

54. Württemberg Superior Church Council to Curate Dipper of Isny, September 29, 1934; Curate Dipper of Isny to Director Diest of the Überruh convalescent home, October 8, 1934; Curate Dipper of Isny to Superintendent Ströle of Ravensburg, October 8, 1934, Dekanatsarchiv Ravensburg 57c.

55. Württemberg Superior Church Council to Pastor Wertz of Isny, June 11, 1935; Pastor Siegle of Isny to Superintendent Ströle of Ravensburg, May 20, 1935; Siegle to Pastor Griesinger of Ulm, May 14, 1935; Griesinger to Siegle, May 15, 1935, Dekanatsarchiv Ravensburg 61a.

56. Pastor Siegle of Isny to Superintendent Ströle of Ravensburg, May 20, 1935, Dekanatsarchiv Ravensburg 61a.

57. Pastor Siegle of Isny to Superintendent Ströle of Ravensburg, March 30, May 9, and June 26, 1935, Dekanatsarchiv Ravensburg 61a.

58. Württemberg Superior Church Council to the Württemberg Education Minister, December 30, 1937, Dekanatsarchiv Ravensburg 57a; Pastor Siegle of Isny to the Ravensburg Superintendent, August 24, 1938, Dekanatsarchiv Ravensburg 61c; Siegle to the Ravensburg Superintendent, February 15, 1937, Dekanatsarchiv Ravensburg 61a; Farewell Sermon from Pastor Siegle of Isny, February 21, 1938, Landeskirchliches Archiv Stuttgart PA S446.

59. Former Pastor Raithelhuber of Waldsee, now in Göppingen, to Superintendent Ströle in Ravensburg, March 17, 1930, Dekanatsarchiv Ravensburg 71b.

60. Paul Birkmeyer et al. to the Württemberg Superior Church Council, February 6, 1930; Parish Councilor Heinrich Notz to the Ravensburg Superintendent, June 22, 1930; "Agreement!" July 26, 1930, Dekanatsarchiv Ravensburg 71b.

61. Protestant Parish of Bad Waldsee, *Evangelische Kirche Bad Waldsee 1889–1989*, 37, Landeskirchliches Archiv Stuttgart; Pastor Hartmann of Waldsee to the District School Office in Saulgau, March 18, 1935, Dekanatsarchiv Ravensburg 72d; Württemberg Superior Church Council to the Ravensburg Superintendent, March 26, 1936, Dekanatsarchiv Ravensburg 72b.

62. Pastor Hartmann to the Ravensburg Superintendent, March 3, 1936; Württemberg Superior Church Council to the Ravensburg Superintendent, March 19, 1936; Superintendent Ströle of Ravensburg to the Waldsee parish council, April 28, 1936; Ströle to the Württemberg Superior Church Council, May 15, 1936, Dekanatsarchiv Ravensburg 72f.

63. Württemberg Superior Church Council to the Ravensburg Superintendent, June 2, 1936, Dekanatsarchiv Ravensburg 72f.

64. Pastor Hartmann of Waldsee to the District School Office in Saulgau, September 10, 1937; Württemberg Superior Church Council to the Württemberg Education Ministry, July 24, 1937, Dekanatsarchiv Ravensburg 72d.

65. Württemberg Superior Church Council to all Württemberg Superintendents, January 19, 1939, Dekanatsarchiv Ravensburg 93a; Württemberg Superior Church Council to the Ravensburg Superintendent, May 25, 1937, Dekanatsarchiv Ravensburg 71a; Pastor Hoffmann of Waldsee to the Ravensburg Superintendent, April 5, 1941, Dekanatsarchiv Ravensburg 72d.

66. Report on the presence of German Christian groups in the Ravensburg district, n.d., Dekanatsarchiv Ravensburg 115g; Württemberg Superior Church Council to all Württemberg Superintendents, January 19, 1939, Dekanatsarchiv Ravensburg 93a; Weingarten Protestant Parish, *Evangelisches Stadtkirche Weingarten 1883–1983* (Weingarten: Franz Harder, 1983), 33-34; Protestant Parish in Wangen im Allgäu, "Excerpt from the Book of Minutes of the Parish Council, Volume III, Page 377 . . . ," November 18, 1939, Dekanatsarchiv Ravensburg 73a; Ravensburg Superintendent to the Württemberg Superior Church Council, March 4, 1946, Dekanatsarchiv Ravensburg Neue Akten B IV 1.

67. Vicar Mauch of Ravensburg to the Württemberg Ministerial Department for the Higher Schools, September 21, 1935, Dekanatsarchiv Ravensburg 152b; Pastor Spellenberg of Fischbach to the Ravensburg Superintendent's Office, January 13, 1939; Württemberg Superior Church Council to the Ravensburg Superintendent, May 22, 1944, Dekanatsarchiv Ravensburg 56h.

68. Copy of the Württemberg Education Minister to the Ministerial Department for the *Volk* Schools, November 26, 1937, Dekanatsarchiv Ravensburg 152b.

69. "Order of the Secret State Police," February 1939; Ravensburg Criminal Police Department to the Mayor and the Gestapo, February 13, 1939, Stadtarchiv Ravensburg AI 3027.

70. Elizabeth Jacquignon to Bishop Wurm, October 24, 1945; Wurm to the French Military Government in Tübingen, March 25, 1946; Württemberg Superior Church Council to the Ravensburg Superintendent, June 25 and July 10, 1946; Minutes of the Tettnang parish council, August 16, 1946, Dekanatsarchiv Ravensburg Neue Akten/Tettnang A I 1; War Chronicle of the Protestant Parish of Tettnang, n.d., Dekanatsarchiv Ravensburg Neue Akten/Tettnang A III 4.

71. Bishop Wurm to all superintendents in Württemberg, December 12, 1938, in Gerhard Schäfer, ed., *Die evangelische Landeskirche in Württemberg und der Nationalsozialismus: Eine Dokumentation zum Kirchenkampf*, vol. 6, *Von der Reichskirche zur Evangelischen Kirche in Deutschland: 1938–1945* (Stuttgart: Calwer, 1986), 113–16.

# Index